Leaves from the Garden

An Anthology of *divrei Torah*
from the
Egalitarian Minyan of Rogers Park

LEAVES FROM THE GARDEN
An Anthology of *divrei Torah* from the
  Egalitarian Minyan of Rogers Park

Authored by members of the Egalitarian Minyan of Rogers Park
Edited by Nava Cohen, Ruth Tupper and Richard J. Tupper

Copyright © 2006 by the Egalitarian Minyan of Rogers Park

Cover art by Gabrielle Emanuel
Cover design by Joshua Burton

All rights reserved. No part of this book may be used or reproduced in any manner whatsoever without written permission except in the case of brief quotations embodied in critical (and not so critical) articles or reviews. For more information, contact the Egalitarian Minyan at its webpage: www.egalitarianminyan.org.

ISBN: 978-1-4303-0973-4

Printed in the United States of America

Published by the Egalitarian Minyan of Rogers Park
Chicago, IL   October 2006

*Her ways are ways of pleasantness,
   And all her paths are peace.*

(Proverbs 3:17)

Contents

Preface .... *v*
Acknowledgments .... *vii*
A Note on Translations from the Tanakh .... *ix*
Abbreviations .... *xi*

Entering the Garden by Richard Tupper 1

Rosh HaShanah Day One by Zeke Emanuel 3
Rosh HaShanah Day One (II) by Joan Katz 11
Rosh HaShanah Day Two by Bev Fox 17
Rosh HaShanah Day Two (II) by Lise Weisberger 23
Shabbat Shuvah by Ruth Tupper 29
Shabbat Shuvah (II) by Richard Tupper 35
Yom Kippur by Richard Tupper 39
Yom Kippur – Mincha by Richard Tupper 45
Sukkot by Karin Klein 51
Sukkot – Shemini Atzeret by Al Hobscheid 55
Sukkot – Shemini Atzeret (II) by Joan Katz 59

BERESHIT **63**

Bereshit by Robert Grannick 63
Noach by Ellen Holtzblatt 69
Lech Lecha by Jonathan Freed 75
Vayera by Richard Tupper 77
Chayyei Sarah by Richard Tupper 79
Toldot by Lise Weisberger 83
Vayeitze by Richard Tupper 87
Vayishlach by Richard Tupper 91
Vayishlach (II) by Richard Tupper 93
Vayeshev by Andrew Kirschner 99
Vayeshev (II) by Lise Weisberger 105
Vayeshev (III) by Richard Tupper 109
Mikketz by Hillel Crandus 113
Mikketz (II) by Hillel Crandus 117

i

Vayiggash by Gail Golden 119
Vayiggash (II) by Benjamin Tupper 125
Vayechi by Richard Tupper 127

SHEMOT **129**

Shemot by Richard Tupper 129
Vaera by Joan Katz 133
Bo by Natalia Emanuel 139
Beshallach by Sam Neusner 143
Yitro by Ellen Holtzblatt 147
Mishpatim by Joan Katz 153
Terumah by Al Hobscheid 157
Tetzaveh by Richard Tupper 165
Ki Tissa by Richard Tupper 169
Vayyakhel-Pekudei by Richard Tupper 177

VAYIKRA **179**

Vayikra by Richard Tupper 179
Shabbat Zakhor by Lise Weisberger 185
Tzav by Richard Tupper 187
Tzav (II) by Richard Tupper 191
Shemini by Peter Levavi 195
Shemini (II) by Richard Tupper 201
Tazriah-Metzorah by Richard Tupper 207
Tazriah-Metzorah (II) by Richard Tupper 213
Achare Mot by Richard Tupper 217
Pesach – The Fifth Son by Hillel Crandus 227
Pesach – Morid HaTal by Al Hobscheid 229
Kedoshim by Richard Tupper 235
Emor by Richard Tupper 243
Behar by Joan Katz 247
Behukkotai by Liz Bennett 253
Behukkotai (II) by Richard Tupper 259

BEMIDBAR **263**

Bemidbar – Erev Rosh Chodesh Sivan by Steve Oren 263
Naso by Joan Katz 267
Naso (II) by Richard Tupper 271
Shavuot by Steve Oren 275
Shavuot (II) by Bev Fox 281
Behaalotecha by Richard Tupper 289
Shelach Lecha by Carol Grannick 291
Shelach Lecha (II) by Richard Tupper 295
Korach by Tamar Fox 299

Hukkat by Gail Golden..303
Hukkat (II) by Andrew Kirschner 307
Balak by Joel Teibloom...311
Pinchas by Shira Eliaser 315
Mattot by Steve Oren...321
Mattot (II) by Jesse Bacon...325
Mattot (III) by Joshua Burton..329
Massei – Rosh Chodesh by Richard Tupper 333

DEVARIM... **337**
   Devarim by Al Hobscheid..337
   Vaetchanan by Miriam Berele..343
   Vaetchanan (II) by Steve Oren 345
   Eikev by Richard Tupper...349
   Reeh by Benjamin Sommer...355
   Shofetim by Bernard Weisberger...361
   Ki Tetze by Nava Cohen 369
   Ki Tavo by Richard Tupper...373
   Nitzavim-Vayelech by Steve Oren 377
   Haazinu by Richard Tupper...379

PREFACE

Members of the Egalitarian Minyan of Rogers Park need no introduction to this book. However, if you happen not to be a member of the Minyan, then a few words of introduction may be necessary.

The Minyan was founded in 1978 by a handful of Jews who sought to form a minyan that was egalitarian in every sense of the word, not just men and women participating equally, but a community that encouraged every member's fullest participation. Today, we have grown to approximately one hundred adult members. The Minyan, to be sure, is not just a place to *daven*. We engage in various forms of *tzedakah*, such as working at the Uptown Café, which provides kosher meals for poor Jews and non-Jews in Chicago, and supporting a sister Jewish community in Kineshma, Russia. From almost its inception, the Minyan has had a Tzedaka Fund, which, you will be happy to learn, will receive all the proceeds from the sale of this book. Of course, like any other congregation, the Minyan together celebrates *simachot*, such as a *bris* or *simchat bat*, a *bar* or *bat Mitzvah*, an *aufruf*, or a wedding. We also care for those who are ill, and seek to comfort those who mourn.

The Minyan is unusual in this respect: though several of our members are rabbis, we have no officiating rabbi or, for that matter, *chazzan*. Consequently, every service is led by different members. A standard feature of every Shabbat service is the *d'var Torah* ("Torah talk") that each week is delivered by a different member. Like any other congregation, the Minyan draws its membership from a variety of backgrounds – doctors, artists, lawyers, homemakers, real estate agents, social workers, psychologists, scholars, professors, recyclers, computer experts, rabbis, accountants, teachers, administrators, clerks, and more. As one can easily imagine, this variety of backgrounds produces many different perspectives on the Torah.

It was Zeke Emanuel who first suggested collecting in a book *divrei Torah* delivered by Minyan members. Some members had written copies of almost every *davar* they had ever given at the Minyan and willingly contributed them. Other members had to be cajoled, prodded, and, in some cases, subtly threatened into writing down *divrei Torah* they had given, while still others never got around to writing down a *davar* they had given (and you know who you are!). The result is this book, a sampling of *divrei Torah* delivered at the Minyan over several years, a sampling that includes many excellent *divrei Torah*, but not all of the best because some were never reduced to writing. To hear some of the Minyan's best *divrei Torah*, you will just have to come and visit us for Shabbat services some day. If you would like to learn more about us via the Internet, you can visit our web page at: www.egalitarianminyan.org.

A brief word about the format of this book. We have succeeded in including at least one *d'var Torah* for every weekly *parsha*, although on occasion the *davar* covers a double rather than a single *parsha*. We have not tried to impose a uniform system of transliteration or even, for that matter, italicization. Furthermore, these *divrei Torah* have not been heavily edited, allowing each person to speak in his or her own voice. If, when copy editing these *divrei Torah*, we failed to catch a major error or, worse, introduced one, we apologize to the author and the reader. Perhaps in this way, this book mirrors the Minyan, imperfect yet refreshingly atypical.

ACKNOWLEDGMENTS

The Egalitarian Minyan sincerely thanks Robert Alter and his publisher, W. W. Norton & Company, for generously granting the Minyan permission to quote from Robert Alter's *The Five Books of Moses* (2004), and *The David Story* (1999). Furthermore, the Minyan sincerely thanks Jacob Milgrom and his publisher, Doubleday/Anchor Bible, who also generously granted the Minyan permission to quote from Jacob Milgrom's *Leviticus: A New Translation with Introduction and Commentary* (volume 3 in 1991 and volumes 3A and 3B in 2000). If you have not yet bought or borrowed these books, make it a point to do so soon. You will be happy you did.

As is the case with almost all Minyan enterprises, this book would never have been completed without the help of many members. The Minyan is grateful to all the members who took the time to submit a written version of one of their *divrei Torah*. Thanks, too, are due Joan Katz, Lisa Liel, and Cheryl Stone, who helped solve formatting problems and all sorts of other related issues. The Minyan thanks Gabrielle Emanuel for her beautiful artwork appearing on the cover of this anthology. Of course, the Minyan also thanks Zeke Emanuel for coming up with the idea of preparing this anthology and for his efforts, meager though they were, to collect *divrei Torah* from members. The Minyan thanks the editors of this anthology, Nava Cohen, Ruth Tupper, and Richard Tupper, for the hours of hard work they put into preparing this book. And finally, the Minyan thanks Joshua Burton, who at crunch time was a lifesaver in the difficult process of formatting this book's cover and putting the book into its final shape.

If someone helped out but was not mentioned here, just contact one of the editors and you will be thanked in the next volume. (And no, Al, you don't get thanked for constantly harping, "Oh, you guys will never finish that thing!")

A Note on
Translations from the Tanakh

When members prepared their various *divrei Torah*, they quoted from a variety of translations of the Tanakh. The Minyan was fortunate to obtain permission from Robert Alter and his publisher, W. W. Norton & Company, and from Jacob Milgrom and his publisher, Doubleday/Anchor Bible, to quote from their translations of portions of the Tanakh. Unless noted otherwise in the text, quotations from Genesis, Exodus, Numbers, Deuteronomy, and I and II Samuel are from Robert Alter's *The Five Books of Moses* (Norton 2004), and *The David Story* (Norton 1999). Likewise, unless noted otherwise, quotations from Leviticus are from Jacob Milgrom's *Leviticus: A New Translation with Introduction and Commentary* (Doubleday/Anchor Bible, volume 3 in 1991, and volumes 3A and 3B in 2000). For translations from the other books of the Tanakh, the editors worked from the 1917 translation of the Tanakh by the Jewish Publication Society ("OJPS"). Because the OJPS is now in the public domain, the editors freely modified the translation to modernize it and, on rare occasions, to incorporate more recent biblical scholarship.

ABBREVIATIONS

Etz Hayim *Etz Hayim*, ed. by D. Lieber (JPS 2001)

Hertz *The Pentateuch and Haftorahs*, ed. by J. H. Hertz (Soncino 1964)

Milgrom, *Leviticus* Jacob Milgrom, *Leviticus: A New Translation with Introduction and Commentary* (Doubleday/Anchor Bible, volume 3 in 1991, and volumes 3A and 3B in 2000)

NJPS *JPS Hebrew-English Tanakh* (JPS 2000)

OJPS *The Holy Scriptures According to the Masoretic Text* (JPS 1917)

Sim Shalom *Siddur Sim Shalom*, ed. by J. Harlow (Rabbinical Assembly 1985)

Slim Shalom *Siddur Sim Shalom for Shabbat and Festivals* (Rabbinical Assembly 1988)

Entering the Garden

Richard Tupper

> Four entered the Garden [*pardes*], namely, ben Azzai, ben Zoma, Acher, and Rabbi Akiva. Rabbi Akiva said to them, "When you arrive at the stones of pure marble, do not say 'Water, water!' For it is said, 'Whoever speaks falsely shall not be established before My eyes'" (Psalm 101:7). Ben Azzai took a look and died. Of him Scripture says, "Precious in the sight of the Lord is the death of His righteous ones" (Psalm 116:15). Ben Zoma looked and was stricken [mad]. Of him Scripture says, "Have you found honey? Eat as much as is sufficient for you, lest you be filled with it and vomit it out" (Proverbs 25:16). Acher mutilated the shoots. Rabbi Akiva departed unharmed.
>
> *Hagigah* 14b

Traditionally, the "Garden" here is thought to be the study of philosophy or natural philosophy or theosophy, but I believe that they went to study Torah. Water was thought of as the primeval source from which everything had sprung. Thales, the Greek philosopher, thought that everything was water, just rearranged, and in many creation stories in the ancient world, even Genesis 1, everything arises out of water. Although Akiba was not bringing his students into the Garden to study the origins of matter, he was warning them of how dangerous it can be to apply this type of thinking to Torah study, namely, that the Torah is water and every verse can dissolve into every other verse. Perhaps, even, this story is a criticism or at least a warning of the dangers of mystical interpretations of the Torah.

Ben Azzai looks and dies and is pronounced blessed. Why does he die? He did not say, "Water, Water." No, ben Azzai did not say this, and we should not think of his death as a punishment; instead the story explicitly tells us that he is "pronounced blessed." How was he blessed? I submit that he was blessed because he "got it." In one moment he was able to grasp with his finite mind the multitude of meanings packed into every verse. Blessed with this incredible comprehension of the Torah, he was translated into a higher realm.

Ben Zoma loses his mind. Why? Because he, too, saw the multiplicity of meanings in every verse and his mind could not endure it. The Talmud says of him here, "Have you found honey? Eat as much as is sufficient for you, lest you be filled with it and vomit it out" (Proverbs 25:16). What is the honey he has found? It is the sweet honey of Torah study, as it says in Psalms 119:103, "How sweet are Thy words unto my taste! Yea, sweeter than honey to my mouth!" But the multiplicity of meaning, the abundance of honey he finds, becomes too much for him. Later in the Talmud, he is reported talking about different verses and applying them in strange ways to different issues. Why? Because he sees the infinite meaning in every verse, and so, verses that seem to have no relevance to each other do have relevance for him. He begins to connect one verse to another in nonsensical ways and ultimately loses his mind. This interpretation is perhaps an ironic criticism of the famous apothegm attributed to ben Zoma, "Who is wise? He who learns from every person . . ." (*Pirkei Avot* 4:1).

Acher (Elisha ben Abuyah of *As a Driven Leaf* fame) mutilates the shoots – becomes a heretic. Why? Because he concludes that if every verse means everything, then it can mean anything, and therefore it means nothing.

Akiba returns unscathed. Why? Because he does not lose sight of the big picture and realizes that interpretation requires discipline, and so he stays within the tradition of the rabbis. He is able to return from the Garden, from this place of incredible insight into the infinite meaning of Torah, and live within the community, and within the interpretations of the Torah accepted by the community.

Torah study can be wonderful yet dangerous. For the rabbis, the message is: study, even dare to glimpse the Torah's infinite meanings, but to stay in the Garden too long is dangerous. One must always return to the community and the communal interpretation of the Torah, which is not infinite, but always unfolding within the bounds of communal acceptance. Otherwise one risks becoming like ben Zoma or Acher. That is good advice for us, as well, as each of us undertakes to study Torah. Let us study together and remain together.

Rosh HaShanah Day One

Zeke Emanuel

Seven score and seventeen years ago, Henry David Thoreau began felling trees to build a one room hut on the banks of Walden Pond among the fourteen acres owned by Ralph Waldo Emerson. He was building the hut because he had come to a rut in his own life. In 1837, he had graduated from Harvard College. His subsequent years were marked by some successes but also a great deal of frustration and failure in becoming a writer. In 1838, he started a school with a loan from Emerson and then he moved into Concord Academy that had recently closed. His brother John joined him to run the school. But, despite individualized instruction, the school floundered and closed because it failed to attract enough students. In 1839-40, Thoreau courted one Ellen Sewall, a woman with whom John had also fallen in love. She turned down marriage proposals from both Thoreau boys.

In 1840, Thoreau's first poem, "Sympathy," and his first article on a Greek satirist were published in the transcendentalist journal, *The Dial*. After his failed marriage proposal and the closing of his school, Thoreau moved in with the Emersons. Yet Emerson also began growing impatient with Thoreau's lack of progress in writing. And tragedy struck. In early 1842, John died from tetanus. His first original work, his first real nature writing, "The Natural History of Massachusetts," appeared in *The Dial* in 1842. In January 1843, he and Emerson had a major fight, Emerson finding Thoreau threatening and generally socially ill-adept. Living together in close family quarters certainly did not help. In May 1843, Thoreau accepted a teaching job in New York City as a tutor to Emerson's nephew. He sold some writing in New York City, but in general he was not happy and hated writing for dollars. In November 1843, Thoreau returned to Concord. In September 1844, Emerson bought eleven acres around Walden Pond and then three more of forest to protect his initial investment. Ellery Channing suggested that Thoreau build himself a cottage on the Pond to write his book about his trip down the Concord and Merrimack rivers with his brother John.

Leaves from the Garden

In the spring of 1845, Thoreau built and moved in, as he famously says, on Independence Day.

Thank Sam Fox for asking Linda and thank Linda for saying she was not prepared to do it. Disclaimer: this speech was not cleared with my boss; it represents the views of the author and not the DHHS or NIH. But it is consistent with President Bush's faith-based initiative, lecturing to enlighten souls, even at religious gatherings as long as my government salary does not contribute to the actual religious service, is fine according to the new rules. So I did not have to do this as an outside activity. Plus as many of you know there is not a spiritual bone in my body, all of them having been crushed long ago, so the chances I would say anything religious is negligible, so the ACLU and its supporters in the room can be happy, too.

Thoreau writes about his reasons for going:

> We must learn to reawaken and keep ourselves awake, not by mechanical aids, but by an infinite expectation of the dawn, which does not forsake us in our soundest sleep. I know of no more encouraging fact than the unquestionable ability of man to elevate his life by a conscious endeavor . . . . Every man is tasked to make his life, even in its details, worthy of the contemplation of his most elevated and critical hours . . . . I went to the woods because I wished to live deliberately, to front only the essential facts of life, and see if I could not learn what it had to teach, and not when I came to die, to discover that I had not lived . . . . I wanted to live deep and suck out all the marrow of life, to live so sturdily and Spartan-like as to put to rout all that was not life, to cut a broad swath and shave close, to drive life into a corner, and reduce it to its lowest terms, and if it proved to be mean, why then to get the whole and genuine meanness of it, and publish its meanness to the world; or if it were sublime, to know it by experience, and be able to give a true account of it in my next excursion.

Walden is Thoreau's true account of his living. He moved away from Concord, but not far, less than one mile, so all in town could still see his experiment, so he could awaken others. Thoreau makes clear he is leaving, giving up the old, especially as he makes clear in "Economy," the first chapter, the money-making economy and life dependent upon the social standards, the unsimple, the being a "tool of our own tools." He moves for the purpose of re-creating his life, of consciously, deliberately making a life that is worthy of contemplation, as he implies, on a death bed. Walden is filled with the actions of re-birth. The listening intently to sounds, the watching of ants fighting, the taking the depths of the ponds and finding them interconnected, and most importantly the cleansing swims in Walden Pond, the baptisms that mark the re-creation of his life. Of course the last chapter, save for the conclusion, is a chapter entitled "Spring." We begin with "Economy" and shedding and end with re-birth in "Spring." This is the chance to shed the life of sin and be renewed. He writes:

> In a pleasant spring morning all man's sins are forgiven. Such a day is a truce to vice. While such a sun holds out to burn, the vilest sinner may return. Through our own recovered innocence we discern the innocence of our neighbors. You may have known your neighbor yesterday for a thief, a drunkard, or a sensualist, and merely pitied or despised him, and despaired of the world; but the sun shines bright and ward this first spring morning recreating the world, and you meet him at some serene work, and see how his exhausted and debauched veins expand with still joy and bless the new day, feel the spring influence with the innocence of infancy, and all his faults are forgotten. This is not only an atmosphere of good will about him, but even a savor of holiness groping for expression . . . .

Thoreau makes clear this is a spiritual journey that is quintessentially human, that "I found in myself, and still find, an instinct toward a higher, or as it is named, spiritual life, as do most men, and another toward a primitive rank and savage one, and I reverence them both. I love the wild not less than the good." He is torn between the beast and angel, attracted to both the animal and God, as we are. He also makes clear this is not just a personal journal but one for all . . . that he is writing to awaken us all.

Walden was originally noted by critics for its nature writing. Readers were told to ignore "Economy" and "Where I Lived and What I Lived For" to concentrate on "Sounds" and "The Bean Field." But Thoreau's self-rebirth is quintessentially American, and *Walden*'s fame justly rests on his expressing a fundamentally American experience.

But it is only one of three characteristically American modes of rebirth, the secular if spiritual one. There is also the religious one epitomized by the Puritans and many subsequent revivals. And there is the materialist one, typified by Benjamin Franklin and labeled by Henry Clay as the self-made man, that is so American.

Leaves from the Garden

So Tupper is muttering, "Did this guy pick up the wrong lecture this morning, get the assignment mixed up in his Palm? What the hell does Henry David Thoreau have to do with Rosh HaShanah?"

Well for one thing, I personally have a bit of identification with Thoreau. In July 2002 the Emanuels moved houses, not to a one room hut I built with my hands on Walden Pond, but to a house on the Lake that we will make our own through changes and renovations. And one of the great pleasures is to see the new day dawn at 6 a.m., the boiling orange sun come up, and to run and sweat and then dive into the Lake to be refreshed, renewed, and rejuvenated. In addition, for the Emanuels this fall represents a new birth with one daughter going off to have a moment of self-creation. Finally, yesterday, *erev Rosh HaShanah*, was my birthday, always a chance for a rebirth.

But more importantly for us, Thoreau is an incomplete forefather. I think there are close similarities between Thoreau's awakening and what we need to feel at Rosh HaShanah, and important differences I will come to at the end.

With today's service we begin the ten Days of Awe. One approach to this time is one of awe, supplication, trepidation, begging God to forget and forgive. This is well captured in the morning *Amidah* which contains words of awe, fear, trembling before God. We are sinners. Every day we commit, knowingly and accidentally, terrible sins. Certainly this year I have been guilty of terrible sins, for which the most severe punishment is called. From the perspective of atonement, we have little to redeem us from our sins. Thinking of our transgressions, appealing to God in three days of prayer, begging to be re-inscribed in the Book of Life, pleading for mercy rather than for justice to be done. This can be seen as a black period in which begging is not too strong a sentiment.

But we are Jews, the people who not only invented the dialectic, but perfected it. That's why we have all the lawyers in the Minyan. Trepidation and supplication are commingled with another perspective. After all, why should God bother with us minuscule beings if we were not important, why should we catch His eye, why should He even expend any energy worrying about whether to put us in the Book of Life? More importantly, why can some humans appeal to His caring to induce Him to act in certain ways, to bargain with Him? These days are filled with awe, but I want to focus on the other side, their being days of liberation from past failures and filled with joy at the possibility of self-renewal and re-creation.

Rosh HaShanah Day One

Rosh HaShanah is the New Year. It begins not just ten days of reflection but a month of endings and beginnings. It ends with Simhat Torah and the ending of the reading of the Torah and re-starting the reading of the Torah. One purpose of this time is to re-think our life, re-examine not just the sins we commit each day, but the direction of our life. We examine who we are, what we have done, our actions and choices. The examination is not sufficient, we believe we have choices and can make different choices. We are told to use the transgression as a means of deepening our understanding and re-directing ourselves. Most of us know that the most powerful moments in our lives are not our successes, but our failures. The old saying is that success is born of wisdom and wisdom is born of failure. It is the failures, our sins and problems, our mistakes, that give us wisdom to see and renew and change.

It is this day that begins our period of *teshuvah*. A distinction is made between atonement and *teshuvah*, between confession and repentance. Confession is about acknowledging our sins to others and asking forgiveness. Atonement is the social part. *Teshuvah* is about self change. Recognizing our transgressions internally leads to self-renewal, rebirth, self-re-creation. The idea that we can, that there is this possibility of self renewal and rebirth, is very much antithetical to supplication, begging trepidation. It is assertive, liberating, the other side of recognizing sin.

This is Thoreau as our forefather, or, more accurately, the Jews as Thoreau's forefather. But there are important differences that I think are worth highlighting which make clear that Transcendentalism and the American style of rebirth fall short of Jewish rebirth. I want to highlight just three differences.

One difference is a matter of timing. There is no calendar that relates to Thoreau's going to Walden. Yes, he went on Independence Day, but that is not the purpose of the day, nor is the day an annual moment of self-reflection. Judaism has built in an annual cycle. Each year a person is forced to confront his transgressions, and is given the opportunity to learn from the errors and sins, to renew and be reborn. Judaism does not leave the possibility of self rebirth to a bolt out of the blue, a moment in a life, individual insight; it builds this into the fabric of life, indeed into the annual cycle, and in some deep ways forces us to choose whether we take the opportunity or not. We cannot miss that there is an opportunity of renewal and re-creation before us, although we can fail to seize it.

There is another difference in timing. The key season for Thoreau is spring, the time of renewal. Spring is the real Jewish New Year, the start of the Jewish calendar, so our real New Year. But Rosh HaShanah, and the time of renewal, occurs not in spring but in autumn. Why? One reason, of course, is that at the time described in the Torah, Jews were an agricultural people. Spring is a busy time, it is rebirth of the land and therefore the time of sowing and tending. For any agricultural people, it begins the busiest time. The fall is the harvest and then a long winter hibernation. Hibernation is the time of thinking, of change, less frenzied and rushed. Alternatively, Jews knew 3,000 years ago that the fall would be the start of the new school year, it would in fact be the New Academic Year. So that for men, if not Nature, the New Year is fall.

A final possibility is that Thoreau misunderstands the importance of spring. To have a spring, when the new bud is born, one needs to put the bulb in the ground in the fall. Things do not spring forth full born, they must develop. To be reborn in spring, requires planting and re-thinking in fall. So Jews appreciate development necessary for renewal and rebirth in a way Thoreau fails to.

Second is the difference of content. For Thoreau and America there is no direction to the self-renewal. It is what an individual feels called to. For Jews there is a direction, a direction set by mitzvot, by *halacha*, by getting closer to God. This is important. God is a mathematician, just ask Josh. He does not like randomness, even a random walk. As a geometrician, He prefers upward slopes. And upward slopes require a direction to the slope.

More importantly, I want to highlight the different role of community. Thoreau goes off to Walden Pond, away, but not out of sight of his fellow townsfolk. He goes alone and his baptismal swims are alone. Yes he is attempting, in his writing, to awaken others, to show them about the possibility of this kind of rebirth and renewal. Nevertheless, it is fundamentally an individual event, an individual rejection of society, an affirmation of his own as separate. Indeed, *Walden* and Thoreau's action are so popular because they are a classic expression of American individualism.

Jews are a clannish people. We do not go away from each other for rebirth; we come together as a community on the Days of Awe for renewal. While this is a moment for self-renewal and self-re-creation, that it is linked with Rosh HaShanah and Yom Kippur and through Simhat Torah, means that it can only occur linked to the community. There is no self to be created apart from the community. Indeed, the self we are creating is ours, it is a self, but it is not individualistic. We all have the same direction, mitzvot, and *halacha*. There is individuality in the path, but the direction is always up and always together. We cannot, as far as Jews, do this alone. We can do it only together.

Rosh HaShanah Day One

This is one of the magical things about Jews; they understand the individual and communal, the inter-digitation. There is no way to be individual without being in the community.

Rosh HaShanah Day One (II)

Joan Katz

Last winter my daughter Miriam and I participated together in a thoughtful series of pre-*bat Mitzvah* classes sponsored by the women's yeshiva Matan. When the teacher dramatized the biblical Hannah of today's *haftarah*, she presented a classic rabbinic interpretation: Hannah as paradigm of the righteous woman. Surely Hannah must not be good enough yet, for God had not answered her prayer with a child. According to the *Gemara, Berachot* 31b, Hannah even challenges God to find fault with her observance of the mitzvot for which women are traditionally obligated, and takes Him to task saying, "*HaKadosh Baruch Hu*, Master of the Universe, of all the multitudes you created in your world, is it so difficult in your eyes to give me one son?" Since God Himself has closed Hannah's womb, Hannah would use *Teshuvah*, *Tefillah* and *Tzedakah* to convince Him to change His decree. The pregnant young teacher of the Matan class painted a compelling model to emulate.

This interpretation is the "old standby." Pray hard, give charity, change your evil ways, and you still have a chance to convince God to change His mind and inscribe you in the book of life. Try hard enough, God will answer. This premise is crystallized in the liturgical refrain of today's *Musaf*, "*U-t'shuvah u-t'fillah u-tz'dakah ma'avirin et ro'a ha-g'zeirah*/But repentance, prayer and charity avert the evil of the decree."

Yet hearing the story of Hannah interpreted in this familiar way in a room of two dozen eleven-year-old girls, I was taken aback. Given the stark statistics we know about infertility, more than a few of these girls are being coached toward a life of unhappiness – if not outright religious disillusion – with most of their loving mothers in the room nodding in agreement!

Thinking of how my fellow classmates – these young girls – could internalize this Torah lesson, I really "heard" this classic interpretation anew. Zeal can be a positive attribute, but I was frightened for the girls in the room who may grow up thinking that we, like Hannah, can expect God to answer

11

us personally if only we pray intensely enough, try hard enough, and make the right choices. Was this the primary meaning of the text I wanted to pass on to my daughter?!

It was shocking, because as adults we know that not all prayers are answered as requested. It is one thing to build a relationship with God through prayer and mitzvot, but another matter to depend on "catching" His attention to convince Him to save us with miracles on our behalf. It is only a small step from this kind of thinking to blaming the victim for her own misfortunes. What a blow to the self-esteem of a young woman unable to conceive or realize her desires! Even the beloved Hannah's self confidence is shaken by her co-wife Penina's taunting.

I am also troubled by this reading of the story because I am personally unwilling to believe that unexpected turns in life – from inability to conceive like Hannah, or a child born with a genetic anomaly, or the untimely death of a loved one – are always in my control or are my fault for being human or not being perfect enough. Or that my faith in myself – or the Divine – is tied to His granting my wishes. I suspect that most of you feel the same way.

This interpretation of our *haftarah* matches a custom not uncommon in our larger Jewish community of responding to the life-threatening illness of a student by petitioning God to save the teen through the communal recitation of Psalms paired with a renewed fight against *lashon harah*/devisive speech. In other words: "*U-t'shuvah u-t'fillah u-tz'dakah ma'avirin et ro'a ha-g'zeirah.*"

But what is the message to our teens when the child we are praying for does die? Which faith is shattered when one's best doesn't work?

So, if we do not expect a direct, one-to-one correlation between prayer and God's intercession, then what do we learn from Hannah's prayer?

In other words, how else can I read this text?

Over Rosh HaShanah, we read not only the story of Hannah, but also selections from three other narratives with common themes: relationships between husbands and mates, their response to infertility, birthing and losing children, and succession.

In the Torah portion for today and tomorrow, we read about Abraham, Sarah and Hagar, Isaac and Ishmael.

In the *haftarah* we just finished, we heard about Elkana, Penina and Hannah, and Shmuel.

Following in tomorrow's *haftarah* is Jeremiah's vision of God and His bride Israel and her return.

Rosh HaShanah Day One (II)

Given the similarities of these themes, I thought I might discover another aspect to Hannah's dilemma by comparing Hannah's experience to these other stories. When I laid out the elements of each story side by side, I could see clearly that the dimension shaping each of these tales was not just concern over progeny but communication with God: prayer.

In Genesis, Abraham talks to God openly, when asking God for direction after Sarah wants to send away Hagar, and, later, when sacrificing his son Isaac.

Sarah talks to God through her laughter when the angels visit her to foretell Isaac's birth. Her silence and death immediately after the *Akeidah* is perhaps another statement.

Isaac asks straightforward questions of his father on their walk up *Har Moriah* in performance of a holy deed, prays in silence, and then participates in God's plan.

Hagar is direct, in the desert, "Do not let me see my son die."

Ishmael wails in the voice of a child.

In Samuel, Elkana visits the temple at Shiloh with his family each year.

Penina visits as well, eating her portion of the sacrifice, but what we read of her is mockery rather than prayer, causing her co-wife Hannah torment instead of joy at the Festival.

Hannah first prays from her heart – silent, private, intense – and later with poetic praise.

Samuel devotes his life to the service of God, hearing His voice.

Jeremiah, the prophet, here relays God's promise that if we turn to Him, there will eventually be a joyful answer to the prayers of our ancestors.

The picture of an archetypical pattern for prayer began to emerge, providing me with a more resonant model for this season. With apologies to the Jeremiah fans, I will focus more on the Genesis and Samuel stories.

As these scenes unfold, what is the pattern for prayer?

First, the setting for each interlude is a potent emotional landscape. Beside the despair from infertility running through these stories, there are other emotional triggers. Watching Ishmael play with Isaac, Sarah is driven to the brink with jealousy. Imminent death is the final provocation for the banished Hagar to call out to God. Balancing fear and trust, Isaac's unrecorded response to the *Akeidah* is no less poignant to our imaginations. We can "get into their moment" with empathy; the stories come to life because we can fill in the text with our own emotional gloss.

There is also a realization that change is needed. Sarah is bothered by the relationship between her son and his half-brother as counter to God's plan.

Hannah realizes that she cannot bear the bitterness eating at her. Elkana, full of love, is troubled by his wife's despair.

Next, the person responds to the problem by getting up and going outside the home, often pushed: Hagar to the desert of Beer-sheva, Abraham to the land of Moriah, and Hannah to the temple at Shiloh.

At the center of each story, as I mentioned above, a communication with God, a "prayer," takes place.

Amazingly, in each episode, God responds! The response when God actually answers is a hearty surprise! Sarah laughs. Abraham is so focused on his son Isaac on the altar that the angel has to call twice, "Abraham! Abraham!" to get his attention. God has to open Hagar's eyes so she can see the well. Hannah is inspired to compose a clairvoyant song of praise.

One senses, particularly by their surprise, that our ancestors were well aware that not all prayer is answered. Stories, such as Moses' repeated but unsuccessful beseeching of God to let him enter the Promised Land, were in their consciousness as well as ours.

Now look at how the response is delivered: through an intermediary, a "*malach*/angel-messenger" speaks to Sarah, Abraham, and Hagar; a priest to Hannah; and a prophet, Jeremiah, to Israel.

There are also long lasting consequences to these prayers. I won't go into the details here, but if you read to the end of each character's life, you will find that after they are blessed with this closeness to God and a place in history, their mundane lives are never the same again.

What does this teach us about how to pray?

Here is the sequence: a problem that needs change, an emotional trigger, a change of scenery, communication with God in words or deeds, recognition of the answer, surprise at getting an answer, and lasting reverberations.

Prayer helps us focus and identify a need for change. Prayer starts with us.

Going outside your comfort zone – away from home or to a holy spot – is not a bad thing.

Prayer has many voices, and we see many examples in these texts.

Prayer can be an empowering experience leading to personal growth. Hagar, feeling helpless, deserted, with her life out of control, leaves the well with the strength to raise a son and marry him off with material blessings – a successful single mother. Hannah, feeling low on self-worth, finds the courage to speak out to Eli, respectfully confronting his authority by challenging him when he mistakes her for a drunken woman.

Rosh HaShanah Day One (II)

The answer to prayer is delivered in many ways. It can be through physical change, pregnancy for example; through an intermediary, such as an angel; or through the vision of a priest or prophet. God does not personally answer the prayer "face to face" in any of these stories – except to tell Abraham to listen to his wife when she complains!

To find the answers, the recipients' eyes need to be opened to seeing differently. The language used in these texts is rich in words like weeping and seeing. God opens Hagar's eyes to see the well of water; Abraham looks and is surprised to see in the bushes a ram for sacrifice. Seeing what was unseen before, God unclouding vision. We have to be ready for the answer – it can sometimes come as a surprise. Finding the right answer is perhaps the real task of prayer.

Lastly, this process can have life-changing impact . . . though not always in the ways we expect. We should be ready to embrace the reverberations.

How *would* I teach Hannah as a model for the eleven-year old girls?

I would argue that Hannah's is not primarily a story of infertility, fertility or bargaining; rather, Hannah's story is a story of prayer heard. It is miraculous because she got precisely what she asked for. We know that God considered Hannah's encounter with Him successful; after Samuel's birth, He eventually blesses her with five *more* children.

But not every prayer is answered in the way we might hope. We bother to pray because the endeavor of prayer itself can bring change; it helps us see different paths. Hannah's prayer also could have been a success if answered in another way. She was consoled, returning to participate joyfully in the Festival, even before she learned of her pregnancy; Eli's blessing does not promise her a child. When her life was changed, she had the vision to understand the gift she was given.

Most of the characters in these texts are introduced to us before they are parents. Children are the desired outcome, but it is not too far of a stretch to understand them as a metaphor for renewal or meaning. These stories can help us understand a process for personal change where "getting what we ask for" is not the primary measure of whether we are "good enough" yet.

I would say to these young girls that Hannah, in distress, actively used the tools she had at her disposal to try to change her situation.

She drew strength from her husband's love and support.

She did not hide out at home, but went with the family to bring the sacrifice and take part in the festivals.

She prayed to God privately instead of grousing about life being unfair.

She took an action to bring change.

She was aware that prayer is a relationship demanding intensity.

Following her vow are the words:

"*ki hirbita l'hitpalael lifnai Adonai.*/As she went on with her prayer before the LORD" (I Sam. 1:12).

There were more words to her prayer we do not have recorded. She continued to pray until she felt she was answered.

Hannah used many voices in her prayer: sacrifices, petition, vow, praise, dedication of her child to the temple . . . and she still continued to pray.

In praying, Hannah's eyes are opened to her future, and even to the future of Israel.

Yes, I would say to the girls that Hannah is a wonderful role model:

Hannah does *teshuvah* by using prayer as a catalyst for change.

Hannah turns to God in *tefillah* to find answers for her life.

Hannah does the ultimate *tzedakah*; dedicating her first fruits to God.

"*U-t'shuvah u-t'fillah u-tz'dakah ma'avirin et ro'a ha-g'zeirah.*/Returning, prayer and good deeds lighten the harshness of the decree."

In this New Year, may we each come to be blessed like Hannah.

Rosh HaShanah Day Two

Bev Fox

As is my custom, I will both begin and end my comments today with a story. The first story is one that Renana sent me from camp this summer. I came home from work to find a letter waiting in the mailbox. Renana wrote that she didn't have time for a real letter, but that she had just heard this story at camp and she wanted to write it down and send it to me before she forgot it. This is what she wrote.

There were two friends in the desert and they only had one canteen between themselves. They got into a fight about who would get the last sip of water and one of them hit the other. The friend who received the slap in the face said nothing, but after a few moments he bent down and, using his finger, he wrote in the sand, "Today my friend hurt my face." The other friend said nothing, but looked ashamed and kept walking.

A few hours later they saw a pool of water, trees and an oasis. They ran to the water and pulled off their clothes. The two friends dove into the water, but only one resurfaced. The friend who had received the slap in the face was nowhere to be found. The other friend dove to the bottom of the pool and saw his friend tangled in some weeds growing in the water. He broke the weeds, grabbed his friend, and carried him to safety. After catching his breath, the friend who had nearly drowned took two rocks in his hands and carved the following words into one of them using the other as a tool. "Today my friend saved my life." The second friend was thoroughly confused and finally asked what the two writings had been done for.

The hurt friend answered, "When you hurt me, it wasn't deep and you didn't mean harm and I didn't want to remember it forever, so I wrote it in the sand. I knew that soon enough the wind would blow it away and it would be as if it never happened. However, when you saved my life, I wanted it to be remembered forever, so I wrote it on a stone which will never be erased." In this way God forgives our mistakes like words in the sand, but God remembers our acts of selfless good forever.

Leaves from the Garden

Taking a closer look at this story should bring us to a better understanding of this season of repentance. Some people would say that the first part of the story is about Rosh HaShanah and the second part is about Yom Kippur. Rosh HaShanah, to some extent the month of Elul preceding it, and certainly the ten days following it, are days when we are supposed to be thinking about our mistakes and asking God's forgiveness and the forgiveness of our fellow man. Yom Kippur is the final day of accounting when God weighs our sins against our good deeds. If we have done true *teshuvah*, then the scale should be tipped in favor of our acts of *hesed*.

What is forgiveness? One might say that forgiveness is giving to the utmost, giving that which is hardest to give – you can only forgive someone if you are ready to accept him as he is.

The biblical concept of forgiveness seems to be associated with a vocabulary of cleanliness and purification. The priest performs a ritual of atonement for the sinner, but forgiveness itself is granted by God. It is not enough for man to hope and pray for pardon; he has to take an active role by humbling himself, acknowledging his wrong and promising not to do it again. The rituals of penitence such as weeping, fasting, rending clothes and donning sackcloth and ashes are seen as useless by the prophets if they are not accompanied by a change of heart. Remorse must then be translated into good deeds. Take a look at the root of the word *teshuvah*, *shuv*, meaning "to return." Man has been empowered by God to turn back and turn his evil into good. The act of "turning" will lead to forgiveness.

Shortly before I received Renana's letter from camp, I attended a wonderful presentation by two of my favorite storytellers, Corinne Stavish and Barbara McBride Smith, entitled: "From Fortune to Misfortune to Forgiveness." In their presentation they were looking at what they called "The Bad Boys in the Bible: Abraham, Moses, David, Jonah, Jacob, Joseph and more . . . ." examining the moment of choice when they had gone from Fortune to Misfortune. As the group of participants tried to brainstorm a list of who the Good Boys of the Bible were, we had trouble finding any who were solely good. For each one that we named, there was some point in time when he faced a conflict and made what we might call a bad choice. As I listened to Corinne and Barbara talk I immediately began thinking of the *Akeidah*. Here was Abraham, the man whom some call the best Jew. It seems as if he passed God's test of faith and yet, every year at this time, I struggled with the problem that he didn't pass my test in terms of the morality of his behavior. What kind of moral example was a man who agreed to sacrifice his only son with no argument, and moreover who didn't even discuss it with his

Rosh HaShanah Day Two

wife? He just snuck off to *Har Moriah* without even giving Sarah a chance to counter his decision or say good-bye to her son. How could I use their point of reference to help me come to terms with my dilemma?

One definition of fortune is a person's condition or standing in life determined by material possessions or money. Another definition is the good or bad luck that befalls someone. If we take the first definition, prior to the *Akeidah* we see that Abraham is in a state of good fortune. He has a wife and two sons, and God has promised him that he will have descendants as numerous as the stars. He has a servant who will do his bidding, and he seems not to be wanting for food or shelter.

In ancient Greek literature, a man of fortune is living at a point of having too much, where others envy you or where you have excessive pride or hubris. We can apply this to Abraham in that he is so confident in his relationship with God that he ceases to question – this is his hubris. Only a few chapters earlier he argues with God about the fate of *S'dom*, but here, when it comes to the fate of his own son, he believes that he is on God's good side and he doesn't need to argue anymore. For me, the point that makes him pass God's test is exactly the point where he fails my test. I don't want him to disobey God, but I want him to ask a question. In my mind, even though Isaac is saved, Abraham's life now changes to one of misfortune – you never see him interact with Isaac again (in fact you aren't sure from the text whether Isaac even comes down the mountain with him), Sarah dies (perhaps of a broken heart) and Abraham's station in the world has changed. The wealth and security of being part of a strong nuclear family are gone.

In using Corinne and Barbara's techniques, I needed to develop a midrash that focused on Abraham's ability to turn back the clock and re-evaluate his own behavior at his moment of choice. There are several moments in the text when we wish we might have heard more than was revealed.

1. When God asked Abraham to offer up his son, his favorite son, Isaac, whom he loved.

Abraham, the man who argued about *S'dom*, must have at least had a conversation with God to understand this request or gone back to Sarah to tell her what was being asked of him. If he has the faith that is attributed to him, I want to know how he communicated it to Sarah. Taking Isaac off to sacrifice him in secret is not only an act of faith, it is also an act of deception.

2. When Isaac asks his father, "But where is the sheep for the offering?"

If Abraham is such a man of faith, would he not take this opportunity to expound upon his beliefs to his son? Can we hear more of this conversation?

3. When Abraham comes down from the mountain.

Leaves from the Garden

What does he say to Sarah? Does he tell her what happened on the mountain? Is she already dead? How does he grieve for her? Does Isaac know that she died?

4. When Abraham sends Eliezer to find a wife for Isaac.

Is this some sort of atonement for his behavior at the *Akeidah*? Is this a promise he made to Sarah? What does he tell Isaac about the need to marry within the clan and show allegiance to his people?

Why do we read this passage every year on Rosh HaShanah? I think that it is precisely because it is such a hard passage. God is asking us to go back, to create our own midrash, to relive that moment of choice and to redefine ourselves with acts of faith based on the new concepts we have found in the unwritten parts of the story.

Rabbi Isaac Kook, the first chief Ashkenazi rabbi of Jerusalem, observed that "what we desire is tied up with what we have done." In this way, the present can change the past. *Teshuvah*, the act of returning to the person you were meant to be, can change who we were. It can't change what we did, but it can change the meaning of what we did. Lawrence Kushner in *Eyes Remade for Wonder* (Jewish Lights Publishing 1998), says that we shouldn't make *teshuvah* because it will make pain go away, but rather because it will send you back to the person you were, change you into the person you were meant to be, and in so doing change you into the person you can still become. "We not only make amends and through them make ourselves into a finer person, we also heal the pain so that now in the light of our present turning, both the one we injured and ourselves regard our original transgression as the initiation of this greater intimacy and love" (*Eyes Remade for Wonder*, p. 136).

Earlier I spoke about Rosh HaShanah as the time we think about our misdeeds and ask for forgiveness, and Yom Kippur as the moment that our good deeds are added to the scale. In the *unetaneh tokef* prayer we speak about the fact that our fate is written on Rosh HaShanah and sealed on Yom Kippur. I would like to suggest a different reading of this prayer. The key to this prayer are the lines "*Ut'shuvah, t'filah utzedakah ma'avirin etroa ha g'zeirah*/But penitence, prayer and good deeds can modify the severity of the decree." I think that we cannot view the decree as life or death in the coming year. In the next paragraph of the prayer it talks about the fact that man's origin is dust and his end is dust. When our time comes, we all will die. Rosh HaShanah and Yom Kippur are our yearly reminder to look back and take an accounting, to make sure that we have lived the best lives that we could, to right our wrongs and to take on new mitzvot, so that when we die we are on

Rosh HaShanah Day Two

the highest plane. In the past few weeks we have seen the loss of many wonderful people – three members of the Weiner family, the Applebaum family and most recently Sue Ellen Schwartz, a beloved colleague and friend. We hope that given the wonderful role models they were to us all, they died at a moment when the scales were weighted down by all of their good deeds.

I promised to end with a story and I will, for I know that while you may not remember my philosophy or my citations, at least a story is something you can take with you and mull over later in the afternoon. This is an adaptation of a story from Elisa Pearmain's book called *Doorways to the Soul*, entitled, "The Messiah is Among Us."

Once there was a little shtetl that had fallen upon hard times. Some of the residents had moved away, and no new families were moving in. Once there had been a great yeshivah there, but now all that remained was a small shul in the corner of town. There were but a handful of learned Jews still studying there with the local Rav. They began fighting among themselves, each blaming the hard times on the faults and failings of the others.

One day a visiting rabbi stopped at the town's synagogue to *daven*. He ate and prayed alongside the other members of the shul. The next day, as the visiting rabbi prepared to continue on his journey, the local Rav drew him aside. He told him of the problems of the town and asked him for his observations and advice.

Upon hearing the Rav's woes, the visiting rabbi was quiet for some time.

"Can you not give me some advice to help my town to thrive again and to help us rebuild the yeshiva?" the Rav begged.

"Your people will not listen to my advice," the rabbi replied. "But perhaps they would benefit from an observation. The Messiah dwells among you here in this shtetl."

"One of us?" asked the Rav astonished. "Which one?"

"Oh that I cannot say," he answered. "Share this with your brethren and in time it shall be revealed to you."

The Rav thanked him and sent him on his way. He then gathered the townspeople together, who listened in amazement to the news.

"One of us! But who?" each one asked out loud. Then to themselves they wondered, "It couldn't be Shmuel the tailor – or could it?"

"Surely not Mottel the cantor's son, but then there are times when . . . ."

"Not Yitzhak the water carrier, well, maybe . . . ."

"Perhaps it is the Rav himself?"

"Could it be me?"

21

Soon things began to change in the town as each began to see the Messiah in the other and to hear the Messiah's words in each word spoken.

Soon people began to wander back to the town, and in time it flourished again as a center of Jewish learning.

If each of us were to take the example of the first story and apply it to the second story, how different our lives would be. Each day we must take the little sins of others and write them in the sand to be blown away by the wind. Then we must take the good deeds and engrave them in stone to be remembered forever. Then we will be able to live in greater peace and harmony as we cease to dwell on the faults of others, and instead bring to life the sparks of the Messiah found in all of us. Let this be the challenge of the coming year.

Shanah Tovah.

Rosh HaShanah Day Two (II)

Lise Weisberger[1]

Our legends say that three women were remembered on Rosh HaShanah with the gift of children. They are Sarah, Rachel and Hannah, and each of them, in some context, is mentioned during the Rosh HaShanah readings. These women are distinguished not only by their initial infertility (after all, that's not uncommon for biblical heroines), but by the intensified frustration of having to deal with a rival wife, who is less-loved but fertile, and who causes them great misery. We hear Hannah's story in full – it is the *haftarah* for the first day of Rosh HaShanah. Of Sarah's story, we hear only the climactic ending, when she is remembered by G-d, conceives and gives birth – that is the Torah reading for the first day. Rachel is mentioned by Jeremiah in the *haftarah* for the second day, but in a very different context than her infertility story. She appears from her grave, a universal mother-figure, weeping for the slain and exiled tribes of Israel:

> A voice is heard in Ramah,
> lamentation and bitter weeping;
> Rachel is weeping for her children.
> She refuses to be comforted for her children,
> because they are no more.
> (Jeremiah 31:15)

I want to explore the relationship between these two portraits of Rachel: the young wife, struggling for dominance over her rival sister, and the bereaved mother mourning her lost children. How does one become the other?

---

[1] Eds.' note: translations and paraphrases from the Torah are Lise's.

Leaves from the Garden

It is somewhat of a surprise to encounter the weeping Rachel in Jeremiah, because we never hear of Rachel crying during her struggle with infertility, or even at her painful death in childbirth. It is Hannah who cries, Hannah who turns the pain of being taunted inward, and weeps, and will not eat, Hannah who makes a private, silent vow to G-d: "If You will give me a son, I will give him back to You for the rest of his life." We overhear both Hannah and Sarah speaking (the one laughing, the other making vows) silently from within their hearts, but we don't hear Rachel's inward thoughts, nor do we need to. Her drives, her desires, her intentions are expressed out loud; her sadness is turned not inward but outward. Her first recorded speech? "Give me children, or I will die!" shouted in frustration at her equally frustrated husband.

Rachel then proceeds to take action to end her infertility. Like Sarah, she tries a surrogate arrangement, presenting her husband with her handmaid to impregnate, with the intention of adopting any resulting child. Unlike Sarah's disastrous experience, Rachel's arrangement works as planned, yet she is not satisfied. She then turns to pharmacology. When Leah's son presents her with a gift of mandrakes, a plant believed to have fertility-enhancing properties, Rachel bargains aggressively for them, ultimately directing Jacob to spend a night with Leah in exchange for the plants. The result is two more pregnancies for Leah. When Rachel is finally remembered and gives birth to a son, she names him Joseph – "G-d should add another son for me." (As someone who has attended hundreds of births, I must comment that it is virtually unheard of for a woman to speak of having more children on the same day that she delivers her first!) But Rachel doesn't stop striving to have children until she dies – ironically in childbirth, at a young age. To me, she is the most recognizably modern of the three – persistent, insistent, with a clear idea of what she wants, and a plan for how to get it.

Understanding Rachel's passionate character helps give depth to the weeping mother who appears in Jeremiah. This is no hopeless, despondent woman letting the tears fall silently. Rather her crying is an insistent plea, even a demand to G-d that He do something to change the intolerable plight of her children – "she refuses to be comforted." Rachel might be a difficult wife and a formidable rival, but she is just the ancestor you'd want on your side in a desperate situation – she'll never give up.

Nevertheless, it's still curious that Jeremiah chooses Rachel, of all the matriarchs, to be the universal figure of mourning, the mother-advocate for all the tribes of Israel. After all, Leah gave birth to more tribes, including the

Rosh HaShanah Day Two (II)

really important ones, like Judah and Levi. How has Rachel managed, once more, to upstage her?

Let me propose two fairly straightforward answers to this question, and then one rather complex one that I find very profound.

The first simple explanation: Jeremiah chooses Rachel as his bereaved mother-figure because he is using Ephraim, the dominant tribe in the Northern confederation, as a stand-in for all of Israel. Therefore Rachel, who is Ephraim's grandmother through Joseph, is a stand-in for all of the mothers. However, this doesn't explain why Jeremiah would not have chosen Sarah or Rebecca as the weeping mother – after all, both of them are the ancestresses of all twelve tribes, and they both have determination and persistence to spare.

The second simple explanation is geographical. Rachel was buried on the road to Ephrat, and the midrash says she was buried there precisely so that the exiles of Israel would pass by her grave and induce her to arise and advocate for them. If you look at a map, this solution actually doesn't make that much sense geographically, but it makes a lot of sense psychologically. Rachel is, in fact, the exile among the matriarchs and patriarchs. She is the only one not buried in the ancestral vault in the cave of Machpelah, and she is the only matriarch who was not able to complete the journey from Mesopotamia to a home in the holy land. Her isolation and her story of unfulfilled longing makes her especially emotionally accessible, and, indeed, modern Jews, mostly descendants of Leah, come to her tomb to ask her support in their prayers for fertility, for healing from sickness, and for protection from harm.

The third complex explanation involves a midrash within a midrash, so let me unpack them one at a time.

The inner midrash undertakes to show that, even though it appears that the rivalry between Leah and Rachel was as intense as that between any pair of brothers in Genesis, in fact, theirs is a history of jealousy overcome. How? Well, Rachel and Jacob, both being skilled tricksters, had figured out that Laban was likely to try to cheat Jacob by substituting Leah for Rachel on her wedding day. Jacob therefore taught Rachel secret signs by which he would recognize her. If his veiled bride did not show him the signs on his wedding day, he would stop the wedding before it became valid. However, as the wedding day approached, it became clear to Rachel that Laban was determined to substitute Leah, and that there was no way for her to prevent it. Rather than have Leah left humiliated and unmarriageable by Jacob's public rejection of her at the wedding, Rachel taught her the secret signs so that she would not be discovered until after the wedding night. Some versions of this midrash say that Rachel actually hid under the wedding bed and answered every time Jacob called her name, so that he would not recognize the voice of Leah.

Now, let me acknowledge that this midrash presents some significant problems. It's a little perverse, and a little farcical, and very painful. It adds yet another layer of deception to the marriage of Jacob. Furthermore, it seems inconsistent with the portrait of Rachel in the Torah. Rachel clearly is jealous of Leah during their marriage; it says so in plain Hebrew. Look at the militant names that Rachel gives to her handmaid's sons – Dan: "God has vindicated me" and Nafatali: "I've struggled with my sister and prevailed." Leah, for her part, accuses Rachel of husband-stealing, not exactly evidence that she owes a debt of gratitude. At first glance, this seems to be one of those tales that whitewash our ancestors; turning them from believable, flesh and blood characters into impossible saints while denying the plain meaning of the text.

However, the more I look at this midrash, the more profound I find it. It speaks to the unique circumstances of Rachel and Leah's story: they are the only rival wives who are also sisters, and they are the first rival siblings who manage to live together. Their competition is unique in that it is vitally productive, resulting in the twelve tribes of Israel. Sarah's introduction of a rival wife into her own family results in the birth of Ishmael, who must be separated from Isaac, and whose relations with his half-brother are hostile and tragic to this very day. In contrast, Rachel and Leah's sons undergo intense enmity, but end up reconciled, sustaining one another, and forming a single nation. This unusual outcome for a bitter rivalry might well be explained if the difficult marriage of Jacob, Rachel and Leah really did begin with a brief, secret act of compassion.

Moreover, the great biblical personalities sometimes do behave contrary to their established character, especially at moments of testing. The obvious example, of course, is the *Akeidah* from today's Torah reading. Abraham has been established as a gentle, hospitable man, hating unnecessary violence, loving justice, and longing for children more than anything G-d can give him. It is completely out of character for him to contemplate harming his son, which is why sacrificing Isaac is the ultimate test of Abraham's obedience to G-d. Likewise Judah, a character who cares deeply about maintaining his blameless image, has his moment of truth when he admits publicly that he has wronged Tamar. So in biblical thinking (and in High Holiday thinking!) it is possible that Rachel, as focused and persistent and passionate and

Rosh HaShanah Day Two (II)

capable of jealousy as she was, might have had a moment, a night, when her compassion for her sister overwhelmed her drive to have things her way. It does not negate this sacrifice, but rather intensifies it that her suppressed feelings of jealousy returned, that her marriage was anything but serene, and that she was ultimately separated from Jacob forever in her death and burial.

With this in mind, we turn to the second midrash, which is from *Eichah Rabbah*: On the day that the Temple is destroyed (due to idol worship) and the wretched survivors are sent into exile, the prophet Jeremiah goes to the graves of Abraham, Isaac, Jacob and Moses and calls for them to arise. Each pleads to G-d to reverse the exile, but to each G-d answers, "Your children have violated every letter of every commandment in the Torah, and how can I reverse My decree?" Then Rachel appears (unbidden!) and reminds G-d of her own story – how Jacob worked for her for seven years, how he loved her and wanted only to marry her, and how she, Rachel, suppressed her jealousy of her sister and taught her the secret signs to spare Leah the humiliation of rejection. "And if I, who am only flesh and blood," says Rachel "could accept a rival into my own house, then how can You, who are the L-rd of the universe, be threatened by idols, who are nothing at all?" And G-d accepts Rachel's plea: "Your children will come back from the land of the enemy."

I want to draw your attention to something remarkable in this second midrash, which is its hierarchy of values. Remember that before Rachel speaks, Abraham, Isaac, Jacob and Moses all make unsuccessful pleas. Abraham and Isaac, as you would expect, invoke the *Akeidah* – Abraham his willingness to make the sacrifice, Isaac his willingness to be sacrificed. Now of course we moderns have problems with the implications of the *Akeidah*. But in traditional thinking, it has always been our ace-in-the-hole when pleading with G-d for merciful judgment. Abraham's ability to suppress his compassion for his son is supposed to guarantee G-d's merciful response for all future transgressions. Yet in this midrash, the *Akeidah* ranks lower than Rachel's sacrifice for the sake of her sister. Rachel's willingness to let her sisterly love overwhelm her dreams of an ideal future trumps Abraham's achievement of suppressing his paternal love for the sake of absolute faith.

What does Rachel gain for this? Not a happy life – her marriage is filled with recriminations, frustration, and jealousy. But her children and Leah's will not destroy one another. And she gains the high moral ground, the power to intercede successfully with G-d, and to plead convincingly for her children:

> Refrain your voice from weeping,
> and your eyes from tears;

for your work shall be rewarded, ...
And there is hope for your future, says the LORD;
Your children shall return to their own border.
(Jeremiah 31:15-16)

Shabbat Shuvah

Ruth Tupper

One of the benefits of my occupation as a journalist is I get to meet all kinds of interesting people with all kinds of interesting stories to tell. The only criterion they must all share is that they live in Deerfield, the circulation area of my newspaper.

One of these stories was so compelling that I felt an obligation to share it with you. I chose *Shabbat Shuvah* because the story is about loss of faith and regaining faith, partially through forgiveness. It is also about wondering why God allows evil to happen in the world. These are all topics that hit very close to home, and may for many of you as well.

Before I tell you the story of Wes Adamczyk, a Catholic Pole who was born in the period between the two world wars, and who is now a retired chemist and accountant living in Deerfield, let me bring you back to 1969 when I was eleven years old. My family and I were taking a European vacation: three days in Brussels, three days in Holland, three days in Switzerland . . . three hours in Germany. I asked my mother why we were not visiting Germany for longer than it took to whiz across the country on the famous autobahn at 100 miles per hour. Her answer: your father is still angry about how the Germans had murdered six million Jews, including his grandparents, aunts, uncles and cousins. He had no desire to visit a country tied to such evil.

At the same time that my great-grandparents and other relatives were being taken by train to death camps from their home in Galicia, then southeastern Poland, Wes Adamczyk, at the age of seven, was experiencing his own nightmare in northern Poland. His father had been an army officer in 1920, fighting the Bolsheviks successfully. The Soviets, under Stalin in 1939, did not forget this. After Germany invaded Poland in September 1939 on the west, the Soviets invaded on the east. Wes' father was taken prisoner by the Soviets, and, in the spring of 1940, he and 15,000 other Polish army officers and "bourgeoisie" were murdered at close range in the Katyn forest

29

area of the Ukraine. But young Wes did not know this, all he knew was that about six months after his father said goodbye to him for the last time, a knock came at the door telling his mother and his two teenage siblings and him to pack their bags and take a train ride. They were taken from their comfortable home, where Wes had prayed to God every night that all would be well, to a packed train foul with the stench of human waste: their bathroom was a hole in the floor of the train car. Wes and his family ended up in the steppes of Kazakhstan, far away from their homeland. In his book, Wes told the story of his brave mother, who resourcefully hid jewels in her clothing when they were forced to leave Poland. My great-grandmother had used the same trick with her daughter, my great-aunt Marcia, to allow our family's only surviving relative to live when she was pushed off the train headed for a death camp.

Wes' mother took her two children to freedom by just walking out of their village of exile in broad daylight, and bribing bureaucrats with the hidden jewelry to allow them to get to what was then called Persia. At the age of twelve, just after they arrived in Persia, Wes saw a trainload of Polish orphan children, some without eyes. He cried out to his mother, "Mama, is God blind too?" And shortly after that, he too became an orphan, when his mother died from malnutrition and disease. He told me that is when he lost his faith in God.

I know that David Bier, who works with Holocaust refugees, has been troubled by this concept because a while back he gave a *d'var* on this issue, saying he, too, had heard stories of those troubled by this whole question of how God could allow such unspeakable evil. If He is omnipotent, why did He not intervene on behalf of the Jews, on behalf of the Polish orphan children?

Wes Adamczyk entitled his book, *When God Looked the Other Way* (Univ. of Chicago Press 2004). That line is also echoed in this and last week's Torah portion, *Vayelech*, Chapter 31 verse 18: *va' anochi haster eesteer pah-nahy b'yom ha-hu* (And as for Me, I will surely hide My face on that day), but then it states: *al kol ha-raah asher ahsah kee pannah el eloheeem achareem* (for all the evil that they have done, for they turned to other gods). According to the commentary at the bottom of page 1176 of the *Etz Hayim*, Martin Buber, a refugee from Nazi Germany, links this image of God hiding and turning away to the terrible things that happen in the world.

In this week's poem, *Haazinu*, the same line recurs in chapter 32 verse 20: *va yomer, eesterah pah-nay may-hem ar-yehg mah acharritam* (Let Me hide My face from them, I shall see what their end shall be) *cee dor tah-*

Shabbat Shuvah

heucctot hamah bahneem lo aymen bam (For a wayward brood are they, children with no trust in them).

So the Torah sets out the precedent that God does warn Israel that He will hide His face from them, but it appears linked to the Jews doing terrible deeds. Few of us want to believe that the Holocaust occurred because we Jews were doing terrible deeds.

Neil Gillman, who spoke at our 25th anniversary Shabbaton last year, tried to tackle this issue in his book, *The Way into Encountering God in Judaism* (Jewish Lights Publishing 2004), Gillman posits the idea that all three statements cannot be true: God is omnipotent, God is good, the Jews (or Job or the innocent child who died) are blameless. When forced to choose which is not true, Gillman went for omnipotent. Maybe God is not omnipotent, sometimes God is just not there, and humans have free will to choose not only between life and death, as Jodie told us last week, but, equally important, between good and evil, as Heschel said in his book, *God in Search of Man* (Farrar, Straus & Giraux 1997).

But Heschel took a different view: God is omnipotent; in fact, He created humans knowing full well they could choose to do evil. Making it more complicated, sometimes humans start off thinking they are doing good, and it sort of transmogrifies into evil. Osama bin Laden, evil though his murder of those 3,000 plus innocent victims was at the World Trade Center, the Pentagon and the field in Pennsylvania, apparently thought he was doing good, in his own warped view.

But we should not think that only 21st century Jews are grappling with this concept of *When Bad Things Happen to Good People.* Clearly, our ancestors were anguishing over the same question in the times of the Bible. Heschel cites Psalm 55: "Fear and trembling come upon me, and horror has overwhelmed me. And I said: 'Oh that I had wings like a dove! then would I fly away, and be at rest.' " And Psalm 83: "O God, keep not silent; hold not Your peace, and be not still, O God. For, lo, Your enemies are in an uproar; and they that hate You have lifted up the head." And Gillman cites Psalms 13 and 44 where he says "in neither of these texts is there even a hint that God's punitive behavior is deserved."

Clearly, the struggle to do good is a constant one for humans, which makes the *Yamim Noraim* and the accompanying soul searching and quest for forgiveness all the more welcome. If we could not purge ourselves of this guilt we feel over our misdeeds every year, think how polluted we would feel. The beauty of Yom Kippur is it can appeal to everyone on the spectrum of belief in God. As Heschel said, in Judaism, we do not look into people's beliefs, we stress only their action, their carrying out the mitzvot.

Now this week as we go around asking those we love and those we know for forgiveness, we can feel better. Still, Judaism teaches there are two sins we cannot forgive each other for, slander and murder: slander, because it is impossible to know how many others heard the *lashon harah* and so impossible to make the victim whole again, and murder, because the victims are dead and they are the only ones who can grant forgiveness.

I asked my father last week if he still would refrain from visiting Germany today, 59 years after the Holocaust. He said yes, he was still angry.

Then, I read an article in Richard's *Yale Alumni Magazine* (Sept./Oct. 2004) on "Why We Hate," an article about the work of Robert Sternberg, professor of psychology and education and the son of a Holocaust survivor, an article which brought many of the pieces of this story together for me. Like my great aunt Marcia, who changed her name to "Maria" after her mother pushed her off the train headed for a death camp, Sternberg's mother survived because she did not "look" Jewish. My aunt Marcia was also helped by righteous gentiles, Polish peasants who chose good, at great personal risk, hiding her and feeding her potatoes to survive.

Sternberg defined the importance of story telling in the human condition, saying narrative was a "fundamental aspect of human cognition" that sets us apart from other animals. These narratives give meaning to our lives. The problem occurs when the narratives all center around the suffering that one group experienced at the hands of another. That is when hate is born, even if the initial injustice occurred hundreds of years ago.

And here is how Wes' story ends: Wes came to Chicago when he was fifteen years old to live with his father's cousin. He finished college, married, had children. He always wondered what had happened to his father. The official line was that the Germans had murdered those Polish officers at the Katyn forest, although the Germans had maintained they had not done it. It was the one crime they, in fact, did not commit during World War II. Then in 1990, under *perestroika,* President Mikhail Gorbachev finally admitted that it was the Soviets who had massacred the Polish officers, with the approval of Josef Stalin. The Polish government then invited the surviving members of the officers' families to come to the Ukraine to lay wreaths on their graves. Wes went with his grown son to represent other Katyn families from the Chicago area. A BBC news crew filmed the visit, which was made into a documentary, "Forgotten Odyssey," which Wes showed me. On the way back from laying the wreaths, the train stopped in a town that Wes

Shabbat Shuvah

remembered from his childhood. Everyone got off the train. Why? Some young Ukrainian soldiers wanted to break bread dipped in salt with the families of the Katyn victims. It was a peace offering. The camera showed Wes sitting stubbornly on the train, refusing to get off. Then he said he felt a divine spirit move him to get off the train, and he went down to where the officers were standing. He dipped the bread in the salt and ate. Wes told me he believed that without forgiveness, this hatred would just continue on and on. The world has too much hate, Wes told me.

I believe we can all show divinity when we say we are sorry to each other, and when we ask each other for forgiveness. Just as God forgives, so can we as God's partners. In so doing, may God's countenance not turn away but shine on us.

Finally, I asked my father if, given the chance, he, too, would get off a train as Wes did, and break bread with the descendents of the Germans, if they made that request. He paused for a very long time, and then said quietly, "Yes."

Shabbat Shuvah (II)

Richard Tupper

Ritual arises from need. When we are faced with some compelling need that we cannot otherwise meet, often we find that ritual answers the need. When we no longer have the need, often the ritual will fall away. Sometimes, if the ritual is aesthetically pleasing, we'll retain the ritual until our circumstances change and ritual becomes a burden. For example, many non-observant Jews will keep a mezuzah on their doors because they like the look of it. But if they move into a community where mezuzot are viewed as alien, they may very well be tempted to dispense with the mezuzah in order to fit in better.

In my *d'var Torah*, I want to focus on the ritual of *Kol Nidre* that will be chanted on *erev Yom Kippur*. Many Jews find *Kol Nidre* the most moving part of the Yom Kippur service. For myself, when it comes to *Kol Nidre*, there is no one whom I like to hear chanting it more than Larry Moss, because, as I've often said, no one fakes a sincere humility better than Larry!

But why is it that Jews throughout history and throughout the world have grown so attached to *Kol Nidre*? Why does this service annulling vows between HaShem and us as individuals have such a grip on so many of us? Is it just that we like the tune, or is it something more?

One popular explanation for the origin of *Kol Nidre* is that it arose to accommodate the *conversos* of Spain, Jews who were forced to convert to Christianity during times of persecution. However, scholars pretty much agree that the *Kol Nidre* service long antedates the needs of the *conversos* in Spain. Thus, while I have no doubt that the *Kol Nidre* service carried a profound meaning for Jewish *conversos*, its origins are in something far more universal than the *conversos'* specific historical context. And that is the reason *Kol Nidre* persists long after, even until today.

Anti-Semites, of course, have always used *Kol Nidre* as an excuse for attacking us, but since anti-Semites ignore that the *Kol Nidre* service is about annulling vows between God and an individual and not about annulling vows between two people, they completely misunderstand the purpose of *Kol Nidre*.

For hundreds of years, the *Kol Nidre* service has been chanted on *erev Yom Kippur* throughout the Jewish world. While the *Kol Nidre* service has its roots in Mishnaic provisions for the annulling of vows, it was, I think it is fair to say, often opposed by rabbinic authorities as inconsistent with Jewish law. The method used in *Kol Nidre* for releasing an individual from vows did not comport in the view of many leading rabbinic authorities with the requirements of the *Mishnah*, and throughout history leading rabbis have tried to suppress the recitation of *Kol Nidre* on Yom Kippur. However, lay Jews – *Am Yisrael* – have always insisted on its inclusion and eventually the rabbis had to give in. I find it striking that even the Reform movement, which dispensed with *Kol Nidre* for years, has decided to reinstitute the *Kol Nidre* service.

Am Yisrael's attachment to *Kol Nidre* is demonstrated also by this: during the Middle Ages, Rabbi Meir ben Shmuel, or the RaM, changed the wording of the *Kol Nidre* from past tense to future tense so that instead of annulling vows made to HaShem in the prior year, the *Kol Nidre* service would serve to annul vows made in the upcoming year. However, I would willingly bet that if you asked the average Jew which vows *Kol Nidre* annuls, past or future, the average Jew would say past vows, not future. Thus, while the rabbis tried to change the meaning of *Kol Nidre* by changing the very words of the service, *Am Yisrael* continues to understand it in the way we want or need to understand it. On the other hand, as my friend, Irv HaCohen, once remarked to me, perhaps the RaM's view was: "You know me, HaShem; on Yom Kippur I get carried away. *Pay no attention!*"

Some speculate that *Kol Nidre* has its roots in the generalized fear that people in the ancient world had about breaking vows. The theory is that while vows were discouraged, people couldn't resist taking vows and when Yom Kippur came around, people feared that HaShem would punish them for having broken their vows; hence, they wanted a ritual that would stave off divine retribution.

I think this last view has merit, but *Kol Nidre* is not rooted in just some generalized fear about the evil of breaking vows.

I can easily believe that a *Baal Teshuvah* (newly recommitted Jew) or a recent convert can go through a few Yom Kippur services and believe that *next year* it will be different, that all the promises they made to themselves and to HaShem about how they would change, for example, by going to services, or lighting candles or keeping kosher, would in fact come true. But

Shabbat Shuvah (II)

after a few years, they, like the rest of us who have been through this more than a few times, know that more likely than not they will have broken these promises.

What was a person supposed to do on *erev Yom Kippur* who last year promised HaShem that he or she would be more observant in some respect and now on *erev Yom Kippur* the person knows that he or she has broken this vow? The temptation is to stay home. After all, why would God forgive those who year after year make these promises that they then break? Why would God want us to come?

Kol Nidre responds to this anxiety. What is God telling us in *Kol Nidre*? God is saying, "Yes, you made Me a promise and you broke it, but I am releasing you of the promise. A broken vow cannot stand between you and Me, it cannot block repentance." A cynic would say that this ritual only encourages us to sin all the more, but the penitent sinner knows better – *Kol Nidre* opens the way to true repentance.

Yom Kippur is about recommitment. HaShem does not want our broken vows to heaven to stand in the way of recommitting ourselves to HaShem. Like the most loving parent, HaShem is always ready to take us back. If I may make a rough analogy used by my law partner, Jacob Pomeranz, who opened my eyes to this insight, *Kol Nidre* is sort of like bankruptcy. In order for a person to start over, we tell the person that all the past obligations are erased and the person begins with a clean slate. So, too, HaShem tells us during *Kol Nidre* that our past broken vows are wiped away, that we are welcome in the House of Prayer to recommit our lives to HaShem.

But *teshuvah* is about more than repentance. Repentance is the first step of returning to God. But to return to God we must walk in His ways. What does it mean to walk in God's ways? The rabbis say in *Sifre Deuteronomy, Eikev*:

> "To walk in all His ways" (Deut. 11:22). These are the ways of the Holy One: "gracious and compassionate, patient, abounding in kindness and faithfulness, assuring love for a thousand generations, forgiving iniquity, transgression, and sin and granting pardon . . . ." This means that just as God is gracious and compassionate, you too must be gracious and compassionate. "The Lord is faithful in all His ways and loving in all His deeds" (Psalm 148:17). As the Holy One is faithful, you too must be faithful. As the Holy One is loving, you too must be loving.

Leaves from the Garden

The most important thing in life is not a Nobel Prize or a Pulitzer or winning a Supreme Court argument, it's not rewards or recognition. The most important thing in life is how we treat others, whether it is our dearest loved ones or the stranger we pass on the street.

Our relationships with others are a series of net-like connections and, just as a net weakens exponentially as each individual strand tears, so too our relationships with others weaken as each individual strand of our connections with them tears. That is why it is so important to repair our relationships. Unless we fastidiously repair our relationships, they can, like a net, tear beyond repair. Repentance and forgiveness are an important part of repairing our relationships with others.

Just as HaShem is forgiving, so we must be forgiving towards those around us. But we humans encounter a problem when it comes to forgiveness that HaShem does not. HaShem has perfect "*binah*" – the ability to discern. HaShem can discern true repentance, we often cannot. Sometimes we refuse to forgive when a person truly repents, sometimes we forgive when the person is not truly repentant.

Often forgiving a person who is not truly penitent has no adverse consequence, they simply get a free pass. But the more intense the relationship, then the greater is the likelihood that feigned repentance and misguided forgiveness will work future injury. The spouse that betrays the other or the parent that betrays a child, after having been forgiven once before, does far more damage to the innocent spouse or child than he or she did the first time around.

I used to think that a relationship ended when one said to the other, "I can't forgive you for what you did." But upon further reflection I think there is an anterior barrier to reconciliation. That is when one person says to the other, "I'm sorry" and the other responds, "I don't believe you." No matter how sincere the penitent may be, the disbelief of the wronged party forecloses any reconciliation.

In this period of repentance, as we each ask forgiveness of each other, may HaShem grant each of us the *binah*, the discernment, to discern in ourselves the sins for which we must seek forgiveness from others and to discern true repentance when we encounter it in others. May HaShem also grant us the grace to forgive. When we truly repent to each other and we forgive each other, we walk in HaShem's ways, and it is when we walk in HaShem's ways that we see in each other the face of HaShem. That, my friends, may be a truism, but, like all truisms, there lies at its core a profound truth.

Yom Kippur

Richard Tupper

"Why are we doing this?" How many times have you asked or been asked that question when performing one of the many rituals that permeate our lives? "It's a mitzvah!" is one answer but often we at least try to grasp the symbolism embedded in the ritual to make it more meaningful.

One challenge of today's portion is that many of the rituals described in it have not been performed since the destruction of the Temple. As a result, we must read the portion very carefully to see just what it is that is being done before we can ask, "Why are they doing this?"

When studying this portion, one question I had was – why must the High Priest change clothes during the Yom Kippur service? Why in the beginning of the portion is he told to put on garments of linen and only linen and then towards the end told to take off the linen garments and to put on his other garments, presumably his customary garments? Although not immediately clear from the text, the commentators (see, *e.g.*, Rashi on v. 4) seem to agree that the High Priest wears the garments of pure linen when he enters the Tabernacle (Lev. 16:3-4) but wears his customary high priestly garments when he goes before the people (Lev.16:23-24). And so, I ask, why is he doing that? Why can't he wear his customary garments into the presence of HaShem?

Of course, one answer is, "because it's a mitzvah!" But if my *davar* were to end with that, it would be short but not very inspiring, so let's slog on.

Rashi suggests that the High Priest must wear linen garments rather than his customary garments because his customary garments contain gold. If the High Priest were to wear garments containing gold in the presence of HaShem, it might remind HaShem of the incident of the golden calf – not the sort of mind-set you want to create on Yom Kippur.

I think the answer to this question may involve not gold but *shaatnes*. We all know the Torah's ban on *shaatnes*, on wearing garments of mixed materials (Lev. 19:19), particularly wool and linen (Deut. 22:11). However, if you thought there was no *shaatnes* among Israel, you would be mistaken.

For instance, the Tabernacle's curtains were made of linen interwoven with costly dyed wool. (See, *e.g.*, Ex. 26:1, 31, 36; 27:9, 16; the dyed material was wool; see, *e.g.*, Rashi's commentary on these verses.) Of course the ban on *shaatnes* applied to garments, but the customary garments of the High Priest contained *shaatnes*. His ephod was made of linen and costly dyed wool (Ex. 39:2), so too were the straps of the breastplate (Ex. 39:8) as well as his robe (Ex. 39:22-24) and his belt (Ex. 39:28). Even his turban was linen with a *techeilet*, a blue woolen strand, threaded through it (Ex. 39:28, 31). On this *techeilet* hung a gold plate, a *tziz*, inscribed with the words, "Holy to the LORD" (Ex. 39:30).

Jacob Milgrom, the JPS commentator on Numbers, has a brilliant essay in the back of this volume, with the pedestrian title of "Excursus 38,"[1] in which he suggests that it is precisely because of the abundance of *shaatnes* in the Tabernacle and the High Priest's clothing that *shaatnes* was banned from common use. Thus, just as some Americans might object to "desecrating" the flag by wearing clothing made from it, so, too, *shaatnes* was seen as reserved for the Tabernacle service and the High Priest's office, and was therefore considered holy and not to be used in common clothing.

If Milgrom is right and *shaatnes* was considered holy, why then would Aaron wear his customary *shaatnes* garments when he went before the people but must only wear garments of pure linen when he stood before God inside the Tabernacle? To answer that, we must grapple with what *shaatnes* represented. If my theory on what *shaatnes* represented – discussed below – is correct, the fact that Aaron customarily wore *shaatnes* except for when he stood in the presence of HaShem is the proverbial "exception that proves the rule."

At first blush, *shaatnes* seems a strange material to be holy since we usually associate holiness with its root meaning of "separate" (*e.g.*, Lev. 20:26). But not every mixture or combination is bad. Some are very good and others even holy. God did not perceive creation as "*tov meod*/very good" until after Adam was created (Gen. 1:31). Adam, unlike the rest of creation, was a combination – made from the dust of the earth and the breath of life from God (Gen. 2:7).

As for combinations being holy, aside from *shaatnes*, there was the incense that was burned in the Tabernacle. This incense was made of a

---

[1] This same essay appears in the back of the *Etz Hayim*, pp. 1468-1470.

Yom Kippur

combination of spices, none of which by itself was considered holy, but the combination of the spices was declared "most holy" (Ex. 30:34-37). So holy was this combination of spices that the people were forbidden from using it for any purpose other than burning it as incense in the Tabernacle (Ex. 30:38). Similarly, there was the anointing oil used in the Tabernacle (Ex. 30:22-33). It, too, was made from a combination of spices, and, just like the incense, this particular combination of spices was holy and could only be used as anointing oil for the Tabernacle service (Ex. 30:32-33). Striking similarities to *shaatnes*.

Holy objects or substances seemingly have the remarkable ability to transform other – presumably pure – objects into holy objects as well. The holy oil is used to anoint the various utensils of the Tabernacle and they then become "most holy" (Ex. 30:26-29). Once the utensils are "most holy," anything that touches them becomes holy (Ex. 30:29). The Tabernacle's altar is described as "most holy" (Ex. 29:37), and whatever touches it is holy (*ibid.*). Likewise, various sacrifices are described as "most holy," and whatever touches them is holy (Lev. 6:7-11, 18-20).

Israel, too, is called to be holy (*e.g.*, Lev. 11:45). How does Israel become holy? By obeying HaShem's mitzvot (Num. 15:39-40).

Thus, just as the white linen, when interwoven with the precious dyed wool, becomes *shaatnes*, a holy material, so, too, when Israel purified itself – made itself white – by sacrifice and confession – and wove into its life God's mitzvot, it would become a holy combination, reserved for a special purpose, "to be a kingdom of priests and a holy nation" (Ex. 19:6).

This may explain why Aaron wears *shaatnes* when he goes before the people but pure linen when he stands before God in the Tabernacle. When Aaron stands before the people in his customary *shaatnes* clothing, he personifies the Covenant, God and Israel intertwined. However, when he stands before God in the Holy of Holies, he personifies not the Covenant but purified, penitent Israel, thus the white linen. This combination – Aaron, as purified, penitent Israel, standing in the presence of God in the Holy of Holies on this day, Yom Kippur – is *shaatnes*, the pure in contact with the Holy and thereby transformed.

One last "thread." There was apparently yet another article of clothing that was *shaatnes* – *tzitzit*. Milgrom in his Excursus 38 posits that *tzitzit* were originally *shaatnes*. The mitzvah of *tzitzit* is found in Num. 15:37-41. Apparently, *tzitzit* or fringes were common among the people of those times, worn by men and women. In Numbers, the people are commanded to add to the fringes of their garments a *techeilet*, a blue woolen strand, just like the *techeilet* on Aaron's turban. The blue dye for the woolen thread was so valued that the color was reserved for royalty. Thus, by adding the blue woolen strand to their *tzitzit*, all Israel became elevated to the status of royalty. Indeed, the Talmud recounts how R. Judah HaNasi made *tzitzit* for his daughter to wear. Remarkably, however, it seems that adding the blue woolen strand to the garment rendered the garment *shaatnes*.

Milgrom points to a portion of a targum (an ancient Aramaic translation) as well as passages from the Talmud discussing how adding the *techeilet* to the garment could render the garment *shaatnes*.[1] (Milgrom apparently believes that the *tzitzit* themselves were *shaatnes*, linen fringes with a blue woolen thread – not the assumption of Rashi and Ramban – but Milgrom is apparently relying upon a targum.) The rabbis conclude, however, that the positive mitzvah of *tzitzit* supersedes the negative mitzvah of *shaatnes*. Indeed, they point out that these two mitzvot, *shaatnes* and *tzitzit*, appear together in Deut. 22:11-12, first *shaatnes* and then *tzitzit*. Thus the rabbis conclude that Israel must add the *techeilet*, the blue woolen strand, to their *tzitzit* even though it may render the garment *shaatnes*. Milgrom reports that the excavation of the Bar Kochba caves uncovered *shaatnes tzitzit*.

When the people are commanded to put the *techeilet*, the blue woolen strand, on the fringes/*tzitzit* of their garments, the purpose is to remind them to keep God's commandments and so be holy (Num. 15: 39-40). Why would looking at *tzitzit* make them think of commandments and holiness? Because, Milgrom suggests, when the people looked at their *tzitzit* what did they see? They saw *shaatnes*, this holy material that was reserved for the High Priest's office and the Tabernacle service. Indeed (whether or not the *techeilet* actually rendered the garment *shaatnes*), the *techeilet* of the *tzitzit* bore a striking resemblance to the *techeilet* on the High Priest's turban, lacking only the *tziz*, the inscribed gold plate. And so, when the people saw this bit of holy material on the fringes of their garments, they would remember that they, too, were to be "Holy to the LORD" (Ex. 39:30; *cf.* Num. 15:40).

The Tabernacle no longer exists. The Temple has been destroyed. No High Priest leads our worship. Even the *techeilet*, the blue woolen thread added to our fringes, is missing. The blue dye later became so costly that only the rich could afford it and so the rabbis decided to dispense with it rather than divide Israel between the rich and the poor. Nevertheless, the next time you pray and you take your *tzitzit* into your hands, and you see the fringes and you also recall the missing blue woolen thread, whose presence

---

[1] See also Rashi on Deut.22:12 and Ramban on Lev. 19:19.

once announced our royalty but whose absence today proclaims our unity, if you ask yourself, "why are we doing this?" then remember that our *tzitzit* symbolize holiness and connect us to Israel of long ago. Our *tzitzit* embody Aaron dressed in white linen as penitent, purified Israel, standing in the very presence of God on this day, Yom Kippur. Remember that we, no less than the High Priest, are called to be holy. Remember that we become holy by purifying ourselves through prayer and *teshuvah* (repentance) and by weaving into our lives God's mitzvot so that we become as it were living *shaatnes*, reserved for a holy purpose, to be "a kingdom of priests, and a holy nation" (Ex. 19:6).

After all, "it's a mitzvah!"

Yom Kippur – Mincha

Richard Tupper

This afternoon, I predict two questions are burning in almost everyone's mind. New members and visitors are no doubt wondering why we are reading Lev. 19 instead of the traditional passage, Lev. 18. Long-time members no doubt are asking themselves, "Why did we ever read Lev. 18 instead of Lev. 19?" But have no fear, I propose to offer answers to both these questions. As for the new members' and visitors' question, the reason we read Lev. 19 instead of Lev. 18 is because the membership of the Minyan in its wisdom voted a couple of years ago to read the alternative Torah portion in the *machzor*, Lev. 19 rather than 18 (and ours is the only *machzor* that I know of that has this alternative reading). Why the membership voted the way they did, I do not know. You'll have to ask the people who voted for it because I was against the change.

The more interesting question to me and hence more burning question is: why is it traditional to read on the afternoon of Yom Kippur the repeated warnings in Lev. 18, indeed repeated seven times (3 [*bis*], 24, 26, 17, 29, 30), against following the practices of the Canaanites or what HaShem describes in Lev. 18:3 (NJPS) as: "copy[ing] the practices of the land of Egypt where you dwelt, or of the land of Canaan to which I am taking you"? Now interestingly, Egyptians and Canaanites are joined by more than the mere fact that Egypt is where Israel is coming from and Canaan is where Israel is going. The Table of Nations in Genesis 10 traces back both Egyptians and Canaanites to a common ancestor – Ham (Gen. 10:6), who, when looking upon the nakedness of his father Noah (Gen. 9:22), arguably may himself have violated one of the prohibitions in this chapter. Indeed, the fact that Egyptians and Canaanites descend from Ham may partially explain why they are both guilty of these forbidden practices.

The rabbis point to a connection between our *haftarah* Jonah and chapter 18 of Leviticus. Jonah is vomited out of the great fish (Jonah 2:10), and HaShem warns Israel that if they do not obey, they will be vomited from *eretz Canaan* (18:28) just as the Canaanites were (18:25, 28). However, that is sort of putting the cart before the horse because generally we think of the *haftarah*, in this case Jonah, as relating back to the Torah portion, and not *vice versa*.

The rabbis relate another reason for reading Lev. 18 on the afternoon of Yom Kippur. In the *Mishnah, Ta'anit* 4:8, we are told:

> Rabban Simeon b. Gamaliel said: There were no happier times for Israel than the 15th of Ab and the Day of Atonement, for on them the daughters of Jerusalem used to go forth in white raiments; and these were borrowed, that none be embarrassed which had them not; [hence] all the raiments required immersion. And the daughters of Jerusalem went forth to dance in the vineyards. And what did they say? "Young man, lift up your eyes and see what you would choose for yourself: set not your eyes upon beauty, but set your eyes on family; for grace is deceitful and beauty is vain, but a woman that fears the Lord she shall be praised [Prov. 31:30]; moreover it says, Give her the fruit of her hands and let her works praise her in the gates [Prov. 31:31]. Likewise it says, Go forth you daughters of Zion, and behold king Solomon with the crown wherewith his mother hath crowned him in the day of his espousals and in the day of the gladness of his heart [Song of Songs 3:11]: In the day of his espousals – this is the giving of the Law; and in the day of the gladness of his heart – this is the building of the Temple. May it be built speedily, in our days! Amen.

It was because of these activities that the rabbis prescribed the reading of Lev. 18 in order to counsel the young men and women against entering into marriages that were forbidden. Of course, I've always wondered about how efficacious this instruction was. If the young men and women are out dancing in the vineyards on the afternoon of Yom Kippur, how will they hear the instruction? Maybe we're supposed to tell them about what was read in shul when they come home raving about their half-sister that they saw dancing or one of the sheep grazing on the nearby hillside.

For better or for worse however, today, on the afternoon of Yom Kippur, we are not graced with nubile maidens dancing in vineyards observed by eligible young men, although I think many members of the Minyan would also have voted in favor of restoring this practice had it been on the agenda. Myself, I would certainly have preferred a vote in favor of restoring this practice than in favor of not reading Lev. 18. But aside from tradition and the historical interest, is there any other reason that we ought to read Lev. 18 this afternoon? Or, as Sam Fox so often insists on asking, "what's the relevance of Lev.18 to us today, man?!"

Before trying to answer that question, however, it might benefit us to pay attention to what Lev. 18 is actually talking about. On first reading we see that Lev. 18 bans certain types of sex. On closer reading, many people find certain things troubling. For example, some people are troubled by its labeling of male homosexual sex as *toevah*/abomination, but I say: what we are troubled by is the interpretation of the verse, and I sincerely believe that over time our interpretation will evolve, but it won't evolve if we stop reading the verses that upset us. Similarly, to the extent that we find Lev. 18 boring or irrelevant, that is all the more reason to study it since it's all the more of a challenge; our understanding will never grow nor our interpretation evolve unless we continue to challenge ourselves by reading the passages we find the most troubling or incomprehensible.

Some are troubled by the fact that missing from the list are the full sister and the daughter, though the half-sister (v. 9) and the granddaughter (v. 10) are listed. Some modern scholars have proposed that they are missing from the list because such incestuous unions were not prohibited. To me this seems to be a reading whose intention is to portray Israel in the worst possible light, a type of reading that is sadly common among modern scholars. The rabbis use a *kal v'chomer* argument – if your half-sister and granddaughter are prohibited, *kal v'chomer* your full sister and daughter are prohibited. But I think a modern scholar by the name of Susan Rattray has offered a fascinating solution to this problem by focusing on v. 6. Verse 6 says no one shall approach "anyone of his own flesh" *el kol sh'er bsaro*; what does this phrase mean? Rattray notes that a similar phrase appears in ch. 21 where it says:

> None shall defile himself (mourning) for any dead person among his kin, 2 except for his closest relatives [*ki im lesh'ero haqarov elav*]: his mother, his father, his son, his daughter, and his brother; 3 also for his marriagable sister, closest to him, for her he may defile himself.

In other words, in Lev. 18:6 a man is prohibited from having sex with his closest kin, and these are, Rattray suggests, those identified in 21:2-3 as the relatives closest to him: his mother, father, son, daughter, brother and virgin sister. The purpose of the rest of the chapter, Rattray suggests, is to explain who else, in addition to the nearest kin, are forbidden:

1. Extended family members are discussed until v. 19.
2. The married sister banned by the ban on adulterous sex in v. 20.

If Rattray is right, why then is "mother" still included since she is included in "nearest kin"? Listing mother with father establishes the principle of affinity that, along with blood, accounts for everyone on the list until v. 19.
1. Two persons that marry are "one flesh."
2. To the extent the one that is related to you by blood is banned, to the same extent that person's spouse is banned.

The real problem in reading ch. 18 is that it reads like our family history. Verse 20 bans intercourse with your neighbor's wife, but David had intercourse with Batsheva. Verse 12 bans intercourse between a man and his father's sister, but, of course, Amram married his father's sister, Yocheved (Ex. 6:20), and she bore Moses and Aaron and from Aaron springs the entire priesthood. Verse 15 bans intercourse between a man and his daughter-in-law, but Judah had intercourse with his daughter-in-law Tamar (Gen. 38:18), from whom descended the tribe of Judah and the entire Davidic line. Verse 18 bans marrying two sisters yet Jacob married Leah and Rachel (Gen. 29:28). And, finally, verse 9 bans intercourse between a man and his father's daughter, but Abram married Sara, his father's daughter and his half-sister, and from them all of us descend. The rabbis define children of forbidden unions listed here as *mamzerim*, and Deut. 23:3 bans *mamzerim* from ever entering the congregation of the LORD.

Now, of course, David was punished for his transgression, but what of these other banned unions from which we spring? Ibn Ezra argues that the prohibitions apply only within the land of Israel, and Nachmanides supports his argument by noting that Rachel dies when she enters the land of Canaan. Abarbanel however argues that the prohibitions apply to Israel outside Canaan as well but further argues that since the Torah had not yet been given, the patriarchs did not violate the prohibitions because the laws do not apply *ex post facto*. If that is true, however, why are Canaanites vomited from the land and the Egyptians condemned for having violated these prohibitions? They had not received the Torah, had they?

We seem to be confronted with a quandary: we are called to be a "kingdom of priests and a holy nation" (Ex. 19:6), yet we are a nation of *mamzerim*. If it is our ancestors who sinned, can we repent for them, and thus rid ourselves of this terrible label?

The answer to our difficulty lies not in repentance, a major theme of today, but in yet another major theme today – holiness, and more specifically in this case, the transforming power of the mitzvot through which holiness is achieved. What do the mitzvot do? They transform us from common to holy. With every *bracha* we say, *"asher kiddeshanu b'mitzvotav"* – "who makes us holy through His mitzvot." Becoming a kingdom of priests and a holy nation is not achieved simply by repentance. Through repentance we become pure, but holiness is achieved through the mitzvot. God is not satisfied with Jews who have purified themselves by repentance. God demands more, that we become holy, and holiness is achieved only through obedience to God's mitzvot. Indeed, the mitzvot are not only the source of holiness but, as Lev. 18:5 teaches us, they are the source of life itself.

And so, what were those young men and maidens doing in the vineyards? They were looking for marriage partners so that they could fulfill the first mitzvah, *pru urvu* – to be fruitful and multiply, and it is through fulfilling this mitzvah that we most easily perceive the connection between the mitzvot and life. Instinctively the young men and women understood that God demands more than repentance, they understood that God demands that we fulfill the mitzvot and thereby become holy, a kingdom of priests and a holy nation.

And the prescription of the rabbis that we read Lev. 18? Thousands of years ago, it had a very practical effect – to counsel the young people as to whom it is proper to marry. But yes, Sam, even today it is relevant. Traditionally we do not read Lev. 19 which contains perhaps the most difficult of all the mitzvot to fulfill, to love our neighbor (18) and even the stranger (34) as ourselves. If traditionally on Yom Kippur we read Lev. 19 with these most difficult mitzvot, we could easily despair of our ability to obey and even to repent because true repentance requires prospective obedience. Instead the rabbis prescribe that we read what for many of us are the most easily obeyed mitzvot – refraining from sex, for example, with animals and our in-laws!

This morning we read the description of the sacrifices offered to atone for our sins and to purge the Temple of the impurities caused by our sins. However, the Temple has been destroyed and not rebuilt so we cannot offer these sacrifices. We do not despair, however, because as the prophet reminds us that "to obey is better than sacrifice and to hearken than the fat of rams" (I Sam. 15:22). God is not satisfied with repentance and neither should we be.

God demands holiness and that is achieved through the mitzvot. So take the instruction of Lev. 18 to heart and do a mitzvah, even if it is only the easiest mitzvah that you can think of, because fulfilling one mitzvah leads to another and so to holiness and to life.

Sukkot

Karin Klein

Chag Sameach. I am glad to have this opportunity to speak for two reasons. One is that Sukkot is my favorite holiday, and I'm delighted to be able to share some of what I love about Sukkot with you. We'll get to that in a minute. The other is that this is really the first opportunity I may have had to talk to some of you. My name is Karin Klein. I am a new member of the Egal Minyan this year. I began coming to services here due to an irresistible attraction to a certain member of the Minyan. But I soon found that the members of this Minyan are, as a group, warm and supportive and inclusive. All of those are things that matter a great deal to me, and make me feel very much at home here. A special nod to Norman and Shira Eliaser, who told me many years ago, at a time in my life that was not as happy as this time is, that I really should come to the Egalitarian Minyan at Ner Tamid, that I would really like it there. Thank you. You were right.

I'll speak only briefly about Sukkot, and I doubt I'll say anything you haven't heard before. But I hope what I say may serve as a reminder of some of the sources of joy in this holiday of joy.

This time of year is near the harvest time in Israel. I grew up in a rural area of Iowa, and I remember what this time of year was like. At the time of harvest, life is good. Among the Israelite farmers (and farmers everywhere) there is a great deal of work to be done. People labor in the fields and vineyards and orchards picking and sorting, separating wheat from chaff, grinding olives into oil and storing away the wine and the corn and the oil that the rich land has yielded. Fruits and vegetables are cooked and canned, and shelves are lined with enough food to feed us through the winter. It is hard work, but when it is finished, the granaries are full, the storehouses are bursting at the seams, and we have a warm sense of confidence about what we have accomplished. Through our hard work and great attention, the land has been coaxed to pour out more food than we can use. There is sustenance and then some for ourselves, our families and our neighbors. We have everything under control.

It is precisely at this time that we are commanded, not encouraged or invited, but commanded to leave our warm and secure houses and dwell in huts in the backyard. In *Vayikra*, Chapter 23, verses 34, 42-43, it says, in part: "On the fifteenth day of this seventh month [there shall be] the pilgrimage-festival of Booths (*Sukkot*), [lasting] seven days to YHWH . . . all citizens in Israel shall live in booths (*sukkot*), in order that your generations may know that I made the Israelites live in booths when I brought them out of the land of Egypt; I am YHWH your God."

This dwelling in huts is very important. At the moment of our profoundest feeling of control and comfort in our ability to take care of ourselves, we are forced out into the elements. Into the insecure shelter of a *sukkah*.

And this *sukkah* is not just any old hut – but specifically an impermanent dwelling with very little roof. The *halacha*, the laws, are quite clear about this. According to the laws, the walls of a *sukkah* can be made of almost anything, even attached to a permanent dwelling. But the roof is a different matter. The *schach* that serves as the roof of the *sukkah* is to be made of materials that come from the ground, but which are no longer attached to the ground (hence the very appropriate use of branches cut from a tree, or corn stalks pulled from the earth, or bamboo poles of various kinds). These things were rooted in the earth, attached, grounded. But they are no longer so stable. Those attachments have been removed. They are just branches. It is forbidden, for instance, to use the branches of trees near a *sukkah* that are still attached to the tree as a covering for the *sukkah*. That would be too much shelter. There are also specific laws about how much *schach* should be used to cover the *sukkah*. There should be enough that most of the *sukkah* is in the shade – so more covering than open spaces – but there should not be so much that a heavy rain cannot penetrate into the *sukkah*. There is also an opinion that the *schach* should be arranged so that we are able to see the stars through the holes between the branches of the *schach*.

So what do we learn from sitting under this roof of *schach* for seven days – under this frail, mostly shady covering over our heads that we can see the stars through? There are many things to be reminded of, and I would just like to list a few of them here.

We are reminded, in this harvest time of plenty, that we are not the ones in control of that bounty. That we are not in charge of the rain – the first time I ate in a *sukkah* was at the home of Rabbi Michael Balinsky, whom I think a number of you know. It was raining – a little – the first night of Sukkot, and

Sukkot

there was a great deal of discussion in the kitchen of his home about whether we should eat in the *sukkah* and whether it was raining hard enough, and what the *halacha* said about rain in the *sukkah* and what was best for the children, and we finally decided to do *Kiddush* in the *sukkah* and then eat inside. So we all traipsed out to the *sukkah* and stood around the table and Michael poured the wine. And as he began to say *Kiddush*, the rain suddenly picked up, and, before he was finished, we were all soaked and rain was dripping off the end of his nose into the *Kiddush* cup. But we finished *Kiddush* before we went in – finished blessing the God who was raining on us in this hut that God commanded us to dwell in for seven days.

We are reminded when the wind blows, that a little bit of pine needles in the chicken soup is not such a bad thing.

We are reminded that *schach* smells wonderful when the sun shines on it and a little bit of a breeze blows through it.

We are often reminded that there are more bees than we thought there would be still flying around in the middle of October.

And if we take the time to look up from our evening meals, through the spaces between the branches, we can see the stars. We can look through the holes in the roof of the *sukkah* that we built and see the roof of the world that was hung there by the creator of the universe. And hopefully, as we sit in our *sukkah* and look at the sky, we'll be reminded that it is that roof, the broad roof of the world, that is our only true shelter.

Shanah tovah. May it be a year of blessings for all of us, and for the rest of the world as well.

Sukkot – Shemini Atzeret

Al Hobscheid

This *d'var Torah* serves as a bookend of sorts to one I gave on the subject of *"morid hatal"* ("You cause the dew to descend") last Pesach[1], so let's take a look at *"mashiv ha'ruach u'morid ha'gashem"* ("You cause the wind to blow and the rain to descend") in the *g'vurot* ("powers") of the *Amidah*.

Although it may seem to suggest it, wind and rain are not meant to be separate concepts. They are clearly interconnected phenomena as understood in nature as well as by the rabbis. Israel lies in a region classified climatologically as "Mediterranean." In the Northern Hemisphere, this indicates that the region is characterized by year-round moderate temperatures and distinctive wet winters and dry summers. After a bone dry summer dominated by subtropical high air pressure, the prevailing westerly winds take over, bringing much needed moisture. Low-pressure cells carried along in this part of the global circulation system spawn winds from the northwest and west that bring moisture, clouds and precipitation fed by the Mediterranean and Black Seas and sometimes from the south via troughs of lower air pressure that form over the Red Sea. This situation is comparable to that of southern California as a point of reference, where nary a drop of precipitation falls in the summertime (the Los Angeles Dodgers have had only five games postponed due to rain since 1959!), and the winters tend to be wetter.

Although we call it the wet season in these Mediterranean zones, it hardly is. Precipitation in Israel varies according to latitude and elevation, but averages annually around twenty inches. In comparison, Chicago averages around thirty inches. Moreover, desert classification schemes normally

---

[1] See pp. 229-233.

require an area to have less than thirty inches annually. But given the ecosystem that has evolved in Israel, it is sufficient.

Geshem is the popular word for rain, yet there are other Hebrew words for rain, notably *matar* (the most used in the Tanakh), *yoreh* (early rain), and *malkosh* (latter rain). But in the Tanakh, *geshem* is associated with those passages that are very concerned with powerful or significant rain. It is used in Noach – 'nuf said. *Geshem gadol* and *hamon hageshem* (abundant rain) are used in the Elijah tale with King Ahav and the challenge of the prophets of Ba'al. And *geshem shotef* (torrential rain) was employed by Ezekiel describing God's power in the struggle with Gog in the *haftarah* from last Shabbat.

To emphasize the relationship, heavy rain is directly related to wind, more specifically to downdrafts out of storm clouds. Why is there this attachment to such potentially dangerous weather? It is a key to survival in these regions. The need for heavy rain is beneficial for the adequate gathering and storage of water. Slow gentle rains tend to be absorbed by the soil or evaporate quickly so much so as to be lost to a society that relies on channeling and storing water into great basins and cisterns. Prime examples are the ones located at Masada or in Qumram. In these regions it is especially critical to corral all water possible to endure the summer.

I saw a thing on the web from a scholar, Joseph Lowin, that reinforces this notion of *geshem* with substantiality. He notes an apparent linguistic connection with the *shoresh*: *gimel, shin, mem*; between *geshem* and *gashmi'ut*, between "rain" and a word meaning substance, matter, concreteness. Lowin relates a contemporary example of the relationship:

להגשים או לא להגשים

"In Israel, youths preparing to join a kibbutz ultimately have to ask themselves: *le-hagshim o lo le-hagshim*? – literally, 'To concretize or not to concretize?' In other words, 'Shall I indeed put the ideology I imbibed in the youth movement into practice and make a commitment to become a kibbutz member or not?' "

Although some scholars, he notes, are dubious of the connection, it seems to me to be more than coincidental.

But I think the significance of the word "*geshem*" and rain itself is found in its position in the *g'vurot*. It is a declaration of God's power in the natural world that affects humanity directly – the water that supports the agriculture that is vital to support society and enables us to live in meaningful and satisfying ways. So nature comes before all of the human behaviors linked to the mitzvot of *tzedakah* and *gemilut chasidim*. So what is the significance of "you give life to the dead" that precedes it? To me it stands as an encompassing statement about the world and its wonders: that everything is in cycles, and that growth leads to decline and back to regeneration. That it is during times of terrific storms that we become very nervous, scared, but also awed. We can really sense God's power, God's wonder, awesomeness, beauty.

We tend to look at rain in our society as a negative thing because we are generally quite removed from agriculture where one has to be more attuned to weather. It is usually a nuisance that keeps us from doing apparently more important things. It's the "in each life a little rain must fall" kind of mentality. It's important to overcome this attitude and that is what the *g'vurot* models for us. The whole concept was succinctly captured by Arthur Freed (*nee* Grossman), the Hollywood producer, in his memorable lyrics:

> I'm singing in the rain, just singing in the rain
> What a glorious feeling, I'm happy again
> I'm laughing at clouds so dark up above
> The sun's in my heart and I'm ready for love!

Sukkot – Shemini Atzeret (II)

Joan Katz

Shemini Atzeret is the holiday when we savor the special relationship between God and Israel. Retelling the story of the dedication of the Temple, chanting *Hallel*, reciting *Yizkor*, and praying for rain reinforce this intimacy as we linger just a little bit longer before leaving the holiday season behind.

We just heard how Solomon finished dedicating the First Temple by praying for an ongoing closeness between God and Israel, asking that they always remember to fulfill their obligations and pay attention to each other with the intimacy of that wonderful moment. We remember this hopeful, joyous time by repeating Solomon's blessing aloud on *Shemini Atzeret*.

In a few minutes, we will recite *Yizkor*, when we, too, look to God for hope and continuity as we remember those close to us who have died.

In today's *Musaf Amidah*, we pray for *geshem*, for the appropriate quantity of rain in its proper season. We chant historical example after example of times when God provided for our ancestors, Abraham, Isaac, and Jacob, Moses and Aaron, in association with water, obliquely reminding God to send the rain: *zachor, zachor, zachor, zachor, zachor.*

What about this theme word *zachor*?

I had emotionally understood the word *zachor* in the heavy sense of remember, do not ever forget, obsess about it, make it a memory, feel it as a weight in your heart. But I learned the simple insight in the course of studying Psalms this year in Ben's class that the word *zachor* has the more straightforward meaning of "remember" as in "notice" or "say it out loud." The action of speaking or mentioning is remembering, is *zachor*.

On a more complex level, our class saw many examples of man calling to God in much the same way we do when we pray for rain.

Specifically, we heard the psalmist speak to God, certain of the right to demand that God show His face, trusting that eventually God will respond because He has in the past. What the psalmist often voices, particularly in laments, is a request for God's attention. It is not tied to a promise of *teshuvah* or repentance on man's part; rather it is tied to the history of a relationship. Man's "threat" to God, if you will, is, as we said today in *Hallel*, "*lo hamatim yihalleluya* – the *dead* cannot praise God."

Actively remembering past occasions when God took action just may catch God's attention, but certainly, equally important, it reminds man. There is a confidence expressed that now, or some time, God *will* notice us, for *God* desires this special relationship.

Noticeably absent, of course, is time context. God's stage for humankind began with creation of the world and continues to eternity, and may well not fit our personal agenda.

However, a sweet satisfaction in just speaking aloud of these historical occasions reinforces our own confidence that, whatever the time frames, we are having a conversation.

One Yom Kippur in the late 70's we *daven*ed at the Jewish Theological Seminary. The *darshan* was the then Chancellor Gershon Cohen, *z"l*. He spoke immediately before *Yizkor* and demanded that each attendee rethink leaving the room for *Yizkor*, a custom he deemed based in folk "*shtus*" or superstition. Dr. Cohen felt that as the generation born on the heels of the Holocaust, we young adults had an obligation to stand to say *Yizkor* on behalf of those who had perished. My memory is not good enough to relate the details of his reasoning, but as I prepared this *dvar* I understood that his charge was not only to stand witness or say *kaddish*. Rather in the sweep of history we were also to *zachor*, to remind God that we, His people, are still here and still waiting for His answer to their prayers. Meanwhile, we enrich our own lives by remembering our personal and national history.

I would like to close with a story, a family story, which had been an enigma to me.

My Polish born great-uncle Leon Berman, *z"l*, told me the following story. Perhaps you may know my Uncle Leon indirectly, as his grandson is the creator of the TV series CSI.

On Yom Kippur in 1919, a pogrom dramatically dislocated the large Berman family. The older boys were of necessity parceled out for apprenticeships. City relatives who had a small business agreed to take in the teenage Leon with a head for math. Unbeknownst to my great-grandparents, these relatives were no longer observant of Shabbat and *kashrut*. Uncle Leon was appalled when he arrived, but felt he had no choice but to hide this from his parents and make do, because they had no alternative for him. The crisis

Sukkot – Shemini Atzeret (II)

came to a head one Shabbat afternoon when he was physically forced to get on the wagon to fetch some merchandise at the dock. He was terrified. He knew, in his heart, as he had well learned, that without doubt he was about to be struck down by a bolt of lightening from Heaven. The horse began to trot. Leon waited. And waited. And waited. And waited. He was in utter disbelief. By the time he arrived at the dock alive, he decided that if God was too busy to notice him to strike him dead for violating the Sabbath, he guessed it was okay to ignore Him, too. He went *frei*, free of observing the mitzvot, making his peace with these relatives until he made his way to America to open his own shoe store and lead the good life here. However, Uncle Leon's personal dialogue with God apparently did not end on the wagon. By the time I was a young girl, he had wandered back to a relatively observant life, treating God and religion seriously. He never articulated to me why he came back, but he told me this story, and he told it to me more than once. It was clear that for him the telling, the remembering, the passing on, the speaking the story aloud, had its own power.

As Uncle Leon would have wished you, a *Gut Yontif*.

Bereshit

Robert Grannick

Alan Hobscheid reminded me that it has been four years since my last *d'var*, and that it was time that I gave one. Other folks who remember the last one said, "Only four years? What's the hurry?"

Based on *Bereshit* and *Noach*, God is an all-powerful and all-knowing creator who rewards the just and obedient and swiftly punishes the disobedient and the willful. Some obvious examples: Adam and Eve banished from the garden for eating the prohibited fruit, the destruction of life on earth for the evil doings of man, "a servant of servants shall he [Canaan] be unto his brethren" (Gen. 9:25 [OJPS]) (resulting from Ham's uncovering his father's nakedness), and the destruction of the tower of Babel (resulting from man's hubris). The pattern here generally seems to be one of cause and effect. Man acts badly, and God punishes him. Justice is preserved in the world through God's actions. God's omnipotence, omniscience, justice, and mercy convey to us a sense of stability, continuity, and equilibrium. There are rules governing man's behavior, and there are mutual expectations between God and man. These are described in God's stated expectations as in *Bereshit* and in the Noachide covenant. This theme continues through much of the Torah and the writings. God remembers the faithful, the righteous and the penitent. We note Hannah, Ruth, and the inhabitants of the city of Nineveh from Jonah.

I think that most would agree, whether children or adults, that the world we know diverges from the world of *Bereshit* and *Noach*. The continuity of collective and individual lives is often ripped apart by unexpected events that do not distinguish the just from the unjust and do not spare the penitent or the righteous. It often appears that the only thing we can count on is indifference. God's hand does not appear to be in control. So we ask, as did Rabbi Harold Kushner,[1] why do bad things happen to good people and what is God's role

---

[1] *When Bad Things Happen to Good People* (Schocken 2001).

in it all? It is this divergence that I want to discuss today. It will spin off of several vignettes:

When I was a young kid growing up in Riverdale, I was something of a *"Vilda Chaya."* You wouldn't know that looking at me now. My mother would threaten, "God will punish you if you hit your little brother or embarrass the family at the restaurant or in company!" Or if I fell and skinned my knee while running away from anticipated punishment, she'd assure me that God had punished me and she would not have to do it herself. These warnings became internalized and conscience took the place of her admonitions. My behavior did improve from time to time. In any case, I had a sense that an all-seeing eye was examining my behavior from above.

I was both impressed and puzzled that God would drop all He had to do in other corners of His universe, find apartment 3G at 3300 Netherland Avenue and administer the appropriate punishment or reward. He would not mistake me for my friend Ricky Goldstein, the pharmacist's son, who lived on the second floor above our family, or for one of the Siegels, one flight up. In time, I found that God often did not punish me when I did something wrong although I felt he should have. Also, I was not always rewarded when I did something right.

In the summer of '49, my family (mother, father, brother Joel, and I) drove toward Merrick, Long Island, to check on the progress of the construction of our new home. I was eight and my brother one year old at the time. We were traveling at 45 miles per hour. My mother's scream informed us that the back door had opened and my brother had fallen out of the car. My father applied the brakes, screeching to the side of the parkway, a three-lane highway in each direction. We found Joel resting on the grassy median strip, not a scratch on him. What if my brother had not survived? What would it have been like for my parents? What would it have been like growing up in such a family? Was it a miracle that Joel survived or was it the realization of an extremely fortuitous event? The Rambam was to have said that a miracle cannot result from what is impossible; rather, it informs us as to what is possible. It was a miracle. My father enveloped Joel in a bear hug; and there on the median strip near the Babylon Turnpike we wept.

When I was in the middle of the fourth grade, we moved to Long Island. My parents regarded this as a step up, and the only drawback seemed to be was that you had to live on Long Island. I guess we wanted to keep up with the Joneses, the Collins, and the Crawfords. A kid down the block, Richard Waters, was a couple of years younger than me and my close friend Jonathan. A year after we met Richard, he was hit by a car while running across the street and died. Nobody I spoke to seemed to know the details. Another time, Lois Richard, a classmate, was pulled out of our fifth grade class and informed that her younger brother, Bobby, was missing. He had a history of running away from home. We later learned that he had drowned in Merrick Bay.

In 1980, my uncle returned to his business in downtown Atlanta, surprised a burglar, and was shot and killed with his own gun. What if he had not gone in that day or went in later after the intruder had left?

Having seen *Waiting for Godot*, I noted with interest the obituary of Samuel Beckett, its author. I learned that once he was walking down a narrow street in Paris with his wife and another couple. Out of the darkness, a man leapt and stabbed Beckett, narrowly missing his heart. Afterward, Beckett visited the jail and inquired of the man: "Why did you do it?" The man's answer: "I don't know."

Jack Eisner, a Holocaust survivor, wrote in his book *The Survivor* (Bantam Books 1982), "Why me? Why not grandma Masha? Why not Hela, Lutek, Mrs. Grinberg? What about Schmeel, the shoemaker?"

Primo Levi wrote in *Survival in Auschwitz* (Touchstone 1995) about a day in which the Germans tested the slave laborers for fitness. The unfit would be sent to the gas chambers. Inmates were asked to run a distance and were then classified by their performance and appearance. When the testing was complete and the selections made, an observant Jew in a bunk near Levi's loudly prayed to God thanking Him for having found him worthy and saving his life. Levi found this contemptible because it was done in listening range of another despairing man, who, although apparently more fit than the first, was selected.

Rabbi Kushner's son Aaron was born with progeria, a genetic disease that causes rapid aging and stunts growth. It led to his death at age fifteen. The rabbi wondered if another sperm had met a different egg, perhaps the outcome would have been different.

So, why must there be misfortune? Why does it seem so random, without cause or purpose? Why would a merciful and just God not endow everyone with an optimal set of parents, long-lived grandparents, equal capabilities, appearance, strength, intelligence, and good character, and the best of genes, rather than endowing these attributes in an uneven way? Why would He not prevent the slaughter of the innocent? There are many ways to address this. We may perceive God as not having some of the qualities attributed to Him; we may re-interpret His role; or we may redirect focus from cause to effect.

Leaves from the Garden

Contending with Inexplicable Misfortune by Perceiving God As Not Omnipotent

Rabbi Kushner concludes that God does not have all the characteristics attributed to him in *Bereshit*. Rather than drop justice and mercy, he drops omnipotence. There are certain things that God is not able to do. Kushner does not say that God can do anything but chooses not to for reasons of His own. He says: "No matter what stories we were taught about Daniel or Jonah in Sunday school, God does not reach down to interrupt the working of laws of nature to protect the righteous from harm." In this case it might be well to understand the relationship of God to nature in order to sort out the sovereignty of each.

Contending with Inexplicable Misfortune by Perceiving God As Not Omniscient

In this, God's un-involvement is due to being unaware of a situation crying out for intervention. This would seem unlikely, given that He knows the future as well as the present. Indeed, He knew that Pharaoh's heart could and would be hardened so as not to let the people go in *Shemot*, or in *Devarim* where He predicts that the Israelites would be punished because they would not adhere to the mitzvot. Nevertheless, there are some ambiguities as described in *Bereshit*. We are informed that God recognized that it was good after He created light, after He separated the light from the darkness, after He separated the earth from the waters and from the heavens, after He created the herbs, and after He created the animals. An omniscient God would know this prior to these works, not after them. God also appears to learn that man is wicked after the fact. "And the LORD regretted having made the human on the earth and was grieved to the heart" (Gen. 6:6). Presumably, an omniscient God would know ahead of time that man would turn out this way.

Contending with Inexplicable Misfortune by Denying Its Paramountcy

Rabbi Kushner cites the reflection of a Holocaust survivor described in the book *The Faith and Doubt of Holocaust Survivors* by Rabbi Brenner.

> It never occurred to me to question God's doings or lack of doings while I was an inmate of Auschwitz, although of course I understand others did. . . . I was no less or no more religious because of what the Nazis did to us; and I was not undermined in the least. It never occurred to me to associate

Bereshit

the calamity we were experiencing with God, to blame Him, or to believe in Him less or cease believing in Him at all because He didn't come to our aid. God does not owe us that or anything. We owe our lives to Him. If someone believes God is responsible for the death of six million because He didn't somehow do something to save them, he's got his thinking reversed. We owe God our lives for the few or many years we live, and we have the duty to worship Him and do as He commands us. That's what we're here on earth for, to be in God's service, to do God's bidding.

This theme is certainly found in our tradition. Abraham's willing sacrifice of Isaac in the *Akeidah* seems in line with this. Also, in reciting the *Kaddish* we acknowledge God's domain as paramount and not our reaction to loss. In reciting the *Kaddish*, we acknowledge, affirm, and praise, not question, demand or blame. On the other hand, an argument can be raised that we should diminish the impact of God's being a shelter and defender of His people Israel and of His alliance with those who sleep in the dust.

Contending with Inexplicable Misfortune by Responding To It

Our Torah is wonderfully adaptive in a prescriptive sort of way. It acknowledges that this is not the best of all possible worlds, and that we are obliged to heal it for ourselves and others. It does not say that accidental death will not occur. Rather, it provides for cities of refuge for unintentional killers. It does not say that man will be created incapable of the self-loathing associated with envy. Rather, God tells Cain and us how to deal with envy:

> Why are you incensed,
>   and why is your face fallen?
> For whether you offer well,
>   or whether you do not,
> At the tent flap sin crouches
>   and for you is its longing
>   but you will rule over it.
>   (Gen. 4:6-7)

It does not say that man will not fall into poverty but rather informs us as to how to respond to your brother who is waxen poor. It does not say that widowhood or orphanage does not occur in this world but what to do when they do occur.

Leaves from the Garden

The existence of inexplicable misfortune makes a greater impact when you are young, when its repetition has not dulled the senses. If the misfortune does not directly affect you, you can only wonder about it and conclude that in this world such a thing is possible. Its existence contains mystery, but with the expectation that its meaning will eventually become clear. This is not the case. In the passage of time, it remains circumstantial and inexplicable and God's relation to it all remains inexplicable as well. God created His world in mystery and enshrouded Himself in mystery and awe. We accept this condition. We also understand that from mystery comes possibility, from possibility hope and then perhaps, but not always, a rainbow.

Noach

Ellen Holtzblatt

A Mid-Autumn Night's Stream (of Consciousness)

Parshat Noach describes how God nearly destroyed all flesh, a mere ten generations after Creation (Gen. 7:19-22):

> And the waters surged and multiplied mightily over the earth, and the ark went on the surface of the water. And the waters surged most mightily over the earth, and all the high mountains under the heavens were covered. . . . And all flesh that stirs on the earth perished, the fowl and the cattle and the beasts and all swarming things that swarm upon the earth, and all humankind. All that had the quickening breath of life in its nostrils, of all that was on dry land, died.

The story clearly depicts the scope of the devastation, but blanks on details that my imagination has since filled in. In my mind's eye, I can see the many human and beastly bodies violently contorted by the gales and torrents. The water carries limbless figures with bloated bellies; people with gaping eyes and open mouths, who give entry to the waters as the boundaries between person and sea diminish. In the beginning, lovers still cling to each other in lifeless desperation as the waters rise around them. Some struggle to fight the powerful currents and pounding assault from above. Like a child willing immortality they plead to God, their hands are enlarged as they grasp for safety and assistance, only to close their shivering fingers around the wind. And the birds, which live their lives winging through the heavens, are forced down into the depths of the rising waters. After the forty days and nights, after the unleashed elements have erased the last traces of humanity and beasts, lonely bodies float peacefully under the cloudless darkness, rhythmically following the lead of the waves.

Leaves from the Garden

What is the significance of God choosing water to be the tool of destruction?

In *parshat Bereshit*, the only element of the world not created by God in the six days of creation was water. Chapter 1, verse 2 states, "and the earth then was welter and waste and darkness over the deep and God's breath hovering over the waters." On the first day God separated light from dark, and named day and night. It wasn't until the second day that God created an expanse called "sky" to separate the waters below from the waters above. Because water pre-dates creation, rain takes on significance beyond its role as the nurturer of soil and supporter of life on earth. When it rains it is as though the world is returning to an existence that pre-dates our conceptualization of God. The waters from above and below reunite. Sometimes this is gentle and pleasing: a drizzle, a sun shower, the first rain after a prolonged hot and dry spell. But sometimes the process is chaotic and violent: lightning, thunder, sleet, hail, tornadoes, hurricanes, and flood.

Another way of perceiving the flood waters can be found in an oceanic metaphor by contemporary theologian Richard L. Rubinstein, "God is the ocean and we are the waves. In some sense each wave has a moment in which it is distinguishable as a somewhat separate entity. Nevertheless, no wave is entirely distinct from the ocean which is its substantial ground."[1] This metaphor enables us to view the flood story as an allegory of humankind merging with God to the point of being unrecognizable, until, like the wave, it again distinguishes itself.

Rashi illustrates the beginning of humankind, "For the purpose of creating man, the depths released a vapor that seeded the clouds and moistened the dust, so that when man was created – like this baker, who adds water to his dough and then kneads it!" So here, first there was a moistening and then, 'God formed man.'" Rashi translates the word, *emheh*, which God uses for destruction (6:7), "He is dust, so I shall bring water upon him and dissolve him." According to Rashi, humankind was created from the combination of dust and the cosmic waters of pre-creation, formulated like clay. Before clay has been fired, when it is still in its natural state, objects created from it are especially fragile and easily broken – vulnerable to ruin from exposure to water. These unfinished products are called *green ware*, with reference to their humble, earthen origins.

---

[1] Quotation taken from *The Sh'ma and its Blessings*, edited by Rabbi Lawrence A. Hoffman (Jewish Lights Publishing 1997), p. 73.

Noach

A physical manifestation of the pre-creation waters that continues from biblical times to the present is the *mikvah*, also called *mayim hayim* (living waters), referring both to the preferred state of natural waters, such as an ocean or lake, and the man-made version which is required to contain a minimum of 200 gallons of rain water. In order to enter the *mikvah* one must remove all physical barriers to the water: cosmetics, jewelry, perfume, dirt and sweat. One becomes like an infant who first enters the world from her primordial womb-pool. The act of submerging in the *mikvah* is meant to result in the cessation of individual ego, and reunification with God – *Adonai Echad*. For those of us who are fond of our egos, this could be experienced as a destructive and scary process. Through immersion in the *mikvah* we merge our dust-life, or clay-self, with the source of life, and symbolically disintegrate in the water, and then emerge spiritually renewed.

The flood could be viewed as the ultimate *mikvah*, returning the earth's residents to the water that pre-existed descriptive life, or following Richard Rubinstein's metaphor, a wave indistinct from the ocean who is God. If the flood was the ultimate *mikvah*, then it logically follows that it also might have been experienced as the ultimate destruction because of the great terror it engendered in the many egos who attempted to stay afloat and separate.

I viewed my fortieth birthday, which took place almost seven years ago, as an appropriate time to return to making art integral and central to my life. I wrestled with finding time and space for making art during my years of birthing and nursing, which were activities that I initially experienced as creative. I witnessed internal squabbles of my primal urges to engage in messy practices against the solid, rational voices which said, "make money, be a responsible member of society," and the damning voices that whispered, "No, no, no. You can't do that."

I ignored the voices and set before me the task of making a drawing every week about an aspect of that Shabbat's *parsha*. When I came to *parshat Noach*, I asked myself, "What did this destruction look and feel like?" I drew dead bodies floating in water with heavy rains beating them down deeper, like a hammer to a nail into soft wood.

I quit this project before I even reached the story of Joseph. My children needed me, there were too many other demands on my time, and I grew tired of the frustration of squeezing in these art explorations as if into a vise between carpool, part-time teaching and my occasional venture at cleaning – not to mention moving my drawing materials from one end of the dining room table to the other.

Leaves from the Garden

Then last June I finally had the audacity to rent a studio and begin spending significant, if somewhat insufficient, amounts of time creating and making messes. Alone in my new studio, I faced the empty space. I was treading deep water without the presence of a lifeguard and no shore in sight. I found a life preserver and attempted to fill the bareness with something familiar; I returned to my question about the destruction of the flood that I had asked six years before in that frustrating and futile art-making attempt, "How did the destruction of the flood look and feel?" Maybe I was exploring the possibility that my artistic soul had died after years of neglect, drowned in a sea of suburban expectations to fit in. After all, I used to panic at the completion of every painting I had ever made, thinking that I could never do that again. I knew that my choice was the adage, "sink or swim."

This is where the ocean current is taking me. What if the flood story compels me, not because of destruction, but rather because of the possibility of rebirth and immersion with God? Like most opposites, destruction and creation are two sides of the same process. We build, and then we take away. Or we take away, and then we build. The potter puts the clay on the wheel and forms the pot, continually removing the excess clay. The painter makes love to the canvas and then sweeps away an entire day's work with the palette knife. The writer edits out whole paragraphs in endless rewrites. God makes the world, and then retreats to allow space for us to shadow the Divine through our own creativity. We cannot take an eraser to our mistakes, or pull out a fresh sheet of paper to replace the ones we are constantly soiling. But there is always God's promise for us to do *teshuvah*, to return to the essential source.

Art, like all passions, is similar to what I imagine to be the experience of drowning. I have visualized the figures of the flood story with their gaping orifices, freely admitting the seas into their bodies, boundary-less with the waters. I have spent the day painting, only to wonder where the hours went, lost as I was in the doing. I think of a person who is drowning in sorrow as emoting with passion. Drowning in one's own tears is a salty reversal of the flood, as the pre-creation waters pour out from the body, melting the dry, unfired clay of one's earthly reality. Perhaps in passion one swallows whole the metaphoric primordial waters, intermingling with the Eternal.

The danger of drowning is, of course, drowning. Isaac of Akko wrote, "Now you my child, strive to see supernal light, for I have brought you into a vast ocean. Be careful! Keep your soul from gazing and your mind from conceiving, lest you drown. Strive to see, yet escape drowning." And so we are warned to balance passion with judgment, to heed our mortal constraints, and against contemplation of God beyond our moral capacity.

The outer garments of the flood story show us a sinful people who are punished for these sins by total annihilation. Peering beyond these garments one can see God's compassion. Water is liquid breath. It is the medium that God uses to embrace the souls on earth and breathe spiritual life into them. In these post-Rosh HaShanah and Yom Kippur days, the story of the flood reminds us that *teshuvah* cannot be willed or controlled, but is ultimately an act of surrender to our desire to be one with our God, who is One.

Lech Lecha

Jonathan Freed[1]

In the tradition of Rabbi Hillel, who, as many of you know, said that all the lessons of the Torah could be explained while standing on one leg, I will stand before you – on both legs if you don't mind – but I will make my *d'var Torah* as *short* as I *possibly* can.

This week's Torah portion mostly concerns Abraham and the significant things he did as the first Jew. I, however, would like to start by focusing on a character in a supporting role, also famous, but not quite as famous as Abraham. I am talking about Lot.

Some have said that on balance Lot – who is Abraham's nephew – does not look very good, especially because he may have returned to the worship of idols after embracing Abraham's belief in one God. But I say that Lot, like all humans, was a mixture of good and bad.

After going to Egypt because of a famine in Canaan, both Lot and Abraham return to the Promised Land with flocks, silver and gold. When a quarrel breaks out between Lot and Abraham's herdsmen, Abraham orders Lot to leave but offers him his choice of location. Abraham says (Gen. 13:9): "If you take the left hand, then I shall go right, and if you take the right hand, I shall go left." So Lot goes to the plain of the Jordan, and Abraham to Canaan.

The text makes a point of stating that Lot saw that his land was good land. Some blame Lot for taking the better property, but I believe he had every right to do what he did. How many of us would do any differently?

Now let's talk about Abraham for a moment. He had a choice to make also, just like Lot. It was too crowded in the land of Canaan. So Abraham said (Gen. 13:8-9), "Pray, let there be no contention between you and me, between your herdsmen and mine, for we are kinsmen ["brothers" (NJPS)].

---

[1] Jonathan delivered this *d'var Torah* on becoming a *bar Mitzvah*.

Is not all the land before you? Pray, let us part company" ["Please separate from me" (NJPS)].

What could Abraham have done to prevent his family from splitting up? Abraham told his nephew to leave, but he could have sold some of his livestock instead. He could have made room for Lot and his herds. But he chose material possessions over people.

This raises the question: what kind of individuals were Abraham and Lot? I believe they were very human ones, full of faults, just like the rest of us. Both Abraham and Lot were flawed, yet history treats Lot as the bad guy, not Abraham.

The problem is . . . Abraham is our role model, the father of the Jewish people, and we tend to think of role models as entirely good.

Let's turn our attention for a moment to parallels with other family relationships in the Bible.

This episode, in which Abraham tells Lot to leave, could be a hint of a coming story. Lot is Abraham's nephew, but in some ways, he's more like a son. Abraham's decision to separate himself from Lot can be seen as a variation of the casting out of Ishmael, Abraham's son by Hagar. Regardless of the relationship – son, nephew or whatever it may be – cutting off family ties in my opinion is almost never a good thing.

In the text, Abraham actually calls Lot his brother. In *Bereshit*, or the book of Genesis as it is called in English, brothers never seem to get along. First there were Cain and Abel. There were Yitzchak and Ishmael, Jacob and Esau, and Joseph and his brothers, to name just a few. This sibling rivalry is prominent in the Torah, even amongst our revered heroes.

Let's move on. At one point, generations after Abraham and Lot, when the children of Israel left Egypt, they were starving. The Moabites, who were descended from Lot, refused to give food to these hungry people and even tried to curse the Jews. What goes around comes around. Had Abraham not chosen material possessions over kin, the incident with the Moabites might never have happened. Mistakes have an effect, even if far down the line.

What have I learned from all this? For one thing, I've learned that mistakes have a way of getting back at you.

But I've also learned that our role models – the Abrahams, the Isaacs, the Jacobs, and even the Moseses of the world – may be far from perfect. Our ancestors were very human, sometimes acting wisely and sometimes not so wisely. Nevertheless, they had important contributions to make. I'd like to think that there's hope for all of us. May we all strive toward the wisdom of our ancestors, while recognizing our many flaws.

Vayera

Richard Tupper

The *Akeidah* is sometimes viewed as a rejection of the practice of child sacrifice, that God is teaching Abraham the lesson that child sacrifice is unacceptable. That interpretation, I think, misses a larger point that the story is making. The premise of the story is that God is putting Abraham to the supreme test. It is precisely because child sacrifice is so unthinkable that the test is so difficult. If sacrificing your child were no more unthinkable than a tattoo or a ham and cheese sandwich, then it would not be as difficult a test. The story only works if the reader assumes that Abraham would never willingly offer up his son on his own. Moreover, the story goes out of its way to stress the father/son relationship between Abraham and Isaac, repeatedly referring to Isaac as "his son" and the two address each other as "my father" and "my son."

If the story is not simply about rejecting child sacrifice, then what is it about?

When one reads the story of the *Akeidah*, obvious parallels appear to *Lech Lecha* in Gen. 12. The text stresses the parallels. For example, in *Lech Lecha*, there is a triplet: Abram is called to leave "your land and your birthplace and your father's house" to go "to the land that I will show you." In the *Akeidah* – a similar triplet: Abraham is told to take "your son, your only one, whom you love, Isaac" and go to "one of the mountains which I shall say to you." In both stories, Abram/Abraham answers the call without hesitation. In *Lech Lecha*, he goes to Moreh; in the *Akeidah*, he goes to Moriah. In both stories, he has an encounter with the Divine. In both stories he receives a blessing, and in both stories he offers a sacrifice.

However, there are important differences in the two stories, and in these differences lies an important message.

One difference is how the stories end. In the *Akeidah*, the Torah relates that Abraham calls the place, "The LORD sees" and refers to an apparently common name of the place Moriah as "on the mount of the LORD there is sight." [Some Bibles mistranslate this as "on the mountain, the LORD will be seen" but better translations recognize that the subject of the verb is unstated.] In *Lech Lecha*, when Abram comes to Canaan, God "reveals" (same Hebrew verb) Himself to Abram.

Thus, in *Lech Lecha*, God is doing the "revealing" and Abram is doing the "seeing." In the *Akeidah*, it is God who "sees" but what does God "see" and who is doing the "revealing"?

The answer, I think, is that God is seeing the results of His test of Abraham, and so it is Abraham who is doing the "revealing." What does Abraham reveal? He reveals that he "fears God" – no matter what. In so doing, Abraham "reveals" that he has come a long way from Abram in *Lech Lecha*.

In *Lech Lecha*, the call and the promise go hand in hand. Abram receives the call and is told he will be blessed. In contrast, in the *Akeidah*, Abraham receives a "call," literally, "*kach nah*" – which can be translated as "take, please" – but no promise. When Abraham is asked to offer up Isaac, God gives him no assurance of blessing. It is only after Abraham follows God's request the blessing/promise is restated.

For many of us, it is not hard to imagine that a childless couple would travel to the ends of the earth to have children as Abram and Sarai did. But who of us can imagine sacrificing our child as Abraham was asked to do? Abraham's conduct attests that he had become so involved in the Covenant, so rooted in God, that he needed no external promise. He was willing to do whatever God asked because he trusted God. Thus, in the *Akeidah*, Abraham reveals and God sees an Abraham who has grown in the Covenant.

The *Akeidah* story is read on Rosh HaShanah, when we look back over the past year. The *Lech Lecha* and the *Akeidah* stories demonstrate that being a good Jew is not a one-step process. As the life of Abraham demonstrates, becoming a better Jew is a lifetime process of continuously learning and doing. May we, like Abraham, constantly recommit ourselves to becoming the sort of Jews God demands so that come the next Rosh HaShanah God will see better Jews.

Chayyei Sarah

Richard Tupper

I chose this portion to give a *davar* on because I had intended to talk about Eliezer, the servant whom we all take for granted that Abraham sent to find a wife for Isaac. I chose it because my namesake is Eliezer and I had planned on talking about what sort of person Eliezer was. However, as I read and reread the portion, it struck me that Eliezer's name is nowhere mentioned. It reminded me of the self-taught Pentecostal preacher I once knew who always preached on the words emphasized in the text. How did he know which words were emphasized? They were the words in italics. Apparently, he had not read the translator's preface to his translation of the Bible that explained that words in italics had been supplied by the translator to fill in the text, to make more sense. So, this preacher often focused on words that never appeared in the original text. I didn't want to make the same mistake by focusing on the personality of Eliezer, since the text seems to make a point of not mentioning his name.

I. If Not Eliezer, Then Who?

If the story doesn't intend for us to focus on Eliezer, then about whom is the story?

Reading the story some more times, I became convinced that the story is about Rivkah. The story seems to make a point of drawing parallels between Rivkah and Abraham.

In *Lech Lecha*, Abram leaves his country, his kin, and his father's house to go to Canaan. In this story, that mission is echoed in Abraham's direction to his servant to go to his country, his kin, to find a wife for his son. Thus, like Abram, Rivkah will similarly leave country, kin and her father's house.

Like Abram, when Rivkah receives the "call," she is ready to obey immediately. She doesn't wish to wait but wants to set out with the servant right away.

The story recounts two apparently important qualities of Rivkah: she is good-looking and a virgin. The Torah doesn't say that Abraham was necessarily good-looking, but Sarah was (and we know that Rivkah's good looks will cause problems for Isaac just as Sarai's good looks caused problems for Abram – see the Pharaoh and the Avimelech stories; indeed, Avimelech is a problem for Isaac and Rivkah). Good looks often (but not always) are associated with virtue.

Now, neither Abram nor Sarai was a virgin at the time of *Lech Lecha* (or if they were that might explain a lot), but they were childless. Their going to Canaan would result in the blessing of children. Rivkah, too, when she leaves home is blessed by her sisters and that blessing promises a heritage very similar to the blessing given by God to Abram at *Lech Lecha* and after the *Akeidah*.

The story also reveals Rivkah's hospitality to the servant. It is reminiscent of Abraham's hospitality to the divine messengers after his circumcision. Hospitality was a very important virtue in the ancient world.

Certainly part of this story is meant to impress upon us that Rivkah is a worthy bride and a worthy participant in the Covenant, and it does so in part by drawing parallels between her and Abraham. Later we see God telling Rivkah about her upcoming pregnancy just as He did with Abraham and Sarah.

But going through this analysis, I realized how much I was thinking about Abraham, even though he only figures in the beginning and then the end of the portion. Maybe the story is also meant to reveal something important about Abraham.

II. What does this story say about Abraham?

Some note that after the *Akeidah*, God never again speaks directly to Abraham, and they conclude that God was displeased in some way with Abraham's response in the *Akeidah* incident, that perhaps he should not have been so willing to offer up Isaac. I disagree.

Certainly when I read this story of Abraham sending his servant to find a wife for Isaac, I can find no hint that God is displeased with Abraham. The story begins by noting how God had blessed Abraham in all things, and it ends by recounting how Abraham had taken another wife through whom he had more children, thereby becoming a "father of nations." The story thus begins and ends in blessing, revealing how God had kept His promise of

Chayyei Sarah

blessings to Abraham, and, I think, reflecting how God was pleased with Abraham.

The servant's speeches to Rivkah and her family stress the important relationship between Abraham and God, how God was faithful to Abraham and had blessed Abraham. The servant tells them how he was acting at Abraham's direction and how God had participated in the task that Abraham had set before the servant. The servant is clearly trying to relay that Abraham had a very special relationship with God. You could almost say that the servant's description of Abraham and his experience with God function almost as a ("pre") eulogy on the life of Abraham.

But it is true that the Torah nowhere recounts that God is speaking to Abraham at this point. What do we make of this?

Although God apparently is not speaking to Abraham, Abraham is making some very important decisions and appears to *know* things without them necessarily having been revealed by God to him.

For example, Abraham not only knows that it's time to find a wife for Isaac, but that one will be found among his kin back home. How does he know this? At the end of the *Akeidah*, it's reported that Abraham learned that his family back home had had more children, including Rivkah, but there's no suggestion that this news came to Abraham in some divine way.

Abraham also knows that under no circumstance should Isaac go back to Abraham's home. Later, God tells Isaac that he should not leave Canaan during a famine, but how does Abraham know that Isaac should stay in Canaan? (We'll skip over the midrash about how Isaac was a "sacrifice" and therefore should not leave Canaan.)

Abraham also is absolutely certain that God will make sure that the servant's mission will be successful. How can Abraham be so certain?

The story, I think, is meant to show us how attuned to God and the Covenant Abraham has become. He knows these things without being told directly by God precisely because he has become so imbued with the Covenant. He knows without being told what it is that God wants, and he does it.

In *Lech Lecha*, Abram answers God's call. He does what he is told. The story of Abram going to Egypt during the famine and the trouble he and Sarai have with Pharaoh demonstrates that Abram might not yet be able to act without divine direction. The *Akeidah* story reveals how Abraham is able to follow God's direction, even the most difficult direction, without questioning God. But this story reveals even more about Abraham: after so many years of living in the Covenant and interacting with God, he knows what God wants, even without having been told by God, and also he does it without being told.

III. What does it mean for us?

Often, I've thought that, compared with us, Abraham had it easy. He had years and years of direct communication with God. God gave him lessons on what the Covenant meant, what he had to do, in essence, how to be a Jew. None of us, I assume, will ever have a direct communication from God, let alone years and years of such communications. However, we have something Abraham didn't. Abraham had just his experiences with God to rely upon. We have set out in the Torah the experiences of not only Abraham, but numerous others. We have the Torah (oral and written), we have the insights/learning of many others, we have a history of Jews struggling with God and the Covenant, we have a community that stretches back in time and around the world. We can draw upon the experiences and insights of so many. None of us will live as long as Abraham, but we have tools to learn how to be a Jew that Abraham didn't.

Whether Abraham had it better than we do doesn't matter. In the end, the task for us is the same as it was for Abraham – to learn about the Covenant, to keep it and to be the sort of Jew that God intends.

May we, like Abraham, do our best to learn what it is that God and His Covenant demand of us and do it.

Toldot

Lise Weisberger

What kind of a story is this for a people to tell about their national and spiritual origins? That our ancestor Jacob was the younger of twins, and that he wished to win the blessing of his father, who preferred the older, is not at all strange – we expect to sympathize with deserving younger brothers in the Bible as well as in folklore. But this younger son steals the blessing by deceiving his aged, blind father into thinking that he is the favored, older brother! Are we supposed to admire this act, find it reprehensible, or accept it as the inscrutable will of Heaven? What can it say about the legitimacy of our own religious inheritance? How can a blessing be valid when it is given under false pretenses? How is it that Isaac has the sole power to pass on a prophetic blessing and yet doesn't have the prophetic knowledge about his sons that has been given to his wife Rebecca? And why doesn't Rebecca act like the other foremothers and talk to Isaac directly about her preferences? Why does it seem like the blind Isaac and the guileless, unsuspecting Esau are the victims in this story? Are we really supposed to sympathize with the ancestor of our enemies?

Almost every year, the *d'var Torah* for *Toldot* focuses in some way on this story of the stolen blessing. The questions it raises are compelling, and none of the answers is definitive enough to end the discussion. Each new way of looking at the issue seems to solve some of the difficulties of the story and to exacerbate others. I have come to the conclusion that the story is irreducibly ambivalent – the multiplicity of interpretations is built into it. I once heard a rabbi say (after expounding his theory that Isaac actually knew he was blessing Jacob): "This is what I believe about the story this year – I'm not sure that I'll reach the same conclusion next year."

And here's what I believe (or don't believe) about this primal, paradoxical, essential story of our origins . . . for this year.

First, I believe that the narrator intends the sympathy that most of us feel for Esau when we directly read this text. Those who are familiar with the midrash on this story may not agree, because the midrash makes Esau out to be the embodiment of brutality – a murderer, a rapist and a scoffer. In the midrashic version, both Rebecca and Jacob act with the knowledge that the future of the covenant people, and indeed the future of the world, is at stake. It is an absolute necessity that the spirit of Esau should not gain the upper hand. The extreme anti-Esau slant of the midrash is understandable, given the violent adversarial relations that the people of Israel had with the Edomites, descendants of Esau, and later with Imperial Rome, symbolized by Esau in the midrash. But Esau doesn't come across as evil in the biblical text. Brutish, perhaps, impulsive and capable of violence, but he is also capable of forgiveness. Most of all he seems piteous in the tale of the stolen blessing – he is so eager to be blessed, and so crushed to discover that he has lost his chance through his brother's trickery.

But perhaps our sympathy for Esau is only an artifact of modern sensibilities foreign to biblical times? One simple explanation for this story is that it was originally a "trickster tale," a legend in which a clever, powerless hero overcomes an adversary with his quick wits. In trickster stories, the use of lies and disguises is applauded, and there is no intention that we should feel any pity for the strong but stupid brute who ends up losing.

Although there are plenty of trickster-type stories in the Bible (one of my favorites is about the midwives, who disobey Pharaoh's order to kill the Hebrew babies, lie to him about why they've done so, and get away with it), I don't think that this story fits the mold. In the first place, Jacob does not merely deceive his loutish brother. He lies directly to his venerable, aged father, the patriarch, on his deathbed! It's hard to group Isaac with the tyrants and enemies who are the usual deceived parties in biblical trickster tales. Secondly, as I've said, trickster tales usually show no sympathy toward the losers. But Esau's tears and Isaac's trembling are details that seem calculated to move us. Thirdly, there seems to be a great effort in the text to reassure us that Jacob did not only receive the blessing through trickery, but also, multiple times, in honest ways. An oracle tells the pregnant Rebecca that her older son is destined to serve the younger. Isaac gives the "blessing of Abraham" to Jacob knowing full well who he is at the time that Jacob leaves Canaan to find a wife among his mother's relatives. And finally, Jacob receives a blessing from an angel after a night of wrestling – with physical effort, no trickery, and an honest answer to the question "what is your name" before he is blessed. The net effect of these alternate versions of how Jacob came to be blessed is to indicate to us that the stolen blessing by itself cannot be authoritative.

Toldot

But the most compelling argument against regarding the story of the stolen blessing as a simple trickster tale is seen in the subsequent events of Jacob's life. Jacob suffers more than either Isaac or Abraham, and much of his suffering reflects back on the stolen blessing. He is forced to leave home for twenty years, and it seems he never sees his mother again. He is deceived on his wedding night in a manner that seems to be a deliberate inversion of his stolen blessing – the younger brother who masqueraded as the preferred older is now deceived by an older sister masquerading as the beloved younger. Jacob, the son who fails to respect his father's prerogatives, suffers the disrespect of his own eldest sons. He is dishonored by his oldest son Reuben, who sleeps with his concubine, and disobeyed by his second and third, Simeon and Levi, who consider him incapable or unwilling to protect the family honor in the rape of Dinah. And finally, that kid goat whose meat he served his father, and whose skins he wore to simulate the hairy Esau, comes back to haunt him. When Joseph's brothers sell him into slavery, they dip his many-colored coat into the blood of a kid goat to convince the devastated Jacob that a wild beast has killed his son.

So, if we set aside the midrashic explanation, that Esau was so extravagantly wicked that Jacob was forced to act as he did, and if we reject the idea that the text simply intends us to enjoy the spectacle of a clever younger brother outwitting the elder, what does that leave us? I can't believe that we are supposed to conclude that Esau was a fine, upstanding fellow (as he appears in *The Red Tent*[1]), and that it's just too bad that our own ancestor is the less likeable, sneaky fellow. I think the story simultaneously maintains that it was the will of heaven that Jacob prevail over Esau and disapproves of the method that Jacob used to obtain his father's blessing. There are a number of tales in the Bible in which our ancestors, prophets and rulers are shown to have all-too-human flaws; they serve as negative examples, even when they have desirable outcomes. When Moses strikes the rock in anger, he does provide water for the thirsty Israelites, but he is reprimanded for having done so in a way that diminished the glory of Hashem. David's adultery with Bathsheba is denounced and severely punished, even though eventually it leads to the birth of King Solomon.

But here's my problem with the "negative example" theory: where does it leave my favorite matriarch, Rebecca? Jacob, at least, has a full life ahead of him, an opportunity to learn what it means to be the victim of deception, and a chance to reclaim his blessing legitimately, through wrestling with the

---

[1] Anita Diamant, *The Red Tent* (St. Martin's Press 1997).

angel. If it was both unnecessary and wrong for Jacob to obtain his father's blessing through trickery, then Rebecca is ending her once-promising life story either as the villain who prompted her son to do the wrong thing, or as a failed prophetess, who never correctly understood what G-d expected of her.

So I want to end by bringing in yet another theory (and there's still more that I won't have a chance to discuss this year!), and this one is inspired by Aviva Zornberg's take on *Toldot*.[1] Suppose that, somehow, it is a necessary maturational experience for Jacob to try on the part of Esau? Jacob, after all, is at first described as a *"tam,"* a simple (childlike?) man, one who is smooth, not hairy; one who doesn't leave his mother's tent. In other words, he is rather like a baby, undeveloped. If Abraham is the pioneer who comes to the land, and Isaac is the settler who stays on it lifelong, then Jacob is the wanderer, the one who needs to go out in the world, to be able to interact with other people, to spread the blessings, and to survive more than one exile. To do this, he needs to become an adult. By putting on the goatskins that make him into a complicated, adult, "hairy" person, by donning Esau's clothes, which smell of the outdoors, Jacob is perhaps transformed, at his mother's prompting, into a person capable of going out into the world. Of course, at the same time, he and his mother are setting into motion the events that will force him to leave home. In this version, Jacob may fool the outer Isaac, but Isaac's innermost soul blesses him correctly, because Jacob has begun to change himself into the man for whom the blessing was meant.

This would make the story of Jacob's stolen blessing rather akin to the story of the Garden of Eden. There is no doubt that Jacob, like Adam and Eve, has done something wrong, and yet the results are mixed. Paradise, or the safety of home is lost, but Adam and Eve, with their new knowledge of good and evil, or Jacob, with his ambivalent blessing, have grown up, and are ready to go out into the world to start the next stage in the development of humanity, or, with Jacob, the development of the people of Israel.

---

[1] *The Beginning of Desire* (Image 1996).

Vayeitze

Richard Tupper

Teraphim – don't leave home without them?

In Gen. 31, we have the puzzling story of Rachel swiping her father Laban's *teraphim*. The theft of the *teraphim* explains why Laban pursues Jacob – because he wants to recover "my gods" (though they are mentioned first, his daughters seem to be of secondary concern to Laban), but the story never tells us why Rachel lifts them in the first place.

Now it could be that from the perspective of the storyteller "why" Rachel stole the *teraphim* is irrelevant. If that is true, then the rest of my speculation here is similarly irrelevant.

On the other hand, it could be that the narrator assumes that his audience would understand why Rachel would take the *teraphim* and think it unnecessary to explain. Thus, perhaps the narrator and the audience share a social/historical context to supply the motive, a context we lack. If you know what credit cards are for, and someone tells you, "my daughter took my credit cards before she left home," you'd know why the daughter took the cards even without being told. However, if you didn't know what credit cards were for, you would be puzzled.

So, assuming there was a reason for Rachel to take the *teraphim*, what was it? Traditionally, the rabbis have taught that she did it to wean Laban of idolatry – a theory that I find hard to accept since as we see below the theft results in a curse upon her. Moreover, Rachel could just have tossed them or broken them, she didn't need to keep them. Ramban speculates that the *teraphim* were used not as idols but as means of foretelling the future, similar to the ephod. However, Laban's description of them as "my gods" seems to cut against that. (Of course, that's not to deny that one's gods might very well help one foretell the future!)

Some modern scholars, relying upon archeological finds, believe the *teraphim* were ancestral or household gods (a view I buy) and argue that by obtaining the *teraphim*, Rachel was staking her claim that Jacob should inherit from Laban. This I do not find convincing. First, the attitude of Rachel (and Leah and Jacob as well) seems to be "let's git while the gittin's good" (vv.14-16). There is no hint that Jacob *et al.* ever intend on coming back to reclaim an inheritance. Second, even if the inheritance went with the possession of the household gods, I don't see how swiping them while Laban was still quite alive would help their claim. Surely, Laban would notice, as he did. If, after his death, Jacob should reappear with the *teraphim*, everyone would know he must have stolen them. Consider the plights of Absalom and the other son of David, Adonijah, who both tried to claim the kingship while David was still kicking. It was not successful to put it mildly.

Moshe Greenberg ("Another Look at Rachel's Theft of the Teraphim," *Journal of Biblical Literature* 81 [1962], 239-248) suggests that it was common to travel with your household gods; they went with you wherever you went. He cited, I think, a remark by Josephus about a Parthian woman refugee. Personally, I think that is right. When I first thought about this issue, I remembered reading some Latin work, about how, when Aeneas fled burning Troy, he took with him his father, his son and his household gods (*penates*). That was the norm in the ancient world. You took your gods with you.

Rachel then takes the *teraphim* because she doesn't want to leave behind the benefit/protection of her household gods. She thinks the *teraphim* will benefit her, but it turns out – as is often the case – her plan boomerangs.

When Laban catches up, he searches the tents of Leah, Bilhah and Zilpah, and then Rachel. Why only their tents? I think because these *teraphim* are household gods, and therefore they wouldn't be of any use to persons unrelated to Laban. We know later that Jacob tells his people to put away their strange gods (35:2), and I think it is fair to assume that Jacob is referring to the household gods of these folks. Each family had its ancestral gods. So, Laban searches Leah and Rachel and their "belongings" – Zilpah and Bilhah. He does not need to search everyone's gear because his household gods would be of no use to anyone else. (Apparently *teraphim* are not quite as easily transferable as a credit card.)

Some think an ancient audience would have found ridiculing humor in Rachel's device to defeat Laban's search by hiding the *teraphim* in a camel saddle, sitting on it, and then telling Laban she can't rise because she is menstruating (31:34-35). Some think that by sitting on the *teraphim* in her ritually impure state of menstruating, Rachel was defiling and showing contempt for the *teraphim*. But I don't think so. I do think it is fair to assume

Vayeitze

that the taboos about menstruating women did apply in some fashion even before Sinai and the rules laid out in Leviticus. But the ridiculing humor only works if we believe Rachel that she is menstruating. I think she is lying. She knows her lie will work because she knows and Laban knows that no woman in her right mind would sit on the *teraphim* while she was menstruating.

So, let's assume that Rachel took the *teraphim* and desperately wants to keep them. She wants them so badly that she's willing to steal them and lie to her father about them. Why?

One reason I think is protection. She believed the ancestral gods would protect her. She may also have believed that the *teraphim* would help her have more children. In naming Joseph, Rachel revealed her desire that God would add more children and perhaps by taking the *teraphim* Rachel was spreading her bets. This isn't so unlikely because we've already seen that Rachel believes in the magical power of mandrakes to induce fertility (Gen. 30:14).

Does her plan work? No. The text goes out of its way to tell us that the *teraphim* had no role in protecting Rachel and Jacob from the pursuing Laban. It is God in His *tête-à-tête* with Laban who protects Jacob, and the *teraphim* have no role. There is also irony in Rachel's ruse of using menstrual impurity to "protect" the *teraphim*. The non-existent impurity she claims does succeed in keeping Laban away, but it turns out that the *teraphim* were making Rachel ritually impure! The idols make people ritually impure, and that is why Jacob has to tell everyone to get rid of their idols (35:2). Stealing the *teraphim* has an even worse result for Rachel. The theft brings about the terrible curse from Jacob (31:32): "'With whomever you find your gods, that person shall not live; before our kinsmen make recognition of what is yours with me, and take it.' But Jacob did not know that Rachel had stolen them."

Rachel does not get put to death immediately but she does die sooner than expected, after giving birth to the son she names son of my sorrow, Ben-oni, that Jacob later renames Benjamin. I think we should see her unfortunate death as the price she paid because of her theft of the *teraphim*. The *teraphim* in part are a lesson about the dangers and impotency of false gods

Vayishlach

Richard Tupper

Reflections on the Death of Deborah, Rebekah's Nurse

Once Jacob leaves Uncle Laban, he seems to age rapidly. No doubt his aging is spurred by the misfortunes he suffers upon his return. His only daughter, Dinah, is abducted and degraded by Shechem, son of Hamor. Levi and Simeon vengefully launch a murderous rampage and his other sons pillage and despoil, causing Jacob to fear clan warfare. Later his beloved Rachel dies when giving birth to their youngest child, a son whom Rachel in her death throes would name Benoni, son of my sorrow, but whom Jacob renames Benjamin, son of my right hand, a name brimming with irony. Very soon afterwards, Reuben wounds Jacob by bedding Jacob's concubine and Rachel's handmaid, Bilhah. Worse yet, Joseph, Rachel's eldest, is taken from Jacob, who imagines Joseph torn to death by an evil beast. Among all these calamities, when Jacob arrives at Beth-El, Gen. 35:8 relates: "And Deborah, Rebekah's nurse, died, and she was buried below Bethel under the oak; and the name of it was called *Allon-Bacuth*," that is, "the Oak of Weeping." We should not overlook the misfortune for Jacob that lies buried in this verse. Jacob returned to Beth-El at God's behest, and immediately after this verse has arguably his most intense encounter with God. However, Jacob quickly leaves Beth-El. Why? Gen. 35:8 hints at an answer.

Gen. 35:8's sparse report forces us to supply details. Who buried Deborah, herself a stranger to Beth-El? Who named the tree? Who else but Jacob? Why does the Torah now tell us that Rebekah's nurse is named "Deborah," a name withheld before (24:59)? It is because the name has special meaning only here.

It is unlikely that Jacob simply found Deborah lying dead at Beth-El. No, he met her alive and she dies afterwards. He buries her beneath a tree he names "the Oak of Weeping." Why this extravagant display of grief?

The Torah never tells us when Rebecca died but, because Jacob never again sees her alive after he leaves home, one infers she must have died before he returned. If so, then true to her name, "bee," Deborah stings Jacob with terrible news when they meet – Rebecca, Jacob's mother who loved him, has died. Then like every other bee, having inflicted her sting, Deborah dies. Jacob must bury her, but his naming the tree *Allon-bacuth* reveals not only his sorrow upon the death of the aged nurse but surely also his overwhelming grief at the news of his mother's death. Just as he is absent when his mother died and was buried, so, too, he is absent from this verse, Gen. 35:8, when Deborah dies and is buried, but we can see him in this verse and his loss and grief. Even though HaShem, like a good Jew, visits the mourning Jacob, the pain from the loss is so great, Jacob decides on his own to leave Beth-El. For Jacob, the Oak of Weeping overshadows the pillar he has erected to God.

Though not excusing Jacob, Gen. 35:8 helps frame Jacob's later treatment of Joseph. Benjamin, whose mother Rachel died giving birth to him, never knew his mother and very likely had a surrogate, perhaps Bilhah. Jacob's others sons have both a father and a mother, all save Joseph. When Jacob looks at young Joseph, his inherited beauty (39:6) a constant, bittersweet reminder to Jacob of Rachel (29:17) and Rebecca (24:16), he sees a boy who alone among his sons knows what it means to lose a devoted mother. In Joseph's pain, Jacob sees his own. With tragic consequences, Jacob, battered by grief into old age, dotes on Joseph, in part, we can reason, to comfort Joseph for his loss but perhaps also to ease his own suffering. And so we read in Gen. 37:3, "And Israel loved Joseph more than all his sons, because he was the child of his old age; and he made him an ornamented tunic."[1] Given their father's sufferings for which they are partly to blame, could not the sons, as adults, have forgiven Jacob an old man's foibles? Could not the brothers have suffered their younger brother Joseph, a motherless child, his cries for attention and his fancy coat?

---

[1] OJPS: "coat of many colours."

Vayishlach (II)

Richard Tupper

The story of Dinah in Gen. 34 can be read from many angles and in fact this is my third take on the story. This time I'd like to focus on the story's setting, what the Torah says both after and before the story of Dinah is told.

Immediately upon the conclusion of this tale, Gen. 35 begins, "And God said to Jacob, 'Rise, go up to Bethel and dwell there and make an altar there to the God Who appeared to you when you fled from Esau your brother.'" Commenting on this abrupt change, Rashi tersely states: "Because you were delinquent in [fulfilling] your vow, you have been punished and this [trouble] of your daughter has come to you."[1] Thus, surprisingly perhaps for many of us, Rashi both connects the Dinah story to Jacob's vow at Beth-El and sees the degradation of Dinah as a punishment visited on Jacob. In this *davar*, I would like to lend support to Rashi's view.

At first blush, the notion that the Dinah story is in fact a story about the punishment of Jacob seems counterintuitive; after all, isn't Dinah the one who was raped? Yet I think Rashi is right.

First the Hebrew verb employed to describe what Shechem did to Dinah, *anah*, does not necessarily imply rape. Literally, it means "to lower," "to humble" or "to degrade." Thus for example, when Laban takes leave of Jacob after having caught up with him fleeing back home, Laban warns Jacob, "Should you abuse [literally "lower"] my daughters, and should you take wives besides my daughters though no one else is present, see, God is

---

[1] According to Moshe Tzippor, "[t]he text of Rashi, 'for you were late along your way,' [Heb. *ba-derekh*] in printed editions, is a corruption and should read, 'for you were delinquent in [fulfilling] your vow,' [Heb. *nidrekha*] a difference of one letter (b/n)." See, "Jacob Kept Silent," at: http://www.biu.ac.il/JH/Parasha/eng/vayishlach/tzi.html n. 2 (2004).

witness between you and me" (Gen. 31:50). Laban is not worried about Jacob raping his daughters. Rather he is warning Jacob not to do anything that will lower the status of his daughters. Similarly, Deuteronomy (22:24) describes as "degraded" the betrothed daughter who is discovered lying with a man in the city. According to Deuteronomy's viewpoint, because she did not cry out in the city, she must have consented. Obviously, then, even though she was "degraded," she was not raped.

Second, according to biblical law, if without the consent of the father another man has sex with that man's unbetrothed daughter, the damages are payable to the father. Thus, Deut. 22:28-29 states:

> 28 Should a man find a virgin young woman who his not betrothed and take hold of her and lie with her, and they be found, 29 the man lying with her shall give to the young woman's father fifty weights of silver, and she shall be his wife inasmuch as he abused ["lowered" or "degraded"] her. He shall not be able to send her away all his days.

Note that Deuteronomy makes a distinction between daughters who are betrothed and those who are not. If a betrothed daughter is found with another man in the city, she is put to death because the legal presumption is she did not cry out (Deut. 22:23-24). If they are found in the field, she is not put to death because the presumption is that she did cry out (Deut. 22:25-27). However, in the case of the unbetrothed girl, there is no distinction in the text between the city and the field. The key for our purposes, however, is that only in the case of the unbetrothed virgin does the father receive payment because the bride price he would receive for his daughter has been reduced. Thus, Jacob has been injured by Shechem having sex with his daughter, regardless of whether Dinah consented. The important point is that *Jacob* did not consent.

So what is Jacob's vow that Rashi is referring to and how did Jacob violate it? When Jacob is on the run from Esau, he stops at Beth-El and has a vision of angels ascending and descending between earth and heaven. Upon arising in the morning he makes a speech which includes a vow (Gen. 28):

> 20 If the LORD God be with me and guard me on this way that I am going and give me bread to eat and clothing to wear, 21 and I return safely ("*v'shalom*") to my house, then the LORD will be my God. 22 And this stone that I set up as

Vayishlach (II)

a pillar will be a house of God, and everything that You give me I will surely tithe it ["give the tenth" (OJPS)] to You.

Does God keep His end of the bargain? We know that Jacob fared very well with Laban, returning a rich man. Moreover, the text makes God's fulfillment of Jacob's request explicit. Right before the Dinah story, when Jacob has returned to Canaan, we are told (Gen. 33:16-20):

> 16 And Esau returned that day on his way to Seir, 17 while Jacob journeyed on to Succoth. And he built himself a house, and for his cattle he made sheds – therefore is the name of the place called Succoth. 18 And Jacob came in peace ("*shalem*") to the town of Shechem, when he came from Paddan-Aram, and he camped before the town. 19 And he bought a parcel of land where he had pitched his tent from the sons of Hamor, father of Shechem, for a hundred kesitahs. And he set up an altar there and called it El-Elohei-Israel.

Thus Jacob asked to be returned safely and we are told he was. Has he gone to Beth-El to pay his vow? Obviously not; instead he built a home in Succoth[1] and then purchased land near Shechem. Rashi was certainly right to conclude that Jacob had been terribly delinquent in paying his vow.[2]

The Torah is very serious about paying vows. For example, it says in Deut. 23:22-24:

> Should you make a vow to the LORD your God, you shall not delay in fulfilling it, for the LORD your God will surely require it of you and there would be an offense in you. 23 And should you refrain from making a vow, there will be no offense in you. 24 The utterance of your lips you shall keep, and you shall do as you have vowed to the LORD your God, the freewill gift you spoke with your mouth.[3]

---

[1] Rashi on Gen. 33:17 states that Jacob spent a minimum of eighteen months in Succoth.

[2] This is in marked contrast to Shechem, whom we are told did not delay fulfilling his word to Jacob's brothers (Gen. 34:19) and he was the most respected person in his father's house (*ibid.*).

[3] See also, Eccl. 4:17 -5:6 which has special relevance to Jacob making a vow at Beth-El.

Now all this is well and good that one must pay one's vows or God will require it of you, but how does the incident involving Dinah fit in? I offer three reasons.

First, there is Dinah's name. Dinah was born after her half-brother, Dan, whose name we are told means "judgment" (Gen. 30:6). When Dinah is born, unlike her brothers, no special significance is assigned to her name. Indeed, her name only assumes significance in this story. It begins, "And there went out Dinah," or, more in keeping with the meaning to the story I am advocating, "And there went out a Judgment . . . ." Remember too that in the story we are never told what Dinah is thinking. It's quite possible that she has been raped and abducted. It's equally possible that she was seduced and now is happily in the city of Shechem awaiting the return of her lover. The narrator has refused to tell us anything approaching Dinah's "side of the story." In so doing he has left us in the same position as Jacob. Jacob cannot know whether his daughter has been raped by or is in love with Shechem, this son of a jackass (Hamor). The only difference between us and Jacob is: Jacob is her father. Thus, Dinah's outing inflicts maximum pain or judgment on Jacob.

Second, there is the matter of Dinah's birth order. At Beth-El Jacob had promised God his tenth, and who is Dinah? She is Jacob's tenth. "No," you'll say, "she's his eleventh." But remember, Reuben as the firstborn belongs to God (Ex. 13:2), and therefore he cannot be dedicated to God since he already belongs to God (Lev. 27:26). Because Dinah is Jacob's tenth (*cf.* Lev. 27:32) and Jacob has failed to pay his vow, God has "required it" of him and has taken away Dinah, his tenth.

Finally, I would point to one more passage explaining why Dinah is taken from Jacob. Lev. 5:1a, 4-6 says:

> If a person does wrong . . . . 4 Or when a person blurts out an oath to bad or good purpose – whatever anyone may utter in an oath – and, though he has known it, the fact escapes him but (thereafter) he feels guilt in any of these matters – 5 When he feels guilt in any of these matters, he shall confess that wherein he did wrong. 6 And he shall bring as his reparation offering to YHWH, for the wrong that he committed, a female from the flock, sheep or goat, as a purification offering; and the priest shall effect purgation on his behalf for his wrong.

Vayishlach (II)

Who is Dinah? She is the female of Jacob's flock.

Vayeshev

Andrew Kirschner

I had a dream last night that I was at a Shabbaton Committee meeting. Nava was there, the Hobsheids, Norman Eliaser, well basically there were about twelve of us all together. We were making centerpieces for the Shabbaton luncheon – Feb. 10-11. All of a sudden my centerpiece rose up above all the other centerpieces and the rest of the centerpieces bowed down low to mine. So I have decided to entitle my *d'var*, "Daydream Believer." And no, it was not inspired by Davy Jones or the Monkees.

So obviously, I have decided to focus on the dream aspect of the *parsha*. I initially thought it would be very easy to tackle this story and I found it very pertinent to the experiences I have had over the last couple of years as a young man looking for ways to find and pursue my dreams. But as I looked into the topic further, and read the *parsha* more closely, I found that this dream *d'var* was turning more into a nightmare as I was becoming conflicted on a major issue.

The issue is: what does the *parsha* tell us about dreams? Not the dreams we have every night about showing up to work in our underwear, and not even the dreams that our forefathers and prophets had that were actually more visions and prophecies than dreams. I am talking about the dreams we have when we are awake, about what we want out of life. Dreams about what great things we are here on earth to accomplish. So hopefully, I don't put you to sleep – pun intended – as we talk about this subject.

First a story that is not biblical or Jewish, but will tie into things quite nicely. I thought it would get us in the right frame of mind for this *d'var*. I was waiting to get a haircut on Thursday and flipping through a *Time* magazine [Dec. 26, 2005] and came across an article entitled, "Six Tales of Courage." And one of the stories was about a cabbie in Washington, D.C., who was originally from Batagram, Pakistan. This cabbie, whose name was

Ihsan Kahn, had a dream to become mayor of his town. When he was nineteen, he came to America to seek his fortune. He met his wife here, studied at Northern Illinois University, and eventually became an American citizen. After divorcing his wife he found his way to D.C. Though he was clearly not living the American Dream as he often slept in his cab, he used to say "It's the worst job in the world. But I told myself I'd go on until I had a heart attack and then people would know what Khan went through."

One thing you should also know about Khan is that he religiously played the lottery. In fact every week he played the same numbers because they had come to him in a dream. In fact his mother on her deathbed informed him that she had a vision of him living like a king some day. And basically that is what happened. In November of 2001, Khan won 55.2 million dollars in the lottery. He decided to cash in his ticket and move back to his hometown where he fulfilled his dream of becoming the mayor.

Now, I'll go back to the Torah. The question that comes out of the *parsha* for me is this. Does God create our dreams and manipulate the universe around us in just such a way so that we will be inclined or maybe in some cases obliged to pursue them? Or do we decide our own dreams, what we ultimately want to accomplish and, as long as it is within the boundaries of God's will, God will give us the strength to influence the universe in such a way that it will allow our dreams to come true? Now, certainly you could also ask a third question and that is – does God have anything to do with it at all – but I figured I would save the agnostic questions for a different *d'var*.

So to start off, we'll go over the evidence in favor of how God remains the primary controller of Joseph's dreams coming true. First of all, after having the initial dreams about the brothers' sheaves bowing down to Joseph's and about the stars, the sun, and the moon bowing down to Joseph himself, the brothers were angry. So Israel instructs Joseph to go find them to "see how your brothers fare, and how the flock fares." On the way to find them he meets a mysterious man who tells him where to go. Some commentaries suggest that this man was actually an angel of God and that is why the Torah does not give us his name.

Further evidence comes later when Joseph is in the pit, and there just happens to be a band of Ishmaelites wandering by, so his brothers can choose to sell him into slavery instead of leaving him in the pit to die. Or how about more blatantly when Joseph goes down to Egypt and ends up in Potiphar's house and the text says that "the LORD was with him, and all that he did the LORD made succeed in his hand." There is also a midrash that says that Potiphar's wife went to see an astrologer and saw that she and Joseph were to

Vayeshev

have children in common – which caused her to try to seduce him and ultimately resulted in Joseph going to jail. And in jail, we see God controlling the story line again. It says, ". . . and God was with Joseph and extended kindness to him, and granted him favor in the eyes of the prison-house warden." This results in making Joseph the head prisoner so he had access to all the prisoners including the baker and the butler, whose dreams he would interpret.

So we see in the story that on the path to Joseph's ultimate success, God is there every step of the way. To make things more interesting, when Joseph tries to take things into his own hands, things don't seem to work out. For example, after interpreting the butler's dream that he will be reinstated to be a chief butler, Joseph asked that the butler remember him because he was stolen away from the land of the Hebrews and was put in jail for a crime he didn't commit. Clearly he is trying to buy his own ticket out of jail. What happens? At the end of the portion we find out that Joseph's interpretations are 100 percent accurate, but the chief butler completely forgets him. According to Rashi, God does this on purpose to show Joseph that people can forget, but God never forgets His own.

But what about the other side of the coin? Is it possible that Joseph was having these dreams because he wanted to be great? And in fact wanted to be the future head of the family? Is it possible that God allowed it all to happen because it was in line with His ultimate goal for the Jewish people some 400 years later? I found some evidence to support this view as well.

For example, why does Joseph insist on telling his brothers his second dream, when he knows the first one already made them mad? It almost seems that he is trying to goad them into attempting to get rid of him so he can find his ticket out of there to seek his fortune. Later on when he was in prison, he approaches the butler and baker one morning because they look so sad, and asks them what is the matter. They say they had dreams and need someone to interpret them. Here an interesting line comes from Joseph, who says, "Are not solutions from God? Pray, recount them to me." If the solutions to dreams are from God, why does Joseph take it upon himself to interpret them? Does he see some gain from interpreting the dreams of these powerful officials of Pharaoh's court?

The last action that Joseph takes to create his own destiny comes after this *parsha* when his brothers come to Egypt to buy grain for their family. There is a series of plots by Joseph: from making them go get Benjamin to planting the cup in Benjamin's sack, all this to achieve his dream of reuniting his family. In fact, Rashi even says that the reason he makes the brothers get

Benjamin in the first place is because he literally wants his earlier dream to be realized. In other words, when ten of his brothers come to him and bow down before him, he notices there is an inconsistency because in the dream there were eleven stars that bowed down, and the sun and the moon. So he makes them go back for Benjamin and later the rest of the family so that his dream can be realized.

So you can probably see why I became conflicted when reading the story as to who was driving the story line. However, in the story of Tamar and Judah, we find evidence that supports the idea that perhaps we do have control over our dreams and can take action to pursue them as long as it does not conflict with God's greater purpose. Tamar, Judah's daughter-in-law, dreams of having a son. When her first and second husbands die and Judah asks her to remain a widow in case the third son dies by marrying her, she takes matters into her own hands. She dresses as a harlot and seduces Judah in order to become pregnant. Ultimately she and Judah become the ancestors of King David and Elijah the prophet. So God allows this to happen because it is consistent with what He wants for the world many generations down the line.

These are the sides to the two cases. A clear answer I have not found. I did find a parallel story that we always tell around the same time as this *parsha*. That is the story of Chanukah. It is a story about a group of religious Jews who decide to organize a revolt in order to stop the Hellenization of their people. What role does God play in this story? Is it their decision to protect their beliefs that prompts God to support them in creating the miracle of victory over the Greeks? Or is it that God desired the Jewish people to survive, so He inspired a revolt and the Miracle of the Menorah that followed?

Perhaps the answer lies in one of Chanukah's most recognizable symbols, the dreidel. The dreidel is an interesting game. You could look at it as symbolizing the earth as it spins on its axis. Just as we spin the dreidel from the top, God spins the earth from up above. We really have very little control over the matter. This would surely explain the miracle of the Maccabees defeating the mighty Greek army.

However, there is another way to look at the dreidel. We must take it in our hands and spin it, but then once we start it spinning, we have no control as to what side the dreidel will land on. Will it be a *Nun, Gimel, Shin, Heh*? We don't know. Presumably it's in God's hands. If that is the case, then it would seem that God just wants us to get the ball rolling or dreidel spinning, so to speak, and He will surely take care of the rest. It could be a bad result

Vayeshev

and land on a loss, or it could be a good result and land on a win. Life is really a game of dreidel. That may still make you feel powerless over your life, but if you think about it, every time we do a mitzvah, it's like getting another spin on the dreidel. The more mitzvot we perform, the more opportunities we get for a better result.

That is exactly what the Jews did when they defeated the Greeks. They cleaned up the Temple and found only one jar of pure oil that they knew would only last for a day. They could have chosen any number of things to do with the oil. Knowing that it would be eight days before new oil would arrive, they could have used the oil sparingly each day. Even if it didn't burn the whole day it would at least burn every day. They could have also waited seven days and lit the Menorah on the eighth day so that there would be no interruption between days. But the ancient Jews knew that their job was not to figure these things out. Their job was simply to start the dreidel spinning and let God figure the rest out. So they lit the Menorah as soon as it was ready because that is what they had been commanded to do. God took care of the rest by allowing the oil to burn for eight days.

As for our friend in Pakistan, Ihsan Khan, it turns out there is an epilogue to his story too. You see, just as Khan was settling in as mayor of his home town, fulfilling his lifelong dream – a dream he achieved, by the way, by playing the Lotto numbers for twenty years that he saw in a dream. Well, just as things couldn't be better, in October of this year, there was an earthquake that killed nearly 80,000 people across Pakistan (4,500 in his own town). Khan was able to use $200,000 of his money to get much needed medicine, supplies, and transportation to hospitals for the people of his village.

One final note to leave you with. One year ago, I fulfilled my lifelong dream of going to Israel. During one part of the trip we visited Mount Herzel. I can honestly say, it was one of the most moving days of my entire life. Of course at the top of the mountain lies Herzel who said *"Eem Tirzu, Ein zo Aggadah* – If you just want it to happen, it will not be just a dream." Surrounding him are where most of the presidents and prime ministers are buried, Chaim Herzog, Golda Meir, Yitzchak Rabin, and others. And then surrounding them going all around the mountain are thousands of fallen soldiers from the wars fought over the last fifty-six years. And as we toured the cemetery I was moved to tears over the thought that these individuals died, and many died young. They were brave and died not just to defend their families but to defend the very existence of their nation. But what really made me sad was knowing that they died so that I could have the privilege of standing in the holiest land on earth on that day. It was perhaps the most humbling moment of my life. I don't know for sure what role God played in all of it, but, given all that I had witnessed, I could not deny that He had something to do with it.

Vayeshev (II)

Lise Weisberger

Many stories in the Bible are mystifying, but few are so tantalizingly obscure as the story of Judah and Tamar, Genesis chapter 38. In a single chapter, this story touches on intermarriage, sudden death, contraception, prostitution, illegitimate pregnancy, capital punishment and high risk obstetrics. The only problem is to figure out what it all means.

I'd like to start by offering what I think are two keys to unlocking the meaning of this baffling story, and then look at the narrative in detail, with an emphasis on its place in the moral biography of Judah.

The first point I want to make is that there is a major clue to the significance of the story buried in the next to last sentence of the chapter, when Tamar's first twin is named Perez. Strangely, there is no hint in this chapter or, indeed, anywhere else in Genesis that this Perez is any more important than any other child of Judah. However, I believe that we, the readers of this text, are supposed to realize, or to find out, that Perez is the ancestor of King David. If we are of a mystical bent, we will also recognize Perez as the ancestor of the messiah, and knowing this casts a very positive glow on the character of Tamar.

Up to the point that we recognize the name Perez, we might think that this story of a woman who disguises herself as a prostitute in order to seduce her father-in-law is yet another story about those insatiable gentile women and the trouble they make for nice Jewish boys – not unlike the story of Potiphar's wife which immediately follows. But once we know that Tamar has given birth to someone essential to the future of the Jewish people, we realize that this is another story about how G-d brings necessary people into the world even when it seems impossible. Far from being like Potiphar's wife, Tamar is like Sarah, who has a baby at age ninety. Or, to be more precise, she is like Ruth – a plucky, steadfast gentile woman who takes unconventional action in order to preserve life in a family that is haunted by death.

Leaves from the Garden

The second key to understanding the story of Judah and Tamar is to see it only *appears* to be an interruption in the story of Joseph. In fact, on every level, from specific words and phrases to overarching themes, the stories are intimately connected. They are about what brothers of capable of doing to each other and doing for each other, and about how G-d's plans become manifest though the impulses and passions of distinctly non-divine human beings.

I would like to explore in detail only the most obvious connection between the story of Tamar and the story of Joseph, and that is the character of Judah.

We first hear Judah speak in chapter 37, verses 26 and 27, and his speech is an interesting one. The brothers have seized Joseph, with the intent of killing him, and cast him into a pit. Judah says, "What gain is there if we kill our brother and cover up his blood? Come, let us sell him to the Ishmaelites and our hand will not be against him, for he is our brother, our own flesh." Notice how Judah almost simultaneously advances a moral argument – It's wrong to kill our brother – and an expedient one – We'll get rid of him more profitably by selling him. It's entirely unclear which argument Judah believes, and which one he's using in order to get the brothers to listen to him. But he does indeed get the brothers to listen to him, and it is consistent throughout the story that people listen to Judah when they will listen to no one else.

Judah then participates with his brothers in covering up their crime. They dip Joseph's torn coat in animal blood, and lead Jacob to erroneously conclude that Joseph has been killed by a wild beast.

At the beginning of our chapter, Judah separates himself from his brothers. The midrash imagines that the brothers, stricken with guilt, turn on Judah, saying, "You were our leader! If you had told us to take Joseph back to our father we would have listened to you! Why didn't you take responsibility for leading us in the right path?"

So Judah leaves his past life and his guilty secrets behind and starts a new life for himself – he gets himself an Adullamite business partner and a Canaanite wife, he raises three sons, and he forges a new identity as a respectable citizen of Canaan. Like any responsible father, he gets a wife for his son when the boy comes of age, a girl named Tamar. But his son is wicked, and dies childless. Judah again acts responsibly and in accordance with tradition; he directs his second son to marry Tamar, in order to provide her with a child who will carry on the name of his deceased first son. But the second son does not wish to create a rival for himself by donating his sperm

Vayeshev (II)

for his deceased brother, and he avails himself of an ancient form of nonprescription birth control in order to avoid impregnating Tamar. G-d is displeased, and the second son dies as well.

I am going to skip over the fascinating and disturbing question of why Judah's two oldest sons, out of all the wicked characters in Genesis, are the only ones to be personally, individually executed by G-d. It is another *d'var Torah* in itself. I want to stick with the point of view of Judah, and the fact is that Judah doesn't have a clue about what just happened. All he knows is that he keeps marrying his sons to Tamar, they keep on dying, and she's still not pregnant. He thinks, in fact, that Tamar is bad luck for his family, and although he should now send his third, his last, his youngest son to her, he's afraid to do so.

But it seems he's also afraid to jeopardize his reputation as an upholder of tradition, or to anger Tamar's family, because instead of telling Tamar that he does not wish to lose another son in her bed, he puts her off – tells her that his youngest isn't fully grown yet, that he'll send the boy to her when he's older.

So Tamar goes back to her father's house to wait indefinitely for Shelah. It's clear that Judah is being unfair to her – by tradition, he owes her a secure, high-status position in his household as the mother of his firstborn grandchild. Instead, he's dooming her to life as a perpetual childless widow. What is not so clear is that he is also sealing off his own future. He has only one surviving son, and we've been told that his own wife has left off childbearing. As long as he must maintain the pretense that his youngest is not ready to marry, he will never have any grandchildren whatsoever, let alone grandchildren to carry on the names of his lost sons, grandsons whom only Tamar can conceive. Between his fear of losing a son and his fear of losing his reputation, Judah has cut his own tribe off at the root.

But luckily for Judah, Tamar has no intention of seeing her future cut off, and she has plenty of courage. After Judah's wife dies, she disguises herself, and positions herself on a public road, at a place called *Petach Enayim*, the Opening of the Eyes. Sure enough, Judah gets an eyeful of her, mistakes her for a prostitute, and enters into a negotiation about her price. He offers her a kid goat, but since he doesn't have one on hand, she asks that he leave certain articles as a pledge – his cord, signet and staff. These are unmistakable articles of personal identification – basically she's holding onto his driver's license till he redeems it with the cash he owes her.

But when Judah sends the payment, the "prostitute" and his personal articles are nowhere to be found. Again, his words are telling: verse 23 –

Leaves from the Garden

"Let her take them [the cord, signet and staff], lest we be a laughingstock." Better to lose a little more of his personal identity than to be publicly shamed. But no sooner is this sexual indiscretion swept under the rug than another scandal erupts. Judah's daughter-in-law, Tamar, has gotten herself pregnant. This time Judah reacts forcefully, with great authority, to restore the family honor: "Take her out to be burned" (Gen. 38:24).

Now Tamar produces the cord, seal and staff and tells Judah that they belong to the man who impregnated her. In the past, I've always read this as a scene of great triumph for Tamar, "Now I've got you, you dead-beat dad, check out these paternity test results!" But the fact is, Tamar is still in a completely vulnerable position. Judah, a man who hates to be embarrassed, will surely not be pleased to learn he was sexually entrapped by Tamar. And if he decides not to recognize his personal articles, who would believe her? He's a respected community figure; she is a single pregnant woman who's been condemned to die.

But, finally, faced with the evidence of his own past, faced with his family's future in Tamar's womb, and faced with Tamar's plea: "*Haker-na*, please recognize," Judah does recognize – himself, what he's done, what he needs to do next. To his credit, when he confesses, there's no attempt to excuse himself or blame Tamar. He doesn't say; "I'd just lost my wife; I was lonely; she sat where she knew I'd see her; she deliberately concealed her identity." Even though all these things are true, Judah sees the deeper truth – not just that he fathered her twin babies, but that he put her in the impossible position from which this desperate act was the only way out.

In *parshiot* to come, we will see Judah again connected with his brothers and father, acting as their spokesman in difficult situations, and taking full responsibility for the life of Benjamin, who has replaced Joseph as the outrageously favored son. His encounter with Tamar has not made him a saint, but it has given him the courage to see himself as he is and to take responsibility for his actions. Combined with his natural abilities as a leader, these changes allow him to speak effectively for the brothers as they unknowingly move toward reconciliation with Joseph.

Vayeshev (III)

Richard Tupper

The teaching of the rabbis that there are 70 interpretations of every verse is based in part on the idea that God gave the Torah at Sinai in the 70 languages of all the peoples of the world. In essence, the rabbis are teaching us that because the Torah was given in every possible language, there are an inexhaustible number of interpretations for every verse. That process of interpreting the Torah never ends and we today are still discovering interpretations to the Torah that God gave at Sinai. "Even that which a distinguished disciple was destined to teach in the presence of his master was already said to Moses on Sinai" (*p. Peah* 17a).

But, of course, we draw back at the idea that every interpretation is true. The rabbis have a fascinating solution:

> Any dispute which is for the sake of Heaven [whose participants are motivated by an honest search for truth and do not merely plead for the sake of argument and provocation] shall in the end be of lasting worth [such a dispute is destined to produce positive insights and permanent solutions of the issues under investigation]; but that which is not for the sake of Heaven [where the basic motive is the achievement of power, or mere obstinate self-assertion], shall not in the end be of lasting worth [such disputes fail to yield substantive results].
> (*Pirkei Avot* 5.17 [comments of R. Kehati[1]])

The paradox as I see it is that you and I can have completely different interpretations, seemingly, and yet both can be for the sake of Heaven, and

---

[1] *Chapters of the Fathers with a Commentary by R. Pinhas Kehati* (WZO 1986).

both can be "right" or lead to "right" interpretations. The classic example is why God chose to give the Torah to Israel. One answer is: "Why did the Holy One, blessed be He, choose Israel? Because all the peoples repudiated the Torah and refused to receive it; but Israel agreed and chose the Holy One, blessed be He, and His Torah" (*Num. R.* XIV.10). Another is: "The Holy One, Blessed be He, inverted Mt. Sinai over them [*b'nei Yisrael*] like a huge vessel and declared, 'If you accept the Torah, well and good; if not, here shall be your sepulcher'" (*Shab.* 88a). We can even dispute whether these two interpretations are irreconcilable, but the key is that our dispute is "for the sake of Heaven."

The multifaceted meanings of every verse are amply illustrated by the verse in this week's *parsha*, "And Israel loved Joseph more than all his other sons, for he was the child of his old age" (Gen. 37:3). Let's assume that this is a correct translation and that the words – "for he was the child of his old age" – are meant to explain why Israel loved Joseph more. Though I won't give seventy, consider three possible different interpretations:

1.) "[C]hild of his old age" is meant to echo Isaac who, at age sixty (Gen. 25:26), had two sons, who loved Esau while Rebecca loved Jacob (Gen. 25:28), and who, when an old man (Gen. 27:1), sought to favor Esau with a blessing meant for Jacob (Gen. 27). We know what trouble that caused and that trouble will be repeated in the Joseph story. That is the meaning of "Israel loved Joseph more . . . ."

2.) "[C]hild of his old age" is meant to remind us of Israel's troubled past and how that past affected Joseph so that Joseph was in need of special attention. Old men look back. Jacob had recently lost Rachel, who died in childbirth (Gen. 35:19). Moreover, the death of Deborah, his mother Rebecca's nurse (Gen. 35:8), reminded him of how much he missed his mother, with whom he was never reunited after he went to Paddan Aram to find a wife (Gen. 28). Jacob remembered how as a boy his father had always loved Esau so that he in essence had only one parent, Rebekah, who was now lost to him.

He looks at Joseph and what does he see? A young boy without a mother who needs more attention than his brothers do. Joseph has no brothers to speak of (Benjamin is too young to mention and, since his mother died in childbirth, did not suffer the loss that Joseph did – a loss Israel keenly understands). If Reuben pesters him for attention, he can say, "Go ask your

Vayeshev (III)

mother!" But he can't say that to Joseph. So, Isaac must be a father and a mother to Joseph – that is the meaning of "Israel loved Joseph more . . . ."

3.) "[C]hild of his old age" is meant to remind us that Jacob may be nearing death and may be concerned about tending to the passing on of the Covenant. Old men look to the future, just like his father Isaac had when he thought he was near death (Gen. 28:1). Isaac had preferred Esau who was clearly unworthy; Israel would not make the same mistake. Israel, who arguably has just had the most vivid encounter with God in his life and the fullest statement of the Covenant and its promises, looks carefully at his sons for leadership.

Reuben, the firstborn son of Leah, had already demonstrated that he was unqualified for leadership. Right after the death of Rachel, Reuben had bedded Bilhah, Jacob's wife/concubine (Gen. 35:22). The enormity of that sin disqualifies him (Gen. 49:4). Moreover, Reuben, rather than recognizing that children are a gift from God, had already displayed an impious belief that the blessing of children could be achieved by magical means. (Reuben gave mandrakes, thought to have magical powers of fertility, to his mother Leah; Gen. 30:14.) If Reuben was disqualified, then perhaps Joseph as the firstborn of Rachel was next. In any case, Israel had already received reports about how the other sons were misbehaving (Gen. 37:2), and while this may have been *lashon hara* from Joseph, a child too young to know better, it was still true, and the evil reports convinced him that Joseph was morally superior to his brothers. By loving Joseph rather than the others, he was acting like Sarah, who recognized that Isaac was more deserving than Ishmael, and Rebekah, who recognized that Jacob was more deserving than Esau. That is the meaning of the words, "Israel loved Joseph more . . . ."

No one of these interpretations is necessarily the "right" interpretation nor is any of them necessarily "wrong." I have come to believe they can all be right. The point I have begun to grasp is that I need to bring that same attitude when I listen to or read the drash of another.

"Yehoshua ben Perachyah said, 'Provide yourself with a teacher; acquire a companion; and judge every person in the scale of merit'" (*Pirkei Avot* 1. 6). How does R. Yehoshua's teaching apply? Every person can be my teacher and my companion.

How do I know whether the person I meet should be my teacher or should be my companion or should be neither? R. Yehoshua says I should "judge every person in the scale of merit." Moreover, in judging another, R. Kehati

111

in the name of Rashi says that when I see another do something that can possibly be taken as either wrongful or meritorious, I should consider it as meritorious and not suspect the worse. (Kehati's commentary on *Pirkei Avot*, *ad loc.*, citing, Rashi, *Shevu* 30a.)

Thus when I hear another's *drash*, I can assume that he or she is making the argument either for the sake of Heaven or not for the sake of Heaven. Since I have no reason to believe that the person is not acting for the sake of Heaven, I should assume that that she or he is making the argument for the sake of Heaven. An argument made for the sake of Heaven produces meaningful results. Once taken to heart, the pool of one's teachers becomes inexhaustible:

> Ben Zoma said: "Who is wise? He who learns from every man, as it is said (Ps. 119:99): 'From all my teachers have I gained understanding.' " (*Pirkei Avot* 4.1)

And ben Azzai added,

> Do not despise any person, and do not dismiss anything; for there is not a person who has not their hour; and there is not a thing that has not its place. (*Pirkei Avot* 4.3)

As Rabbi A. Steinsaltz has written, "One of the greatest talmudic commentators, the Maharsha, often ended his commentaries with the word '*vedok*' (continue to examine the matter). This exhortation is an explicit admission that the subject has not been exhausted and that there is still room for additions and arguments on the question. To a certain extent the whole of the Talmud is rounded by this *vedok*, the injunction to continue to search, to ask, to seek new aspects of familiar problems" (*The Essential Talmud* [Bantam Books 1976] p. 273).

Occasionally, I have become so convinced of my interpretation that I have failed to listen to what others have to say. In my worst moments, I have suspected them of making an argument not for the sake of Heaven. By my actions, I have robbed myself of the opportunity to obtain another teacher and a deeper understanding of the Torah.

The Minyan is a place where we come to argue for the sake of Heaven, and from our arguments may come deeper understandings of the multifaceted Torah and, as we all know, "the more Torah, the more life."

Vedok!

Mikketz

Hillel Crandus

The Interpreters of Egypt

Parshat Mikketz opens with Pharaoh having two dreams. In the first, he watches seven healthy cows emerge from the Nile. Seven sickly cows follow and consume the healthy ones. Pharaoh awakens, but the dream has not bothered him, so he goes back to sleep only to have a similar dream. This time, he sees ripe corn swallowed by seared corn. Now Pharaoh awakens and he is disturbed. To regain his calm, Pharaoh calls "all the wise men" and "all the magicians" of Egypt to interpret his dreams, but they cannot. Why not?

One response to this question underscores the notion that prophecy of the Divine Will comes only to those who are favored by God. The Egyptian interpreters are no doubt called to Pharaoh because of their ability to understand the secrets that the Egyptian gods intend to be hidden. However, the Divine Will is unfathomable unless God grants a person the power to see it. And God has not granted the interpreters of Egypt this privilege. Understood in this way, the episode works as a tacit diatribe against the ancient world's notion that Man, when empowered by his understanding of the meta-divine realm, could defeat even the will of the gods. In addition, the whole sequence that follows Pharaoh's dream can be read as an example of how the Divine Will guides history, in this case, granting Joseph prophetic ability, which leads to his liberation and ascent in Egypt (Gen. 45:5-9).

Though this view offers a sturdy starting point, it minimizes human participation in the prophetic process. Arguably, the act of prophecy has several stages. From seeing to understanding to articulating, an individual not only must be favored by God to be a prophet, but also must be ready for the call. Solomon Ashtruc, a 14th century scholar who lived in France and then Spain, makes this point in his *Midrashei HaTorah*: "Some of the wizards did perceive the essential significance of the dream, but none of them could verbalize the calamities that the dreams portended." (This translation from the ArtScroll *Bereishis* volume,[1] as are all following translations.) In other words, divinely inspired "seeing" is only one part of the prophetic process. Pharaoh sees, but does not understand; some of the Egyptians understand ("perceive the essential significance"), but cannot speak. Certainly, God chooses those who will be granted an intimation of the Divine Will, but humans also have a role to play in the process.

The wise men and magicians fail in this role because they live in a religious/political culture that has not allowed them to cultivate the independence or the singular devotion to God, which is necessary for prophesying the explosive intimations that God sends into the world. The story that leads up to *parshat Mikketz* suggests that fear of Pharaoh's wrath is a condition of Egyptian life. In this previous story, Pharaoh tosses two courtiers in jail for some unspecified crime. One is re-instated, the other put to death. The one who lives, the cup-bearer, stands next to Pharaoh, an omen of Pharaoh's wrath for the wise men, magicians, and the reader. After the Egyptian interpreters fail to explain Pharaoh's dream, the cup-bearer narrates how he came to meet Joseph in jail. He recalls that, "Pharaoh had been furious with his servants, and he placed me under guard in the house of the high chamberlain – me and the chief baker" (Gen. 41:10). Here, the cup-bearer *explicitly* tells us of Pharaoh's volatile temper. In addition to serving as a conduit to introduce Joseph to Pharaoh, the cup-bearer's presence allows us a glimpse into the workings of the Pharaoh's governance and is a useful lens for understanding the pressures weighing on the wise men and magicians.

Pharaoh's anxiety over his dreams intensifies his usual intimidating presence. So desperate is Pharaoh to have his dreams interpreted that he straightaway asks for two different types of thinkers: those who can offer rational explanations based on experience (the wise men) and also those who can conjure explanations through some sort of mystical practice (the magicians). Pharaoh is not concerned about how he gets at the meaning of his dreams; he will resort to using any interpretive approach. Rashi offers that Pharaoh really asked for wise men and "necromancers," or those who "excite themselves with" the bones of the dead to understand the happenings in the present. (These days, we call 'em "historians.") Eventually, he will turn to a nobody – Joseph – for help. Pharaoh's desperation is revealed by his comprehensive call for anyone who can help to soothe his anguished soul.

---

[1] Edited by N. Scherman and M. Zlotowitz (Mesorah 1986).

Mikketz

If we take into account Pharaoh's penchant for pouring out wrath and his desperation to calm his mind, we can begin to understand his interpreters' failure. The wise men and magicians are the first ones called to Pharaoh. Chances are that they have gained a position of primacy because of their political savvy – their ability to understand how to treat Pharaoh and how to respond to the complex situations that arise in Egypt. Ever aware of their immediate situation *vis-à-vis* Pharaoh, they know that he can make or break a man. Find an explanation and prosper; fail Pharaoh and who knows what type of punishment might ensue. As Shakespeare makes clear in Part II of *Henry IV*, "the first bringer of unwelcome news/ Hath but a losing office." Pharaoh's presence stymies the interpreters' ability to articulate a clear expression of the Divine Will.

There is a more compelling way to put this: the interpreters of Egypt, devoted as they are to Pharaoh, do not have the emotional or psychological strength to be messengers of the Divine Will. Nothing in their culture has taught them the independence to confront Pharaoh with bad news; and nothing in their culture has prepared them to show devotion to messages sent by the God of Israel. Left to their own devices, with no help from God, trembling before their master, these men cannot articulate their understandings.

This reading of the situation becomes more plausible if we look at the Egyptians' response after Joseph successfully interprets Pharaoh's dreams. After he finishes, the Torah tells us that "the thing seemed good in Pharaoh's eyes and in the eyes of his servants" (Gen. 41:37). No jealousy or skepticism is recorded; if anything, they are relieved. The Egyptians immediately recognize good interpretation when they hear it. This recognition makes sense if we accept Ashtruc's reading that the Egyptians could perceive the dreams' significance, but they could not articulate it. As Ralph Waldo Emerson says in *Self Reliance*, they "recognized [their] own rejected thoughts: they came back to [them] with a certain alienated majesty." In other words, when Joseph interprets Pharaoh's dreams, the wise men and magicians recognize their own prophetic thoughts cloaked in the language of a different speaker.

Joseph is the opposite of the Egyptians. He is entirely devoted to God and, therefore, he is able to articulate the Divine Will, despite the suffering this causes others and himself. Joseph demonstrates his unabashed devotion to truth when he is in prison, and he interprets the dream of Pharaoh's baker. Joseph gives the baker the straight dope: he is certain to die in three days. The Midrash is uneasy with Joseph's insensitivity in this scene. *Oznaim*

LaTorah counters that, "Joseph did not offer to tell its meaning, but when the baker pressed him to do so, he responded." It seems more accurate to suggest that Joseph has made a choice to keep his eyes focused on the Divine Will and not the feelings of the baker. Similarly, he speaks the truth of his own dreams though it inspires his brothers' murderous wrath.

Usually, we think of *tikkun olam* in positive terms: working in soup kitchens, driving around in a *Sukkah* mobile, or visiting the sick. These types of activities rest easily in our liberal culture. However, Joseph's example is troubling because it is a negative form of *tikkun olam*. Joseph brings the Divine Will into the world even when it is painful for those around him. His insensitivity and bluntness seem obnoxious. However, Joseph is a *tzaddik* precisely because he remains single-mindedly devoted to God, despite the trouble it causes him and the pain it causes others. We, too, must cultivate the necessary independence from worldly masters and the proper devotion to God, so that we, like Joseph, are prepared to bring the Divine Will into the world.

Mikketz (II)

Hillel Crandus[1]

*P*arshat *Mikketz* begins with the following four words: "And it happened at the end of two full years" (Gen. 41:1). On the surface, these words seem to function simply as a link between two episodes; however, they point to a deeper problem. Joseph, the protagonist, has been locked away in jail for two years, and he is almost unknown in Egypt with the exception of one irresponsible attendant to Pharaoh. The fact that, not one, but two years have elapsed indicates that trends are solidifying, and they do not include Joseph. Egypt and the world are sailing along just fine without him.

"At the end of two full years," God intervenes in Egyptian history, since there is no other way to liberate Joseph. God sends Pharaoh a dream, in which seven healthy cows leap out of the Nile and graze along its banks. Seven skinny cows follow and devour the fat ones. At this moment, "Pharaoh awoke. He fell asleep" (Gen. 41:4-5 [NJPS]). God's attempt to kick-start history fails; the dream He sent produces almost no effect on the complacent, self-satisfied Pharaoh. God rolls up His sleeves, as it were, and sends a second disturbing dream, which finally rouses Pharaoh from his bovine contentment. Presumably, God would have sent as many dreams as necessary to move the story of Joseph – and the history of Israel – forward.

Pharaoh's anxiety provides the tension that is needed for the story to progress. The standard story shows Pharaoh seeking someone who can tell him the meaning of his dreams. Through a series of circumstances, Joseph is called before Pharaoh, he interprets the dreams, and he becomes Pharaoh's second in command.

---

[1] Hillel delivered this *d'var Torah*, not at a Shabbat service, but at his *chatan's tisch* ("groom's table") on the morning of his wedding to Nava Cohen.

While the story of Joseph's ascent in Egypt is the primary result of the dream, the story of Pharaoh's suffering might be a more interesting story for a modern audience. Consider what happens to Pharaoh after the second dream: "Next morning, his spirit was agitated, and he sent for all the magicians of Egypt, and all its wise men; and Pharaoh told them his dreams, but none could interpret them for Pharaoh" (Gen. 41:8 [NJPS]). The dream has raised a few problems for Pharaoh. First, the complacent and self-confident Pharaoh no longer feels comfortable in his own, exalted skin. He cannot sleep, and he is forced to reach out to others for help. Furthermore, none of the men on whom he calls, his wise men and magicians, can explain his dreams or offer him the least bit of solace. As with Humpty-Dumpty, "All the Pharaoh's magicians and all the Pharaoh's men couldn't put Pharaoh together again."

Put another way, Pharaoh is half a prophet: he has a vision, but he cannot understand it. The vision absorbs his attention, hints at a profound and consequential meaning, but eludes his understanding. Pharaoh desperately seeks someone to put his mind at rest by translating the opaque, inscrutable images that mystify and torment him. Not prepared for Divine revelations, he *needs* someone to alleviate his awesome burden. Joseph fills this need. He gives form and meaning to the inscrutable and haunting images that had taken over Pharaoh's mind. If Pharaoh is half a prophet, Joseph is the articulate second half, who completes him.

Pharaoh's gratitude gushes forth directly after Joseph interprets his dreams. Pharaoh says, "'Could we find a man like him, in whom is the spirit of God? . . . See, I have set you over all the land of Egypt.' And Pharaoh took off his ring from his hand and put it on Joseph's hand and had him clothed in fine linen clothes, and placed the golden collar around his neck" (Gen. 41:38-42). After his great distress, Pharaoh rapidly promotes Joseph, not merely for interpreting the dream, but for comforting him when no one else could. Joseph is not just a savvy, well-connected advisor; he saves Pharaoh from loneliness and a possible breakdown.

I can understand Pharaoh's gratefulness to Joseph, the one person in all of Egypt – in all the world – who gives voice to Pharaoh's dreams and who comprehends and shares the most intimate and confusing corners of his mind. Pharaoh declares, without hesitation, that he is willing to share all that is his with Joseph. Nava also has given voice to the confusing feelings in my heart, freeing me from loneliness. She is my other half. She interprets me to myself. She comforts and completes me. For that I am grateful and look forward to sharing all that is mine with her.

Vayiggash

Gail Golden

Why is our religion called Judaism?

One of the things I enjoy about the Minyan is how each of the people who presents a *d'var Torah* brings his or her own lens to the text. Historians, doctors, lawyers, business people – each of us has a unique personal and professional way of interpreting what we read. As a psychologist, what fascinates me in the Torah are the people. I read the text like case studies – who are these people? What makes them act the way they do? What can I learn from how they responded to the challenges in their lives? And believe me, there is plenty of material for a psychologist in this book of ours.

In our *parsha* today we read the climax of the story of Judah. Judah's story is an interesting one to explore, because he is often around the edges of some of the more well-known episodes, and the ones in which he plays a major part are some of the more obscure ones. I was also curious about Judah because, after all, our religion is named after him. Although Abraham and Moses would seem to be far more important figures in the development of our way of life, it is not called "Abrahamism" or "Mosesism." And while I am well aware that Judah was the surviving tribe, at the same time it is perhaps not an accident that we are named after this particular person.

So who was Judah? As a psychologist, of course I have to start with family background and sibling order. Judah is the fourth son of Jacob, the youngest of the first four born to Leah, the less preferred wife. His big brothers are Reuben, Simeon, and Levi, and, as we will see, they are a pretty wild clan. He has eight younger brothers, and at least one younger sister. His name comes from the word "*odah*," which means thanksgiving or praise.

Judah is born while Jacob is still working for Laban, his unscrupulous father-in-law. When the whole clan leaves Haran, by my calculation Judah would have been about nine. It would have been a time of great upheaval for the whole family. And Judah would have witnessed how his father, in preparation for the highly threatening encounter with his estranged brother, Esau, places his children according to the status of their mother, with Leah's children in more danger than those of Rachel.

The next time we encounter Judah is following the rape of his sister, Dinah. Simeon and Levi convince all the men in the city where the rape occurred to undergo circumcision, and then they massacre the entire population. Although Judah is not one of the organizers of the massacre, he and his other brothers participate in looting and taking captives. This is vigilante justice at its most horrifying – the brothers are operating like a gang of hoodlums.

Next, the family travels on to Bethel, and Rachel dies in childbirth. Big brother Reuben has sex with Bilhah, Jacob's concubine, once again illustrating the wild, out-of-control behavior of the brothers. Grandfather Isaac dies.

The story now focuses on the brothers' hatred for Joseph – the tattletale, the favored child. Their hostility toward him grows because of his dreams of domination over them, and they plot to kill him. Reuben stops them from shedding his blood, suggesting instead that they throw him in a pit. It is chilling to read about how they sit and have a picnic within sight of the waterless pit in which they have cast him. Then, fortuitously, a gang of Ishmaelites comes along, and Judah suggests selling Joseph to them.

This is the first time we see Judah taking a leadership role and doing something principled. But although his suggestion saves Joseph's life, it is hardly a humanitarian act. The rabbinic commentators are very critical of Judah, stating that he already had enough influence with his brothers that he could have saved Joseph from slavery as well. And Judah then goes on to participate in deceiving his father about Joseph's disappearance.

At this point, Judah takes the first important step toward becoming a decent human being. He leaves his brothers. The text does not explain why, but I would suggest that he is disgusted by what they have done to Joseph and to Jacob, and he realizes that as long as he stays with them he will be under the influence of their immorality. As a psychologist, I know that often the first step toward change is to separate yourself from an environment that is holding you back from becoming who you can be.

However, Judah does not turn instantly into a wonderful human being, by any means. First of all, he marries Shua, a Canaanite woman, a choice the rabbis criticize strenuously. Shua gives birth to Er, Onan, and Shelah. Judah finds a wife for Er, Tamar. But Er dies because "what he did was evil in the

Vayiggash

eyes of the LORD" (Gen. 38:10). Judah orders Onan to impregnate Tamar, which may be the first example of levirate marriage. Onan will not cooperate, and instead practices *coitus interruptus* (not masturbation, as has been frequently misinterpreted). So God kills Onan. So far this family seems destined to continue the dysfunction of the previous generation.

Judah tells Tamar to stay in her father's household as a widow and wait for Shelah to grow up. Shua dies, and Judah mourns for her. The commentators say that the death of his wife and two sons was punishment for causing his father's suffering over the alleged death of Joseph.

Now the story gets even more interesting. Judah goes up to Timnah for sheep shearing. Tamar is fed up because Shelah is grown up but nothing has been done about getting him married to her. So she disguises herself as a prostitute and waits by the roadside. Judah the deceiver is deceived – by clothing, just as he had done to his father. He has sex with Tamar, and she takes a "pledge" for the payment – his seal, cord, and staff.

Tamar becomes pregnant and goes back home. Judah sends payment to the prostitute but cannot find her. He is concerned he will be a "laughingstock." Three months later, Judah finds out Tamar is pregnant. He is furious and announces, "Take her out to be burned!" But she puts before him his own belongings and he realizes that he is the father.

Now Judah takes the second step toward becoming a decent human being – he admits his wrong and apologizes (Gen. 38:26: "She is more in the right than I, for have I not failed to give her to Shelah, my son?"). He is not intimate with her again. She gives birth to twins, Perez and Zerah, and there is a mix-up about who is born first. Perez is the ancestor of Boaz, and therefore David, so out of this strange and forbidden union comes the line of Israel's kings.

Then famine strikes the land of Egypt, and Judah goes to Egypt with all his brothers, except Benjamin, to get food. Joseph recognizes his brothers but does not acknowledge them, and they do not recognize him. Joseph accuses them of being spies, locks them up, and says they must bring Benjamin to Egypt. After three days, Joseph offers to keep only Simeon and let the others go back with the rations, as long as they return with Benjamin. There is an amusing midrash that when the Egyptian soldiers try to restrain Simeon, he goes nuts and is impossible to control. Joseph, watching, signals to Ephraim to take charge, and Ephraim goes up to Simeon and decks him with one punch. As Simeon is coming to, he mutters, "That was no Egyptian punch! I remember blows like that in father's house!"

Unbeknownst to the brothers, Joseph puts their money back in their sacks and they depart. When they find the money, they are dismayed. Back home, they tell Jacob what has happened, but he absolutely refuses to let them take Benjamin to Egypt.

In the first visit to Egypt, Reuben is in the leadership role. When he realizes it is necessary to go back to get more food, he tries to convince Jacob to let them go back with Benjamin. "My two sons you may put to death if I do not bring him back to you. Place him in my hand and I will return him to you" (Gen. 42:37). Not surprisingly, Jacob is not convinced. So Judah steps in and reasons with his father. In contrast to Reuben, Judah offers to make himself fully accountable: "I will be his pledge, from my hand you may seek him: if I do not bring him to you and set him before you, I will bear the blame to you for all time" (Gen. 43:9). And thus he takes the third step toward becoming a decent human being – he puts himself on the line to be held accountable for his actions and their consequences.

The brothers, including Benjamin, go back to Egypt with twice the money and other gifts.

Joseph invites them to his palace for dinner. They are frightened, and admit finding money when they left the last time. Joseph reassures them, releases Simeon, and they dine together. Joseph then secretly orders their money to be once again put back in their sacks, as well as a silver goblet in Benjamin's sack. He sends guards after them and the goblet is found. The midrash says that the brothers beat up Benjamin, saying he is a thief just like his mother. The guards take them back to the city.

Judah admits guilt, and says they are all guilty. But Joseph disagrees, saying he will punish only Benjamin. And it is at this point that we see the man Judah has finally become, in his magnificent speech to Joseph. Judah steps forward, "*vayiggash.*" The commentators tell us that this word is used as introduction to three kinds of action – to do battle, to conciliate, and to pray – and Judah was ready for any of them. The word can also be translated as "he drew near." To whom? To himself, for only when Judah became himself at his best was he able to speak as he did:

> Please, my lord, let your servant speak a word in my lord's hearing and let your wrath not flare against your servant, for you are like Pharaoh. My lord had asked his servants, saying, "do you have a father or brother?" And we said to my lord, "We have an aged father and a young child of his old age, and his brother being dead, he alone is left of his mother, and his father loves him." And you said to your

Vayiggash

servants, "Bring him down to me, that I may set my eyes on him." And we said to my lord, "The lad cannot leave his father. Should he leave his father, he would die." And you said to your servants, "If the youngest brother does not come down with you, you shall not see my face again." And it happened when we went up to your servant, my father, that we told him the words of my lord. And our father said, "Go back, buy us some food." And we said, "We cannot go down. If our youngest brother is with us, we shall go down. For we cannot see the face of the man if our youngest brother is not with us." And your servant, our father, said to us, "You know that two did my wife bear me. And one went out from me and I thought, O, he's been torn to shreds, and I have not seen him since. And should you take this one, too, from my presence and harm befall him, you would bring down my gray head in evil to Sheol." And so, should I come to your servant, my father, and the lad be not with us, for his life is bound to the lad's, when he saw the lad was not with us, he would die, and your servants would bring down the gray head of your servant, our father, in sorrow to Sheol. For your servant became pledge for the lad to my father, saying, "If I do not bring him to you, I will bear the blame to my father for all time." And so, let your servant, pray, stay instead of the lad as a slave to my lord, and let the lad go up with his brothers. For how shall I go up to my father, if the lad be not with us? Let me see not the evil that would find out my father!

(Gen. 44:18-34)

That speech gets to me every time I read it, and it got to Joseph. He weeps and reveals himself to his brothers. What makes the speech remarkable is how clearly it illustrates the man Judah has finally become. His speech is about empathy, about the ability to feel what another feels. He finds it unbearable to contemplate his father's pain. He has finally become a mensch.

The brothers go back to get Jacob, and Judah, now the clear head of the clan, leads the way back to Egypt. They settle in Egypt, and when it is time for Jacob to die, he blesses each of his sons. His blessing to Judah is:

> Judah, you, shall your brothers acclaim –
>   your hand on your enemies' nape –
>   your fathers' sons shall bow to you.
> A lion's whelp is Judah,

> from the prey, O my son, you mount.
> He crouched, he lay down like a lion,
> > like the king of beasts, and who dare arouse him?
> The scepter shall not pass from Judah,
> > nor the mace from between his legs,
> that tribute to him may come
> > and to him the submission of peoples.
>
> (Gen. 49:8-10)

After Jacob's death, the brothers are afraid of Joseph, fearing that now that his father is gone he will finally exact retribution. They tell him that Jacob on his deathbed said that Joseph should forgive them, and Joseph does. Judah's death is not recorded.

So once again, I ask myself, why is Judah the leader after whom our religion is named? It seems to me that the story of Judah is the story of how a hoodlum manages to transform himself into a mensch. He shows us four important steps along the way – leaving an evil environment; admitting wrongdoing and making an apology; taking responsibility and putting oneself on the line; and developing the capacity to understand another's pain.

I would suggest that all of us face the same challenge – to overcome the hoodlum within us, and to learn how to be menschen. Judah, and Judaism, can show us the way.

Vayiggash (II)

Benjamin Tupper[1]

This week's *parsha* is the famous reunion of Yoseph and his brothers. Yehuda makes his passionate speech and Yoseph reveals himself to his brothers, they cry, they hug. But I'm sure you all have heard that story many times, so I'm going to concentrate on the part of the story that most everyone skips over, where Yoseph enslaves all of Egypt.

In the reading of the seventh *aliyah*, we see that Egypt is in a famine, as Yoseph predicted. But the famine doesn't really go as planned. Yoseph says: "And the food will be a reserve for the land for the seven years of famine which will be in the land of Egypt, that the land may not perish in the famine" (Gen. 41:36).

Which sounds good, but in practice, Yoseph takes their money, their cattle, their land and then, finally, their freedom.

After enslaving Egypt, he sets up some laws. The first thing he does is move everyone around in Egypt. I think he does this to keep them from revolting. If the whole country has just been moved around, it's hard to organize revolt. Next, he gives the Egyptians grain for seed and makes them work the land. He makes them give a fifth of their produce to Pharaoh. And most importantly, they are slaves to Pharaoh, and will always be working off their debt. And later on, we see that Yoseph wasn't really being the person he should have been, because when *b'nei Yisrael* are ready to go into Canaan, God, in Leviticus chapter 25, sets up laws that completely contradict Yoseph's actions.

In *eretz Mitzrayim*, the land is Pharaoh's, whereas in *eretz Canaan*, it is clear that the land is to be God's. In *Mitzrayim*, the Egyptians are to be slaves to Pharaoh forever. But in Canaan, *b'nei Yisrael* are not slaves to any king, but they are slaves to God. In *eretz Canaan*, if one Israelite becomes deeply indebted to another, he can work for the other, and the wages he earns can be

---

[1] Ben delivered this *d'var Torah* on becoming a *bar Mitzvah*.

used to pay off debts. But even these debts must be forgiven every Jubilee, which occurs every fifty years. In *eretz Mitzrayim*, the Egyptians are permanently removed from their land. But in *eretz Canaan*, every Jubilee the Israelites must be allowed to return to their families' holdings.

So it is clear that Yoseph is not really trained or ready to be a leader. He mistreated and took advantage of the Egyptians, and his actions seem to go against what God later sets up for Israel. This is where everyday morals come in. What goes around comes around. Eventually, the Egyptians revenge themselves against Yoseph's people by doing the opposite, enslaving *b'nei Yisrael*.

And so if how you are treated depends in part on how you treat others, I'd like to thank everyone for coming in this horrendous Chicago winter weather .... [Rest omitted.]

Vayechi

Richard Tupper

The Blessing of Ephraim and Manasseh

Gen. 48:20 reads:

> And he blessed them that day, saying:
> "By you shall Israel bless, saying,
> 'May God set you as Ephraim and Manasseh[.]'"

True to Jacob's words, each Friday night we bless our sons saying "May God set you as Ephraim and Manasseh." (Okay, so sometimes at my sons' insistence I'll add, "and as Michael Jordan.")

Why do we say "as Ephraim and Manasseh" and not, say, like Judah and Levi or any of the other offspring of Jacob? One traditional explanation is that Ephraim and Manasseh were the first Jews born and raised in exile, yet remained Jewish. I don't quarrel with that explanation. (However, weren't all the sons of Jacob, except Benjamin, born outside of Canaan and didn't they all spend the greater portion of their lives in exile, either in Paddan-aram or in Egypt? Just asking.)

But I'd like to offer a different take on why we are told to recite this blessing each week over our sons. This interpretation requires you to put aside the tradition that the woman that Joseph married in Egypt, "Asenath daughter of Potiphera, priest of On" (Gen. 41:45), was the daughter born to Dinah after she was raped by Shechem. Instead, I assume that Joseph's wife, Asenath, was indeed a true blue Egyptian woman.

Throughout our history, we Jews have had mixed feelings about proselytism and conversion. Still, whatever our thoughts about the "concept" of proselytism or conversion, the Torah, the rabbis, and we Jews in general have embraced proselytes individually. Indeed to mistreat or disrespect a proselyte because he or she is a proselyte is a serious offense. Sadly, there are among us some – hopefully very few – Jews by birth who, for whatever reasons, nevertheless look down upon proselytes and don't consider them "real" Jews. Likewise, there are among us, some – hopefully very few – Jews by choice who question their own place in our community and tend to doubt their own legitimacy.

If Ephraim and Manasseh were the sons of an Egyptian woman and assuming the rules of matrilineal descent apply to them (and please I don't mean to start a debate about that issue), then they were either the sons of a proselyte or they themselves were proselytes. If so, what a lesson for us today!

Those who would look down on a proselyte are reminded every week that they and millions of others Jews throughout the world are blessing their sons by asking that their sons become like Ephraim and Manasseh, two proselytes or sons of a proselyte. What a reassurance to proselytes of their legitimate place among us. In short, we all, regardless of how we have become Jews, have the same obligation, to study and to keep the mitzvot, to become better Jews regardless of our circumstances – whether we are born Jews, proselytes, learned, ignorant, rich, poor, in Israel, outside of Israel, smart, slow, or whatever.

May we all, with God's help, make ourselves like Ephraim and Manasseh.

Shemot

Richard Tupper

Shemot begins by reciting the names of the sons that came to Egypt with Jacob, and how all Jacob's descendants in Egypt numbered 70 soul (*sic*). Next, *Shemot* tells us, Joseph dies, then his brothers, "and all that generation."

Comes verse 7: "And the sons of Israel were fruitful and swarmed and multiplied and grew very vast, and the land was filled with them." A traditional take on that verse has been, "What blessing! Look at how we grow just like God said we would. In fact, the more we are oppressed, the more we grow (1:12)! We go from 70 soul to 600,000 men plus (12:37)! Them's my people!"

If you like that take and aren't interested in considering another "facet," stop listening now.

So often in the Torah, blessings can be curses and curses can be blessings. It depends on you.

I first wondered about v. 7 when I thought, doesn't it seem odd that we are more prolific in Egypt than we were in Canaan? You could almost say that, except for living in the land of Canaan, we more easily obtained the Covenant's promised blessings in Egypt than Canaan. But that can't be right!

Then I noticed the word in v. 7 "*vaiyeshretzu*," translated above as "swarmed." The verb is related to the word "*sheretz*," used to describe swarming things, whether in water or on land. Before, God had promised how we would grow in Egypt (*e.g.*, Gen. 46:3), and we had (Gen. 47:26), but God had not said we would "teem" or "swarm" in Egypt. Verse 7 makes it sound as if we are swarming on the land. Are we like "land swarmers"? Is that all good?

Concerned by the hinted description of us as "land swarmers," I sought expert (*i.e.*, priestly) advice by looking at Leviticus 11. Land swarmers are peculiar. *Behaymot*/quadrupeds can be pure or impure and can make you impure (Lev. 11:2-8). Water swarmers (11:9-12) are not described as "impure" but, if they lack fins and scales, are "abominable" (*shekketz*) and you must "abominate" (*t'shakaytzu*) them. So water swarmers can be abominable, but they don't make you impure. The same is true of air swarmers (11:13-23).

Land swarmers (Lev. 11:29-30, 41-43), however, are unique. Not only are land swarmers "abominable" and to be "abominated," but they are also "impure" and can make you impure!

Here's an unsettling connection. The Canaanites, like land swarmers, also possess this unique combination of abomination and impurity so that by their abominations they make impure the land, and the land vomits them out (Lev. 18:24-30)(*cf.* Lev. 20:22-26). Are we being vomited out of Egypt just like Canaan vomits out the Canaanites? Maybe in someone else's story but not in ours. Nevertheless, is it coincidental that this generation of land swarmers brought up out of Egypt (*cf.* Lev. 11:44-45) cannot enter Canaan?

So, in Egypt we have this incredible proliferation that the Torah likens to the fecundity of land swarmers. If that's not unsettling, think about this – what is something else that exhibits incredible lifelike increase? Leaven.

Plant a seed in soil and, if blessed, it takes a season to increase a hundredfold. Take that grain and mix it with leaven and BOOM overnight (slower acting leaven back then) you have an incredible increase. But it's not really alive; in fact, it is dying and soon dead.

Repeatedly, the Torah reminds us that during Passover we can't have leaven (*e.g.*, Ex. 12). We usually tie the leaven prohibition to when in Egypt we didn't have time to let the leaven work so we ate unleavened bread. Of course, we also had to roast our meat rather than boil it because we were so rushed (Ex. 12:9). But there is no prohibition on boiled meats during Passover. Leaven is banned, I'd say in part, because it has the fake appearance of life but is, in fact, death. The incredible growth associated with leaven is actually a sign of death. Leaven is expressly banned from the altar (Lev. 2:11). Is it coincidental that this leaven-like generation of the exile cannot go up onto the land of Canaan, which itself has altar-like qualities?

The Torah even hints that Israel is dead or at least dying in Egypt. When Moses tells the people about the coming liberation, "they did not heed Moses out of shortness of breath [*ruach*] and hard bondage" (Ex. 6:9). We are short on *ruach*/spirit! If you don't have *ruach*, you are just dead meat.

But wait, didn't God promise we'd be like the "dust of the earth"? Yes, but the Torah often associates dust with death (*e.g.*, Gen. 3:19; dust is associated with land swarmers too, *e.g.*, Gen. 3:14). So let's go back and look when we first get "dusted."

Shemot

Avram gets dusted in *Lech Lecha* but not in the first promise/blessing that God gives (Gen. 12:1-3), nor the second (12:7), but the third (Gen. 13:14-17). Dust/*aphar* is used twice in v. 17. What has happened in between the second and third times God blesses/promises Avram? Avram went to Egypt on account of a severe famine, tried to pass Sarai his wife off as his sister, and walked out a rich man. He was so rich that now the land of Canaan was not big enough for him and Lot, so he asks Lot to split – a pattern of division on account of material things we see replayed time and again. Ramban at least recognizes that Avram's decision to go to Egypt and to pass Sarai off as his sister was a "great sin," an unintentional sin but a great sin nonetheless. I submit that the promise that his descendants would be like dust was a mixed promise, one that they and we can make for a blessing or a curse.

Isaac never gets dusted. He never leaves Canaan even during a famine (Gen. 26). God promises him seed like the stars of the heaven but not like the dust of the earth (Gen. 26:4). He alone of the patriarchs sows the land and reaps a hundredfold (Gen. 26:12). Jacob gets dusted. When? When he is leaving Canaan, on the run, on account of having cheated Esau and tricked Isaac to get a material blessing. Then God tells him his descendants will be like dust (Gen. 28:14). Tellingly, later when recounting this blessing/promise, Jacob substitutes "sand of the sea" for "dust of the earth" (Gen. 32:13). Water is preferable to earth, just as water swarmers are preferable to land swarmers.

I won't go into how Jacob's sons' actions contributed to extending our exile in Egypt. Suffice it to say, no one ever chose to say, "Thanks Pharaoh but we have to go back to Canaan now," and then left. Perhaps because they were afraid he'd say "no." If so, the exiles already were becoming enslaved.

We get "dusted" one more time in the Torah before reaching Canaan. Bilaam, in the first of his three blessings of Israel, ends his first blessing: "Who has counted the dust of Jacob or numbered the stock of Israel? Let me die the death of the righteous and let my end be like his" (Num. 23:18 [NJPS]). This parallel of dust, Israel and death, coincidental?

The good news is that God will not allow Israel to die in Egypt. Once Israel finally cries out to God, God remembers His Covenant, sees Israel and "knows" them (Ex. 2:24-25). God tells Moses to tell the people that they are going to encounter HaShem (Ex. 3:14-25). God explains to Moses that the patriarchs did not "know" God by the name "YHWH" (Ex. 6:2-3). The rabbis teach that, of course, the patriarchs knew of this name of God but had not "known" the name in the sense of "experiencing" so fully that aspect of God. (*E.g.*, sort of, my kids know my first and last name but they call me

"Abba." My wife knows I'm called "Abba" but she uses other names for me.)

So what does "YHWH" mean? Let's look where this name first appears, in Gen. 2. That is where we first see HaShem. What does HaShem do? HaShem takes dust/*aphar* and makes it alive, a *nephesh chayah* (Gen. 2:7). That is what HaShem has in mind for Israel. Israel is going to get to "know" HaShem, the Dust-into-a-Living-Being-Maker, in a way that Abraham, Isaac and Jacob had not. Perhaps because the patriarchs, no matter what, never became land swarmers, leavened dough, or dust.

When does HaShem revivify Israel? I don't think the Torah tells us precisely when, but, maybe Moshe Rabbenu is less interested in telling us just when HaShem does it than in telling us how. And Moshe Rabbenu tells us how in Deut. 30:15-20:

> See, I have set before you today life and good and death and evil, that I charge you today to love the LORD your God, to go in His ways and to keep His commands and His statutes and His laws. And you shall live and multiply, and the LORD your God shall bless you in the land into which you are coming to take hold of it. And if your heart turns away and you do not listen, and you go astray and bow to other gods and worship them, I tell you today that you shall surely perish, you shall not long endure on the soil to which you are about to cross the Jordan to come there to take hold of it. I call to witness for you today the heavens and the earth. Life and death I set before you, the blessing and the curse, and you shall choose life so that you may live, you and your seed. To love the LORD your God, to heed His voice, and to cling to Him, for He is your life and your length of days to dwell on the soil which the LORD your God swore to your fathers, to Abraham, to Isaac, and to Jacob, to give to them.

Dust or stars. Death or life. We can turn promises into blessings or curses. The choice is ours. Yes, but also remember, choosing life is a mitzvah!

Vaera

Joan Katz

"I appeared," God says.
"I was seen," God says.
"I made Myself seen," God says.

The synopsis that opens *parshat Vaera* brings the period of intimate dialogue between God and the patriarchs to a definitive close, while at the same moment setting the stage for the relationship between God and Israel in the saga that occupies the book of *Shemot*.

"*Vaera*"
The root is "*resh, alef, hay*" like the word "*Ra-ah*"/see.
The stem or *binyan*/construction is *Niphal*, the causative.
In the first person singular, God appeared.
What began as an ongoing, incomplete, personal relationship between God and the patriarchs is transformed by the "*vav hahepooch*" into a completed, full, finished relationship relegated to history and the opening, in an intimate moment of revelation, to the nature of the future dialogue between God and Moses.
"*Vaera*"
"I appeared," God says.
"I was seen," God says.
"I made Myself seen," God says,
"to your fathers Abraham, Isaac and Jacob."

"But these fathers did not know Me by the same name that you will know Me by."
They did not see Me the same way you will see Me.
I did not appear to them in the same way you will know Me.
Perhaps you *cannot* see Me the same way.

Leaves from the Garden

Perhaps I will not *let* you see Me the same way.
I am changing the way I appear to you.
Your fathers saw Me/knew Me as *El Shaddai*.
You will know Me as *YHVH/Adonai*. – *ahiye asher ahiyeh*/I will be what I will be."

You Moses are of a different generation.
You Moses are a different person.
You live in a different time and place.
We will experience each other differently.
We will weave the tapestry of this new relationship with a new name.
We will build it together detail by detail.
It will appear differently from what has come before.

God may be the all powerful deity *El Shaddai*, or the all powerful deity *YHVH/Adonai*, but it is in the details of a reciprocal, personal relationship that the history of Israel is revealed.

These details, they are delicious.
Human. Physical. Horrid.
Listen to the description of the plagues and imagine:
The handful of soot, the torment of boils, the total eclipse of darkness, the stench of dead livestock, the wail of grief.

These are not visual descriptions. They are the kind of tactile, all five senses engaged, detail that can make your skin crawl in a hit movie thriller.

What follows in *parshat Vaera* in specific – and on through the Exodus saga in general – is rich descriptive prose helping us, the readers, to personally understand what happened, so that we can remember and retell a saga where most of the characters involved do not see or grasp the whole picture or the truth at all.

They do not see God as He appears.

God – as told to us in our recorded history, the Torah – uses example after graphic example to convey His fairly consistent message.
Why does God need more than one plague?
Why does Israel need more than one miracle?
Why do we need the whole saga retold in *Devarim*?
Why do we need forty years of repetitive wandering in the desert to "get it"?

Vaera

Why do we lose two Temples and kingdoms and wait still?

The same story of relationship building – even within this *parsha* – is retold over and over. Not once but ten times does God plague the Egyptians until Pharaoh "gets it." Still Pharaoh races after Israel into the Red Sea.

It takes time and repetition to recognize the details that enable change.

The story of the exodus from Egypt is our script. It is a story told from many perspectives, each time with a new twist. Within this same repeating text we are even commanded to retell it to our children . . . as we do each year in the *Haggadah*. On Pesach, we chant a ritual with sound bites collected from across the generations, each telling approximately the same story – this story. Those *haggadot* are resplendent in their flavors, insights and special agendas; however many are written, there is no end.

We experience the same during the *Yamim Noraim*/the High Holy Days as we chant sometimes endless variations of the same theme, expressions of dozens of poets in *piyutim* (liturgical poems) from different eras, hoping that one twist of the language will enlighten us or stir us in a new way.

We act it out on Hanukah when we light the candles eight nights – perhaps neither increasing nor decreasing the light as Alan Hobscheid or Richard Tupper would have it (in their joint *d'var Torah* last month) – but eight different patterns to light the way.

What is this connection between detail and seeing, between action and repetition, between appearance and understanding?

As an artist, I love detail. This may sound strange coming from one whose artwork is generally abstract, panoramic and loose. But I have learned, from teachers of art as well as teachers of Torah, that the details are what make a story engaging. They give perspective and universal interest. In every one of my abstract landscapes, ceramic platters, paintings or beaded necklaces, I know the exact spot I want to sit and explore, where I personally want to enter the space I have imagined, where I am connected to the story being told, where I can learn from the perspective offered.

My Viennese-born Jewish teacher of art directors, Henry Wolf – a man who transformed the visual vocabulary of America with his ad and magazine imagery – understood the prize of the image and word perfectly turned to be unforgettable. He changed people's actions – be it their buying choices, their clothing style or their vision. You may not have become so familiar with surrealism had not Henry Wolf taken images from Magritte paintings, transforming bowler hats and openings in clouds into a new medium, giving voice to the American frustration with the reign of propriety and façade over content and feeling in the middle of the last century. His eye for detail and his ability to use it to engage the viewer not only sold the products he was advertising, but also helped foment the societal changes of the 60's and 70's by opening eyes and providing vocabulary which helped give Americans permission to act and think differently.

Details express the vision which makes a story personal, communicating my voice and my ideas, as opposed to someone else's vision of the same subject. I answered a definitive "Yes!" to Carol Grannick when she asked me last year whether visual artists speak of voice in the same way writers do. The variety of detail in our *parsha*, the many voices which tell the story, each time a bit differently, underscore for me the importance and role of artists as catalysts in society.

Not every individual is moved emotionally or engaged intellectually by the same voices or details. We need lots and lots and lots of examples before we find the perfect motivator!

Seeing through another's eyes is both the appreciation of the multitude of God's creations from the outside as well as occasionally the satisfying closeness that comes from identifying with another human being and being able to view the world through his or her eyes. Both of these visions can change the world . . . one detail at a time.

The big picture *is* the important part. It *is* the story worth telling: the context, the message, the universal quality. Here in *Vaera*, it is the furthering of God's covenant with Israel by freeing His people. Without global perspective one can certainly get lost in the minutia and lose sight of the meaning, but only by stepping in close and looking at the individual deed can one change the big picture, change history, change relationships and discover one's own purpose.

We see this in the business world with its emphasis on systems and productivity. We see it in schools where one skill is learned and tested before moving on to the next subject. We see it in the kitchen where one spice can change a soup from Italian to Moroccan.

As many of you know, for the past year and a half Ben Sommer has been teaching a class for the Minyan on the Book of Samuel. We are examining the larger picture of the David stories . . . one word at a time.

Vaera

I would like to take a moment aside to publicly thank Ben and Jennifer for this gift – for the luxury of engaging together with a holy text without the worry of finishing in a time frame, as well as for the detailed planning and preparation needed to have the children in bed and the table cleared off in time for class each week, a feat which is no less critical than the preparation of text.

Our careful focus and turning over of each verse has given me such a rich relationship with these characters.

Like our *parsha*, the beginning section of *Shmuel Alef*/First Samuel is also a story about being able to see God when He appears, about new relationships begun. The book starts with the familiar story of Eli the priest, a man who often overlooks the details – like mistaking Hannah for a drunkard when she is praying. Eli got the details wrong often; he was *not* the best observer. But ultimately, through enough examples, he did understand the larger drama of his role according to God's plan. Eli was accepting of his own humanity, unselfishly teaching Shmuel in turn to hear God's voice when God first appeared to Shmuel. Without the total context, this may not have been a story worthy of canonization, but without the details we would not identify with its depth of feeling and remember it.

Why do this? Why is this engagement with text a Jewish priority?

To devote the time and concentration to any subject, to know it well, is a great "*meshivat nafesh*," a restoration of the spirit. This studying of Samuel and its grammar has flowed over personally to enrich my understanding of the *daven*ing as well as to return me to a renewed contemplation of the role of underlying detail as a mother and an artist.

To be engaged with details can at its best feel like Jacob wrestling with the angel, building intimacy with the Divine.

To me, relishing the details is a form of communication with God. To stop and turn them over is to comprehend the wondrous and innumerable ways in which God has created the world. Not only to see, but to understand and foster creating my own relationship with God. Perhaps each of us has a relationship with God that, like Moses, demands a new name, a personal name for the God who appears to each of us as we recognize Him.

A popular twist of a common proverb is the oft-quoted phrase, "The devil is in the details." I think here, however, of the original proverb, attributed variously in Internet sources to Gustave Flaubert or Michelangelo or Mies van der Rohe, each of whom understood that the road to great art and expression is based in the personal knowledge that "God is in the details."

In our *parsha*, God challenges Moshe, warning that while I am the same God who appeared to your fathers as *El Shaddai*, from now on My relationship is with you and Israel, not your fathers. We have had our watershed experience at the bush. Ours will be a different kind of relationship, so it demands a different name to acknowledge that.

Watch what is coming, Moses. Look carefully at what appears. I will make Myself known to you. *Vaera*. I will provide the cues by how I reveal Myself. Study. Focus. Take good notes. You will learn who *you* are and who *I* am as we go forward together in time, engaging in holy work over and over, until we, God and Israel, get the details of this covenant right.

Bo

Natalia Emanuel[1]

Good *Shabbes*. I just have to say before beginning how wonderful it feels to have all the people who matter to me crowded into this room. It is really special to know the treks people have made to be with us today. Grandpa and Grandma have overcome an unbelievable number of obstacles to be here, coming all the way from England. This means a lot to me, so thank you to them and everyone else sitting here for sharing this.

Just to warn you, this is on the longer side. So you might want to get comfortable.

When sitting down to read my portion, I had in mind one of the common perceptions of God, as loving, kind and merciful. But, as I began to read, it seemed as though God did not quite fit this description. Although we are supposed to have an intimate relationship with God, this portion suggested to me that perhaps we do not really know God. Still, as we grow up we become acquainted with different sides of God.

Parshat Bo starts in Egypt with the quest of the Israelites for freedom from an oppressive Pharaoh. God hardens Pharaoh's heart and subsequently Egypt is struck by the plagues of locusts and darkness. Before the last plague, the death of the Egyptian firstborn, God tells Moses and Aaron what to do in the holiday of Passover so that their children will not die in the plague. Scared by this final plague, Pharaoh commands the Jewish slaves to leave. Before escaping, they pause only for a moment to follow God's instructions, asking their neighbors for valuables. The *parsha* ends with a commandment to remember the Passover and what it means through the act of telling the story of Passover to younger generations and also through the act of laying on *tefillin*, a physical sign on one's arm and forehead.

The way the past generations have told me the story of Exodus was generally through children's stories. In these stories, the Egyptians and the

---

[1] Natalia delivered this *d'var Torah* on becoming a *bat Mitzvah*.

Leaves from the Garden

Pharaoh are portrayed as awful and cruel in the extreme, while God, on the other hand, is usually portrayed as loving, kind and parental. And although we see God commanding destruction with the plagues and the closing of the sea on the Egyptians, it did not seem that bad because I saw it as legitimate for such evil people as the Egyptians to be killed. And God's role at the end was emphasized, bringing *b'nei Yisrael* out of bondage. We went back to some of the actual stories that I was read which we still have in our basement. In *Bible Stories for Little Children*, "The Hebrews had crossed the Sea of Reeds . . . safely. But the soldiers could not get across. And the Hebrews were free at last. They thanked HaShem. They sang a prayer to God. Who is like You, O God, among the mighty? Who is like You glorious in holiness, awe inspiring, working wonders? Amen." The Artscroll *Youth Pirkei Avot* said, "Whatever Hashem does is good even if we do not understand why He does something we must have *emunah*, faith, that it is good." As I grew and learned prayers I still saw descriptions of God as the same kind, merciful parent figure. For example, in the *Baruch Sheamar* prayer that we said this morning, it describes God as a "merciful," or "compassionate Father."

But when rereading this *parsha* I was confronted with descriptions of God that were much more complex and challenging. For example, God hardens Pharaoh's heart. God makes decisions for Pharaoh but then punishes him for these decisions. Exodus 10:1-4 of *Bo* says, "Come into Pharaoh, for I Myself have hardened his heart and the heart of his servants, so that I may set these signs of Mine in his midst . . . . How long can you refuse to humble yourself before Me?" Then, "For if you refuse to send off My people, look, I am about to bring about tomorrow locust in all your territory." God seems to want to show God's miracles even if they cause destruction. God destroys all of the land of Egypt when Pharaoh does not listen to Him. It seemed a little much because, for one, Pharaoh did not harden his own heart and also Pharaoh did not know God previously.

Although this is slightly contradictory, it is not the only time it happens. On the one hand God lets the Israelites remain enslaved for 430 years and on the other hand, when Pharaoh does not let them go in a snap, God brings terrible punishment. So on the whole the characteristics that are shown in *Bo* seem to be ones that *in a human* we would not like. But maybe for God there are better reasons.

So one obvious question is: why is there a difference between the way people seem to perceive God versus the way God is represented in *Bo*? As with all questions posed to Jews, there are many possible answers. One

Bo

explanation is that our readings change as we grow up because when stories are geared for young people, generally we do not like to show the more challenging sides of God. Similarly as a child grows up, a parent's role changes so maybe these different perceptions of God are because God is like a parent who is raising the children of Israel. So God might then do what is appropriate to make the nation of Israel grow given the circumstances. And, therefore, in the different situations of *tefillah*, approaching God on a day-to-day basis, versus our history, the birth-of-our-nation God would interact differently. Perhaps it is not God who changes but our relationship with God. One way of understanding this is that God is so big that we cannot know all of God, and so we relate to different sides of God in different circumstances.

This can be seen in the prayer *Avinu Malkenu* said around Yom Kippur, the annual day of repentance. In just the title, two main characteristics of God are named: *Avinu*, which means "our Father," and *Malkenu*, which is defined as "our King." The Father title seems to represent the close, approachable, caring, and forgiving side of God that I was more acquainted with as a smaller person. The kingly side of God seems to me to be the side that holds people accountable and punishes them. This is especially relevant now that I am becoming a *bat Mitzvah* and will have to be responsible for my own deeds.

But both roles of *Avinu* and *Malkenu* are important because on Yom Kippur God has to be punishing so that there's a reason to repent, and people have to be accountable of their sins and mitzvot which are elements of the *Malkenu* side. But you also hope God is forgiving so that repentance can achieve something, and you can explore and make mistakes, like a parent would allow, which is more the *Avinu* side of God.

But this raises another question. Why is God displaying these different roles at these times? As to why God is more *Avinu*-like in prayer, it seems obvious. It seems as though in *tefillah*, people must approach God and therefore we hope that God is forgiving and listening.

So why is there a kingly God in *Bo*? Especially since after 430 years in Egypt, *b'nei Yisrael* do not really know God, and God might want to be approachable. Again, there are several possibilities. One is that *b'nei Yisrael* do not know what it means to have a compassionate leader and won't respect one. An idea inspired by the *Etz Hayim chumash* is that God could appear this way to make the point that God, not Pharaoh or any other human, is freeing the Israelites from Egypt (*Etz Hayim* p. 351). God uses all of the plagues and afflictions leading up to the exodus to show *b'nei Yisrael*, Egypt and all the other nations that it was really God releasing them from bondage.

A linked idea is that God might be trying to teach us compassion for those still in bondage and gratefulness for our freedom, which would not have been learned if *b'nei Yisrael* had come easily out of Egypt.

Another possible reason as to why the kingly side of God appears in *Bo* is because *b'nei Yisrael* are just getting acquainted with God and freedom. Therefore, they do not know God, but only know what it means to have a king. However, in this explanation, would God then be falling to Pharaoh's level, or letting one of God's creation's actions determine God's own actions?

A related idea is that God is doing something like many teachers do. Setting up authority before softening up. In this scenario, God's actions show that God is powerful and has authority. The Israelites probably needed these actions because they had not seen any leader as worth following unless he was powerful. This may have been one of the reasons that Moses was not sure if the Israelites would believe him, which is *pasuk* 1 of chapter 4. Later on, God becomes more approachable and allows Moses and *b'nei Yisrael* to behold God to an extent at Mt. Sinai.

In the first *pasuk*, God says, "Come into Pharaoh, for I Myself have hardened his heart and the heart of his servants, so that I may set these signs of Mine in his midst, and so that you may tell in the hearing of your son and your son's son how I toyed with Egypt, and My signs that I have set upon them, and you shall know that I am the LORD." This suggests that the point of the plagues is to have humans recognize God. The quote also shows the moving from physical signs such as the plagues to a spiritual understanding, the belief in God. But even now that we have recognized God, there are still physical things that are very important to the nation of Israel. For instance *tefillin* and the pascal lamb are two *things* to remind us of God. This, too, is tied to growing up because the mezuzah originated from the wiping of blood of the pascal lamb on the doorposts. This movement from sacrifice to prayer is one that shows how the Jewish people grew up and not just individuals. This generational evolution is linked when God commands *b'nei Yisrael* to "tell in the hearing of your son." As the people grow up it shows a reason why God changed from *Malkenu* to *Avinu*. This growing up of the nation is especially relevant now that I am becoming a *bat Mitzvah* and trying to understand my relationship with God, both the parental and kingly sides.

Good *Shabbes*!

Beshallach

Sam Neusner

Deborah – Jewish Caesar

Introduction

Great leaders have laid the solid foundation for the Jewish people. Abraham had strong beliefs. Jacob displayed super paternal instincts. And Moses had a one-of-a-kind intellect. Still, there is one great leader who does not receive quite the same respect as these forefathers. She is Deborah, who should be considered the greatest Jewish general.

This *d'var Torah* will show how the battle at Mt. Tabor should elevate her to the greatness of our forefathers.

Prewar Plans

Just after the Israelites destroyed the city of Jericho and settled in the land of Israel, the Canaanites, lead by Sisera, attempted to retake Israel with a swift and powerful invasion. Sisera had at his disposal 900 chariots and 9,000 soldiers. His invasion called for his troops to start at the base of the Golan Heights in present day northwest Jordan and cut through the Galilee. From there, his army would head directly south through central Israel. Nowhere in the Bible does it discuss Sisera's invasion route. However, it is safe to guess that he would take this path. Ever since Abraham, traders have taken this same route from central Israel, through the Sinai and eventually into Egypt. It is the same route that Abraham and Sarah used to travel to Egypt and the same highway that Jacob and his family traveled to settle in Egypt. A trade route is a country's lifeline, and, if an enemy can cut this route off, the enemy has essentially suffocated its opponent. This was Sisera's plan to quickly defeat the Israelites.

Fortunately, the Israelites were lead by a very able person, Deborah, who saw the invasion coming. Her plan was to defend Israel at Mt. Tabor, a hill that oversees much of the Galilee region. It is a high point that intersects the trade route between Jordan and Egypt. Mt. Tabor is also a strategic point that intercepts the opponent's ability to communicate with and supply its troops. An army that cannot supply or communicate loses its ability to command, control and fight.

Even before the battle, Deborah is now faced with a major dilemma. She is a highly respected judge from the Naphtali tribe. Yet, she knew that she could not lead the troops. The strategist needed a general and tactician to execute her plan. Deborah hears of an able general named Barak, who at first was very reluctant to battle the Canaanites. When they meet, Deborah uses a tremendous amount of leadership skill to motivate Barak. The conversation is legendary, yet does not by itself make Deborah one of the greatest Jewish leaders. Many prior (Joshua) and after (Moshe Dayan) have experienced similar situations. Great leaders are able to motivate, yet there is another factor about this war that makes Deborah one of the greatest.

The Battle

From their base camp, the Canaanites quickly close in on Mt. Tabor. The Israelites are at the top of the hill and the Canaanites are at the foot. At this point, Sisera has two options. His troops could surround the Israelites in a manner similar to when the Israelites encircled the residents of Jericho. Or, he could charge up the hill. As we recall Sisera charged. This tactic may not make sense because the Israelites were on top of a hill with no vegetation and water. All the Canaanites had to do was surround the Israelites who would have capitulated within a few days. Not quite. There were two sound military reasons for Sisera's decision to attack and not encircle the enemy. The Israelites were a weak nation, which made it vulnerable to attack. During the period of Judges, the Israelites consisted of twelve tribes who did not get along. And, relations within the tribes were poor. Sisera knew that and believed that this was the best time to attack.

The second reason for this charge centers on military economics 101. The 9,000 Canaanites were squaring off against the 10,000 Israelites representing the tribes of Naphtali and Zebulun. Being a smaller army, the Canaanites wanted a fast war and not a war of attrition. If they had surrounded the Israelites, Sisera feared that the southern tribes would come to the aid of their northern brethren. The Canaanites would lose the initiative and fight a type of war that they were hoping to avoid. Sisera wisely charged up the mountain only to see his troops slaughtered by the ingenious trap that Deborah had devised.

Beshallach

Conclusion

The greatest are always the standard bearers. Moses is considered to be the greatest prophet because he established the laws that other prophets followed. If Moses is the greatest prophet, then Deborah should be considered the greatest Jewish general. For the first time in its history, the fledging Israelite nation was threatened by a formidable foe. The Jewish nation only succeeded thanks to the courage and smarts displayed by Deborah. It is also these same leadership traits that set the example for all future Jewish military leaders. Gideon selected the finest troops to defeat the Midianites. King David utilized his cunning to kill a clumsy Goliath. And, Moshe Dayan instilled his courage in battle to develop a modern well-disciplined Israeli Defense Force. All of these military generals might claim Julius Caesar, Napoleon or Alexander the Great as their role models. However, they are overlooking the obvious. Deborah set the example for all future Jewish military leaders. And, if she is the standard bearer, she should therefore be considered the greatest Jewish general.

Yitro

Ellen Holtzblatt

The Taming of the Jew

Tame: 1: to reduce from a wild to a domestic state, b: to subject to cultivation, c: to bring under control, 2: to deprive of spirit, humble, subdue, 3: to tone down (*Webster's Ninth New Collegiate Dictionary*).

The Little Prince

In *The Little Prince* Antoine de Saint-Exupéry wrote about the process of taming through relationships between the little prince with a rose, and the little prince with a fox. The little prince came from a small, baobab seed-infested planet on which there were two active volcanoes, an extinct volcano, and a beautiful, but demanding rose, which the little prince protected from danger and drafts.

The prince left his planet to travel to other planets, including earth, where he met a fox. The fox pleaded with the little prince to tame him, a request that the little prince eventually agreed to honor. The fox instructed the little prince to follow a daily ritual, in which he was to move closer to the fox day after day. The fox instructed the little prince to be patient, and to come at the same time every day.

After the fox was tamed, the little prince prepared to leave. This made the fox sad, which caused the little prince to question the wisdom of taming in the first place.

The fox told the little prince that the wheat field, which used to mean nothing to the fox, would now evoke special feelings because the color of the wheat was the same as the prince's hair.

The fox also gave the gift of a secret, "One sees clearly only with the heart. What is essential is invisible to the eyes." The last truth that the fox told the prince was, "You become responsible forever for what you've tamed."

The Story of Tricky
We bought a parakeet for our youngest daughter, who bestowed the name "Tricky" upon her pet. Within a couple days we realized that Tricky was a fearful bird and did not trust us. She only wanted to be in her cage, and flew away in fear whenever we came near to feed her or talk to her. We tried to follow the example of the fox by observing the taming ritual: slowly, patiently and steadily drawing closer and staying longer. We covered three-fourths of the cage, and every day pulled the cover away a little bit more. We put our hand in the cage – at first a little, then a little more, and then still more. A month went by and still Tricky avoided all contact with us. She clung to the bars or flapped around the cage in a panic.

We brought her to a veterinarian who diagnosed Tricky as having parasites. "This bird is very afraid of humans, probably from experiences at the pet store," she told us. "It will take months to train her." To help with the process we had her wings clipped, and returned home with medicine. We felt sad and discouraged.

Parshat Yitro
In God's first message to Moses at Sinai He expressed His love for the Israelites (19:4), "You yourselves saw what I did to Egypt, and I bore you on the wings of eagles and I brought you to Me."

In her book, *The Particulars of Rapture*, Avivah Zornberg states (p. 258), "The effect of the image is, of course, to convey intimacy, protection, love, speed; but also, I suggest the enormous power of the adult eagle, effortlessly carrying its young through the air. In other words, it engenders in the people a sense of their own lightness. It deflates their grandiosity, and evokes a relation to God, in which their *kavod*, their weightiness, becomes insignificant."

She also writes, "Past identities are swept up in a rush of God's wings. History is driven entirely by God's motion. The human reality, the gravity of personal experience, is absorbed into that surge" (p. 258).

The effect of participating in the taming process is transformative. This process can be subtle. "What is essential is invisible to the eye," the fox told the little prince.

The fox also said, "It's the time you spent on your rose that makes your rose so important." It was the same between God and the Israelites. What

Yitro

would have happened if God had not hardened Pharaoh's heart, and the Jews had been set free after just one plague? Or if the Israelites had been saved from the Angel of Death without needing to take the possibly life-threatening action of sacrificing the Paschal lamb, an Egyptian deity, and smearing the blood on their doorposts? It is through the rituals of doing for others, and others doing for you, through the patient and time-consuming process of earning trust that one becomes tame. It cannot be a one-way process. As one carries and the other is borne, they both can feel the connective touch. The Israelites needed to learn to know God. And as God acts for us, He more firmly embeds us in His heart.

When we resist being tamed, we are resisting death. In the union of one soul with another – and taming is nothing less – the fear is of disappearing entirely into the new entity created by the integration, as though it were a black hole. One is afraid that control, power, and safe boundaries – however illusory – will be lost.

Taming can also be alluring. Remember that the fox asked the little prince to tame him, despite the knowledge that there was a strong potential for future loss. The urge to belong is potent, and often supersedes rational thought. This isn't unlike the desire a woman might feel to become a mother, which can take the form of emotional and physical longing in which experienced reality may have no place. How many people rationally say, "I can't wait to lose my figure, develop permanent dark circles under my eyes from lack of sleep, forgo interesting peaceful vacations, know the joys of carpool, and never again be able to form a complete thought or remember if I do"?

Jews are continually forming, joining, abandoning, and re-joining synagogues and community groups. Why? Are we masochists seeking new thrills? Or are we acting out our conflicts of attraction to and fear of the taming process?

This internal conflict and external acting out extend to our relationship with God. Both Jews and non-Jews long for, seek, question, pray to and reject God – sometimes in the same morning service.

Imagine, for a moment, your longest and most committed relationship. Can its continued existence always be rationally understood and explained? Like the fox, is the precious quality of the relationship more acute in part because all living relationships are inherently fragile and fleeting? In our relationship with God, perhaps it is the limitations of our perceptions that impress the fear of loss on us. After all, how can we conceive the infinite? Taming does not happen in the realm of the intellect.

Leaves from the Garden

In *My People's Prayer Book, The Sh'ma and Its Blessings*, Lawrence Kushner and Nehemia Polen quote Shneur Zalman of Liadi, the Alter Rebbe of Lubavitch Chasidism (1745-1813), who takes the process of diminished ego and merging souls to a new level. "God is not only the basis of reality, God is the only reality. Creation is continually brought into being through the divine word. If our eyes could truly see reality we would see no material world at all, but instead, behold God's continuous utterance of the Hebrew letters, the real matrix of all being."

In the *Sh'ma* we pray, "Enlighten our eyes with your Torah and cause our hearts to cleave (*dabek*) to your commandments." Lawrence Kushner and Nehemia Polen write,

> In Chasidism, however, the word *dabek* ("cleave") means more than simply remaining close. It comes from the same root letters that give us the noun, *d'vekut*, arguably the goal and the fulfillment of Chasidic spirituality. Usually translated as 'cleaving,' 'intimacy,' or 'staying attached to,' *d'vekut* is nothing less than a fusion with God, a loss of self in the enveloping waters of the divine, the *unio mystica*, a kind of amnesia in which we temporarily lose consciousness of where we end and begin, a merging with the Holy One(ness) of all being.
>
> Yechial Michal of Zlotchov (1731-1786) explained that a person who experiences *d'vekut* loses all self awareness and considers him or herself to be nothing (*ayin*), like a drop which has fallen into the sea and returned to its source, now one with the waters of the sea, no longer recognizable as a separate entity.
>
> *My People's Prayer Book*, p. 73

But Judaism does not allow the individual to retreat into pure meditation of the divine. While we have breath and ability, we are obligated to work to make this world in the image of God's world, just as we are created in God's image. By doing mitzvot we raise *nitzotzot*, sparks of God's light. The little prince learned through his journeys that he belonged back on his planet with his beloved and annoying rose. We also must live in our experiential world.

When we engage in the process of taming – whether it is with a bird, a fox, a rose or a dear friend – we mirror our relationship with God. We undergo a temporary death of our ego, which submerges in the metaphoric ocean and is reborn, unique not only to our partner in taming, but to the entire world.

Yitro

The rose was unlike all the other roses, not by any objective criteria, but because of the loving labor that was done for it. Because of what God did for us in bringing us out of Egypt, we are a holy people – not better than anyone else, and certainly not more spiritually beautiful – just separate. It is our own responsibility to bring beauty to our souls.

The paradox of becoming tame is to integrate both qualities of uniqueness and nothingness, existing in concurrent time, on the same plane in a shared ocean.

Back to Tricky

The Talmud says (*Berachot* 22a), "The Torah was given in dread and fear and trembling and shuddering." We were trying to give friendship and love, but Tricky was skinny, wide-eyed and quivering in our presence.

The veterinarian prescribed medicine for Tricky that we had to dispense twice a day directly into her mouth with an eye dropper. I read about an alternative taming method in a book about parakeets. While I practiced holding her in order to give her the medicine, I held her close to my chest so that she could hear my heartbeat. I spoke softly to her and told her how beautiful she was, and how happy we were to have her live with us. When she tried to bite me I gave her millet seed to chew on. We repeated this ritual intermittently that night and the next morning.

Because Tricky's wings were clipped, we decided to try bringing her out of the cage. She settled onto the kitchen floor and predictably retreated into a distant corner. When I tried to put her back in the cage, she jumped up and down trying to escape. During one of Tricky's leaps she accidentally landed on my extended arm. She stood still, probably as surprised as we were. After a long, motionless moment, I put my finger near her tummy and she climbed onto it.

One day after cleaving Tricky to my heart, she became a tame bird. Now she voluntarily leaves the cage, borne on the hand that carries her.

Leaves from the Garden

Tricky taming Emma

Mishpatim

Joan Katz[1]

Imagine writing a book report on the suspense-filled story of the suspicious children of Israel, led by the reluctant leader Moses, encountering God at Mt. Sinai and agreeing to be partners in a difficult ברית or covenant. How is this story, as recounted in the Torah, told so convincingly that generations later we will still be moved to action by remembering it and studying it?

What I would report on first is how God appears to the children of Israel, introducing Himself as a personal, almost human God, trying hard to find a way to create a relationship with His people.

He takes the time, like a patient teacher, to guide the children of Israel.

In *parshat Vaera* a few weeks ago, God tells Moses directly that He is changing His name. He will no longer be seen with the name *El Shaddai*, as He appeared to the matriarchs and patriarchs, but with a new name for a new relationship, *YHVH*, *Adonai*.

Next *Adonai* promises that He did not forget us or abandon us to slavery forever – the invitation to be His people was *not* lost in the mail . . . it just took 400 years to be delivered.

Then *Adonai* shows off His great powers with all the magic . . . the miracles . . . the drama . . . turning staffs into serpents, raining ten plagues down on Egypt, and splitting open the seas for the children of Israel to cross to safety.

Oh, the partying comes next. Israel provides the entertainment: *Shirat HaYam* from the men, the women dancing led by Miriam. *Adonai* provides the feast with manna from heaven.

They barely recover when nature goes wild: the mountain trembles, the people see – not hear – thunder, lightning flashes around Sinai, clouds that

---

[1] Joan delivered this *d'var Torah*, not at the Minyan, but to her daughter's fifth grade class.

protected the people now enshroud the mountain, the fire from the burning bush now smokes from the mountaintop.

Then *Adonai* restricts access: you fast for three days, put on clean clothes and circle the mountain. Only the elders can step forward. Only Moses goes up the mountain.

At last, at long last, after all of this build up, *Adonai* appears to Moses – face to face – and delivers His message.

We the people of Israel are paying attention! We are ready!

The Jewish philosopher Franz Rosenzweig suggests that this moment itself was the whole of revelation. That moment itself on Sinai when *Adonai* appears is enough for us to feel forever commanded, and everything else that follows is just detail or commentary.

I suggest further that in the moments after *Adonai* reveals Himself on Sinai comes the most important part. What has occurred up to now has been the flash, the falling in love, the learning about each other, the deep recognition.

As Moses now comes down off the mountaintop, he describes the fine print in this *brit*/covenant. *Adonai* begins with the Ten Commandments and follows in *Mishpatim* with mitzvot describing how people should relate to each other and the rituals which will bind us together.

First He gets our attention by showing us Himself, next He reveals His holiness in a way so awesome that we feel it to our day, and then He shares the rules of the game.

Moses, He commands, tell the people these very words.

And then, only then, is the climax of the story. *Adonai* asks us, the children of Israel, if we will be His partner in the covenant. He asks us to choose to be His people of our own free will.

Adonai is no longer the *El Shaddai*, the Father figure making decisions for the patriarchs and matriarchs. He is now *Adonai*, the One who commands, who partners in a covenant.

The suspense mounts.

Has He convinced us? Will we choose to follow His rules, the mitzvot? Are we willing to make this commitment to Him?

What do the people answer? You know the answer; we the people said with one voice:

Naase v'nishma!

We are doing it! We are listening!

There is a virtual handshake as *b'nei Yisrael* agree to obey the terms of this *brit*. The agreement is sealed in royal style and Moses records the events

Mishpatim

in the Torah. Today we honor it as if we ourselves stood at Sinai and personally answered: *Naase v'nishma*!

Not we heard and we agreed. Let's move on.

Not, as in modern Hebrew future tense:

Let's do it, let's hear it, when we get around to it.

But we answer in a grammatical form which in biblical Hebrew conveys ongoing action and unfinished business.

Naase v'nishma!

We will continue to do it! We will continue to hear!

We will hearken! We will obey now and into the future.

The flash is over and the hard work of building a holy nation begins. *Adonai* teaches us in this *parsha* how to take action, how to treat other people, how to act fairly in school and the workplace, how to celebrate the holidays, how to pray. By engaging in these mitzvot, we build our relationship with *Adonai* and seal the *brit*.

And each time we "*naase*" or do one of the mitzvot, each time we "*naase*," we recreate the experience at Sinai and we are able to "*nishmah*," to hear.

Naase v'nishma. When we do, if we listen carefully, we can hear *Adonai* talking directly back to us.

Terumah

Al Hobscheid

You know, I do have a more than passing interest in architecture; after all as an undergrad, I did take one class in modern architectural history. So it was two years ago and I was reading along in the *Terumah haftarah* text in the *Hertz (vay-ya-as' la-v(eh)-yeet cha-lo-ney sh-ku-fim a-tumim)* which is translated as *"and for the house he made windows broad within, and narrow without."* It's a nice little detail; extremely mundane, yet somehow important enough that it needed to be included in the Tanakh. And then to my delight Hertz had some commentary (p. 157); so I scanned down the page to read it and thinking right there in front of God and the entire congregation and everybody – "what the hell?"

> This translation follows the Targum. The Rabbis, however, explain that the windows were narrow within and cut obliquely through the wall, widening towards the exterior – teaching that the Sanctuary required no outward light, rather was its spiritual radiance to spread abroad and illumine the world outside.

To elaborate, I turn to Rabbi Mordechai Silverstein, senior lecturer in Talmud and Midrash at the Conservative yeshiva in Jerusalem for further elaboration.

> The interpretation of these two terms among the various commentators reflects the technology available in their own day. *Targum Yonathan*, the 7th century Aramaic translation of the Prophets, explains that the windows were open [broad] on the inside and closed [narrow] on the outside. This particular design was thought to provide the maximum amount of light from the outside while providing for the maximum protection inside. The Rabbinic tradition adapted

the same technological understanding. However, the sages maintained that the source of light was not found outside the Temple precinct but rather inside, provided by God. The windows were constructed, according to the sages, in the opposite manner in order to provide the world with God's light.

And so you have it. Targum says one thing and the Rabbis pull a total 180 on it. How can these translations be so far apart? Isn't the Hebrew straightforward here?

Big problem . . . . I don't know Hebrew so well, so I really couldn't understand the ramifications of the commentary until I obtained some independent translation from somewhere. So during *Kiddush* I grabbed someone (who shall remain nameless) who I believed had an adequate grasp of the language and asked them to translate the verse. Confusion washed over this person's face and, privately, this person wondered to me if Hertz had lost his marbles. This reaction just whetted my curiosity, so I sought a person who had spent an inordinate amount of time in Israel and made my query; and this person said, "It says that the windows are light and dark, or opaque." Light and dark – at the same time?? What does that mean??!! I then asked a preeminent scholar who happened to be enjoying some creamed herring on a Tam Tam® and he translated with "and he made windows for the house, transparent (and) blocked up." Gee, thanks so much, preeminent scholar! Transparent and blocked – at the same time? What does that mean??!! Light, dark, transparent, opaque, blocked?? I was getting nowhere and to make matters worse, *Kiddush* had gone on so long, all of the ice cream sandwiches had been devoured.

If you look in your *Etz Hayim* (and this is true in several other Tanakhes), the generally accepted translation is that '*sh'kufim*' means 'recessed' and '*atumim*' is taken to mean that the windows are latticed. The New English Bible gives "and he furnished the house with embrasures" which means that it is latticed (learn something new everyday!). This would certainly seem to solve the apparent conundrum of windows being transparent and opaque at the same time; and latticing windows in places with high bright sun certainly makes sense, but what about my original issue – the rabbinic reversal alluded to by Hertz? These translations are still screwy because if *sh'kufim* means light, why is it translated as recessed? And why does Hertz, using a Targum translation and the rabbinic commentary, make no apparent reference to latticing, only the recess?

Terumah

As I searched for answers to my problem, I turned to another house of God; one that moves me as much as the Temple, designed by one of the big three architects of the 20th century, along with Frank Lloyd Wright and Mies van der Rohe. I speak of the Swiss master, Charles-Edouard Jeanneret, who called himself "le Corbusier," or just "Corbu" to his good friends, including *moi*. In 1955 he designed one of the masterpieces of modern architecture, Chapelle de Nôtre Dame du Haut (my French ain't much better than my Hebrew). It is located in Ronchamp, which is a town in eastern France near the Swiss border. Long a pilgrimage spot, this structure replaced the previous one which was destroyed during the Second World War. Using some of the existing stone, he created something so totally different that nowadays it generally draws more pilgrims to see the architecture than are there to celebrate Mass (kinda like Henikoff Hall). According to Horst Janson, who wrote in the seminal, *History of Art*, it is "the most revolutionary building of the mid-twentieth century." Its exterior is consciously "brutal," "*brute*" as Corbu called it, using exposed unfinished reinforced concrete. It smacks of prehistory and seems to resonate with a Stonehenge or ancient Middle Eastern structures. Externally it is a sanctuary that invites discovery. There are no obvious doors. To quote Janson, "we must seek them out like clefts in a mountainside." The crazy roof is one of its most striking elements. Many have noted that it resembles the wimpels of nuns in the region (think "The Flying Nun"). It is

Leaves from the Garden

intriguing to think that "chapeau," French for "hat," has the same root as "chapelle" and that its roof should resemble headwear. I'm sure that was not lost upon that old punster Corbu!

But back to the topic – the windows are also unconventional. Once inside the church, one can see the function that the windows perform. A complex interplay of light and color designed not only to illuminate the space but to disorient the viewer into an otherworldly dimension. This illusion is created in part by its arrangement (he was a huge fan of the modernist painter, Piet Mondrian, whose abstract paintings the design resembles) but more importantly by the handling of the recesses through the massive poured-concrete walls. Some casements are concave relative to the interior, allowing light to diffuse and flood in; while some are convex relative to the interior which pinpoints the light and stabilizes it. This was Corbu's attempt to create a spiritual atmosphere to the chapel. It creates a dazzling space that I personally would just love to *daven* in. It may be interesting to note that Le Corbusier was not a practicing Catholic, yet had a great capacity for spirituality, so much so that he wanted to create a universal religion which hinged on a vision of the cosmos in which masculine and feminine elements would exist in balance – very egalitarian. As an added treat, I also searched extensively and found no anti-Semitic attributions to him, *yet*.

Terumah

Let's follow the idea of concavity and convexity to the present day and to Skokie. I present another architect, Stanley Tigerman, who won the design proposal for the new Holocaust Memorial Foundation of Illinois museum and education center. Tigerman is the classic outspoken, foul-mouthed, uncompromising architect type who sees this project as the pinnacle of his career. A typical zinger from Tigerman goes, "you know I'm Jewish and the Jewish god established a quota for Jewish architects. They can only work on so many suburban homes for Jewish American princesses and I reached my quota five years ago." This will be his first specifically Jewish work and he has created a two-part building that symbolizes the horror and the hope of the

Holocaust. The dark portion is the horror and its basic design as one approaches is a cambered cone, a convexing space that encloses and suggests no retreat from the inevitable. When one continues to the white side of the structure, the space slowly opens up and accepts light and a sense of hope and future is presented. For Tigerman, the great theme is *choice*; that there were no choices for Jews caught up in the Holocaust and it is only through choice today that we can be educated to work against future holocausts.

Tigerman is using architecture as a teaching tool. In the same fashion, the rabbis are taking advantage of a sufficiently vague architectural reference and making it a learning opportunity. As Silverstein noted above, the verse is taking into account the available technology. It is safe to assume that architectural elements that represent "light and dark" such as mullions, louvers, shutters and lattice were not utilized in ancient Israelitish construction. Once it is assumed that light and dark must be referencing a cambered recess (*i.e.*, narrow end = dark, broad end = light), the obscurity that remains is which end of the recess (the interior or the exterior) is dark or light.

Leaves from the Garden

So let's talk about windows, or more accurately, openings in walls. They serve several functions. Of course, number one is windows made Bill Gates rich. But they also reduce the load bearing of the wall (especially in ancient and medieval construction where masonry construction was necessarily thick to support its weight as at Nôtre Dame du Haut). They allow light and ventilation into the interior as noted before. Of course, windows permit the occupants to view what is outside of the structure. And they also serve one other function; they allow for egress and ingress, not for humans necessarily, but for flying objects. Everyone probably has noted window construction in a castle or fort. You don't see big ol' picture windows, because large open spaces in walls are not very practical – they were difficult to engineer, they would be a significant source of heat loss, and they would be vulnerable during times of crisis. Windows act as entry points, and during warfare they become sensitive areas for defense and offense. So normally you see those vertical slits on the exterior, but there are two varieties. As noted above to allow the maximum light into a room, the casement should cut concavely to the interior, to spread it widely. Moreover, the deep recess affords greater protection from external aggression. You should stay away from the window during a pitched battle anyway. However, this window is not the best for fighting the enemy at the gate. If you were an archer, let's say, you wouldn't want to come right up to the slit and fire away because you could become way exposed. The better approach is to be in a casement that cuts concave to the exterior wall, thus permitting a wide range for shooting while remaining protected thanks to the deep recess. So in practical terms, one window serves a domestic and passive function. The other is more aggressive, if you will, serving a military function.

It appears to me that the Targum's translation (broad within, narrow without) could be interpreted as a response to uncertain times – Judaism is Templeless, in diaspora, in retreat, on the defensive; trying desperately to hold onto light, keeping it close, drawing it into ourselves. On the other hand the rabbinic outlook on 6:4 is the complete opposite; it is reminiscent of the shape of a shofar – trumpeting light and hope – the light of God that is thrown out confidently into the world. While dropping the militaristic connotation, it remains aggressive, in the sense that it is a proclamation that God is in da house and we are damn proud about it. If you think of Corbu's chapelle as more reclusive in nature, it may reflect what Janson opines, that the chapel has a strangely disquieting aspect about it which is "a nostalgia for the certainties of faith that is no longer unquestioned." But when you think of Tigerman and his architectural expression, it affirms the uncertainty and

Terumah

these questions – as a reality of the world. It is a condition that we are not to shy away from; rather we are to seek it out and understand it, and it is from this perspective we can all become genuinely participating members of society and guiding lights of humanity.

By the way, "le Corbusier" comes from *la corbeau*, which means "the crow" in French (the Latin for the family of crows, ravens and jays is *Corvidae*) and he adopted his maternal grandfather's name because (according to him) he wanted to see the world in its totality, to see society as a functioning whole – from a bird's-eye view if you will, and wanted his architecture to foster and promote this unity of mankind. Corbu is essentially a cognate to the Flying Nun, who as Elsie Enthrington, a blithe surfer girl from California (remember Gidget?!), decided to become a nun and, as part of the process, adopted a new name (as did Charles-Edouard Jeanneret) by calling herself, Sister Bertrille. In this way she demonstrably cast off her materialism and shallow outlook on life, in order to find a deeper dimension to her existence and to become a tool, a force to aid humanity, giving something back to society.

Tetzaveh

Richard Tupper

To praise a scholar, it is customary to praise that scholar's teacher. And so I considered entitling my *davar*, "Pomegranates and Golden Bells," the title of a *Festschrift* composed in honor of Professor Hayes' teacher, Jacob Milgrom. However, since I intend to discuss only golden bells and not pomegranates, I decided to entitle my *davar*, "The Bells," which I consider more "*Poe*tic."

Before examining the bells attached to the *Kohen HaGadol*'s robe, I'd like to say a few words about one way of approaching these chapters dealing with the construction of the *Mishkan*, the manufacture of the priestly clothing and the initiation of the sacrificial cult. In his eye-opening book, *The Art of Biblical Narrative* (Basic Books 1983), Robert Alter discusses the "narrator's reserve," how the biblical narrator tells us who does what in a story but often does not tell us why, which then draws us into the story. Thus, for example, we are told that Itzhak loved Esav because of the game that Esav brought him, and that Rebekkah loved Jacob (Gen. 25:28), but we are not told why she did. This of course invites readers throughout the ages to consider why Rebekkah loved Jacob. Omissions such as these compel us as readers to supply what the narrator has not explicitly revealed.

If we see the narrator's reserve in the patriarchal stories in *Bereshit*, we find the narrator's reserve in spades here in the description of the *Mishkan*, the priestly clothing and the sacrificial cult. The narrator describes the *Mishkan*, the clothing and the cult in great detail but frequently does not explain the reasons behind the details. This reserve on the narrator's part has then what I would call "the vacuum effect." From a distance, a vacuum looks as if there is nothing there, but once you draw close enough to examine it, the vacuum sucks you in. I submit that the narrator's reserve in these chapters in frequently not explicitly explaining the reasons behind the many details is intended to draw us into these chapters and to cause us to ask, what does it all mean?

Leaves from the Garden

Turning to the verses I would like to focus on, *Shemot* 28:31-35, we are told that golden bells must be affixed to the blue/purple (*techeilet*) robe that Aaron must wear. We are even told why bells must be attached to his robe – "so that its sound be heard when he comes into the sanctum before the LORD and when he goes out, that he shall not die." The explanation that the purpose of the bells is to make sound so that Aaron not die when entering and exiting the *Mishkan* is even more explicit information than we are usually given, but that of course makes us ask – why does Aaron risk dying when entering and exiting the *Mishkan*?

Some modern scholars have described the bells as "vestigial" – a remnant from a time when demons were believed to crouch at doorways, especially of temples, and would kill intruders. The sound of the bells was thought to frighten away the demons.

I don't find this "vestigial" explanation very convincing. First, the Torah doesn't treat the bells as vestigial since it says that their purpose is to prevent Aaron from being killed. The threat of immediate death hardly sounds "vestigial" to me. Second, the notion that demons would be crouching at the entrance of the *Mishkan* seems particularly out of place. The Torah has very little to say about demons, certainly nothing good, and it seems highly unlikely that the Torah would be telling us that demons inhabit the *Mishkan*. To quote a great modern rabbi, Benno Jacob *z"l*, who was paraphrasing Schopenhauer, "Demons belong here as little as pork chops at a Jewish wedding" (*Exodus* [Ktav 1992], p. 924). This demonic interpretation reflects a condescending modern attitude that because the Torah is old, its religious concepts must be primitive, an attitude I reject.

To answer the question, we must consider these verses in the context of the Torah's narrative. Two prior verses frame this entire narrative. When Israel comes out of Egypt and complains because they lack water, they are reported to have asked (Ex. 17:7), "Is the LORD in our midst or not?" Subsequently, HaShem answers Israel's question by telling Moses that He intends to make Israel "a kingdom of priests and a holy nation" (Ex. 19:6). These two verses stand like pillars, they are the Boaz and Jachin that frame the narrative. The construction of the *Mishkan*, the manufacture of the priestly clothing, and the initiation of the sacrificial cult are the beginning of HaShem's answer of how He intends to dwell among Israel. The necessity of the bells then must tell us something about the nature of HaShem's dwelling among Israel.

The key to unlocking the purpose of the bells is the phrase "ולא ימות / that he shall not die" in v. 35. This phrase, as Prof. Hayes' teacher explains in

Tetzaveh

his commentary on *Vayikra*, generally denotes death by divine agency (see Milgrom, *Leviticus*, pp. 609, 613, 946). The phrase "ולא ימות" appears with some frequency in the Torah, and we see it in such verses as those warning that the priests approaching the altar must wear breeches to cover their private parts (Ex. 28:43), that they wash their hands and feet before entering the *Mishkan* or officiating at the altar (30:19-21), and that they be sober when officiating (Lev. 10:9). Milgrom argues that death by divine agency in such contexts is the penalty for profaning the holy as opposed to polluting the holy for which the penalty is "*karet*" or divine excision. I won't confuse you again by making distinctions here between the holy and the common, the impure and the pure. Suffice it to say, we must remember that Israel has just been rescued from years of slavery. They know almost nothing about how to serve HaShem properly and so HaShem must instruct them in the very basics. It reminds me of me with my children. When we come to the dinner table, I've had to tell my children, "Ben, you wear a shirt when you come to the table! Lewie, did you wash your hands? Sophie and Jonathan, be careful not to spill!" The purpose of the bells then was to remind Aaron that he was coming into the presence of HaShem Himself when he entered the *Mishkan*. Aaron had to remember to come into and take leave from HaShem's presence with the proper respect. Coming into the presence of HaShem was not like going to the market. It surpassed in holiness all that Aaron had previously experienced. This also explains why Aaron didn't wear the belled robe when he enters the Holy of Holies on Yom Kippur. Remember, he wears the belled robe when he goes into the *Mishkan* to perform his normal duties, but on Yom Kippur, when he entered the Holy of Holies, he wore only a simple linen garment. Why no bells? Because entering the Holy of Holies only once a year ensured that it wouldn't become so routine for Aaron that he would forget the sanctity of the presence of HaShem. However, the same could not be said of Aaron's daily trips into the *Mishkan* to perform his duties there.

If we had only this passage, the concept of coming into the presence of HaShem might seem terribly forbidding. Moreover, while warning of the danger of coming unprepared into HaShem's presence, it might also seem so totally involved with Aaron and the priesthood that it would appear to have little to do with making the people as a whole a kingdom of priests and a holy nation. But it is important to remember that this is just the beginning of HaShem's instruction. While most of these chapters focus on the *Mishkan*, the priesthood and the cult, they also repeatedly remind Israel of HaShem's ultimate plan. Thus, for example, in the sixth *aliyah* that Ben read, HaShem reminds Moses that the *Mishkan* will serve as the place where HaShem will meet with Israel. Moreover, in next week's *parsha*, there is the beautiful chiastic passage we discussed last year in which HaShem explains that He is giving Israel Shabbat so that by observing it as HaShem did at Creation, all Israel will become holy (Ex. 31:13b-17).

While much of the first part of Leviticus deals with the importance of disposing of impurity and keeping it away from the holy, the latter half of Leviticus instructs Israel that not only must Israel limit impurity but all Israel must strive for holiness. This message reaches its apex in chapter 19 that blends the ritual mitzvot with the ethical mitzvot, so that by observing them, all Israel, not just the priests, can become holy. Then, as if a bookend to this instruction, we have in *Bemidbar* (Num. 15:38-41) the beautiful instruction that Israel attach a blue woolen thread to their linen fringes so that by their *shaatness tzitzit* they will be reminded to keep the mitzvot so that they become holy just as the High Priest's *tziz*, the gold plate he wears on his forehead, proclaims that he is holy to HaShem. Thus the *tzitzit* bring us back to this passage.

If Israel keeps the covenant by keeping the mitzvot, HaShem promises: "I will establish my presence in your midst" (Lev. 26: 11) and "I will walk about in your midst" (Lev. 26:12). This language should ring a bell. It evokes the image of HaShem walking about the Garden of Eden (Gen. 3:8; Milgrom, *Leviticus*, p. 2302). If Israel follows the mitzvot, the *Mishkan*, which serves as an introduction to HaShem, will be surpassed by the reality of HaShem walking among us. The picture is thus transformed from Israel going to the *Mishkan* to HaShem coming down and walking among us.

It is an astounding vision. While at first Israel's approach to HaShem might appear daunting, the promise is that we will be restored to that original relationship that HaShem intended for us, HaShem walking among us. Yes, coming unprepared into HaShem's presence is dangerous, but HaShem has not merely given us the promise that we can, but He has also given us the means. Indeed, He has restored to us the means. The Torah is our path back to our relationship with HaShem, back, as it were, to Gan Eden.

עֵץ-חַיִּים הִיא לַמַּחֲזִיקִים בָּהּ !

She is a tree of life for them that lay hold upon her!

(Pr. 3:18)

Ki Tissa

Richard Tupper

"Turn it, turn it," the sage Ben Bag Bag taught concerning the Torah, "you will find everything in it. Scrutinize it, grow old and gray with it, do not depart from it: there is no better portion in life than this" (*Pirkei Avot* 5.24).

I have been blessed to have been taught to *lehn* Torah by my sons Ben and Lewie and have benefited from the incredible patience of Sam Fox, who always tutored me when I was learning a new passage. However, because I do not possess a natural facility for *lehn*ing Torah, I have to practice a passage a hundred times or more to get it down reasonably well. A positive side effect of my disability is that reading the same passage a hundred times or more often helps you see things you otherwise would easily have glided over.

One of things that caught my eye when I was practicing this passage was verses 13b-17 of chapter 31 in this week's *parsha*. This passage is the seventh in a series of instructions by HaShem to Moses. The first six passages dealt with the construction of the *Mishkan*; this seventh instruction, fittingly, focuses on observing Shabbat.

Some modern scholars have criticized this passage as "clumsy," repetitive, the product of carelessness and marred by secondary insertions. (See, *e.g.*, Martin Noth, *Exodus* [Bill West 1962, trans. by J. S. Bowden], pp. 240-241.) However, as I practiced *lehn*ing this passage, I began to see in it a pattern that modern scholars often refer to as "chiasmus" or "inversion." I tried to diagram the structure of this passage and was delighted by what I found. Later, I learned that I was by no means the first to note the chiastic style of this passage, having long been preceded by real Bible scholars, among them an Israeli biblical scholar named Meir Paran, who in his book, *Forms of the Priestly Style in the Pentateuch* (Jerusalem: Magnes, 1989)(Hebrew), focused at length on the chiastic patterns in the Torah. Long before me, he had diagramed and discussed the chiastic pattern in Ex.

Leaves from the Garden

31:13b-17, and I was happy to discover that he and I saw pretty much the same pattern in these verses. The sheets that I've handed out are my diagrams of this passage, in Hebrew and English, which differs somewhat from the diagram set out by Paran in his book (Paran, p. 167).[1] As you can see, this passage does not exhibit clumsiness or carelessness. Even from the perspective of modern scholarship, there is no reason to suspect subsequent additions. What this passage reveals is a very sophisticated, "architectural" skill in its construction.

Modern scholars call this passage's form "chiasmus," often diagramed as ABXB'A', where A' repeats an idea in A, and B' repeats an idea in B. Frequently in chiasmus, that which lies at the X connecting the two wings of the chiasmus is what is intended to be stressed. This passage begins with the instruction, "My Shabbats you shall keep." It proceeds from B to H and then repeats in chiastic style from H' to B'. At the heart of the chiasmus lies X, which again is an instruction to keep the Shabbat. At the end of the passage, A' forms a parallel panel with X that links the mitzvah that we keep the Shabbat to HaShem's own observance of Shabbat after creation. If we may extend somewhat the striking anthropomorphism of the last line, one message in this passage is that if we observe Shabbat then we will be "refreshed," "*nephesh*ed," "enlivened," just as HaShem was when He rested from creating the world. Our work during the six days of the week parallels and continues HaShem's work in creation and our observance of Shabbat enlivens us as did HaShem's rest on the seventh day.

The assertion that HaShem was "refreshed" on the seventh day is all the more striking when one considers that this rarely used verb "*naphash*" appears earlier in connection with Shabbat in Ex. 23:12,[2] but there we are told that we must rest on Shabbat so that our female slave's child and the *ger*/stranger may be refreshed. Hence we have in the conclusion to this passage in Ex. 31 not only an anthropomorphism, but an anthropomorphism which links HaShem with the lowest rung of Israel's society.

I would also point out that lines F and F' stand in chiastic relationship to line A. Line A puts first "My Shabbats" followed by the verb, "you shall

---

[1] My diagrams are set out in the last two pages of this *davar*. My translation tries to follow the Hebrew structure as closely as possible.

[2] The verb "*naphash*" only appears again in 2 Sam. 16:14, where David and those with him take a breather after their flight from Absalom and his supporters.

Ki Tissa

keep." In contrast, lines F and F' reverse this order, putting first the verb, the requirement of keeping, followed by the direct object, the Shabbat. This change in structure reflects a change in focus. Lines A-E and E'-A' focus on the Shabbat, whereas lines F-H and H'-F ' focus on the verb and its subject.

F' repeats line F but subtly changes it. When examining a chiastic passage, one cannot help but notice places where the chiastic pattern "breaks down," so to speak. I say "so to speak" because it isn't fair to say that the chiastic pattern "breaks down" when we see differences in the various lines of a chiastic pattern. After all, a perfect chiasmus with no variations could be rather boring. Instead of seeing a discrepancy in the chiastic pattern as a flaw, we should be ready to consider whether the discrepancy is a signal that some important information is being imparted. An obvious difference between F and F' is the subject of the verb. The subject in line F is "you," plural, whereas the subject in line F' is "the children of Israel." One could conclude that the same people are being addressed, just referring to them in different ways, but the text gives us other indications that this is not the case. The second half of the chiasmus in lines D' and B' adds words not appearing in lines B and D of the first half. In line D' we are told that for the generations of the children of Israel the Shabbat is part of a "covenant forever," and line B' stresses that it is a sign "forever." In effect, then, the first half of the chiasmus is addressed to the generation at Sinai, whereas the second half of the chiasmus is addressed to future generations, which, of course includes us. Thus as we all know, when HaShem spoke at Sinai, He spoke not only to those living then but to us living today, and to all Jews at all times.

The parallelism between E and E' is not as tight as the parallelisms in other lines; they share only a similar verb form and sentence structure. Nevertheless, the chiastic structure is telling us that the two lines are related. I would suggest as one interpretation that if we want to know or experience HaShem sanctifying us (E), then we must make the Shabbat (E'). This accords with the rabbinic interpretation of what Israel says at Sinai, "*na'aseh v'nishma*" – "we will do and we will hear" (Ex. 24:7). In other words, through performing a mitzvah we come to experience HaShem. If we continue to apply this idea that differences can serve as emphasis and we focus only on what I label the "positive statements" (lines A-F, X and F'-A'), we see that line E adds "who makes you holy," not appearing in E', and F adds "for it is holy to you," not appearing in F'. This emphasis on holiness is picked up again in line X5, "it is holy to HaShem," connecting lines E and F to X5 by the concept of holiness. Indeed, line X5 "it is holy to HaShem," is a clear parallel to line F, "for it is holy to you." Pushing further the passage's anthropomorphism, the Shabbat then is a *sanctum* which Israel and HaShem share.

Moreover, the idea that HaShem sanctifies us (E) through our making Shabbat (E') makes an interesting contrast to the statement in Ex. 20:11 and Gen. 2:3 that HaShem sanctified the Shabbat. To phrase differently the message of lines E and E', the holiness of Israel and Shabbat is maintained by the relationship between HaShem and Israel; to the extent Israel obeys HaShem by keeping the Shabbat, Israel and Shabbat are sanctified; to the extent Israel disobeys HaShem by not keeping the Shabbat, Israel and the Shabbat are profaned.

The parallelism between the two panels X and A' breaks down at line 5. X5 says that the Shabbat is "holy to HaShem," whereas line A'x5 says that Hashem "was *nephesh*ed." As I've said, the idea transmitted here, I think, is that observing Shabbat sanctifies and enlivens us. D' adds "a covenant forever," not appearing in D, and B' adds "forever," not appearing in B. As I said, these differences signal that HaShem is speaking to all future generations of Jews. Looking back then at the positive statements, obedience is connected to holiness, life and an eternal, perpetual bond with HaShem.

If we turn our attention to what I label the negative statements (G-H and H'-G'), G adds the concept of profanation not appearing in G', and H adds the concept of the *nephesh* being *karet*/excised not appearing in H'. Thus in contrast to the person who, by keeping Shabbat, becomes holy and is *nephesh*ed, the person who doesn't keep Shabbat profanes the holy and his *nephesh* is cut off. The idea of a *nephesh* being *karet* is not simply another way of expressing the death penalty (*contra*, Noth, *ibid.*). There are competing theories of what it means for a *nephesh* to be *karet* (see Milgrom, *Leviticus*, pp. 457-460), but some at least agree that the penalty of *karet* is worse than the death penalty. According to the rabbinic view, the phrase "*mot yumat*"/"he shall be put to death" signifies execution by human agency. In contrast, the penalty of *karet*/excision is meted out by HaShem. I won't review the competing theories of what it means for a *nephesh* to be *karet*. For myself, however, I think that when HaShem cuts off a *nephesh*, it may mean that after death a person's *nephesh* will not be "gathered to his fathers" in the biblical phrase, but will be cut off from his ancestors. Moreover, the Bible at least hints at the notion that the living can somehow tend to the souls of the dead. If this is so, a person who is *karet* will not enjoy this benefit. The *nephesh* that is *karet* is totally separated after death from his kin, living and dead, from all Israel and from HaShem for all time.

Ki Tissa

If we look at the ideas grouped into these positive and negative statements, we see that on the one hand obedience is connected to life, holiness, and an eternal, perpetual bond with HaShem, whereas, on the other hand, disobedience is connected to death, profanation, and *karet* – eternal excision. This dichotomy between obedience and disobedience is succinctly summarized later in Lev. 18:5, "You shall keep my statutes and my rules, which if one does them, he shall live by means of them. I am YHWH." (See Milgrom, *Leviticus, ad loc.*)

HaShem has given us life and holiness; it is for us to choose by how we choose to live.

Leaves from the Garden

A(x, -f)	[13]But My Shabbats you shall keep
B	for it is a sign
C	between Me and you
D	for your generations
E	to know that I am HaShem who makes you holy
F(-a)	[14] You shall keep the Shabbat for it is holy to you
G	One profaning it shall be put to death
H	For everyone that makes on it work cut off shall that *nephesh* be from among his people
X1	[15] Six days
X2	may be done work
X3	but on the seventh day
X4	it is a Shabbat Shabbaton
X5	it is holy to HaShem
H`	Everyone making work on the Shabbat day
G`	shall be put to death
F`(-a)	[16] The children of Israel shall keep the Shabbat
E`	to make the Shabbat
D`	for their generations a covenant forever
C`	between Me and the children of Israel
B`	[17] it s a sign forever
A`x1	for in six days
A`x2	made HaShem the heavens and the earth
A`x3	but on the seventh day
A`x4	He "Shabbat-ed"
A`x5	and was "*nephesh*ed."

Ki Tissa

A(x, -f)	אך את-שבתת תשמרו
B	כי אות הוא
C	ביני וביניכם
D	לדרתיכם
E	לדעת כי אני ה' מקדשכם
F(-a)	ושמרתם את-השבת כי קדש הוא לכם
G	מחלליה מות יומת
H	כי כל-העשה בה מלאכה ונכרתה הנפש ההוא מקרב עמיה

X1	ששת ימים
X2	יעשה מלאכה
X3	וביום השביעי
X4	שבת שבתון
X5	קדש לה'

H'	כל-העשה מלאכה ביום השבת
G'	מות יומת
F'(-a)	ושמרו בני-ישראל את-השבת
E'	לעשות את-השבת
D'	לדרתם ברית עולם
C'	ביני ובין בני ישראל
B'	אות הוא לעלם

A'x1	כי-ששת ימים
A'x2	עשה ה' את-השמים ואת-הארץ
A'x3	וביום השביעי
A'x4	שבת
A'x5	וינפש

Vayyakhel-Pekudei

Richard Tupper

D'var Light

This constitutes a "*d'var* light" not because it is particularly insubstantial (though some might disagree) but because it is filled with reflections on light.

Certainly the most dramatic moment in this *parsha* comes in the final moments when, after the Tabernacle is completed, God's *kavod*/glory rests upon the Tabernacle and fills it, demonstrating to the Children of Israel that the LORD does dwell among them. The Torah goes on to say that God's *kavod*/Glory guided them through the wilderness, a pillar of cloud by day and a fiery pillar at night.

I've often wondered what it must have been like, especially at night, to view that pillar of fire which the Torah says was visible to all of Israel. I can't help feeling a little envy. The rabbis identify this *kavod*/glory/pillar as the *Shechinah*, God's Presence. The rabbis say that the *Shechinah* still rests upon Israel, for example, upon a minyan when it prays, a family celebrating a Shabbat meal, or two studying together. While I wouldn't argue with the rabbis, I can only say that I have never seen the *Shechinah* on any of these occasions, at least, I don't think I have . . . .

I once heard a rabbi give a *d'var Torah* in which he asserted that the light from the *Shechinah* was so intense at night that the people could not look at it directly. Now, I happen to think that the rabbi was mistaken because the text makes it pretty clear that the people could see the fiery cloud. However, his *davar* appealed to my ironic side – here I was longing to see what the people themselves never saw directly. But then I had an enlightening experience while camping a couple of summers ago.

My wife, unlike me, loves to camp. But, since I love my wife, we packed up our kids and along with my wife's brother and his family went camping in the great north woods of Wisconsin. Late one night, I happened to be sitting outside by the campfire talking to my brother-in-law. As we talked and watched the campfire burn, it suddenly struck me that I did not need to look directly at the fire to see its light; I only had to look at the face of my brother-in-law, and there in his face I saw the light reflected. That reminded me of this portion and the rabbi's *davar*. I wondered – thousands of years ago in the wilderness, as the people sat outside their tents at night in their camp illuminated by the fiery pillar, did any of them look up at the faces of their family and neighbors and realize that what they saw in their faces was God's glory reflected? At that moment it struck me that perhaps I had been looking for the *Shechinah* described by the rabbis in the wrong place. The place to find the *Shechinah* is not somewhere in the air hovering over us when we worship, or celebrate Shabbat or study but reflected in the faces of those around us, in their lives and in their deeds.

Vayikra

Richard Tupper

Gut Shabbos and welcome to our many visitors, including those from the Chicagoland Jewish High School. My *davar* today focuses on the *chattat*, the purification offering described in Lev. 4. I think much of what I have to say will be new to our visitors. As for long-time Minyan members, they may recognize it as a revision of a *davar* I gave a few years ago, but a little review never hurt anyone.

Religious rituals are theology encoded in actions. If we see a baseball player go up to bat and make the sign of a cross before he steps into the batter's box, most of us know what that ritual means and we could tell someone else about the God he believes in. However, if you were a Martian with no knowledge of human history and religion, you would not understand that ritual and you might not even notice it. For many of us, when we read *Vayikra*, we are like Martians – we don't understand the code and often we don't even notice when a ritual is being performed. We Jews today have the good fortune of having a modern day code-breaker by the name of Jacob Milgrom, a Conservative rabbi and the leading authority on the book of *Vayikra*. More than any other scholar, Milgrom has succeeded in decoding the rituals described in *Vayikra* and revealing their underlying theology. Milgrom's chief method of investigation is to compare Israel's rituals to those of the surrounding cultures and note the similarities and differences, both in actions and the underlying theology. The results of his investigations help us understand *Vayikra*.

Thanks to Milgrom, the *chattat*, formerly translated as "sin offering," is now correctly understood as a "purification offering" and that is the translation used in Lev. 4 of the new *Etz Hayim chumash*. Purification offerings and procedures were common in the ancient world but the underlying theology of their rituals differed significantly from the theology underlying Israel's purification rituals.

Leaves from the Garden

The purification rituals of Israel's neighbors arose from their understanding of the universe's origins, and their concept of how the world arose was very different from the creation story in Gen. 1.

In the pagan creation story, there is first chaos, which is conceived of as a vast, unbounded primordial sea. Inhering in that sea are forces of order and forces of chaos. Over time the primordial sea separates, and from this separation there arise the gods who try to bring order to the universe. Pitted against them are forces of chaos, which are also inherent in or arise from the primordial sea. For these natural forces of chaos I will use the shorthand of "demons" or "demonic powers." The initial gods give birth to more gods and by means of battles bring a semblance of order to the universe. However, they are under constant attack from the demonic forces who are trying to bring back the original chaos. To aid them in the fight, the gods create mankind. Mankind builds temples to house the gods, and mankind feeds and tends to the gods through sacrifices. However, the gods residing in their temples are constantly being attacked by the demonic forces that send impurities that attach themselves to the temples and, if the impurities become sufficiently severe, the gods will abandon the temple and the human beings who tend the gods in the temple. Consequently, human beings constantly perform purification rituals to rid the temples of impurities lest their gods abandon them.

In Israel's theology, our God does not arise out of a primordial sea; He exists apart. Although HaShem creates in part by acting upon the primordial sea, the primordial sea poses no threat to HaShem. The question then arises – why must Israel bring purification offerings? In Israel, there are two sources of impurity – those that arise from nature and those that arise because of the actions of humans. In this *davar* I will not discuss impurities that arise naturally, such as when you come into contact with a dead body. However, I will note that in Israel, natural sources of impurity have been reduced to a mere handful and can be readily neutralized through various purification procedures, which usually do not require sacrifice. The chief source of impurity in Israel, however, is human conduct, and chapter 4 of Leviticus details how this impurity is caused and how to be rid of it.

The chief source of impurity in Israel is human sin, or, as Lev. 4:2 says, when you inadvertently do what HaShem has commanded that you not do. If you violate one of HaShem's negative commandments, a "Thou shalt not," this causes impurity. I would also note that the mitzvot focused on in Lev. 4 are laws regulating relations between God and man, not relations among

Vayikra

human beings. Thus, Lev. 4 is prescribing what you must do if, for example, you accidentally work on Shabbat.

Now suppose you are a typical Israelite as described in vv. 27-31, and you accidentally work on Shabbat; let's say you didn't realize Shabbat had started and you lit a fire, what happens? Well, first, either you realize that you violated the mitzvah against working on Shabbat or someone tells you that it was Shabbat; and then you "feel guilt/*v'ashem*." *Asham*/Guilt is a key concept. *Asham* or guilt is Leviticus' way of talking about *teshuvah*/repentance. In Leviticus we don't find the word *teshuvah* used as repentance; instead, *asham*/guilt is how Leviticus talks about repentance. Once you feel *asham*/guilt, then you are ready to be forgiven.

So, you have reached the first step, *asham*/guilt, what do you do next? You bring a *chattat*, a purification offering. Why must you bring a *chattat*? Because sin generates *tuma*/impurity and you must remove the *tuma*/impurity as part of the process of repentance. So, if you are a typical Israelite, you bring your female goat or sheep as a *chattat*, and its *nephesh*/life-force, contained in its blood, is the substance used to remove the impurity. But where is the *tuma*/impurity that your sin has generated? We can answer that question by looking at where the blood, the purifying substance, is put. It is not put on the person who sinned but on the outer altar, the altar of burnt offerings. This is important. The person who accidentally sins does not become impure. His guilt is enough to remove his sin and his accidental sin does not make him impure. The accidental sinner is never required to bathe or engage in some other purification ritual, unlike the person who has become impure from some natural cause, such as menstruation, who always must bathe or engage in some sort of purification ritual. But his sin has generated impurity and the impurity has attached itself to the outer altar, because, just like in the pagan world, impurity is attracted like a magnet to holiness. The blood of the *chattat*, the purification offering, has to be used to remove the impurity and sure enough the *kohen* daubs the blood of the *chattat* on the horns of the outer altar thereby purifying it and removing the impurity. Once the ritual is completed, assuming that the person is sincere in his guilt or, as we would say, in his repentance, the sinner is forgiven and the impurity is removed.

Suppose you are not a common Israelite, but a big-shot, a *nasi*, a chieftain, like the chairman of our Minyan, CB. As described in vv. 22-26, the chieftain also must feel guilt, and he, too, must bring a *chattat* because his sin has generated impurity. The chieftain brings not a female goat but a male goat. Why the difference? At first it seems counter-intuitive but it may be because male goats are less valuable than female goats. Male goats are not nearly as valuable as female goats because they produce no milk. Consequently, it's more efficient to raise females than males, so the ordinary Israelite would very likely quickly eat male goats, keeping only one male goat alive for every fifty or so female goats in order to keep producing more goats. Excess male goats, then, were a luxury that ordinarily the typical Israelite might not possess. So in effect, requiring the chieftain to bring a male goat, a luxury, imposes a higher "tax" so to speak on the chieftain who sins than on the ordinary Israelite. Aside from this difference, the ritual for the chieftain is the same as the ritual for the common Israelite – he feels guilt about having violated the mitzvah, he brings his *chattat*, and the *kohen* uses the blood of the *chattat* to purify the outer altar that was polluted by the impurity generated by the chieftain's sin. If he sincerely feels guilt, the impurity is removed and he is forgiven.

Now suppose the entire people of Israel accidentally violate a prohibitive mitzvah; suppose, for example, they thought Pesach started on Thursday so they all worked on Wednesday and only later realized that Pesach started on Wednesday. They have accidentally violated HaShem's mitzvah by working on Pesach. As described in vv. 13-21, the procedure is very much the same. They, too, must feel guilt and must bring a *chattat*, in their case a bull, which is a much more expensive animal than a goat, because their accidental sin has generated *tuma*/impurity, which has attached itself to the Tabernacle and must be removed. However, the impurity has attached itself to a different place in the Tabernacle, and we can tell that by what the *kohen* does with the blood. This time the *kohen* does not put the blood on the outer altar, the altar of burnt offerings, but brings it inside the tent and sprinkles it in front of the curtain which is in front of the holy of holies, and also daubs some of the blood on the horns of the altar of incense, which is inside the *Mishkan*.

This ritual of placing the blood in different areas of the *Mishkan* is crucial for understanding how sin, impurity and the *chattat* function:

> *The more serious the sin, the deeper into the Mishkan its impurity penetrates.*

The chieftain's sin is no more serious than the sin of the ordinary Israelite, and so the impurity generated by the chieftain's sin attaches itself to the same place – the outer altar. However, the sin of the entire people is more serious than the sin of the chieftain or the common Israelite, and so it penetrates inside the *Mishkan* but outside of the holy of holies.

Now suppose you are the *kohen hagadol*, the high priest, and you accidentally violate a prohibitive mitzvah, then you must follow the

Vayikra

procedure described in vv. 3-12. Curiously, here we are not told that the *kohen hagadol* feels guilt. How can this be explained? It is a puzzle but two explanations have been offered. First is a *kal v'chomer* argument – if the typical Israelite or the *nasi* or the entire congregation feels guilt when they realize they have sinned, *kal v'chomer*, how much more so would the *kohen hagadol* feel guilt and therefore his feelings of guilt are assumed. Second, we are told in v. 3 that when the *kohen hagadol* sins, his sin brings guilt upon the entire people. Since the entire people are now guilty, the *kohen hagadol*'s sin requires all Israel, including the *kohen hagadol*, to feel guilt, and his *chattat* is brought in conjunction with the *chattat* of the entire community. The feeling of guilt is experienced by the entire community, including the *kohen hagadol*.

Like the blood of the *chattat* brought on behalf of the entire community, the blood of the *kohen hagadol*'s *chattat* is brought inside the *Mishkan*, sprinkled in front of the curtain hanging in front of the holy of holies, and daubed on the horns of the altar of incense. Thus, the unintentional sin of the *kohen hagadol* is just as serious as the sin of the entire community, and it pollutes the *Mishkan* to the same extent.

However, we know from reading Lev. 16 that the blood of the *chattat* brought on Yom Kippur is actually brought into the holy of holies and sprinkled on the *kapporet*, the gold cover that sits on the ark. What sins are so serious that they create impurities that pollute so deeply into the *Mishkan*? The text tells us. This blood of the *chattat* brought on Yom Kippur is used to purify the pollution of the *kapporet* caused by Israel's *avonot* and *peshaim*. An *avon* and a *pesha* are different than an unintentional sin whose impurity is removed according to the directions given in Lev. 4. An *avon* is an intentional sin, like when you know it's ham in the sandwich but you decide to eat it anyway. A *pesha* is a brazen sin, like when you know it's ham in the sandwich and your family knows it, but you decide to eat it in front of your family anyway. Intentional and brazen sins are the most serious sins, and it doesn't matter whether you are an ordinary Israelite or the *kohen hagadol* – intentional and brazen sins committed by no matter whom pollute the very heart of the *Mishkan*.

But how can a *chattat* which was used to remove impurities generated by unintentional sins remove impurities caused by intentional and brazen sins? The key difference between the *chattat* brought for unintentional sins described in Lev. 4 and the *chattat* brought for intentional and brazen sins described in Lev. 16 is confession. For the *chattat* brought on *Yom Kippur* to be effective the *kohen hagadol* must confess the people's sins. The intentional and brazen sinner cannot bring the *chattat* because as we are told in Numbers 15:30-31 he is cut off, barred from bringing an offering; therefore the *kohen hagadol* must bring it on his behalf. Confession, then, is the key to removing impurities caused by intentional and brazen sins. Says Resh Lakish in the Talmud (*b. Yoma* 86b), "great is repentance which converts intentional sins into inadvertent ones" (Milgrom's translation, *Leviticus*, p. 373). If we commit intentional or brazen sins but feel guilty and confess our sins, then HaShem graciously treats our intentional and brazen sins as if they had been unintentional and forgives us and removes the impurity.

Why the compelling need to purify the *Mishkan* of the impurity caused by sin? In this respect, Israel agrees with its neighbors – HaShem's presence will not remain in a polluted sanctuary. If the people sin and do not sincerely repent, HaShem's sanctuary will become so polluted that, as in the vision of Ezekiel the prophet, the cherubim will lift their wings and will fly out of the Temple, and with them will depart HaShem's presence (Ezek. 10).

Thus, the *chattat* embodies an important part of Israel's theology. There are no demons or forces in nature that threaten HaShem. The chief cause of impurity in Israel is man's sin; and man's sin, if not sincerely repented of, can drive HaShem away from us. Unrepented sin separates us from HaShem. Another important point: no man is an island; if one Israelite refrained from sinning or sincerely repented when she did sin, but her neighbors did not, the *Mishkan* would still be polluted and she, too, would experience the loss when HaShem's presence departed. We are all in this together. But the good news is that HaShem is always willing to forgive. Although today we have no temple, our unrepented sins still separate us from HaShem; but if we truly repent, our relationship with HaShem can always be restored.

It is my sincere hope that we learn and apply the lessons which the *chattat* has to teach us.

Shabbat shalom!

Shabbat Zakhor
Haftarah I Samuel 15

Lise Weisberger

On the Shabbat preceding Purim, without the softening effects of alcohol, noisemaking or disguises, we confront two disturbing texts about our relationship with our enemies. The special *maftir* portion, from Deuteronomy, commands us to remember and to blot out our hereditary enemies the Amalekites, ancestors of Haman. The *haftarah* relates how King Saul fell short of this command, and how he was rejected as king for this failure.

The issue of violent retribution is acute and painful from the very beginning of this *haftarah*. Samuel announces to Saul that God has commanded him to wipe out every last Amalekite: women, children and beasts included. Saul musters his troops, pursues and destroys the enemy, but spares the life of King Agag, as well as the lives of the best animals. For this he is ferociously and publicly upbraided by Samuel, who executes Agag himself. Saul is still King of Israel, but this is the beginning of the end for him – ahead lies displacement by David, depression, murderous paranoia, military defeat and suicide.

Why does Saul incur such devastating punishment for failing to take a man's life? A classic midrash portrays him as objecting to the whole project of exterminating the Amalekites – he quotes Torah to God, argues that the loss of life would be too great. God silences Saul by quoting Ecclesiastes: "Be not overly righteous" (7:16). What can this mean? Well, continues the midrash, because of Saul's misplaced pity for Agag, the enemy king gained one extra night of life, during which he managed to sire one more Amalekite, the direct ancestor of Haman. If Saul had not tried to be more merciful than God, he could have averted endless threats to future generations.

This midrash may raise greater problems than it solves. The very same God who listens respectfully to Abraham's arguments for clemency for Sodom and Gomorrah, the same God who works hard to teach Jonah pity for the innocent children and beasts in Nineveh, here refuses even to engage in a dialogue with Saul. Moreover, the midrash doesn't really fit the biblical text. In the bible story, whatever motivates Saul is not mercy. To destroy the animals that are damaged or feeble and save the ones that are vigorous and useful is not an act of compassion, but a practical economic and political decision. The Israelite warriors who have risked their lives to fight with their king feel entitled to the fruits of their victory, and Saul, who has always had problems maintaining the respect and discipline of his troops, chooses not to take the risk of explaining to them that this is a holy war, and that taking spoils is forbidden. In the matter of the animals, the issue is one of failed leadership.

But what moves Saul to spare the life of Agag? Again, it cannot be mercy – Saul has not hesitated to kill every other Amalekite, including women and children. Therefore it must be Agag's kingly status, and not his human worth, that persuades Saul to spare his life. Perhaps Saul fears that by killing a king, he will remind his own troops that kings are merely mortal. Perhaps he believes, or desperately hopes, there is something divine, something inviolable about kings that prevents their being subject to execution.

Poor Saul. He has no idea that his whole life story is an object lesson about the non-divinity of kings. He has been anointed for the very purpose of illustrating what happens to kings when they cannot hear the divine voice – and Saul, who seems to mean so well, is so sadly out of touch with what God wants and expects. What this *haftarah* has to teach is not that we should avoid excessive mercy, but that murderous kings like Agag are subject to retribution, and weak or disobedient kings like Saul are subject to replacement.

And perhaps that is the connection to keep in mind as we start to read the *megillah*, and enter the luxurious and imposing castle of Ahasuerus, ruler of 127 provinces, with the power of life and death over his wives, princes and subjects . . . . After all, he's only a king.

Tzav

Richard Tupper

Picking up where I left off at the Shabbaton,[1] there are two ways that we can experience HaShem's presence. One way is through the mitzvot. As Lev. 26. explains, if Israel keeps the mitzvot, HaShem comes down and walks among us. The second way is through worship. In ancient Israel, the people worshipped chiefly by means of *korbanot*/offerings. The word "*korban*/offering" is derived from the word "*karav*," which means to "draw near," and it was through their offerings that the people drew near to HaShem (*e.g.*, Ex. 29:43). *Parshat Tzav* focuses on worship through sacrificial offerings and begins with a review of the various sacrificial offerings that the Israelites brought. Today we have no Temple and hence no sacrifices and so instead we worship through *tefillah*/prayer, but there is not a vast discontinuity between sacrifice and prayer. As the prophet Hoshea says, we offer now "the bullocks of our lips" (14:2). Hence, sacrifice can still teach us much about prayer.

As I said, *parshat Tzav* begins with a review of the various sacrifices brought by ancient Israel and instructs the *kohannim* on how to handle the sacrifices. Several of the sacrifices brought by individuals are also incorporated into the public cult – the regimen of *korbanot* brought by the priests daily and on holidays on behalf of all Israel. Thus, the *olah*/whole burnt offering, the *mincha*/grain or tribute offering and the *chattat*/purification offering are regularly brought by the *kohannim* on our behalf. Even the *shelamim*/peace offering is brought by the *kohannim* on behalf of Israel, uniquely on Shavuot according to Lev. 23:19. (For an explanation of why this is, see Milgrom, *Leviticus,* pp. 2006-2007.) However, not all of the individual *korbanot* are incorporated into the public cult. One of them that is not is the *todah*/thanksgiving offering, which is described in Lev. 7:12-15, and I would like to focus on that offering.

---

[1] See pp. 165-168.

Leaves from the Garden

The *zevach todah*/sacrifice of thanksgiving is a subspecies of the *shelamim*/peace offering. Like the *shelamim*, the *todah* is eaten by the offeror. The main difference between the two is that the *todah* must be eaten on the same day that it is offered (Lev. 7:15, 22:30), whereas the *shelamim* may be eaten the following day (Lev. 7:16-18).

Another distinction between the *todah* and the *shelamim*, as I noted above, is that Israel is commanded to bring a *shelamim* offering, and it is even offered on Israel's behalf by the *kohannim* on Shavuot (Lev. 23:18), but Israel is never commanded to bring a *todah* offering, nor is the *todah* ever offered on Israel's behalf by the *kohannim*. The closest that Israel comes to being commanded to bring a *todah* offering is the *korban pesach*, which, as I talked about last Pesach, mirrors the *todah* offering except for dispensing with the *todah*'s requirement that it be accompanied by leavened bread (Lev. 7:13). That, of course, would be forbidden during Pesach (*e.g.*, Ex. 34:25). But even the *korban pesach* is never offered by the priests on Israel's behalf. The head of each household must bring the *korban pesach*.

Why is the *zevach todah* never offered by the priests on behalf of Israel? One purpose of the *todah* is thanksgiving, or perhaps better – public grateful acknowledgment – to HaShem for His salvific acts, and the rabbis, based upon Ps. 107 (see, *b. Ber.* 54b), teach that it is brought on four occasions – a person who has successfully completed a desert journey (Ps. 107:3-6), a person rescued from imprisonment (vv. 10-16), a person who has recovered from illness (vv. 17-22), and the seafarer who has returned safely (vv. 23-32). One can easily see why the *todah*, which is brought on these sorts of occasions, could have been modified to serve as the *korban pesach*. However, one can also see that these are circumstances that are unique to the individual, and so it makes sense that a person would bring it personally. But I believe that the answer to the question why the *todah* is never offered by the priest on behalf of Israel lies deeper, and we can discover the answer by examining similarities between the *zevach todah* and prayers of thanksgiving.

Following in the footsteps of the prophet Hoshea, the rabbis also made the connection between *korbanot* and *tefillot*. Moreover, they explicitly connected the *todah* offering to prayers of thanksgiving. Most famously, in *Midrash Rabbah* on Leviticus (IX 7),[1] it says:

---

[1] Cited by Milgrom, *Leviticus*, pp. 413-414.

Tzav

> R. Phineas and R. Levi and R. Yochanan said in the name of R. Menachem of Gallia: In the Time to Come all offerings will be annulled but that of thanksgiving will not be annulled, and all prayers will be annulled, but [that of] thanksgiving will not be annulled.

Thus, the rabbis teach that in the World to Come, the only sacrifices we will offer will be sacrifices of thanksgiving, and the only prayers we offer will be prayers of thanksgiving. This, then, is a characteristic that the *todah* and prayers of thanksgiving share.

However, there is another characteristic that they share. Where do we say prayers of thanksgiving in the *Amidah*? In the second to last blessing that begins, "*Modim anachnu lach* . . . . /We give thanks . . . . (*Sim Shalom* translates it "We proclaim . . . ." One could also translate it as, "We acknowledge.") If we turn to the *modim* (*Sim Shalom*, p. 360), you will notice that there are actually two prayers laid out in parallel. There is the regular *modim* that we recite when we each individually recite the *Amidah*, but there is also the *modim d'Rabbanan* that each of us recites when the *shaliach tzibbur* (congregation's emissary) repeats the *Amidah*. The *modim d'Rabbanan* is compiled from a number of personal declarations of the rabbis that are recorded in the Babylonian Talmud, *Sotah* 40a. There the rabbis discuss what should the congregation say while the *shaliach tzibbur* repeats the *modim anachnu lach*. The interesting question is: why only here in the *Amidah* when we express our thanks to HaShem does each member of the congregation express thanks while the *shaliach tzibbur* repeats the *modim anachnu lach*? Why don't we rely upon the *shaliach tzibbur*'s repetition?

A great 14th century rabbinic commentator on the *siddur*, Abudarham, offers an explanation in his treatise on prayer. Abudarham teaches that while one may send an emissary, the *shaliach tzibbur*, to present one's requests, one should always express one's thanks personally.[1] Hence, when we come to the *modim*, we members of the congregation do not rely upon our emissary but we each individually express our thanks. In so doing, we are continuing Israel's practice with the *todah*. Just as our prayers of thanksgiving today in the *modim* are offered individually and not through an emissary, so too in

---

[1] To be precise, Abudarham says one should always personally acknowledge what God has done for him/her lest, if you send an emissary instead, you might be tempted to disavow the words of your emissary.

ancient Israel, offerings of thanksgiving were always brought by the individual and never brought by the priests on behalf of a thankful person.

So Sam, since you are always demanding "relevance," here's relevance for you. The next time you are at services and begin reciting the *modim d'Rabbanan* while the *shaliach tzibbur* repeats the *modim*, remember that you are following the same custom that the ancient Israelites did when they brought a *zevach todah*. Moreover, if there is any sacrificial offering that you ought to study up on it is the *zevach todah*, since it, along with prayers of thanksgiving, is the only offering that you and I are ever likely to bring.

From the *Modeh Ani* we recite when we rise each morning, to the *Modim Anachnu Lach* we recite when we rise at every service, to the *zevach todah* we will bring when we rise again, gratefully acknowledging by word and deed HaShem for all that He has for us is an essential quality of being a Jew, which makes perfect sense since we are, after all, *Yehudim*/Those who gratefully acknowledge HaShem.

Tzav (II)

Richard Tupper

When I volunteered to give this *davar*, I didn't realize that it was for *Shabbat HaGadol*, the Shabbat before Pesach, so unfortunately I won't be telling you how to *kasher* your home for Pesach in thirty minutes. Besides, if I spoke for thirty minutes, Sam Neusner would throw me out.

Instead, I will talk about sanctification, the process by which people and things become holy.[1] We've already been introduced to one type of sanctification in the latter (and better) part of *Shemot* where HaShem instructs Moses to take the holy anointing oil manufactured according to HaShem's recipe and anoint the *Mishkan*, its utensils, and Aaron and his sons (Ex. 40:9-15). Automatically, they become holy (Lev. 8:10-12).

We see another instance of sanctification in today's portion. Chapter 6:17-22 discusses the procedure for the purification offering, the *chattat*. Vv. 20-21 states:

> 20 Whatever touches its [the *chattat*'s] flesh shall become holy; and if any of its blood is spattered upon a garment, the bespattered part you shall launder in a holy place. 21 An earthen vessel in which it is boiled shall be broken; if it has been boiled in a copper vessel, that shall be scoured and flushed with water.

I'd like to draw attention to three aspects of these verses. First, the holiness that is conferred is not just automatic but it is even accidental. Regardless of the priest's intention, whatever touches the meat of the *chattat* becomes holy. Second, what if the flesh touches not an object but a person?

---

[1] For Milgrom's discussion of "*sancta* contagion," see, Milgrom, *Leviticus*, pp. 443-456.

Does the person become holy? Milgrom translates the word "*kol*" which begins v. 20 as "whatever." However, some argue that the word should include persons. (I'll ignore for the purposes of this *davar* Baruch Levine's comment on this verse in the *Etz Hayim*.) One could argue that since the only persons who should be handling the flesh of the *chattat* are priests, and since they are already holy, there is no reason to fear the accidental sanctification of common Israelites. However, it is conceivable that a common person might somehow come in contact with the meat, and the verses pointedly do not prescribe any desanctification ritual in such an instance. Regardless of the arguments, our tradition teaches that the meat does not sanctify common persons. Finally, does the garment spattered by the *chattat*'s blood and the vessel in which the *chattat* is boiled become holy? Surprisingly, Jacob Milgrom in his Anchor Bible commentary on Leviticus discusses these articles as if they had been made impure by contact with the blood and the meat, although in his discussion of this passage, he seemingly cannot bring himself to say that the garment and the pot are actually impure, only that they are treated as if they are impure. However, the verses do not say that these objects are impure. Although the purgation rituals prescribed are consistent with removing impurity, they are also consistent with removing holiness. Furthermore, if, in fact, for example, the bespattered garment is impure, it seems strange that the text would prescribe that it be washed in a holy place. Why deposit impurity in a place that is holy?

We see another instance of this instruction to wash in a holy place in chapter 16. After Aaron on Yom Kippur has made the rounds purifying the *Mishkan* with the blood of the *chattat* offerings, vv. 23-24 instruct:

> And Aaron shall go into the Tent of Meeting, take off the linen vestments that he put on when he entered the adytum, and leave them there. 24 He shall bathe his body in water in the holy place and put on his vestments; then he shall go out and sacrifice his burnt offering and the burnt offering of the people, effecting atonement for himself and for the people.

The first question to be asked about this passage is: why is Aaron instructed to leave his linen garments inside the *Mishkan*? Remember, these are the garments that Aaron wore when he entered the Holy of Holies to purify it. Perhaps surprisingly, Milgrom in his early writings suggested that the garments are left there because they are impure, having become polluted when Aaron was purifying the *Mishkan*. Later, however, he came around to the view of the Ramban that the garment is holy, having been sanctified

Tzav (II)

when Aaron entered the Holy of Holies. The Ramban's most persuasive argument: having spent all this time purifying the *Mishkan*, why would Aaron leave inside it an impure garment?

The second and perhaps more interesting question is: why must Aaron bathe? I'm not sure but I would hazard the guess that the majority view is that Aaron must bathe in order to remove the impurity that he contracted when purifying the *Mishkan*.[1] However, I see several problems with this interpretation. Why would entering the Holy of Holies sanctify Aaron's clothing but pollute him? It seems counterintuitive though admittedly not impossible. In addition, if Aaron is indeed impure why is he instructed to bathe in a holy place? If we say that Aaron's clothing would not be deposited in a holy place if it were impure, why should we think that Aaron should wash off his impurity in a holy place? Finally, you'll note that after Aaron bathes, he goes right about performing his duties; there is no waiting period prescribed. Normally (*e.g.*, Lev. 15) when persons are instructed to purify themselves from impurity, there follows a waiting period before the purification process is complete. Yet Aaron is subjected to no waiting period.

In sum, we can say two things about these passages: either holiness is not imparted to persons by contact with the holy, or it is imparted but only in the unique circumstance of entry into the Holy of Holies.

Interestingly, there is a dissenting view in the Tanakh. The priest and prophet Ezekiel gives lengthy instructions for the Temple he envisions being rebuilt. Strikingly, Ezekiel warns that the priests cannot wear their priestly garments when they go among the common people, nor can they carry the meat of the *chattat* among the common people. Why? Lest the priests' clothing and the meat sanctify the common people by contact (Ezek. 44:19; 46:20). For Ezekiel at least, sanctification of persons is not only automatic by contact with holy garments but can even be accidental.

Now I'm sure some, like Sam Fox, are asking how is this relevant. After all, the Temple, the sacrifices and priestly garments no longer exist. There is nothing holy anymore that might confer holiness. However, we have the anomaly of the Torah scroll. A Torah scroll is holy, and the rabbis instruct that after touching a Torah scroll one must rinse one's hands. Why? The rabbis teach that a Torah scroll imparts a very low level of impurity. Now washing is consistent with removing impurity, but it is also consistent with

---

[1] After giving this *davar*, I checked and saw that Milgrom's view is that the high priest is washing away holiness (Milgrom, *Leviticus*, p. 1048). No doubt I learned this from him but forgot.

removing holiness. I would offer the unorthodox hypothesis that at one point there were those, perhaps a majority and perhaps even originally, who like Ezekiel believed that contact with holy things could impart holiness to persons. For them the washing of hands was to remove not impurity but holiness. The rabbis, however, rejected this view and therefore championed a different explanation for washing hands, an explanation that is our view today: after touching a holy Torah scroll, we wash to remove not holiness but impurity.

Thus our Torah and our tradition teach us that we cannot become holy by contact with holy things. Nevertheless, we are commanded to be holy (Lev. 19:2). If we cannot become holy by contact with the holy, how are we to become holy? We answer that question with every *bracha* we recite: *asher kidishanu b'mitzvotav* – who sanctifies us by His commandments. We become holy by following the mitzvot that HaShem has graciously given us. Loving our neighbor, keeping kosher, caring for the poor, and keeping Shabbat; obeying such mitzvot are the means to holiness. Holiness comes not in an instant, not by accident, but over a lifetime of obedience to HaShem's commands.

Shemini

Peter Levavi

The story of Nadav and Abihu near the beginning of *Shemini* is one that has fascinated and perplexed me for many years; this year I struggled to find an adequate explanation for the strange events reported in the Torah. I thought of three possible theories. I will offer up two which I encountered in the sources, and one original explanation, as far I can tell.

The text 10:1-3 (NJPS):

> Now Aaron's sons Nadav and Abihu each took his fire pan, put fire in it, and laid incense on it; and they offered before the LORD alien ["strange" (OJPS)] fire, which He had not commanded them. And fire came forth from before LORD and consumed them; thus they died in the presence of LORD. Then Moses said to Aaron, "This is what the LORD meant when He said: 'Through those near to Me I show Myself holy, and gain glory before all the people.'"

This passage raises three questions for me:
What is strange or alien fire?
Why were Nadav and Abihu punished with death?
What is the meaning of Moses' quote?

I. *Korach – Crushing a Challenge to God's Authority*. One way we can try to understand a passage in Torah is to find a similar set of circumstances and see what we can learn from them. One passage that is strikingly similar to the story of Nadav and Abihu comes in the book of *Bemidbar* in *parshat Korach*. Korach, together with 250 big machers, presents a challenge to Moses' authority. The gang complains, "Why should you raise yourselves up over the LORD's assembly?" Moses responds with a passage much like the quote in this week's *parsha*. He says, "In the morning, the LORD will make known who is His, and him who is holy He will bring close to Him and him whom He chooses He will bring close to Him." He then tells Korach and his followers to put fire in their firepans and bring them to *Adonai*'s Tabernacle. After they perform this request, the Presence of *Adonai* appears and speaks to Moses and Aaron saying, "Divide yourselves from this community, and I will put an end to them in an instant." Moses pleads with God not to kill them all. God then tells everyone to move away from the wicked men who have challenged God's authority, and the earth opens up and swallows all the men with Korach; a fire then consumes the 250 men who offered up the incense in the Tabernacle.

Based on what we learn in *Korach*, one possible explanation for the events in our *parsha* is that Nadav and Abihu may have been offering a challenge to Moses and Aaron's authority by bringing strange or alien fire, and God destroyed them to keep the line of authority clear within the Israelite camp. While this explanation is possible, it is improbable, since these sons of Aaron were being groomed for the priesthood leadership; there is no evidence in the text that they were posing a serious challenge to Moses' authority the way Korach and his band were.

II. *Midrash – Punishment for Disrespect for a Rebbe*. The Midrash offers another interpretation of what transpired. On the eighth day of the inauguration of the Tent of Meeting, the heavenly fire descended and consumed the sacrifices. Nadav and Abihu decided that they should place their own fire on the *mizbayach* (altar) based on a verse from Torah which they interpreted, despite the presence of *Adonai*'s own heavenly fire. I think it is in this sense that what the two brought into the tent was an alien or strange fire. It was alien in the sense that God's glory was already present, what they offered was unnecessary, and superfluous. It was strange in the sense that it was odd. In a way it was like "bringing coals to Newcastle." Why would you need to bring a fire into a place where a heavenly fire was consuming sacrifices?

According to Midrash, the problem wasn't so much the strange fire, but the fact that they were making law. They formulated this *halacha* that you should bring fire into the Tent without consulting Moses, who was the chief authority on *halacha* at that moment. They did it right in his presence. This affront constituted an embarrassment to Moses and therefore earned them a heavenly death sentence. The crime they committed was that they violated the prohibition against pronouncing a halachic decision in front of one's teacher. It is taught that a student who puts his rebbe to shame, acting in his

Shemini

presence as if the latter were incapable of a decision, deserves death since his conduct was similar to that of a murderer. This view is predicated on the belief within Jewish tradition that the previous generations should be venerated because they possess more knowledge than we have today, that we are spiritual dwarfs compared to our Torah fathers. This view is extremely conservative in the sense that all ideas must come from the elders.

This authentically Jewish view is out of sync with our current view of knowledge as being progressive, or cumulative over time; one way to put a positive spin on the midrashic view of knowledge is to say that we do know less than our preceding generation, and they knew less than the one that preceded them, but even if we know little, we benefit from the knowledge gained by the past generations. That is, we are standing on the shoulders of the giant scholars of the past, so we dummies get a head start. One problem with this approach is that it assumes that knowledge grows in continuous progression. But Kuhn has taught us in his *The Structure of Scientific Revolutions* that knowledge does not always grow in a straight upward path. Sometimes we are confronted with mounting situations in which our current knowledge can't explain events; there is a paradigm shift and everything we knew before as truth (like the world being flat) all of a sudden is proven to be explained in a completely different way. It is unlikely that these insights or paradigm shifts would always come from the elders. It often takes someone looking at a problem a new way to think of a different approach.

All of this is to say that I don't accept the explanation in the Midrash of the justice in Nadav and Abihu being killed because they disgraced Moses by having their own views on how *halacha* should be interpreted. There is a legitimate countervailing Jewish view that holds that the young possess the ability to see more clearly than the old and corrupt. I will quote a Jewish canon proof text by Rav Zimmerman of Duluth to present an example of this view:

>Come mothers and fathers
>Throughout the land,
>And don't criticize
>What you can't understand,
>Your sons and your daughters
>Are beyond your command,
>The old road is rapidly agin'.
>Please get out of the new one
>If you can't lend your hand,
>For the times they are a changing.

Leaves from the Garden

III. *Pardes – Price for Unpreparedness*. The story of Nadav and Abihu also reminds me of another enigmatic story, the story of the *Pardes*, found in the Babylonian Talmud, Tractate *Hagigah* 14b.

> Four entered an orchard: Ben Azzai, Ben Zoma, Acher, and Rabbi Akiva. Rabbi Akiva said to them: "When you reach the stones of pure marble, do not say: 'water water!' For it is said: 'He that speaks falsehood shall not be established before mine eyes.'" Ben Azzai gazed and died. Of him Scripture says: "Precious in the sight of the Lord is the death of the saints." Ben Zoma gazed and was stricken. Of him Scripture says: "Has thou found honey? Eat as much as is sufficient for thee, lest thou be filled, and vomit it." Acher cut down the shoots. Rabbi Akiva departed in peace.

The Jewish mystics say that the *Pardes* or orchard refers to the *merkavah*, the heavenly chariot, and the halls of the angels on high. One must be spiritually grounded, prepared, and follow exact procedures to have a personal experience with the divine and come away, like Rabbi Akiva, safe and sound. The four who enter the *Pardes* were at different levels of preparedness and therefore suffered different fates. Ben Azzai wasn't prepared and died immediately upon seeing the vision. Ben Zoma wasn't prepared, saw the vision, and was driven mad by it. Acher was ready, but was not sufficiently grounded and misinterpreted what he saw, and became an apostate. Only Rabbi Akiva was grounded, was prepared for what he saw, and knew the right procedure for seeing visions, without either being killed outright, frightened out of his mind, or caused to adopt heretical ideas. What is the preparation required to experience a divine vision? What are the proper procedures to adopt for a direct encounter with the divine?

The Hai Gaon from the tenth century said that when a man is worthy and is blessed with certain qualities, and he wishes to gaze at the heavenly chariot and the halls of the angels on high, he must follow certain exercises. He must fast for a specified number of days, and, with his head between his knees and his face toward the ground, he must softly whisper praises to God. As a result he will gaze into the innermost recesses of his own heart and it will seem as if he saw the seven halls with his own eyes, moving from hall to hall to observe that which is therein to be found.

We are told that the prerequisites to the study of Kabala are the attainment of forty years, being male, being a father to a son, and being knowledgeable in all of Torah. Now that I have satisfied the first three of the four conditions, I can understand exactly why there are these prescriptions. When a guy is over forty and has a son to worry about, who has the mental energy to study mystical texts? Only a very small and well grounded percentage of the population qualifies, one that is unlikely to flip out when exposed to the mystical secrets, and is unlikely to turn apostate.

To conclude, for me, the story of the *Pardes* provides the most plausible explanation to what happened to Nadav and Abihu. Entering the holy of holies in the Tent of Meeting where God's glory is present is a mystical experience, equivalent to entering the *Pardes*. It seems to me that the young sons of Aaron, no matter how learned they were at that young age, were insufficiently grounded and unprepared for the awesome experience of a direct meeting with the divine. They most likely directly looked upon the glory of God. As God says to Moses on Sinai, "No human can see Me and live." It is likely that the two had not yet consulted with Moses on how to approach the inner chamber, and, unaware of the Hai Gaon's method of approaching a vision of the divine, suffered the same fate as ben Azzai in the *Pardes*. Tragic, yes, but what a way to go . . . with a vision of God in one's eyes.

Finally, remember the quote from Moses in the text, "Through those near to Me I show Myself holy, and gain glory before all the people"? If we view these events through the lens of the *Pardes*, then the quote might mean that the nearness of Nadav and Abihu caused them to see God and lose their lives through the vision, which, in turn, heightened the awe of God of those who witnessed or heard of the events that transpired that day – which may be why we continue to tell the story of Nadav and Abihu even today.

Shemini (II)

Richard Tupper

So why do Nadav and Avihu get toasted? The text tells us that they offered strange fire before the LORD which He had not commanded (Lev. 10:1). At which point, fire comes out from before the LORD and consumes them (Lev. 10:2). From this we are to conclude that God is not only picky but extremely irascible?

And what's with Moses? Here his nephews are incinerated, his brother is stunned, and what's Moses' reaction? A sort of "super-duper" I told you so! He tells his grieving brother, "This is what the LORD meant when He said: 'Through those near to Me I show Myself holy, and gain glory before all the people' " (Lev. 10:3 [NJPS]). What is Moses talking about? And if Moses is quoting God, when did God say this before?

Why does God warn Aaron not to drink on the job (10:8-9), and what is the point of God's instruction to Aaron that it is his job to distinguish between the holy and the common, the impure and the pure so that he can teach God's laws to the children of Israel (10:10-11)?

A close reading of the text yields some answers to these questions though, of course, I don't claim that these are *the* right answers.

Over the centuries, commentators who fault Nadav and Avihu have criticized virtually every aspect of their conduct. Among the major criticisms are:

1) What did they think they were doing? In Lev. 9, God had given very explicit instructions on the sacrifices that were to be offered at the dedication service of the Tabernacle, and God had not specified any incense offering. Thus, while chapter 9 is filled with repeated instances of Aaron doing as God had commanded, here we have Nadav and Avihu doing something that God had not commanded (10:1).

2) Who did Nadav and Avihu think they were, bringing this offering? In Ex. 30:7, we were told that it is Aaron's job to offer incense on the altar of incense. Why then did Nadav and Avihu take this duty upon themselves?

3) Were they bringing "strange incense" as well as strange fire? In Lev. 10:1, we are told that the sons brought "incense/*k'toret*" but the text does not say that they brought "aromatic incense/*k'toret samim*" which God had specified in Ex. 30:7 and had given the secret recipe for in Ex. 30:34-38. Any other incense offered was forbidden as "strange incense/*k'toret zara*."

4) Others note that the text seems to stress that each son brought his own pan upon which to offer the incense – "each took his censer" – and they suggest that the offering was improper because the sons used their personal utensils rather than those of the Tabernacle.

But surely, the text seems to stress that the major flaw in the sons' offering was that they used "strange fire/*aysh zara*" (10:1), and it is the "strange fire" that is mentioned in later accounts (Num. 3:4; 26:61). How can fire be strange or alien? To answer that question we must first decide what fire they should have used. On this question all commentators seem to agree that the fire they should have used was that which burned on the altar of burnt offering in the Tabernacle courtyard. Recall that when Aaron had completed the offerings specified by God, then "there came forth fire from before the LORD, and consumed upon the altar the burnt-offering and the fat . . ." (Lev. 9:24 [NJPS]). (That there was something to be consumed after Aaron had already lit the sacrifices should not be surprising since normally it would have taken several hours at least to burn up the carcasses of the offerings.) The offerings brought by Aaron were then consumed by fire sent by God. Recall that God had already commanded that the fire on the altar of burnt offerings was to be maintained perpetually (Ex. 29:42; Lev. 6:2, 6). Throughout the Torah, fire is used as a symbol of God's presence.

The fire continually burning on the altar of burnt offering signified God's constant presence with Israel. Just as the perpetual fire burning on the altar of burnt offering represented God's continuing presence among Israel and His acceptance of their various burnt offerings, so too the fire perpetually burning the twice offered incense on the altar of incense (Ex. 30:8) represented God's continuing acceptance of the people's purest offering.

What then was wrong with the fire used by Nadav and Avihu? Apparently they did not use God's fire, the fire from the altar of burnt offering. Whose fire did they use? The story doesn't tell us. And from the story's perspective, it doesn't matter. As long as it is not God's fire, the fire is unacceptable.

Shemini (II)

However, the phrase "strange fire/*aysh zara*" calls to mind the phrase "strange god(s)" that Israel is accused of or warned against worshiping elsewhere in the Bible (Deut. 32:16; Psalm 44:20; Psalm 81:9; Isaiah 43:12). In short, I think what the story is describing is religious infidelity of the first order – similar to the Golden Calf incident. Nadav and Avihu were offering incense using fire other than God's fire so that in essence they were proffering an offering inside the Tabernacle to some deity other than God. It's as if you came home and found your spouse with someone else in your very own bed. No wonder the fire from God consumed Nadav and Avihu.

However, it is Moses who explains the import of this event. He says to Aaron, "This is what the LORD meant when He said: 'Through those near to Me [*bekrovai*] I show Myself holy, and gain glory before all the people' " (10:3 [NJPS]). This verse is intended to explain the event but one problem is that Moses appears to be repeating what God has said before, yet despite numerous clever suggestions by commentators, no one seems to be able to locate such a statement by God before. Without reviewing the suggestions made by other commentators, I think that what is going on here is that God, by way of Moses, is illuminating the message of the preceding chapter.

A more literal but less felicitous translation of "*bekrovai*" as "through those near to Me" would be "through near-drawers" or "through presenters" or "through offerors." I think "*bekrovai*" is a pun on the use of "*korban*/offering" in Chapter 9. Chapter 9 begins with God instructing Moses to tell Aaron to offer ("*v'hakrev*")(9:2) various sacrifices and to instruct the people to bring various sacrifices "for today the LORD will appear to you" (9:4). So the congregation draws nigh ("*yikrvu*") (9:5) and stands before the LORD. Then Moses says, "This is that which the LORD commanded that you do, that the Glory of the LORD may appear to you" (9:6 [NJPS]). Then Moses instructs Aaron to come forward ("*k'rav*") (9:7) and to sacrifice the various sacrifices including the people's "offering/*korban*" "as the LORD commanded" (9:7). So Aaron "draws near/*yikrav*" (9:8), slays the purification offering, and his sons "presented/*yakrivu*" the blood to him (9:9). Later, Aaron offers ("*yakrayv*") the people's offering ("*korban*"). The text continues describing the various offerings offered and, at the completion of the process, "the glory of the LORD appeared to all the people and fire came forth from before the LORD and consumed the burnt offering and the suet pieces on the altar." We have seen this manifestation of God's glory before when Moses erected the Tabernacle and offered sacrifices (Ex. 40:26-29, 34-35), and this same pattern is repeated when Solomon finishes the Temple (I Kings 8:10-11; II Chron. 5:11-14; 7:2-3).

But if the people thought the message of Chapter 9 was that God's glory could be accessed or somehow manipulated through an offering (*b'korban*) then the message of Chapter 10 – of Moses' statement to Aaron – is that God's glory is revealed through the offerors (*bekrovai*). The offering is seen as the extension of the offeror. The two are conflated. Deficiencies in the offering reflect deficiencies in the offeror, and an offering no matter how technically correct is still unacceptable if brought by an unacceptable offeror. The story begins by stressing how each man (*ish*) brings his own censer to offer "strange fire/*aysh zara*." Because the *aysh* is strange, so, too, is the *ish*, and God rejects both. God sees both the external and the internal. "Who shall ascend into the mountain of the LORD and who shall stand in His holy place? He that has clean hands and a pure heart" (Ps. 24:3-4).

But how then is God sanctified and how is His Glory revealed before the people through the offerors? A commentator named Peretz Segal[1] has noted a close parallel to this verse in Ezekiel 28:22: "Thus says the Lord GOD: Behold, I am against you, O Zidon. I will be glorified in the midst of you; and they shall know that I am the LORD when I have executed judgments on her, and shall be sanctified through her." A similar theme is expressed in Numbers 20:12-13: "And the LORD said to Moses and to Aaron: 'Inasmuch as you did not trust Me to sanctify Me before the eyes of the Israelites, even so you shall not bring this assembly into the land that I have given to them.' These are the waters of Meribah, where the Israelites disputed with the LORD, and He was sanctified through them."

God's is sanctified and His Glory is revealed when God executes judgment (Ps. 99:2, 9). When the priests and the people bring acceptable offerings, when, in short, they keep the Covenant, God is sanctified and His Glory is revealed. However, when the people transgress and bring unworthy sacrifices, when they break the Covenant, then God is still sanctified and His Glory is still revealed because God executes judgment. "You only have I known of all the families of the earth; therefore I will visit upon you all your iniquities" (Amos 3:2). That is the downside, so to speak, of the Covenant. Israel is intended to be a light to the nations (Is. 42:6) and if God's Glory is not reflected by their adherence to the Covenant, then God's Glory and sanctity are revealed when God executes judgment on the people for having broken the Covenant.

---

[1] "The Divine Verdict of Leviticus X 3," *Vetus Testamentum* 39:91-95 (1989).

Shemini (II)

This is why Aaron and his successors must maintain their sobriety when they draw near to offer the people's offerings (Lev. 10:9). The High Priest has an awesome responsibility. He brings offerings on behalf of the entire community when it errs (Lev. 4) and enters the Holy of Holies once a year on Yom Kippur (Lev. 16). The acceptability of the people's offering depends in part upon the acceptability of Aaron.

But Aaron has an even more sobering task: he must distinguish between the holy and the common, the impure and the pure (Lev. 10:10) and must teach the children of Israel all the laws which God gave to them through Moses (10:11). If Aaron and his successors fail to distinguish between the holy and the common and between the impure and the pure, then the sacrifices the people offer will be unacceptable. Moreover, their error will be compounded if they fail to instruct the people on how to obey God's mitzvot.

All Israel is called to be a "kingdom of priests and a holy nation" (Ex.19:6). The sacrifices we offer today are not bulls, goats and sheep, but prayer (*e.g.*, Ps. 141:2; Prov. 15:8; Hosea 14:2), study (Hosea 6:6) and good deeds (Prov. 21:3; Hosea 6:6). Just as in the case of Nadav and Avihu, so too with us the quality of our offerings depends upon the qualities within us. Our offerings reflect ourselves.

May the offerings we bring through the choices we make be such that through our lives God is sanctified and His Glory is revealed to all the peoples of the earth.

Tazriah-Metzorah

Richard Tupper

The double *parsha Tazriah-Metzorah* describes the diagnosis of the disease "*tzaraat*" (often mistranslated as "leprosy" but the disease cannot be identified), and the ritual for restoring the *metzorah*, the person afflicted with *tzaraat*, to the community once he or she has recovered from the disease. The prevailing opinion holds that HaShem has inflicted this disease upon the person because she or he has sinned. While the rabbis posit a variety of sins that can result in *tzaraat*, the best known sin is that of *lashon hara* – speaking evil of another. Indeed, Miriam's slander of Moses (Num. 12) is the parade example for this view. On the other hand, my hero, Jacob Milgrom, suggests, chiefly because of the presence of the *asham*/reparation offering in the rituals for restoring the healed *metzorah* to the community, that the *metzorah* may have been suspected of profaning the holy, and thus incurred divine punishment. (See, Milgrom, *Leviticus*, pp. 820-825.)

I do not dispute that, elsewhere in the Tanakh, *tzaraat* is caused by sin. However, I am focusing on Lev. 13-14 because these chapters spring from "P," the "Priestly" source, and I am asking whether P teaches that *tzaraat* always is caused by sin.[1] Read closely, Lev. 13-14 indicate that the priestly writers, at least, drew back from concluding that all instances of *tzaraat* in humans were caused by the person's sin.

Aside from non-P stories in the Tanakh that expressly attribute *tzaraat* to sin, many people perhaps conclude that the *metzorah* has sinned because the

---

[1] I will not discuss Lev. 14:33-53, which scholars such as Milgrom and Israel Knohl, *The Sanctuary of Silence* (Fortress Press 1995), ascribe to "H," the "Holiness source." According to Milgrom and Knohl, although H inherits P's traditions, H wrote later than P and did not necessarily adopt all of P's views. Interestingly, H (Lev. 14:34) states that HaShem does inflict the disease on houses, but, strikingly, does not expressly attribute HaShem's action to the homeowner's sin.

metzorah must bring sacrifices before being restored to the community. However, I hope that by now you have been persuaded that P distinguishes sacrifices (chiefly the *chattat*/purification offering) brought for sin from those brought for severe physical impurity, and that P does not equate human impurity with sin. If you have not yet been persuaded on this point, you will find none of what I say about *tzaraat* persuasive. In order to determine whether the *metzorah* brings sacrifices on account of sin or on account of physical impurity, we must examine closely how P treats the *metzorah*'s sacrifices.

P treats sacrifices brought because of sin differently than those brought because of severe human impurity. P begins by grouping these sacrifices separately. P discusses sins which require a *chattat* chiefly in Lev. 4-5. P discusses physical impurities which require a *chattat* chiefly in Lev. 12 and 15. Where does P discuss *tzaraat*? Not in Lev. 4-5, but in Lev. 13-14, in the very middle of its discussion of physical impurities.

When describing sacrifices brought because of sin, P regularly identifies the sin on account of which the sacrifice is brought. Thus, P says a person must bring a *chattat* for inadvertently violating a prohibitive command (Lev. 4:1, 13, 22 and 27), for failing to testify after hearing an imprecation to do so (5:1), for forgetting to purify oneself after becoming impure (5:2-3), and for failing to fulfill an oath (5:4). Similarly, P requires that an *asham*/reparation offering be brought when a person is remiss with regard to *sancta* (5:14), suspects that he or she may have profaned *sancta* (5:17), or has lied under oath (5:20). In contrast, when discussing offerings brought because of severe physical impurity, P never identifies any sin that the person has committed. Rather, P describes the impurity which occasions the need for the *chattat* (childbirth [Lev. 12], or an unusual genital discharge lasting more than seven days [15:1-12, 26-28]). When discussing the *metzorah*, P makes no mention of sin. Rather, consistent with its description of sacrifices brought because of severe physical impurity, P describes at length the signs of the *metzorah*'s physical impurity (Lev. 13).

When P discusses sacrifices brought because of sin, P requires not only that a person bring a sacrifice but also that the person feel guilt (4:13; 22, 27; 5:4, 17 and 24). Sacrifices for certain sins require confession (5:5, see also 16:21); the restitution required by P for certain sins perhaps may also serve as a confession (5:16, 23-24). However, in no case is the person required to engage in any purification ritual such as bathing, laundering or waiting before bringing the sacrifice. Presumably, this is because in P's system sin pollutes the *Mishkan* but not the sinner. In contrast, when P discusses

Tazriah-Metzorah

sacrifices brought because of severe physical impurity, P never mandates that the impure person feel guilt, nor does P ever require confession by the impure person. However, P does mandate that the impure person always purify himself or herself through such rituals as bathing, laundering or waiting before bringing the required sacrifice (Lev. 12:5; 15:13, 28). What of the *metzorah*? P does not specify that the healed *metzorah* feel guilt, nor does P require any confession. Instead, like its treatment of the impure person, P requires that the healed *metzorah* engage in physical purification rituals before bringing a sacrifice to the *Mishkan*.

Finally, when P discusses sacrifices brought on account of sin, P states that the sacrifice's purpose is *kaper* and forgiveness (4:20, 26, 31, 35; 5:6, 10, 13, 16, 18, and 26). The precise meaning of *kaper* is hotly disputed, ranging from "rubbing" and "purgation" to what the King James translators conceived of as "effecting at-one-ment," whence the KJV neologism of "atonement." But surely the concept of *kaper* is not always joined with sin because it is also used in conjunction with the sacrifice brought by the person with a severe physical impurity who has not sinned (15:15, 30). Moreover, when discussing sacrifices brought on account of sin, P frequently states that the need for *kaper* is because of sin (4:26, 35; 5:6, 10, 13, and 18). In contrast when discussing sacrifices brought on account of a person's severe physical impurity, P uses the word *kaper*, but states that the sacrifice is necessary to effect purgation, not for sin, but for the person's impurity (15:15, 30). If we turn to P's treatment of the *metzorah*, P does not say that the *metzorah*'s sacrifice is to obtain forgiveness, but rather, as in the case of other persons with severe physical impurity, its purpose is to effect purgation for the *metzorah* who is being purified of his impurity (14:19).

Thus far, based upon the similarities and differences discussed above, P has given us no indication that the *metzorah*'s sacrifices are because of sin; rather, P's treatment of the *metzorah* is consistent with its treatment of persons with severe physical impurity.

Before concluding, I would like to discuss the two rituals described in Lev. 14:1-9 and 10-18. The first ritual, employing wild birds, cedar, crimson yarn, hyssop and fresh running water, is a dispatch ritual, designed to remove impurity, and akin to the purification ritual of the Red Cow and the Yom Kippur scapegoat. This ritual carries away impurity regardless of whether the impurity source is a person's sin or severe physical impurity. Thus, it does not force us to conclude that the healed *metzorah* has sinned.

The second ritual, described in Lev. 14:10-18, mandates that the healed *metzorah* bring an *asham*/reparation offering, and, for Milgrom at least, the *asham* is telling evidence that the *metzorah* has sinned in some way. Before concluding that P does not attribute sin as the cause of a person's *tzaraat*, Milgrom's view must be considered.

Milgrom notes that the *asham* is brought for the sin of *maal*/profaning the holy. Milgrom notes that, for profaning the holy by presuming to perform the priestly function of officiating at the altar, King Uzziah is stricken with *tzaraat* (II Chron. 26). Moreover, Milgrom brings evidence from surrounding roughly contemporaneous cultures that profaning the holy can result in divine punishment. However, the story of King Uzziah is in Chronicles and is not a P story, assuming with Milgrom that P wrote before the exile. Moreover, while evidence from surrounding cultures may be helpful, we should not let it determine our understanding of P if there is evidence in P that conflicts with the ideology of the other cultures.

As Milgrom has explained, the *chattat*/purification offering and the *asham*/reparation offering, which is a subspecies of the *chattat*, purge the *Mishkan* of impurity caused by sin or by severe physical impurity. The purgative element is the blood of the *chattat* or the *asham*. Sin pollutes the *Mishkan* and so does severe physical impurity. Depending upon the severity of the impurity caused by the sin or the physical impurity, the purgative blood is placed on different parts of the *Mishkan* and purges the *Mishkan* of the impurity caused by the person's sin or severe physical impurity.

If we turn to the *metzorah*'s *asham*, we see that its blood is not placed on any part of the *Mishkan*, and, therefore, we must conclude that its blood is not being used to purge the *Mishkan* of impurity, whether caused by sin or by the *metzorah*'s severe physical impurity. We would more logically conclude that the blood of the *metzorah*'s *asham* is used to remove severe impurity from the healed *metzorah*.

The use of the *asham*'s blood also indicates that the *asham* is not intended to atone for sin. The priest daubs the *asham*'s blood on the *metzorah*'s ear, thumb, and toe (Lev. 14:14). This procedure copies the ritual used to ordain Aaron as high priest in which Moses daubs blood on Aaron's ear, thumb, and toe (Lev. 8:23). In Aaron's case, the blood is taken from the ram of ordination (8:22), and, quite reasonably, has the effect of ordaining Aaron as high priest. Why then is an *asham* used in the healed *metzorah*'s case? An *asham* is brought when something holy has been profaned by depriving HaShem of what is rightfully His. In the *metzorah*'s case, what has been profaned, what has HaShem been deprived of? The *metzorah* himself. The *metzorah* has been expelled from the camp because of his severe impurity. The *metzorah*, in effect, is no longer part of Israel, which is intended to be "a

Tazriah-Metzorah

kingdom of priests and a holy nation" (Ex. 19:6). The *metzorah*'s *asham* ritual is a rite of passage. Just as the blood of the ram of ordination elevates Aaron from Levite to high priest, so, too, the blood of the *asham* elevates the healed *metzorah* from the status of one excluded from the camp to that of one included in the camp. The *asham* is particularly appropriate because its purpose is to restore, to repair. Thus, rather than conclude that the *metzorah*'s *asham* evidences the *metzorah*'s sin, we should conclude that the *metzorah*'s *asham* serves to restore him to communion with God and the community of Israel.[1]

If P does not teach that the *metzorah* has been punished with *tzaraat* for having sinned, what then can we conclude? First, the priestly writers demonstrate a certain humility. They do not claim always to know the mind of God, to be able to determine in every case whether a person's illness is due to sin. Second, the priestly writers evidence a humanistic tendency, a willingness to accept that illness is not always a sign of divine displeasure because of sin, but is simply part of the human condition. Finally, the priestly writers demonstrate their compassion for the *metzorah*. They do not hold him up as a sinner, but rather simply as a person who has suffered a terrible illness and who, now having recovered, must be reintegrated into fellowship with God and with the community of Israel. This is a model which would serve us all well.

---

[1] Moses sprinkles blood from the whole burnt offering and the well-being offering on the Israelites when they enter into a covenant with God at Sinai (Ex. 24:5-8). Thus, applying blood to a person does not necessarily mean that the person has sinned. Rather, the blood ritual at Sinai seems to be part of a rite of passage. Might we say the same of circumcision?

Tazriah-Metzorah (II)

Richard Tupper

In *Metzorah*, we have the discussion of the impurity resulting from menstruation (Lev. 15:19-24). Many moderns who read these verses find them boring or irrelevant. Often the rituals surrounding menstruation are seen as shrouded in superstition, fear and oppression. Moderns say, menstruation is perfectly healthy and normal; why should a woman who menstruates be considered impure? What has she done wrong? Many conclude that the rituals surrounding menstruation reflect a male dominated priestly system that uses superstition to oppress women.

Of course, I do not share this view. A woman who menstruates and must subsequently purify herself has done nothing wrong. Various things that we do result in impurity, but it is not a sin to become impure. To bury the dead, to have sex and to give birth are all mitzvot, yet they render one impure. It is not a sin to become impure; it is only a sin not to purify yourself when the time is appropriate.

It's important to distinguish between impurity arising from physical causes (Lev. 12-15) and impurity arising from violating the mitzvot (Lev. 4-5) (see Milgrom, *Leviticus, ad loc.*). Every transgression of a prohibitive mitzvah pollutes the Tabernacle (ch. 4). In contrast, very few physical causes of impurity are severe enough to pollute the Tabernacle – the woman who gives birth, the person with the skin disease, the man and woman with the genital drip/flow. Persons who sin never undergo any sort of purification procedure because their sin pollutes not themselves but the Tabernacle. In contrast, persons with the physical impurities always undergo purification procedures because they are physically impure, though most likely their physical impurity has not polluted the Tabernacle. Most importantly, those who pollute the Tabernacle by sinning bring a *chattat*/purification offering *so that they may be forgiven* (Lev. 4:20, 26, 31, 35; 5:10, 13, 16, 18, 26), but this is never said of persons who bring a *chattat*/purification offering because of a physical impurity. Instead we are told that at the conclusion of the *chattat* that they are *pure* (Lev. 12:7, 8; 14:20). Similarly we are repeatedly told that the sinner brings a *chattat* on account of his/her sin (*e.g.*, Lev. 4:26, 35; 5:10, 13, 18, 26); in contrast, the person with the severe physical impurity brings a *chattat* on account of his/her impurity (*e.g.*, Lev. 15:15, 30). Consequently, it is clear that a person with a physical cause of impurity has not done anything wrong.

More importantly, it is a mistake to view mitzvot as tools of oppression. Ritual mitzvot spring from human need. HaShem sees a profound human need and responds to it by transforming the need into a mitzvah. For example, the *chattat* brought on account of sin (Lev. 4) is not a means of inducing guilt in people. Rather it is a means of relieving guilt. A person has sinned and feels a profound sense of guilt. How can s/he relieve her/himself of that guilt? The *chattat* is the answer to that need. The question we must ask concerning the menstruating woman is: what profound human need do the rituals surrounding the menstruating woman answer?

However, before answering that question, it is important to note that the system set out in Lev. 15 appears to relax the restrictions that encircled the menstruating woman in ancient Israel.

From other verses in the Tanakh (*e.g.*, Isaiah 30:22; Ezekiel 7:19-20; Lam. 1:7; Ezra 9:11) we get the definite impression that women who were menstruating were secluded, separated from the rest of society and even abhorred. We know that similar restrictions were observed in other cultures, some even existing today. In contrast, the menstruating woman in Lev. 15 remains at home with her family. She can prepare food, eat at the table and interact virtually normally with the family. True you cannot touch her skin without becoming impure. But, assuming she must observe rules similar to that observed by the man with the genital discharge, so long as she rinses her hands after tending to her bodily needs, she can touch you without rendering you impure (*cf.* Lev. 15:11).

Still, we must ask, why should a woman who menstruates go to a *mikvah* to purify herself? Isn't menstruation perfectly normal?

To answer that question, we must consider the context in which she lives. For modern women in industrialized Western societies, menstruation often begins before the age of 13 and continues past the age of 50. Women delay marriage until their 20's and then they have only two children, nursing, if at all, only briefly. As a result, these women will often menstruate several hundred times in their lives. Menstruation is the norm, not the exception.

In contrast, in the ancient world and in pre-industrialized societies today, women often begin menstruating as late as 17 years of age and end as early

Tazriah-Metzora (II)

as the ages of 35 to 40. For these women, earlier marriage, more pregnancies, lengthier and more frequent breastfeeding, poorer nutrition and less body fat severely curtail menstruation. In these societies, a woman will typically menstruate ten to thirty times in her entire lifetime, unless, of course, she is barren.

What is the one thing that women in the Bible want? Children! What does Rachel say to Jacob? Give me children or I will die! A modern woman who is 17 and unmarried or who is 40 and hopes she is done having children, if she misses her period, this is a cause for alarm. In contrast, in the ancient world, women longed to become pregnant as often as possible. For this woman, her menses did not signal normalcy but disappointment; her menses signaled that the seed within her had died. If this continued month after month, despair would deepen.

The *mikvah* answered this need. It separated women from the mini-death of their menses. The month of infertility was put behind them and they were inspired with new hope for a successful pregnancy.

Let me give one modern example of how the mitzvah is viewed positively. In the February 2002 issue of *Hadassah* magazine, a Linda Bergman wrote the editor, saying:

> The article "Old Springs, New Currents" in the December issue demonstrates how rituals can cut across lines of religious affiliation.
>
> As a Reform Jew, I never thought that the mikve would have any relevance to my life. That all changed last year when I was diagnosed with breast cancer, followed by surgery, mastectomy and then chemotherapy.
>
> As the end of the chemo approached, I felt myself becoming more anxious (a common feeling, I have since learned) and was searching for peace. I went to the mikve to mark the end of treatment and the beginning of being a physically and spiritually cleansed woman.
>
> It is the best thing I ever did for myself.

This woman gets it. If you told her that the *mikvah* was a tool of male, priestly oppression, she would laugh in your face. She knows that the *mikvah* answers a deeply rooted human need.

Leaves from the Garden

In a phrase striking to the modern ear, the prophet Jeremiah calls HaShem the "*mikvah* of Israel," a "*makor mayyim chayyim*/spring of living waters" (Jer. 17:13). Why is HaShem our *mikvah*? Because HaShem separates us from death and infuses us with hope for life and holiness through the mitzvot. Without HaShem there is no hope for holiness or life. And, after all, "hope" is what "*mikvah*" means, both for the menstruating woman and for all of us.

Achare Mot

Richard Tupper

> Lev. 18:22 (OJPS): "Thou shalt not lie with a male, as with a woman; it is abomination."
>
> Lev. 20:13 (OJPS): "And if a man lie with a male, as with a woman, both of them have committed abomination: they shall surely be put to death; their blood shall be upon them."

How does a person, such as myself, who takes the Torah seriously and believes that it should guide one's life deal with these verses when they are so contrary to one's experience? How do I reconcile these verses with my experience? I know Jewish homosexual couples who are fine people, people whose contribution to the community is invaluable. Must I view their union as an "abomination"?

There are different approaches when confronted with texts that contradict our experience and deeply held views. One is to ignore our experience and conform our views to what we see expressed in the Torah. So, I could say, "Yes, I know that I do not believe homosexual conduct is immoral but the Torah says it is, so I will change my belief." I suppose if I did this, I would begin considering the feasibility of instituting the death penalty for practicing Jewish homosexuals. However, I am not likely to change my views and therefore must consider another approach.

A second approach is just to excise these verses from the Torah. I believe that these are the only verses which on their face seem to condemn homosexual conduct, and it would be easy to excise them and solve the problem. However, excising texts is not part of our tradition (at least since the canon was fixed). Although we sometimes try to glide over troubling texts, we do not rip them out of the Torah. That is not how we do things.

A third approach is to interpret or reinterpret these verses. Interpretation and reinterpretation are an integral part of what we as Jews do. After all, the Torah "is not in heaven" (Deut. 30:12). And let's not kid ourselves, everyone who reads these verses is engaged in re/interpretation at some level. No one I know is advocating the death penalty for Jewish homosexuals.

There has been a variety of reinterpretations of these texts, none of which I find satisfying. (I am not claiming that I have reviewed all attempts to interpret these texts.) One Orthodox rabbi has advocated interpreting these verses very narrowly, *i.e.*, the prohibition against lying with a male, as with a woman, applies only to anal intercourse. Other rabbis have distinguished persons we would normally consider homosexuals from the person spoken of in the text on the grounds that the person in the text is assumed to be able to make a choice, but "modern" homosexuals are supposedly incapable of choice since they are under some sort of compulsion due to being genetically homosexual. Therefore, they supposedly are incapable of complying with the command. (Are they incapable of abstinence?) Others argue that these verses only apply to male homosexuals not female homosexuals (though the rabbis later disapprove of lesbian sexuality as well). Jacob Milgrom has argued that these verses apply only to Jewish men and to gentile men who live in Israel, but not to gentile men who live outside of Israel. (The Canaanites are vomited from Canaan for engaging in homosexual acts, the Egyptians engaged in the same conduct but were not expelled from the land of Egypt. Therefore the ban must only apply to *Eretz Yisrael*.)

I find none of these explanations acceptable. In my view, they are too niggardly. At best they tolerate homosexuals. If female homosexuals are "let off the hook" by stressing that the texts deal only with men, is that sufficient? Should we adopt an interpretation of these verses that implicitly condemns a homosexual union if only in quieter terms? Must we view homosexuals as somehow deficient because they are "incapable" of making a moral choice?

Some have focused on the texts' description of homosexual conduct as an "abomination/*toevah*." They argue that *toevah* is associated with cultic acts and therefore only homosexual conduct that is associated with paganism is condemned. Without going into detail, I am not persuaded that *toevah* is limited to cultic contexts. *Toevah* can include social mores (*e.g.*, the Egyptians' refusal to eat with Hebrews [Gen. 43:32]) and immoral conduct in general (*e.g.*, Prov. 6:16-19, haughtiness, lying, murder, *etc.*). In Ezekiel, the word "*toevah*" is used to describe the conduct of the people of Sodom, who you'll recall demanded of Lot that he surrender the two messengers visiting him so that they could "know" them (Gen. 19:5). However, when the prophet Ezekiel reviewed the faults of Sodom, he did not focus on the attempted homosexual rape of the messengers but proclaimed (16:49-50): "Behold, this was the iniquity of thy sister Sodom: pride, fullness of bread, and careless ease was in her and in her daughters; neither did she strengthen the hand of the poor and needy. And they were haughty, and committed abomination before Me; therefore I removed them when I saw it."

If limiting *"toevah"* to cultic acts does not solve the problem, will a broader reading of the texts be more fruitful?

One approach is to consider the abominable nature of homosexual conduct within the overall context of the Torah. Why would homosexual conduct be considered *toevah*/an abomination? For two reasons, I think. First, the first mitzvah was *pru urvu*, be fruitful and multiply (Gen. 1:28). A homosexual union would not result in children; it would have been viewed as a sexual union that was not part of fulfilling God's command, just as, not surprisingly, bestiality is condemned (Lev. 18:23). Men are viewed as naturally heterosexual and so for a man to lie with another man was going against God's creation and command to *pru urvu* at the completion of creation.

Second, homosexuality in the Tanakh is virtually unheard of. When it does occur, we see it in the context of rape, as for example in the Lot story. A similar instance occurs during the days of the judges when certain base men of Gibeah, populated by Benjaminites it seems, attempt to gang rape a visiting Levite, and, when unsuccessful, rape and kill his concubine instead. This outrage results in fierce intertribal war (Judges 19-20). Ham's viewing the nakedness of his father Noah – if read as intimating sexual union (and this is controversial) – again would be an instance of rape if we assume (correctly I think) that Noah was incapacitated due to being drunk (Gen. 9:22).

Homosexuality is also associated with the Canaanites, who were descended from Ham. The attempted gang rapists of Sodom were Canaanites. Homosexual conduct is forbidden in Lev. 18 and 20 precisely because it is connected with the immoral conduct of the Canaanites (18:3, 24-30; 20:23). I think it is fair to characterize Israel at the time as a very patriarchical society in which men tended to marry young. No doubt, homosexuality was severely suppressed. A man that engaged in homosexual conduct would quite likely be doing so while married and, given the suppression of homosexuality in Israel and its apparent practice among the people of Canaan, is it not at least possible that an Israelite homosexual male might turn to a Canaanite homosexual male? (After all, Judah is portrayed as believing he is having sex with a Canaanite prostitute when he has sex with Tamar (Gen. 38).) This too would be forbidden since it would be mixing Israel with the forbidden peoples of Canaan.

In short, homosexual conduct in those times would be seen as a sort of "anti-natural" immorality. Man by nature was viewed as expressing his sexuality only in a heterosexual manner and, therefore, homosexuality could be equated with bestiality. Homosexuality might also be seen as disloyalty to the Covenant since the homosexual union might involve a Canaanite. It would also cause social turmoil if, more likely than not, the man found committing homosexual acts was married.

Against this background, can we re/interpret these verses in Leviticus? The "reality" of homosexuals as portrayed – rarely – in the Tanakh is far different than our reality. We do not view homosexuals as rapists or as persons who are heterosexual by nature but choose to engage in homosexual acts. We view homosexuals as people who by nature are homosexual, and therefore it is natural for them to seek union with another man if they are male, or with another woman if they are female just as others of us who are heterosexual naturally seek union with the opposite sex. Fulfilling our natural sex drives is not intrinsically wrong, it is a part of our createdness.

If we accept that a homosexual is homosexual by nature just as a heterosexual is heterosexual by nature and that both are exhibiting God's good creation, what do we say about the fact that homosexual unions cannot result in children, cannot be part of *pru urvu*/be fruitful and multiply? But the barren woman also cannot be fruitful and multiply. True, sometimes, barrenness is a punishment for disobedience in the Tanakh. However, other times, it is just the way the woman is and not a reflection of the woman's morality. Even in the Torah, a woman's barrenness was not treated as an insuperable obstacle; natural avenues are used to circumvent it. Abraham contemplates that his servant Eliezer may be his son if Sarah was unable to produce children (Gen. 15:2), and Rachel gave her handmaid to Jacob to raise up children in her place (Gen. 30:3) as did Leah (Gen. 30:9). Today, we have other or similar avenues to circumvent the "natural" barrenness of homosexuals. Homosexual couples may adopt children; lesbian couples may use artificial insemination; both ways allow homosexual couples to be fruitful and multiply just as adoption and surrogates were used in the days of the patriarchs.

Moreover, Jewish homosexual unions need not involve disavowing being Jewish. Jewish homosexual men can unite with other Jewish homosexual men; Jewish homosexual women can unite with Jewish homosexual women. They can set up Jewish homes in which the Covenant will be observed and children raised, just as is done in the homes of Jewish heterosexuals. A

Achare Mot

Jewish homosexual couple can be just as vital a part of our community as a Jewish heterosexual couple.

Jewish homosexual couples are no different than Jewish heterosexual couples; both need our support and both desire and need to participate in the community.

How then to re/interpret these verses? I suggest that we reinterpret them as follows:

> Thou [*i.e.*, a heterosexual man] shalt not lie with a heterosexual male, as with a female; it is abomination.
> (Lev. 18:22)
> And if a heterosexual man lie with a heterosexual male, as with a female, both of them have committed abomination.
> (Lev. 20:13)

Can there be any justification for such a reading? Textually, I think not. But Jews throughout the centuries have dared to reinterpret seemingly clear texts to harmonize the Torah with their experience, the classic example being Hillel who reinterpreted the Torah's ban on lending money to accord with the times he lived in. We "presume" to reinterpret because it is our job to apply the Torah; as I noted earlier, the Torah "is not in heaven" but has been given to us to apply.

As a "proof text" for so bold a reinterpretation, I would point to Deut 23:2-5:

> 2 No one with crushed testes or lopped member shall come into the LORD's assembly.
>
> 3 No misbegotten [*mamzer*] shall come into the LORD's assembly. Even his tenth generation shall not come into the LORD's assembly.
>
> 4 No Ammonite nor Moabite shall come into the LORD's assembly. Even his tenth generation shall not come into the LORD's assembly ever.
>
> 5 Because they did not greet you with bread and water on the way, when you came out of Egypt, and for their hiring against you Balaam son of Beor from Aram Naharaim to curse you.

Leaves from the Garden

These verses caused serious problems later on. On their face, they seem to ban from joining the assembly: eunuchs (v. 2); *mamzerim* (children of illicit unions) (v. 3) and descendants of Moabites and Ammonites (v. 4).

How did these verses cause problems? Descendants of Moabites and Ammonites are doubly banned. Remember that the Moabites and the Ammonites descended from the illicit relationship between Lot and his two daughters (Gen. 19:30-38).

Why is that problematic? Because on its face it delegitimizes the entire Davidic line!

Ruth was a Moabite (Ruth 1:22) and from her descended David (Ruth 4:21-22). To make matters worse, Rehoboam was David's grandson and Solomon's son but his mother was an Ammonite, Naamah (1 Kings 14:21, 31; 2 Chron. 12:13). Thus, the entire Davidic line suffers from a triple whammy: they are descended from *mamzerim*, Moabites and Ammonites! And who is to descend one day from the line of David? The *moshiach* no less.

How could Deuteronomy's ban on *mamzerim*, Moabites and Ammonites be harmonized with the Davidic line? Should David be viewed as an illegitimate king as well as all his successors, including the *moshiach*?

The rabbis understood the ban on permitting into the congregation Moabites, Ammonites and *mamzerim* as a ban on intermarrying with them. In order to respect this ban but still preserve the legitimacy of the Davidic line, the rabbis viewed the ban as applying to Jewish women, but not men, intermarrying with Moabites and Ammonites (*Mishnah Yebamot* 8:3). By so doing, this interpretation spared the Davidic line since it was the product of a Jewish man, Boaz, marrying a Moabite woman, Ruth, and another Jewish man, Solomon, marrying an Ammonite woman, Naamah.

One problem with this inventive reinterpretation – Deuteronomy's ban on intermarriage with these sorts had already been interpreted as applying to Jewish men marrying foreign women.

In 1 Kings 11:1-4, King Solomon is taken to task for marrying the foreigners banned in Deuteronomy:

> 1 Now king Solomon loved many foreign women, besides the daughter of Pharaoh, women of the Moabites, Ammonites, Edomites, Zidonians, and Hittites;
> 2 of the nations concerning which the LORD said unto the children of Israel: 'You shall not go among them, neither shall they come among you; for surely they will turn away

your heart after their gods'; Solomon did cleave unto these in love.

3 And he had seven hundred wives, princesses, and three hundred concubines; and his wives turned away his heart.

4 For it came to pass, when Solomon was old, that his wives turned away his heart after other gods; and his heart was not whole with the LORD his God, as was the heart of David his father.[1]

Similarly, in Ezra (9:1; 10:3, 19, 44) and Nehemiah (13:1-3, 23-28), Deuteronomy's ban on intermarriage is applied to Jewish men who intermarried (and it seems it applied not only to intermarriage with Canaanites, Moabites, or Ammonites but to all foreign women).

Nevertheless, despite these passages, the rabbis were compelled to adopt the "narrow" reading of Deuteronomy that they did because otherwise the Davidic line would have been delegitimized.

I do not quarrel with the rabbis' interpretation. The Torah is not in heaven but has been given to us to interpret. In fact, I think the rabbis were preceded by the prophet Isaiah who had an even more "liberating" reading of these passages.

Prior to the exile, foreigners generally were viewed as not being permitted to join the congregation. In Lamentations 1:10, at the time of the exile, the prophet declares: "The adversary has spread out his hand upon all her treasures; for she has seen that the heathen are entered into her sanctuary, concerning whom You did command that they should not enter into Your congregation." The heathen here are not Canaanites, Moabites or Ammonites, but the Babylonians. So, I think it is fair to conclude that the prohibitions of mixing referred to in Deut. 7:3-4 and 23:2-4 had been broadened to include all foreigners by the time of Lamentations.

However, during the exile, it seems that foreigners did join themselves to Israel. Upon the return from captivity, the issue arose – what to do with the foreigners who had joined the congregation. Should they be put out as was done by Ezra and Nehemiah or was there another solution?

The prophet Isaiah in chapter 56 addresses the issue. Some modern commentators suggest it was written after the return from the exile. Traditional interpreters would not accept that contention but would, I think,

---

[1] This passage is referring to a similar passage in Deut., Deut. 7:3-4, as well as Deut. 23:4 and 9.

agree that chapter 56 prophesies about the conditions in Eretz Yisrael after the return from the exile.

What should be done with the foreigners who had joined themselves to Israel? One view was that such persons were banned from the congregation and therefore should be put out. Another view was that foreigners who had joined themselves to the congregation and sought to be part of the Covenant should be accepted.

What does the prophet Isaiah say? He boldly pronounces:

> 3 Neither let the alien that has joined himself to the LORD speak, saying: "The LORD will surely separate me from His people;". . . .
>
> 6 Also [concerning] the aliens that join themselves to the LORD, to minister unto Him, and to love the name of the LORD, to be His servants, every one that keeps the sabbath from profaning it, and holds fast by My covenant:
>
> 7 Even them will I bring to My holy mountain, and make them joyful in My house of prayer; their burnt-offerings and their sacrifices shall be acceptable upon My altar; for My house shall be called a house of prayer for all peoples.
>
> 8 Says the Lord GOD who gathers the dispersed of Israel: Yet I will gather others to him, beside those of him that are gathered.

The prophet Isaiah also has good news for the eunuchs. But before discussing the eunuchs let me say a few words by way of explanation.

Why did Deuteronomy 23:2 state: "No one with crushed testes or lopped member shall come into the LORD's assembly"? I think it is an expansion of the rule applied to offerings and priests. Offerings in general must be "without blemish" (*e.g.*, Lev. 1:3). Unacceptable blemished animals include animals with "crushed testes" (Lev. 22:24). (See, Milgrom, *Leviticus, ad loc.*) The same ban on blemishes applies to priests who, if they have blemishes, may not draw near the altar to offer sacrifices (Lev. 20:17-24). Among those banned are those with crushed testes (Lev. 20:20). In Deuteronomy, this ban on blemishes is expanded to exclude all persons with crushed testes not only from offering sacrifices but from joining the congregation (Deut. 23:2) – and, if they are excluded from the congregation, they are excluded from the Temple/Tabernacle.

When Israel was independent, it is unlikely that a man would have castrated himself, although perhaps he may have done so as part of another

Achare Mot

pagan cult. Excluding such a person from the assembly coincided with the general prescription of holiness applied to the people as a whole, extrapolating from offerings and priests, and also had the effect of denouncing pagan castration if it in fact existed.

However, after the exile the situation was different. The Hebrew word "eunuch" that was used in Isaiah applied to both governmental officials and to eunuchs. It seems that when foreigners were made part of the conquering power's governmental system, they may have been castrated. Hence the term eunuch would be applied both to governmental officials and to actual eunuchs. It seems that when Judah was conquered, her sons may have been made eunuchs and governmental officials of the ruling power. Upon their return to Eretz Yisrael, should they now be excluded from the congregation?

Just as the prophet Isaiah had good news for the covenant-keeping alien, so, too, he had good news for the eunuch. In many ways, I see a parallel between the situation of the eunuch and that of the modern day homosexual. The eunuch in post exilic times had been made a eunuch without choice just as a homosexual (and a heterosexual for that manner) does not choose his/her sexual orientation. Just as the eunuch was incapable of *pru urvu* because of his physical condition, so, too, the homosexual because of his/her physical condition cannot "naturally" fulfill *pru urvu*. Should either or both be excluded from the congregation because of their condition?

Concerning the eunuch, Isaiah answers emphatically "no" and goes beyond merely tolerating the eunuch. Isaiah resoundingly asserts the legitimate place of the eunuch in the congregation and in the Temple. I think Isaiah's words of liberation can apply equally to the homosexual and can speak to us today. Therefore, permit me the liberty of substituting the word "homosexual" for "eunuch" in Isaiah's message:

> 3 . . .[N]either let the [homosexual] say: "Behold, I am a dry tree."
> 4 For thus says the LORD concerning the [homosexuals] that keep My sabbaths, and choose the things that please Me, and hold fast by My covenant:
> 5 Even to them will I give in My house and within My walls a monument and a memorial better than sons and daughters; I will give them an everlasting memorial, that shall not be cut off.

If we can re/interpret the Torah so that its apparent ban on aliens does not reach the proselytes who have joined themselves to us, if we can re/interpret the Torah so that from its banned unions spring not only the Davidic line but the *moshiach* himself, if we can re/interpret the Torah so that its ban on those with crushed stones becomes a promise of a monument in My house and within My walls and a memorial better than sons and daughters that shall not be cut off, then we can also re/interpret the Torah so that the Jewish homosexual who holds fast to the Covenant and keeps the sabbaths is just as legitimate a part of the congregation of the LORD and as welcome a participant as every other covenant-keeping Jew.

Re/interpreting Lev. 18:22 and 20:13 does not excise them. They still have a message for people like me. I must respect how God created me and must respect sexual union. Particularly as a married man, sex for me is part of *pru urvu*. However, for the homosexual, we should not interpret these verses as demanding that a homosexual Jew defy how he has been created. Homosexual Jews like heterosexual Jews can and must respect the sexual act. We view sex as part of the expression of commitment between two people. Homosexual Jews just like heterosexual Jews can have faithful and committed relationships. They, too, have an obligation to hold fast to the Covenant, to live lives that exhibit Covenant keeping. They, just as heterosexual couples, have an obligation of fidelity and commitment to their partners.

No less than the proselyte, no less than the eunuch, no less than the *moshiach* himself, a Jew who is homosexual is a treasured part of the congregation of the LORD.

Pesach – The Fifth Son

Hillel Crandus

In the more than seventy seders that I have attended, the personalities of the four sons have always upstaged the fifth son, the one who says the *Ma Nishtana*. After the youngest impersonates him by singing his song, the fifth son recedes into the wings and disappears in the shadows. And yet he is the only worthy one of the whole lot.

The fifth son's curiosity fuels the seder. He senses all the differences around him: people are leaning, there are bitter herbs on the table, and the bread is bumpy and flat. These differences ignite the fifth son's imagination. As the authors of *A Different Night Haggadah* explain, "The four questions are not formulated as questions but as statements of wonder. [In the Mishna] they are stated by the parent, not by the child – and only if the child lacks the intelligence to ask [about this night's special quality] spontaneously!" The fifth child feels no skepticism: he steps through the opened portal of the seder, accepting that the night is different and ready to explore how it is so.

Yet the fifth son is not impetuous: he poses his question carefully, shaping his enthusiasm like a mensch. Though excited, the fifth son knows better than to blurt out disparate observations until he has gathered his impressions and looked for a pattern. First, he notices that one thing is different and looks around for more evidence of difference. Next, he crafts the main question – "Why is this night different from all other nights"– to give focus and form to his observations. Finally, he organizes his four original impressions beneath the focusing question in four parallel clauses. The fifth son resists the desire to blurt out his striking observations; instead, he shapes them into a pleasing form that adds to the discussion. It is no wonder that we have fit a song to his thoughts.

All of the four sons we speak of later are outsiders and full of unpleasant attitudes. Even the wise son, when he asks – "What are these testimonies, statutes, and judgments which the Eternal, our God hath commanded you?" – shows that he has not yet entered the seder, for his concern has only to do with rules. Hopefully, these details serve as a bridge for the son to find his way into the Exodus. There is no anxiety about the fifth son's entrance into the discussion of the Exodus from Egypt, however. By *Ma Nishtana*, he has already suspended his disbelief and made the imaginative leap required by the holiday. Accordingly, his question is followed by the story of the five rabbis of Bene-Berak, who lose track of time as they discussed the Exodus from Egypt. Like them, the fifth son escapes his own time and place to participate in the Exodus from Egypt.

The major reason the four sons overshadow the fifth son has to do with the enjoyment that comes from mixing and matching the pungent personalities of the wise, wicked, simple, and silent sons to our own personalities. While it is certainly enjoyable to discuss the fascinating psychologies that sojourn around a seder table, it is beside the point. As the fifth son suggests from the outset, the seder challenges us to leave ourselves behind so that we can travel backward to experience a miracle.

Pesach – Morid HaTal

Al Hobscheid

On the first day of Pesach, we begin the *Musaf Amidah* with the prayer for dew, called *"Tal,"* which is analogous to the recitation of *"Geshem"* (prayer for rain) at *Shemini Atzeret.* But unlike the days and months following *Shemini Atzeret* when the *daven*ers dutifully say *"mashiv haruach umorid hagashem"* ("You cause the wind to blow and the rain to fall") during the *g'vurot* (blessings extolling God's powers) of the *Amidah,* following Pesach there is usually silence (from my limited experience in Conservative shuls, very few recite *"morid hatal"* ["causes the dew to fall"]) in the said same spot. Being a recent convert to Judaism, I often have questions about various aspects of the religion, and that includes the text of the only *siddur* that I have ever used, the Conservative movement's *Siddur Sim Shalom.* So my question is why doesn't *Sim Shalom* contain the phrase *"morid hatal"* in the appropriate place in the *Amidah* when *Geshem* is not being recited? Is dew somehow less important to Conservative Judaism than rain?

To find my answer, I began at the source and submitted my question to the "Ask-a-Rabbi" page via the website of the Rabbinical Assembly (the publishers of the *Siddur Sim Shalom*) and then waited. Soon after, I received a pleasant and informative e-mail response from Rabbi Avram Israel Reisner. His first paragraph outlines the basic conflict:

> The matter of reciting *"morid hatal"* is subject to liturgical custom. Primarily, the Ashkenazi custom was not to recite it, whereas Sephardic custom was to do so, as reported in *Shulchan Arukh, Orach Chayyim* 114.3 where [Josef] Karo (Sephardic) indicates one should say it, and

Leaves from the Garden

[Moses] Isserles (Ashkenazic) appends a note that [states] "We, the Ashkenazim, do not say it."[1]

Because R. Isserles provided no reason for his curt rejoinder, Reisner continues:

> This goes back to the Talmud's discussion on *Ta'anit* 3a which accepts those who do and do not say "*morid hatal*," but specifically justifies those who do not by arguing that "*tal*," that is dew, is never withheld (unlike rain in time of drought), therefore, presumably, there is no real need to request it.[2]

I, unfortunately, do not see this as relevant. This line of reasoning would surely be applicable to the *shanim* benediction in the body of the *Amidah* when moisture is requested – we pray for moisture in their appropriate seasons, but I do not believe it applies to the *g'vurot*, which is a section that exclusively extols the powers of God and is not intended to be an appeal for the benefits of such power.

To summarize the next section of his response, Reisner details the *minhag* of "*morid hatal*" being followed by not only the Sephardim (as intimated from the Karo reference above) but also by the Chasidim, who were emulating the mystical elements of the Sephardi customs, and bringing that practice, geographically speaking, into the domain of the Ashkenazi, that is Eastern Europe (and later, elsewhere). Such developments have led to the overall inconsistent usage in various congregations all over the globe that has come down to this day and, ultimately, influenced the text of *Sim Shalom*.

Reisner concludes with the final decision of the editor of the *siddur*, Rabbi Jules Harlow:

> R. Harlow followed pure Ashkenazic custom and did not include "*morid hatal*." More recently, the *Siddur Sim Shalom for Shabbat and Festivals* (known colloquially as "slim shalom") circulated a preliminary edition without "*morid hatal*" which came under pressure to include it since some wished to use it. The Solomonic compromise, the text

---

[1] Personal correspondence with Rabbi Avram I. Reisner. The Rabbinical Assembly, March 29, 2001.

[2] *Ibid.*

Pesach – Morid HaTal

is Ashkenazic standard (no *"morid hatal"*), but there is an asterisk by "mashiv harua[c]h" referring one to a note below a line at the end of the page, which reads "some add '*morid hatal*'."[1]

So by going with the dominant (Ashkenazic) practice, *morid hatal* gets dropped. So one would get the distinct message from R. Reisner's response that dew isn't as important as rain. But I would argue strongly that this can hardly be true, given the geographic reality of *Eretz Israel*.

The noting of rain in winter and (for a few of us) dew in summer in the *g'vurot* is, of course, purely about the climate of Israel. These two passages exist for the sole reason to hearken ourselves (especially those in the galut) to that fundamental reality three times a day.

A little geography: the climate around the Mediterranean Sea is quite distinctive. Temperatures throughout the year remain fairly temperate and fairly consistent, being only slightly colder during the winter months. Its annual pattern of precipitation is marked by two distinctive seasons: a dry (not a drop of rain during the summer months) and a wet (certainly more precipitation during the wintertime, but only slightly so, relative to summer – we are not talking tropical rain forest here!). It is so distinctive a climate that it has been classified and named, ironically, the Mediterranean climate. It is the climate one would find in Southern California and South Africa, for example.

As we are quite aware, Israel by and large is an arid area with desert occupying a significant portion of its land mass. The appropriate and sufficient rains of winter are critical for the agricultural success of the region. It is no wonder that we Jews, as well as Israeli farmers, pray for it in the *Amidah*. But what about the summers? Do all the plants just shrivel up and die waiting for winter? Hardly, because there is an appropriate and sufficient water supply available while the sun beats down, and that supply is dew.

To explain further, it will be useful to know what dew is. Dew is, of course, water and it forms via condensation upon the surface of objects within a very shallow layer of air hugging the earth. Typically dew occurs at twilight, when air that has been heating all day suddenly loses solar radiation (the source of the heating). This heat energy radiates into outer space and, in the process, rapidly cools a thin layer of air adjacent to the Earth's surface.

---

[1] *Ibid.*

This cooling can be sufficient to condense gaseous water molecules into liquid form and deposit itself upon objects.

The dew-making process happens all over the world, but it is especially prominent in arid environments such as Israel. Because there are no clouds in deserts during the summer months to slow the loss of radiational heat back into outer space at day's end, the opportunity for dew to form increases significantly. Just as the rain is critical to replenish the aquifers, rivers and lakes of the region, the dew is the sole, critical supply of water during the long summer. One may not think of dew in the same league as rain when it comes to copious moisture, but if you have not experienced it, then you may be surprised. A friend related to me his first experience with Israeli dew in the Negev after a night's sleep in the desert. He woke up in utter amazement because he found himself fairly well soaked. It took him a few minutes to realize the source of the moisture was dew and not some practical joke played on him overnight!

And to emphasize further, I reviewed an article entitled, "Dew Absorption by Plants of Arid Zones," by Yoav Waisel, a botanist from the Hebrew University of Jerusalem. His study concentrated on the viability of different plants in the Negev in terms of dew. After many pages of exciting details on the methodology of measuring dew absorption capacity utilizing the vaunted "V-method," the research concluded that there are some indications, dependent on various factors, that dew is critical to the survival of these plants.[1]

I believe that the reason for the discrepancy of *Geshem* and *Tal* is based on a cultural disconnect influenced by a climatic disconnect. Does rain mean more to us than dew? For those Jews who do not live in arid regions, the whole dew thing is foreign. For us, dew is something you see on the car on some mornings – maybe thick enough to turn on the windshield wipers for a couple of passes. Dew is taken for granted here in the Midwest and, more importantly, in Eastern Europe, because its effects are negligible. We and the Ashkenazi don't see dew as significant, because the pattern of precipitation here and in Eastern Europe is fairly consistent throughout the course of the year (slightly wetter in summer). Agriculture here is not dependent on the

---

[1] Waisel, Yoav. "Dew Absorption by Plants of Arid Zones," *The Bulletin of the Research Council of Israel, Section D: Botany (Vol. 6D, No. 3),* April, 1958. Pp. 180-186.

Pesach – Morid HaTal

successful formation of dew, but totally bound to the cycles of rain, hence, Isserles' comment.

Oh by the way – why wouldn't we say *"mashiv haruach umorid hatal"*? Because the coming of dew is not delivered by global circulation patterns as is the rain. Also, the presence of wind would increase the likelihood of evaporation and subsequently decrease the ability of dew to sustain itself. Thus, one would not want to mention wind during the dry season when trying to preserve as much moisture as possible!

My initial goal for all of this was to make an appeal to the Rabbinical Assembly to include *morid hatal* as a full-fledged part of the *g'vurot* in future editions of their *siddur*. I also intended this as an appeal to members of my congregation who do not normally include *"morid hatal"* to consider adopting the practice. The significance of dew to our Jewish heritage cannot be underestimated. The manna that sustained *b'nei Yisrael* in their wanderings was transported by God via the morning dew – an obvious recognition of dew's power.

In fact it is the manna story that underscores for me the spiritual dimension of dew. As the Torah says in *Shemot*, the manna came *down* to the people. *Tal* was understood by the rabbis as water that comes down from above, similar to the process of rain. Both dew and rain are part of the "waters from above" as described in the creation story of *Bereshit*. But as has been noted previously, the scientific process behind dew is really the opposite of the rabbinic view. Dew is formed as heat is radiated *up* from the earth. In a sense, if we extend this "directional" framework, rain is a downward process and dew, an upward one. This apparent duality of *Geshem* and *Tal* can provide us a framework for increasing our *kavana*, our awareness of God, during the *Amidah*. We can believe that for half a year the falling of rain symbolizes God's goodness blessing us; and for the remainder of the year, the rising of dew represents our goodness being sent to God. It is a reciprocal relationship in which both parties are crucial participants and without which creation would have no meaning. We, as Jews, cannot allow ourselves to become disconnected from the design of creation. To leave *"morid hatal"* out of the *daven*ing is to not acknowledge the mutual love that defines our relationship to God.

Shabbat shalom.

Kedoshim[1]

Richard Tupper

In Lev. 19, the children of Israel are instructed to "be holy," and in Lev. 18 they are instructed not to pollute the land. My *davar* addresses a question that lurks in both chapters and that is, why is the land of Canaan, later called Israel, never referred to as "holy"? Even though the people are told to be holy and instructed not to pollute the land, nowhere in these chapters are we ever told that the land is holy or that it, like the people, should be sanctified. In fact, nowhere in the Torah is the land of Israel ever referred to as holy.[2] To answer this question we must first look at the relationship between holiness and impurity in the Torah, particularly in Leviticus.

ulehavdil ben hakodesh uven hachol uven hatame uven hatahor

"You must distinguish between the sacred [or "holy"] and the common, and between the impure and the pure" (Lev. 10:10). This is part of HaShem's instruction to Aaron on priestly duties and one could argue that the principles encapsulated in this verse are what Leviticus is all about. Many of us, however, are not accustomed to viewing the world through this paradigm of the holy and the common, the impure and the pure, and so a review of the basics of this paradigm can be helpful. To save time, I will describe this

---

[1] This *d'var Torah* is based on the work of Jacob Milgrom, *Leviticus*, and his more recent, shorter commentary, *Leviticus: A Book of Ritual and Ethics* (Fortress Press 2004). Insights herein are his; mistakes are my own.

[2] The sole apparent exception in the Tanakh is Zech. 2:16 (Engl. 2:12); however, Moshe Weinfeld argues that the strip of land referred to is around the Temple in Jerusalem. See his *The Promise of the Land: The Inheritance of the Land of Canaan by the Israelites* (Berkeley 1993), p. 203.

paradigm using a number of what I am labeling "rules," which set out the basic structure of the paradigm, but I will not make this *d'var Torah* even longer by a detailed review of proof texts.

The paradigm in Lev. 10:10 sets out four states: the holy, the common, the impure and the pure. Commonness and purity are similar in that commonness is simply the absence of holiness and purity is simply the absence of impurity. Preliminarily then, I will formulate the first rule of the paradigm as: the common and the pure are inert, whereas the holy and the impure are dynamic.

If something that is common touches something holy, the common object has no effect on the holy object. The common object does not profane (*i.e.*, make common) the holy object; it remains holy. Similarly, if something that is pure touches something impure, the pure object does not purify the impure object; it remains impure. Thus we see that the common and the pure are inert, having no effect upon the holy and the impure.

In contrast, however, the holy and the impure are dynamic, and the more holy or the more impure something is, the greater its effect on the common and the pure. True, if something that is holy touches something that is common, there is generally no effect. But if something that is described as "most holy" touches something common, the most holy object by contact sanctifies or makes holy the common object. Thus, for example, a common object becomes holy whenever it touches the outer altar or the furnishings of the *Mishkan* that are described as "most holy" (*e.g.*, Ex. 30:29). Impure objects impart impurity to pure things by contact and generally the greater the impurity of the impure object, the greater the impurity it imparts to the pure object. If Reuven touches a corpse, which is forever impure, he becomes impure. But, assuming he follows the prescribed purification rituals, his impurity lasts only seven days (Num. 19:11). If I, however, touch Reuven while he is impure, I become impure, but my impurity lasts only until evening (Num. 19:22).

So, let me restate the first rule as follows: The common and the pure are inert, but the most holy sanctifies the common and the impure pollutes the pure.

This first rule, however, must be qualified by a second rule because, unlike objects, humans do not become holy by contact with the most holy. For humans, unless they possess a very high degree of holiness, contact with the most holy can be lethal. Thus, whoever even looks at the ark without its covering dies (*e.g.*, Num. 4:20). Humans, however, can become holy. For

Kedoshim

humans and also objects there is another way to become holy: humans and objects can become holy by choice, either divine choice or human choice.

If, for example, a person consecrates a sheep to the *Mishkan* by means of a vow, the animal thereby becomes holy (Lev. 27:2, 9), but obviously the rest of one's flock does not. At the conclusion of the Creation story, HaShem distinguishes the seventh day from the preceding six days by blessing it and sanctifying it (Gen. 2:2-3). The seventh day thus becomes holy but the other days remain common.

There is an apparent exception that, however, proves the rule. Aaron and his sons are sanctified when Moses anoints them with the blood from the ram of consecration and the holy anointing oil (Ex. 29:20-21). Thus, just as the furnishings of the *Mishkan* are sanctified when Moses anoints them with the holy anointing oil (Ex. 30:25-29), so too Aaron and his sons become holy through anointing. However, we are explicitly told in Ex. 29:44 that, in fact, it is HaShem who sanctifies the *Mishkan*, its furnishings, and Aaron and his sons as well. Aaron and his sons are holy because HaShem has chosen them from among all the people to serve as priests. Thus, it is HaShem's choice that sanctifies Aaron and his sons; the anointing is simply the ritual that demonstrates this choice.

We now come to the third rule: the more holy something is, the more susceptible it is to impurity. A woman who gives birth to a son is impure for seven days (Lev. 12:2). During this period, the woman can impart impurity to other persons and things. However, after undergoing purification rituals on the seventh day for a son, the woman no longer imparts impurity to common things or persons, but for the next thirty-three days until her final purification procedures she still may not go to the *Mishkan* or come into contact with holy things (Lev. 12:4). Although the purification rituals have substantially reduced her impurity so that her impurity can no longer pollute the common, she cannot go near holy things since the holy is more susceptible to impurity than the common and would be polluted by contact with her.

A corollary of Rule 3, namely that the more holy a thing is, the more susceptible it is to impurity, is that the more common (in the technical sense) a thing is, the less susceptible it is to impurity. Impliedly, if something is entirely common, it is immune to impurity. If something is entirely common, the only way it can become impure is if it is first made holy. It is then susceptible to impurity. Thus the common and the holy are pure, unless of course they have been polluted. Consequently, we can deduce that the true antithesis of holiness is not commonness but impurity.

Finally, I would like to make one more distinction and that is between ritual impurity and moral impurity.

Ritual impurity arises from natural causes – death, the emission of semen, a woman's loss of menstrual or lochial blood, and a very limited number of physical diseases associated with death or fluids oozing from sexual organs. There is nothing sinful about becoming ritually impure; it is often unavoidable and also often a mitzvah – such as procreating, burying the dead, and purifying those who have become impure by contact with a corpse. However, it is a sin to come in contact with the holy while impure (Lev. 7:20-21) and to delay purification when one is permitted to purify oneself (Num. 10:20). Moreover, ritually impure persons can pollute others (*e.g.*, Lev. 15:5). Such persons must similarly undergo purification rituals and, until purified, must not come into contact with the holy (*cf.* Lev. 22:5-6).

In contrast, certain sins,[1] some of which are the focus of Lev. 18, defile a person (vv. 25, 30), but while his sins defile him and the land of Israel (v. 25), he does not defile others. Furthermore, no physical purification rituals are prescribed for a person whose moral sins pollute him and the land. His impurity is purified, perhaps, by sincere repentance or punishment or both (Lev. 16, 26). The land's purity is restored by exile of the people and the passage of time (Lev. 18, 20, 26).

Thus we have Rule 4: Ritual impurity is not sinful but the person who is ritually impure defiles others by contact; in contrast, moral impurity by

---

[1] Milgrom argues that in the "Holiness Source" ("H"), only certain sins pollute the land: specified sexual sins, Molech worship and consulting the dead, and homicide. However, Lev. 20:22 states: "You shall heed *all* my statutes and *all* my regulations and do them, so that the land to which I bring you to settle in will not vomit you out" (emphasis supplied). I believe the author of this strand of H intended the reference to "all my statutes and all my regulations" to refer at the very least to those included not only in Lev. 20 but also in Lev. 18 and 19. The laws set out in Lev. 19 extend far beyond the three types of sins identified by Milgrom. Hence, I believe that this strand of H in Lev. 20:22 has expanded the more limited polluting sins identified by an earlier strand of H and asserts that the land will be polluted and induced to vomit out the people whenever they consistently violate God's commands. This is picked up in Lev. 26 where the people's continual violation of the covenant's mitzvot results in their expulsion from the land. (Compare Num. 15:22-29 which mandates a purification offering whenever Israel violates any mitzvah, not just a prohibitive mitzvah as in Lev. 4.)

Kedoshim

definition arises from sin, and it pollutes the land and the sinner, but the sinner does not pollute others.

These then are the four rules that I will apply when looking at Lev. 18 and 19.

> Rule 1: The common and the pure are inert, but the most holy sanctifies the common, and the impure pollutes the pure.
>
> Rule 2: Humans do not become holy by contact with the most holy, but humans and objects as well can become holy by choice, either divine choice or human choice.
>
> Rule 3: The more holy a thing or a person is, the more susceptible is that thing or person to impurity.
>
> Rule 4: Ritual impurity is not sinful but the person who is ritually impure defiles others by contact; in contrast, moral impurity by definition arises from sin, and it pollutes the land and the sinner, but the sinner does not pollute others.

If we turn to Lev. 18, we see that the Israelites are instructed not to follow the practices of the land of Egypt nor those of the land of Canaan (v. 3). The Egyptians and the Canaanites share a common ancestor, Ham (Gen. 10:6), and it was Ham who sinned by looking upon his father Noah's nakedness (Gen. 9:22), a sin that perhaps foreshadows sins listed in Lev. 18. Lev. 18 equates the customs of the Egyptians with those of the Canaanites, but there is a twist. We are told that the sins of the Canaanites polluted the Canaanites and the land, and therefore the land would vomit them out (Lev. 18:24-28). But if the Egyptians committed the same sins as the Canaanites, why are the Egyptians not vomited out of the land of Egypt? The implied rationale is this: the land of Canaan is more susceptible to impurity than is the land of Egypt. From this we can deduce one of two things: either the land of Egypt is completely common and therefore immune to impurity or, at the very least, it is far less susceptible to impurity than is the land of Canaan. Otherwise, the land of Egypt at some time would have vomited out the Egyptians for polluting the land by their immorality just as the land of Canaan vomits out the Canaanites and will in the future vomit out the Israelites. Implicit in this explanation is the conclusion that the land of Israel is holier than the land of Egypt.

That the land of Israel is holy as compared with the land of Egypt and all other lands for that matter is evident not only from the different way that the land of Israel reacts to impurity. As described above, holiness can be established by divine choice. Several verses in Leviticus tell us that the

Israelites belong to God, and, therefore, God intends for them to be holy. Lev. 25:55 states: "For it is to me the Israelites are slaves. They are my slaves whom I freed from the land of Egypt. I am YHWH your God." Similarly, Lev. 20:24 states, "I YHWH am your God who has set you apart from other peoples." Consequently, we read in Lev. 20:26, "You shall be holy to me, for I YHWH am holy; therefore I have set you apart from other peoples to be mine." Just as the people of Israel belong to God and therefore must be holy, so too the land of Israel belongs to God. Lev. 25:23 states in relevant part: "Furthermore, the land must not be sold beyond reclaim, for the land is mine." If the land belongs to God, then in the priestly system it therefore must be kept pure because implicitly it is holy.

Based upon the foregoing, we see the dynamic relationship between God, the Israelites, the land of Israel and the mitzvot. Because the Israelites and the land of Israel belong to God, God intends for both to be holy and undefiled by sin. We are told explicitly that the Israelites through their sins pollute themselves and the land (Lev. 18:24-30). In contrast, by keeping God's mitzvot, the Israelites sanctify themselves (Lev. 20:7-8) and the land remains unpolluted. Thus, the land serves as a barometer of Israel's obedience. If Israel disobeys God's mitzvot, they defile themselves and the land until ultimately the land vomits them out. If they obey God's commands, they sanctify themselves. Moreover, by observing the mitzvot, the Israelites explicitly (Lev. 18:27-28) maintain the purity of the land. We know from the above that the land is holy because it is more sensitive to impurity than other lands and because it is peculiarly God's land. However, the Torah never states that the land is holy.

I conclude that the Torah never makes explicit the land's implicit holiness because the Torah is focused on the holiness of the people. Therefore the Torah stresses how the people's sins pollute the land because the land's pollution serves as a measure of the people's holiness, *i.e.*, their obedience to HaShem's mitzvot. God's explicit plan is that the people of Israel should through obedience become holy, living on a land that is not polluted by their sins (Lev. 18-20). Of course, implicitly the land HaShem has chosen for us to live on is holy or it would not be so susceptible to the polluting effects of sin. (Parenthetically, I would add that it is a terrible irony that so many of different religions have shed so much innocent blood over their claims to this holy land because the shedding of innocent blood is one of the chief polluters of the land (Num 35:33-34).)

If God's focus is on our holiness and not the land's, then the fact that we in the Galut do not live in Israel should not distract us from God's primary

Kedoshim

objective – that we should become holy by observing the mitzvot. I would like, however, to draw a further lesson. God intends to be holy all that belongs to Him. The Psalmist tells us (24:1): "The earth is HaShem's and the fullness thereof, the world and they that dwell therein." Since God intends His land to be pure and His people holy, then God intends ultimately that the whole world be pure and its inhabitants holy. But the purity of the earth and the holiness of its inhabitants depend upon the conduct of people who live on it.

Emor[1]

Richard Tupper

Continuing on his personal jihad against the popular notion that rabbinic midrash consists of unbridled rabbinic eisegesis, Ben Sommer last Shabbat focused on the word "shabbat" in Lev. 23:15 in *parshat Emor* to defend the rabbis of the midrash. In his view, rabbinic midrash is built upon two pillars: the rabbis' incredibly close reading of the Tanakh as a divinely authored organic whole, and their desire to harmonize the Written Torah with the Oral Torah. Ben focused on the age-old chestnut of just what does "shabbat" mean in Lev. 23:15, where we are told to begin counting the *omer* after "the shabbat." Some believe that "shabbat" here means the weekly Shabbat during Pesach (Samaritans and Karaites), while others believe it is the weekly shabbat after Pesach (Qumran and Boethusians – Jacob Milgrom suggests that Boethusians = beth Essenes and hence they are the same). Others believe the shabbat refers to the day of rest of the first day of the festival (Pharisees) or the seventh day of the festival (Peshitta and modern Falashas).

Ben championed the reading of the Pharisees (*i.e.*, the rabbis) that the counting begins on the day after the first day of Pesach, in other words, on the 16th of Nisan. However, Ben defended their position in, dare I say, an unorthodox way.

Ben argued that the rabbis read the word "shabbat" in this somewhat unusual way because they were harmonizing the text with a tradition that had been observed and handed down to them, *Torah sheh-b'al peh*. But where could have come this notion that "shabbat" meant the first day of the festival?

---

[1] What follows is not a *d'var Torah* offered at Shabbat services but rather a critique published in the Minyan's newsletter of a *davar* offered by Minyan member Benjamin Sommer.

Leaves from the Garden

Relying upon an argument by Michael Fishbane (see, *Biblical Interpretation in Israel* [Oxford 1985], pp. 149-151), Ben argued that "shabbat" in Lev. 23:15 is related to the ancient Akkadian word "*shaputtu*" which means "full moon." Thus, beginning counting after the "shabbat/*shaputtu*" would mean, in consonance with age-old practice and rabbinic interpretation, beginning on the 16th of Nisan. And so, Ben concluded, the rabbinic interpretation was not unbridled eisegesis but relied upon a close reading of the text (including Josh. 5:10-12 and Num. 33:3) and tradition founded upon Torah *sheh-b'al peh*.

However, there are several problems with this theory, as Ben himself would acknowledge. If in Lev. 23:15 the first "shabbat" appearing in the text from which we are supposed to count means "full moon," what does the word "shabbats" means later in the same verse where we are told to count seven shabbats? No one thinks you count seven months. Moreover, this passage is thought by many modern scholars to reflect the writing of the source designated "H," which, if you are a Knohlite like Ben, you date to Hezekiah or later. Why would someone writing in Hezekiah's day adopt this ancient usage of "shabbat" as "full moon," and, if so, why make it so confusing by having shabbat also bear the traditional meaning of seventh day in the same verse?[1] Furthermore, some scholars do not think that the word "shabbat" in Hebrew ever meant "full moon." (See, Milgrom, *Leviticus*, pp. 2058-2059, citing authority.) Finally, whatever the tradition it was that the rabbis were observing, many scholars, my guess even Ben himself, believe that originally the counting was not tied to Pesach by full moon, shabbat, or festival. Originally, people began counting "when the sickle is first put to the standing grain" (Deut. 16:9), and then fifty days later brought their offering to their local shrine. Because harvest time varied by geographic location, Shavuot would be celebrated at different times throughout the land depending upon when the harvest began. The lack of uniformity did not matter until, presumably, the days of Josiah, when the local shrines were abolished, and hence everyone was required to show up in Jerusalem at the same time.

---

[1] Subsequently in support of his position, Ben pointed out "that *Mishnah Megillah* 3.4 does exactly that: its first sentence uses the word 'Shabbat' to mean 'Sabbath,' and the second uses it to mean 'week.' Context makes clear what it means in each place."

Emor

Why my long harangue? (*Filler!*) Because if we cannot equate "shabbat" with "full moon," then we must think twice about what it means to say that the rabbis are preserving *Torah sheh-b'al peh*. Counting from the day after Pesach is *Torah sheh-b'al peh*, but it is tradition that evolved over time. In other words, the custom of beginning to count after the first day of Pesach is one that grew and, pardon the pun, had not been carved in stone. Just as changes in the society influenced how the counting was done, so, too, these changing social conditions influenced how the rabbis subsequently, and Ben himself, read the text.

If midrash arises from the interaction among Israel, Torah, and HaShem, then we can't ignore the human element. The questions the rabbis asked, the answers they found, and the answers they found acceptable were based in part upon the world in which they lived. The same is true for Ben and for all of us. Ultimately however, midrash eludes any comprehensive explanation because it involves not only Torah and Israel, but HaShem as well.

Behar

Joan Katz

Growing up on the cusp of egalitarianism, my educational exposure to the *haftarah* was limited to training by a *chazzan* who grudgingly prepared girls for the short-lived custom of a Friday evening recitation of a *haftarah*. The experience left me rather uninformed and uninterested in *haftarot*.

In contrast, my father-in-law, Henry Mosbacher, "Opi," relishes preparing the *haftarah*. So I thought in honor of his 85th birthday, which we are celebrating today, I would take the opportunity to learn more about *haftarot*.

I hope those of you with better *bar* or *bat Mitzvah* training will indulge me, or correct me where I err.

What does the word *haftarah* mean? Unlike the rumors in my Hebrew school, it does not mean a half-baked or secondary Torah. It does not, in fact, have anything do with the word Torah. The name comes via the Aramaic "*Aftara*/leaving off" from the Hebrew root *peh-tet-reish* meaning discharge of obligation or adjournment, in other words: successfully finishing the Torah-reading ceremony.

According to traditional sources, reading from the prophets began in the time of Antiochus Epiphanes IV in the second century BCE. As part of his oppression which eventually fostered the Maccabean revolt, the king banned the public reading of the Torah, and the *haftarah* was substituted.

Combining verses from Torah and Prophets followed by a *drash* or homily is already referred to in the Christian Bible and discussed in the Mishnah. The combination reinforces the three sources of Divine authority: written law, prophecy and oral tradition.

In earlier times, the person called to read the *haftarah* would himself choose the prophetic text to read. The idea was to select verses with some loose linguistic or thematic connection to the Torah portion. The reader could chant relevant passages from any single book of the prophets, the *Trei Asar* /12 Minor Prophets being considered one book as it was written on one scroll. The reader could skip forward to leave out the irrelevant parts, as long as he did not waste too much time finding his place. The custom we follow here in the Minyan of adding a few verses from a second *haftarah* on occasions when two special ones would be read, for example when *Shabbat Shekalim* is *Rosh Chodesh*, is apparently an old one – but was a subject of heated debate regarding skipping around.

Suggestions for special Shabbatot like *Rosh Chodesh*/the New Month were discussed in the Talmud, but the annual cycle of *haftarot* was fluid long after the Torah reading cycle was set. Though most of the *haftarot* were agreed upon by the end of the Gaonic period, about 1,000 years ago, only 500 years ago, the *Shulchan Aruch* was still actively discussing the rules for choosing *haftarah* text. One contemporary authority suggests, although it is no longer the custom, that it would not be "wrong" for someone to choose their own text even today. This tradition is reflected in the many variations that are still in place in our time in different communities.

Reading the *haftarah* has not become democratic in the sense that an *aliyah* to the Torah has. While a shift took place allowing one honored with an *aliyah* to designate a reader, chanting the *haftarah* is still almost universally reserved for the *maftir* himself. Though generally read from printed books, some communities prefer a special *haftarah* scroll written with punctuation and trope. In western communities, the reading of the *haftarah* has become the most common ground for *b'nei Mitzvah* to prove their abilities.

Now, a few statistics: The Shabbat *haftarah* is a minimum of twenty-one verses, fifteen on a festival, parallel to the minimum number of verses to be read from the Torah. Only two complete books are read: Jonah on Yom Kippur and Obadiah on *VaYishlach*. The most commonly read selections are from the books of Isaiah, Jeremiah and Ezekiel, although my favorites are from *Niviim Rishonim*/the Early Prophets. Besides Shabbat and *Yom Tov*, a *haftarah* is read on fast days in the afternoon, at *minchah*, with an abbreviated blessing, and in most communities on *Yom HaAtzmaut*/Israel's Independence Day in the morning, the presence or absence of *brachot*/blessings still signaling the crossroads of politics and theology. The *haftarah* blessings themselves can be found in the 9th century *siddur*/prayerbook of Rav Amram Gaon.

*   *   *

Behar

Rereading the context for the *haftarah* in the *siddur*, it became clear to me that the *haftarah* is not just tacked onto the Torah reading; it is part of a liturgical framework.

Let's review the sequence:

After the seventh *aliyah*, the gabbai recites the *Hatzi Kaddish*.

A *kaddish* generally serves as an intermission between "acts" or parts of the service.

Next, the *maftir* is called up for an *aliyah*. The *maftir*, or "the one who concludes," recites the *Barchu* as part of the blessing on reading Torah, a portion is read from the scroll itself, followed by the ending blessing.

The *magbiha* and *golel* then lift and dress the Torah, creating a mini-procession paying honor to the Torah, not unlike when it is taken out and returned to the Ark.

The *maftir* recites the introductory *haftarah* blessing, its message reinforcing the legitimacy of the prophets' words alongside those of Moshe. Next s/he reads the *haftarah*, concluding with four more blessings.

Seven blessings are spoken aloud in total by the *maftir*, perhaps parallel to the seven *aliyot* to the Torah.

Then we recite the *Ashrei*, as in the morning and afternoon *tefillot*/prayers, and conclude with various prayers for well being. Following that we put the Torah away, pausing with another intermission, a *Kaddish Shalem*.

Imagine here a "mini-*tefillah*" with all the essential elements: *Barchu*, seven blessings like an *Amidah*, Torah, a Torah procession, Prophets, a *drash* or sermon, an *Ashrei*, concluding compositions, set off by a *Kaddish* on either end.

Certainly, if this is the case, it is handy for those who hold by the "tradition" of coming to *shul* very late!

* * *

What do the *haftarah* blessings say?

They establish a continuum from the word of God in the Torah, to His word through prophecy on to establishing His kingdom through David, all the while reminding us that His word is true, *ne'eman*.

Several of the expressions in these blessings drew me to the notion that the seven blessings the *maftir* says could instead be related to the seven blessings of the Shabbat *Amidah*. The vocabulary resonates.

Rereading the concluding four *haftarah* blessings and Shabbat *Shacharit Amidah* side-by-side, the thematic and language parallels started jumping off

Leaves from the Garden

the page. Though the concepts were the same, the two points of view reflect a major shift of time frame. The *Amidah's* frame of reference is the past, while the *haftarah* blessings focus on the future.

I would like to go over just the highlights with you.

I am handing out a chart of the seven *brachot*/blessings of the Shabbat *Shacharit Amidah* on one side, with the blessings said after the *haftarah* in the next column, which we will review together. The translations are thematic rather than literal. (Review chart that follows.)

Comparison of Shabbat *Shachrit Amidah* to Concluding *Haftarah* Blessings

Bracha	*Amidah*	*Haftarah*
I אבות Ancestors	מגן אברהם Blesses God the protector of the Patriarchs	מגן דוד Stands by His Word to His Prophets and protects David
II גבורות Creative Force	מחיי המתים Changes the world for good and affects even the end of life/time	המדבר ומקים Whose every word will come true
III קדושת השם Holiness of God	ה' הקדוש God who is holiness	בשם קדשך Swore to David by Your holy name
IV קדושת היום Holiness of the day A Joy	ישמח Brings Moshe joy with the gift of Torah and Shabbat	שמחינו Bring us joy through Elijah your prophet and the kingship of David
B Recipients	לא נתתו Won't give other peoples the Shabbat or Torah as an inheritance	לא ינחלו Won't let a foreign king inherit Israel's throne, or future
C Shabbat	מקדש השבת Sanctifies the Shabbat	מקדש השבת Sanctifies the Shabbat
V עבודה Restores Zion	המחזיר שכינתו לציון Returns to Zion restoring Temple worship	משמח ציון Brings joy to Zion by restoring hope for the future

Behar

VI הודאה *A* Thank You	מודים אנחנו לך Thanks we give You	אנחנו מודים לך We thank You
B Praise	שמך .. נאה להודות Your Name is good and wonderful to praise	יתברך שמך בפי כל חי Your Name will be praised by all living creatures forever
VII שלום Peace	שלום Gives us all good things and brings peace	Gives all good things and brings messianic age – which is *peace*

In short, the blessings after the *haftarah* reading seem to compose a short prayer reflecting the major themes of the Shabbat *Amidah* – and the person chanting it also utters seven blessings, the same number.

I read one suggestion that this seven blessing formulation was, in fact, an alternate version of the Shabbat *Amidah* preserved from a time before the *Amidah* was formalized in Yavneh. It was preserved in the same tradition that includes different blessings before and after the *Shema* in *Shacharit* and *Aravit*, morning and evening. We learned another example here a few weeks ago from Richard Tupper: the two formulations of *Modim Anachnu Lach* in the *Amidah*.

This "*Amidah*" preserves a view for the future of Judaism with a different emphasis. By shifting the perspective from looking back to looking forward, this other vision favors messianism over law and prophets, and kings over patriarchs and Moshe.

Just as the prophetic message often viewed Israel's actions "long term" on the stage of history, so, too, do these blessings take the long view on God's promises being kept. This is language of certainty, expectancy and hope.

The "keyword" to me is *ne'eman*/faithful/believable/trustworthy/reliable, a word picked up from the *Amidah*, but expounded here. We are reminded to not lose our trust in God just because His predictions have not happened yet. Every word of God's true prophets is His word, and He will stand by them unshakably until it is the right moment to deliver.

I want to end by thanking my father-in-law for all he teaches us by his example, and for so often sharing the pleasures of Shabbat with us.

Opi, *ad meah v'esrim*/to one-hundred and twenty.

Shabbat shalom.

Behukkotai

Liz Bennett

Several weeks ago when I was sitting in this room listening to *parshat Kedoshim*, I read the *Etz Hayim* commentary on the *parsha*. In the context of thinking about the *d'var Torah* I was to give today, the words jumped out at me and summarized what I had been thinking: I would like to read a little of the commentary (p. 693):

> To be holy is to rise to partake in some measure of the special qualities of God, the source of holiness. Holiness is the highest level of human behavior, human beings at their most Godlike.

The commentary (pp. 693-694) further reflects in the second *pasuk* of the *parsha* that the commandment to be holy is in the plural "*kedoshim teheeyou*":

> In Hebrew, this summons is phrased in the plural, implying that the capacity for holiness is not restricted to spiritually gifted people; anyone may attain holiness. God does not demand the impossible. The plural phrasing suggests further that holiness is most achieved in the context of a community. It is difficult for a person to live a life of holiness without others. . . . When a community dedicates itself to the pursuit of holiness, its members support and reinforce each other.

It is in the context of this framework of community that I want to speak briefly about two prayers that are at the heart of my *d'var* today. The first one I want to concentrate on in detail is the *mi sheberach* which we usually think of as part of our Torah service. This prayer is also appropriate in the context of a visit to the sick, doing the mitzvah of *bikkur cholim*. In our minyan, we follow the tradition of saying a collective prayer for those who are ill toward the end of the *aliyot*, which is individualized by inserting specific names of people who are in need of healing. The traditional name given is the person's Hebrew name as the son/daughter of their mother. Using the mother's name is a reflection of the nurturing role of the mother. The Hebrew word for compassion is *rachamim*, which comes from the word *rechem*, or womb, thus invoking the image of the mother. Perhaps in our egalitarian environment this is or should be adapted to include either or both parents. Although the prayer asks God to do something, the mention of someone's illness can also be viewed as a public announcement of *tsuris* and possibly a call to action.

The format of the general *mi sheberach* prayer is a medieval French invention and provides for the granting of God's blessing in a variety of circumstances, from providing healing to sick people, to blessing a *bar* or *bat Mitzvah*, to wishing for the wellbeing of a mother after childbirth. The language of the *mi sheberach* prayer for one who is ill includes a reference to our forefathers and mothers, and wishes for a restoration of health and vigor to the person who is ill. There is a mention of both physical and emotional health. In the Shabbat/*Yom tov mi sheberach*, we apologize for petitioning on those days on which petitioning is generally not allowed, but nonetheless, pray that healing will come speedily.

In *Or Chadash*,[1] the commentary on the *Slim Shalom*, there is a section written by Michael Paley (p. 145) which I will read:

> Prayer is an intimate activity. But blessing of another is grounded in relationship. Prayer's roots are in intimacy but its branches are in community. The traditional forms of the mi-sheberach prayer emphasize the importance of this connection by ending with phrases such as "together with all Israel," or "among the other sick of Israel . . . ."

For me, there were many poignant stories of people who said the *misheberach* prayer on my behalf. By highlighting a couple of these, I do not mean to take for granted any one of you who said it for me once or on a regular basis or just thought of me in their prayers. It gave me great comfort to know that it was happening, and I like to think it went straight to God's ears.

---

[1] Reuven Hammer, *Or Chadash* (Rabbincal Assembly 2003).

Behukkotai

The first story came from Kineshma and I will read Bev's e-mail:

Dear Liz and Barry:

I haven't written anyone else about our trip yet, but after reading your e-mail about Liz's chemo, I had to share the story of her mi sheberach. Saturday morning we met at the Kineshma Jewish Community Center. Normally the men pray in one room and the women discuss the Torah portion in another room. Since we were visiting, after the women discussed the Torah portion, led by Lucy, my regular correspondent from Kineshma, Anne, Rhonda and I read the first aliyah. Then Ellen read a part of the haftarah. They had never heard of a haftarah and had never heard either chanted before. Before we began I explained that we had a tradition in our community of saying a mi sheberach when someone was ill. I told them about you having your first chemo treatment on Friday and said that we would say a special prayer for you in English. One of their students had just had some neck surgery and we said a prayer for her as well. Then I went around the room and many people added names and prayers of their own. I think it was a very moving experience from both sides of the table and I wanted you to know how saying prayer for you opened up a whole new experience for these women. May God be with you and heal all those who are sick.

A second story comes from a Reform temple where Mitchell was attending a *bar Mitzvah*. As I heard the story, Mitchell was about to call out my name, when he heard another man, whom he didn't know, say my name. Afterwards, he introduced himself to the person who turned out to be my cousin. I had no idea either one was saying it on my behalf.

I also found out that children, friends of Nathan and others, were saying it for me without even being instructed by their parents. I appreciated that Norman Eliaser made sure that my name was read each week, paying attention to when Barry or the kids were here to say it themselves, and saying it when they weren't.

The *mi sheberach* prayer emphasizes the connection of the person who is ill with the entire Jewish community with the phrase *"eem sha'ar cholei Yisrael."* Even a simple greeting of *"refuah shlema"* or a sincere "how are you" or a heartfelt hug has the power to impart concern, caring and a community connection. Thank you for doing all of these and helping me feel connected at a time I might have otherwise felt isolated.

The second prayer on my mind today is *Gomel* which I benched today after my *aliyah*. Several weeks ago Richard mentioned it in his *d'var Torah* about, what else, the sacrifices. This blessing is the prayer that substitutes for the sacrifice one makes as a thanksgiving offering. The requirements are found in the Talmud, in *Brachot*, which talks about four groups who are required to say it. The four groups, based on verses from Psalm 107, are those who go to the sea in ships, those who lost their way in the wilderness, those who were bound in cruel irons and those who cried unto *Adonai*, and He healed them. Loosely translated, these apply to people who go on a dangerous journey, those who are freed from captivity and those who escape from a dangerous situation such as an illness.

The prayer, recited after an *aliyah*, translates as follows:

> Praised are you *Adonai* our God, who rules the universe, showing goodness to us beyond our merits for bestowing favor upon me.

The congregation responds:

> May God who has been gracious to you continue to favor you with all that is good.

The one phrase "showing goodness beyond our merits" deserves a second look. I will read again from *Or Chadash* (p. 142), the commentary on the *Slim Shalom* prayerbook:

> Literally, "granting favors to those who are guilty." This is based on the often-expressed idea that none of us is really deserving of the gifts granted to us by God. Therefore, we give thanks not for that which we have earned or deserved, but for that we have been granted because of God's gracious nature.

This is spoken in the collective, as on Yom Kippur, so that we can share our burdens. Again, the idea of community is reinforced by the interactive nature of this prayer.

A brief journey into the history of the sacrifice which preceded this prayer, presuming this is okay with Richard. This particular sacrifice was called the *zevah shelamin*, translated in the *Etz Hayim* as an offering of wellbeing. The commentary explains that this offering was always given by an individual who had something to celebrate on a personal level. The name of this sacrifice, *shelamin*, comes from the word "*shalem*," which can be interpreted as wholeness or being at peace with oneself, the priests and God. Another interpretation given is that this sacrifice brings shalom with one's neighbors because they are invited to share in the feast from the sacrifice. Later rules about the sacrifice included the commandment to eat the entire sacrifice on the same day or at least by the following day. The reasoning suggested is to encourage someone bringing the sacrifice to invite friends and poor people to join him. The logical conclusion to my benching *Gomel* today is to make sure that everyone eats and enjoys the *Kiddush* today, in its entirety.

Why did I wait so long to bench *Gomel*? Originally, I had thought to bench it after surgery, and then I decided to wait until after chemotherapy, and then I decided that after radiation would be the right time. I felt better physically, but the emotional recovery was taking a little longer. Then I had a dream. At the end of a long and complicated dream, involving friends and car crashes, I was meeting with my doctor who eventually morphed into a frum doctor. I asked the doctor, "When should I bench *Gomel*?" He said "*lag ba'Omer.*" I woke up from the dream and thought about it. I looked at the calendar and it made sense to do it on *lag ba'Omer*, or at least the first Torah reading day thereafter. This week marks the one-year anniversary of my diagnosis, I just had a clean mammogram, and after all *lag ba'Omer* is the day that commemorates the day when Rabbi Akiva's students stopped dying from a terrible plague.

One more reason this week is right. Although I chose this date a while ago, I looked at this week's *parsha* to see if I could make a connection and of course I could. If you look at the last line of today's *haftarah* from Jeremiah (17:14), it says:

> *Refaeni Adonai ve'ayrape, hoshieni ve'eevasheyah, ki tehilati atah.*
> Heal me, O LORD, and I shall be healed; save me, and I shall be saved; for You are my praise.

The central theme in this *d'var* is community. It is a privilege to be part of this community, but I also recognize it carries an obligation of service to make it what it is. We collectively need to take care of each other, to help heal each other, in body and in spirit, when the need arises. Our family could have made it through this past year on our own, but we are grateful we didn't have to.

This is my public chance to say thank you, to God, to this community, and to my wonderful family. *Kiddush* today is also in honor of Barry's 51st birthday and Jake's 17th birthday. Both birthdays, coming in the next several weeks, can be celebrated properly as they couldn't be last year. We are also celebrating Nathan's and Ben's graduations from elementary school and middle school respectively since we won't be here next week for the graduation *Kiddush*. *Kiddush* is in honor of this minyan community.

Chazak, chazak, vinitchazek!
Be strong, be strong, and strengthen one another!

Behukkotai (II)

Richard Tupper

To the untrained eye, perhaps, the Judaism we practice today seems very different than that practiced by our ancestors thousands of years ago. For example, each day we praise God for forgiving our sins, but when was the last time one of us brought a goat to an altar, slaughtered it, and had a *kohen* daub its blood on an altar? Well, when is the last time one of *you* did it?

How do we account for religious evolution? New circumstances and new questions present new challenges. A religion can ignore the new circumstances and questions and become irrelevant, or it can address them head on and in so doing evolve, but it evolves by revolving, by returning to central truths and applying them to the new questions and circumstances.

We see a perfect example of this in today's *parsha*, in chapt. 26:40-45, which addresses the situation of Israel in exile. One of the central truths of Judaism is that sin or disobedience to God breaches our relationship with God, and the relationship must be repaired. This central truth is amplified in chapter four of Leviticus. There we are taught that even unintentional violations of God's prohibitive commandments pollute the Tabernacle. This pollution is removed and the relationship is repaired when the sinner, motivated by genuine guilt, brings a purification offering. The combination of the sinner's genuine guilt and purification offering purges the pollution and obtains forgiveness from God, thus repairing the relationship between God and man. It is noteworthy that in Leviticus the role of the purification offering is used in only in a handful of cases involving physical impurities, but it encompasses every violation of prohibitive commandments. This, itself, was most likely an evolution.

Chapters five and sixteen of Leviticus deal with a different question – how can the breach caused by intentional sin be repaired? Again there is the requirement of guilt and a purification offering but a new requirement is added – confession. The significance of confession was captured by Resh Lakish, who noted its importance by teaching, "Great is repentance, which converts intentional sins into unintentional ones" (*b. Yoma* 86b). While intentional sins are more serious than unintentional sins, polluting not the outer altar but Holy of Holies itself, intentional sins do not present an insuperable obstacle to our relationship with God. Confession when coupled with sincere guilt and sacrifice removes the pollution caused by the intentional sin, obtains forgiveness for the sinner and restores our relationship with God.

Lev. 18 to 20 addresses a different situation. Lev. 1-16 addresses the situation of the Israelites in the wilderness. Beginning with chapter 18, Leviticus addresses the future situation of the Israelites in the land of Israel. With the movement of Israel from the wilderness into the land, the focus on the effects of the pollution caused by sin shifts from the Tabernacle to the land. Sin causes a breach in the relationship between God and man but the sin is described as polluting not the Tabernacle but the land. Israel is warned that polluting the land by sin is very serious and will cause Israel's expulsion from the land. Chapter 26 addresses how God will punish Israel for its sins, culminating in Israel's exile from the land.

And now the question arises: how can Israel repair the breach in its relationship with God when it lives outside the land, where there is no Temple and no sacrificial cult? Leviticus 26 answers that sacrifice is not absolutely necessary. What is necessary is that Israel must humble itself and confess its sins. Leviticus 26 teaches that for Israel to restore its relationship with God, sacrifice is not indispensable, but humbling oneself and confession are. As the Psalmist says (51:17), "The sacrifices of God are a broken spirit: a broken and a contrite heart, O God, You will not despise." It is because of this teaching that we today believe we can be reconciled to God through repentance even though we are unable to bring a sacrifice.

It is interesting to note the language that Leviticus uses when describing God's reaction to Israel's humbling and confession. It does not say that God will forgive Israel, but rather that God will remember the covenant and the land. What does it mean to say that God will remember? When the Torah says that God will remember, it is not telling us that God forgot. Rather, this language signifies that God will take action. For example, in Exodus, we are told that God remembered Israel when it was in captivity in Egypt and this stirs God to redeem Israel from Egypt.

In Lev. 26, we are told that when Israel humbles itself and confesses its sins, God will remember the land and the covenant between God and Israel.

Behukkotai (II)

We are being told that God will take action in response to Israel's confession. But what is the action that God will take? Though not explicit, surely it is implicit that God will return Israel to the land. Part of the covenant is the promise that obedient Israel may live on God's land. In effect, there are not just two parties to this covenant, God and Israel, but three, God, Israel and the land. The prophet Isaiah personifies the land and describes how the land suffers while Israel is in exile. For example, in chapter 49:14-18, the prophet consoles Zion who suffers because of Israel's exile and says,

> But Zion says: "The LORD has forsaken me, and the Lord has forgotten me." Can a woman forget her nursing child, that she should not have compassion on the son of her womb? Yes, these may forget, yet I will not forget you. Behold, I have engraved you upon the palms of My hands; your walls are continually before Me. Your children make haste; your destroyers and they that made you waste shall go forth from you. Lift up your eyes round about, and behold: all these gather themselves together and come to you. As I live, says the LORD, you shall surely clothe yourself with them all as with an ornament, and wrap yourself with them like a bride.

God's promise that He will remember the land and the covenant signifies that He will act upon the covenant and restore Israel to the land if Israel humbles itself and confesses its sins.

Another question remains; this is a question that I do not propose to answer but only to raise. However, how we answer this question reveals how we think about God, Israel and the land.

Leviticus 26 says that God will restore Israel to the land not only after Israel has humbled itself and confessed its sins but also after "*yirtzu avonot.*" The NJPS translates these two words as "they shall atone for their sins;" it has also been translated as "they accept their punishment in full" (Milgrom, *Leviticus*). It seems clear that the reference is to Israel's exile and the question then arises: is punishment necessary for forgiveness? Can Israel be reconciled to God without exile? One answer is that this is the nature of God; God forgives but requires punishment. He may reduce the punishment but not remit it in full. A different answer is that this is the nature of Israel. Punishment is necessary for Israel to be humbled. Without punishment, Israel will not humble itself. A third answer is that this is the nature of the land. The land has been polluted by Israel's sins. Just as the altar requires a purification offering to be purged from the pollution caused by sin, so, too, the land requires the exile of Israel so that it can be purged of the impurity caused by Israel's sins. Just as we might set aside for a year a *milchich* china plate on which meat has mistakenly been served in order to *kasher* it, so, too, the land must be rid of Israel for a prescribed period of time for it to be purified. This seems to me to be the rationale of v. 43.

I will follow up that question with an observation, and that is that what is true on a macro scale is also true on a micro scale. Unless we take Judaism seriously and are not afraid to seek from it answers to the troubling questions in our lives, our relationship to God will never grow but will simply wither away.

Bemidbar – Erev Rosh Chodesh Sivan

Steve Oren

Some years ago, the Israeli Knesset was debating the legalization of homosexuality. Various Knesset members from the parties that call themselves religious spoke in opposition, citing a variety of *pesuqim* in opposition to the legislation. At last Yael Dayan of Labor, the learned daughter of a learned father, got up and said that indeed all those *pesuqim* existed. But there was another one: "Very dear you [masc.] were to me. More wondrous your [masc.] love to me than the love of women." This *pesuq* has an address. It is in II Samuel 1:26 and forms part of David's eulogy for the fallen Jonathan.

Now the suggestion that there was a sexual component to David's love for Jonathan is not without traditional support. For instance, the Radaq (R. David Qimhi) at this place citing the Aramaic text says the "love of women" is not the love of women in general (which could be of a non-sexual nature) but refers explicitly to David's then two wives. Again, if we look in today's *haftarah*, see what Saul says about his son (I Sam. 20:30): "O, son of a perverse wayward woman! Don't I know you have chosen the son of Jesse to your own shame and to the shame of your mother's nakedness?" This quite clearly seems a sexual reference.

But the text would seem to be naturally understood quite differently. Saul is at least half crazy with paranoia, but even paranoids have real enemies. What is Saul's problem? He is king, but he has been told (I Sam. 15:26) that the kingship will be taken from him and given to another. And by this time, he knows who that other is. It is David. He has heard this in the women's proclamation (I Sam. 18:7): "Saul has struck down his thousands and David his tens of thousands."

What does Saul do about this? He fights for himself and his family. And if you asked him why, why does he think he can defeat a god, I don't think he would say much more than mumble about how, "A man's gotta do what a man's gotta do."

Leaves from the Garden

But if David is a threat to Saul, how much more so is he one to Jonathan, who is the next generation. What Saul says to Jonathan (I Sam. 20:31): "For as long as the son of Jesse lives on the earth you and your kingship will not be unshaken!" is absolutely true, regardless of how loyal David may appear to be.

And what is Jonathan's response? Could it be that he is too stupid to see the problem? No. Look at I Samuel 20:15: "do not cut off your faithfulness from my house for all time." Who is speaking to whom? This is Jonathan, the crown prince, begging for mercy from David. Jonathan is perfectly aware that David will be the next king. And Jonathan does not fight this. Why not? All that Saul can think of is that his son is a sissy. Rashi to I Samuel 20:30 says the word "perverse" suggests femininity: "You sissy, you are not behaving like a man." And notice that this also explains David's eulogy. You, Jonathan, who should have fought me, behaved like a woman and gave in to me, abandoned the kingship to me. Neither Saul nor David, both macho men, can understand Jonathan's actions. It is not enough to say that Jonathan's motivation was his love for David (whether or not there was a sexual aspect to that love). How could Jonathan so revolt against the norms of the culture to which he belonged?

And so we turn to the narrator for these are the narrator's characters. The narrator makes two points. The first is much later in the text (II Sam. 21). It is a generation later, and everyone is dead except David who is king – surrounded by intrigues – he has become a Saul. And David either finds or makes an opportunity (one can read the text either way) to bump off part of Saul's family, who are obviously an ongoing threat to him. And yet (v. 7): "And the king spared on Mephibosheth son of Jonathan son of Saul because of the LORD's vow that was between them, between David and Jonathan son of Saul." This is the very vow that we find in today's *haftarah*. Yes, Mephibosheth was handicapped but the text shows that such was not the issue. For all of Saul's fighting and Jonathan's giving in, it is Jonathan's way that in the end is more effective in preserving the family, although Mephibosheth and his descendents as "the oldest son of the oldest son" would be the greatest threat to David and his family.

But this does not answer our question. Granted that what Jonathan did proved effective, how could he defy cultural expectations? Here, we must turn back. Saul, we said, is not to be king. Why not? Because in the battle with the Amaleqites he had defied the word of the prophet Samuel. He had not wiped out all the sheep and cattle. He had let the people keep them (I Sam. 15).

Bemidbar

Where is Jonathan in this incident? Seemingly nowhere. But, look just before (I Sam. 14). Here, the Israelites are battling the Philistines. And Jonathan, who could scarcely have been more than a young teenager in his first battle, does something very brave. But meanwhile Saul has sworn an oath that no one should eat anything that day. And at the end of the day, Saul finds out that YHWH is displeased. And Saul tells his people that whoever erred, even be it himself or Jonathan, he will be put to death. And they go through the lots. Behold, it is Jonathan who ate. Since he did not know of his father's command, he tasted some honey. And what happens to Jonathan? Nothing, for the people – the same people as in chapter 15 – resist. And Saul gives in.

Jonathan is thus in a cleft stick. I am not to be king because my father did not have the qualities to be king. But had he had those qualities, I would not become king because I would have been killed. I want to suggest that the narrator is telling us that it is out of this shock that Jonathan is able to defy cultural expectations, and is able to love David rather than compete or fight with him.

Naso

Joan Katz

My husband and I have been partaking of one of the jewels of Chicago for many years with our subscription to the Chicago Symphony Orchestra. There is nothing like climbing to the top of the gallery, losing ourselves in the beautiful music and enjoying the beautiful spectacle of this world class orchestra. What a way to restore the mind and soul, to remind us of why we put up with all the indignities of life in a big city and to be dazzled by the sounds that man can create.

But for the first time in all these years, at the last concert in last year's series, I couldn't wait for the music to end. I was fidgeting in my seat. I could barely stifle a cough. I needed the bathroom. I was hot. I was cold. Any excuse: I needed out. The music was that seriously disquieting. Something about the tempo, the rhythms, the endless dragging on of something that just couldn't finish, aggravated my soul.

But when it ended, to my surprise, the mostly Russian audience went crazy with delight. Obviously, the worldview of Shostakovich does not match mine. Never again, I thought. Thank God I never have to ride the train across Siberia.

Some weeks later, we did an unusual cultural stop. My husband called Friday morning and said, "Let's go see the opening matinee of the final Stanley Kubrick film, *Eyes Wide Shut*. You're done cooking, aren't you?" Well, this was one fascinating film – a visual feast and a moral wrench – but I could not sit still in my seat. I mean I fidgeted non-stop. OK, I thought, it is one stirring film, but I am old enough to watch this.

Imagine my surprise when I read the credits. Guess whose music was used to create the intense drama?

None other than Mr. Shostakovich.

Talk about music resonating!

What, you may ask, does this have to do with a *d'var Torah*?

Leaves from the Garden

Some years ago we had a visitor at the Minyan, a nurse from Minneapolis named Dan. He taught us a beautiful *niggun* or melody to some of my favorite words in *Shacharit*. I no longer remember the exact tune, but I do remember the lesson I learned from the words.

The words are found in *Nishmat:* "*eelo pinu maleh shira cayam*//If only our mouths were as full with song as is the sea."

It is a poem about rhythm. The hope that our praise of God will fill our mouths with the constancy of the waves in the sea. Eternal appreciation for the world that God has created. A prayer for the sensitivity to God's creation to allow us pleasures of continued awe. The antithesis of cynicism. A vote for constancy.

The slow lapping of waves. A peaceful calming in a scattered world. Just listening to the repetition, the *kevah* – if you will – lulls one back into a rhythm from which one can – from which I can – slip back into *kavanah* – or awe at the world God has created.

Most importantly, this poem teaches about listening. Learning to hear the world speaking to us.

My grandmother, Flora Katz, has a favorite song: Maleguena. When each of her dozen grandchildren was old enough for music lessons, she made us each the same offer: $10 to play the whole song for her. What a sum!

I still wonder if this little bribe has anything to do with eight of that dozen growing up with serious avocations or professions in the arts. From some depth of repetition, we learned to hear the music.

Like Maleguena, *eelo pinu* goes on to changing winds. It speaks of *hamon galav*. Many waves. Maybe it refers to number, as in "many." I like to imagine the poet also intended *hamon galav* – the many waves – meaning an endless variety of waves.

Sometimes our rhythm is quiet and gentle. Some days the sky threatens. Other days a hurricane is brewing. Nonetheless God's hand is in it all.

It is keying into these differences at the right times that causes music to resonate so fully.

Now I will take a leap. Please forgive me as I certainly stand among the "*avaryanim*" – the sinners.

I think that we in the Minyan have let our ear for our rhythm wander. Our group listening skills have strayed. As a result, our *daven*ing is lagging in invigorating energy.

Naso

I think that on a personal level most of us understand this connection to music and the words of this poem. Otherwise we would not sit here singing together week after week.

But we have lulled ourselves into the endless repetition. The constant calm and quiet are reassuring. But we are no longer, as a group, listening to the variety that makes music so stirring.

We do not listen to our *shaliach tziboor* leading the *daven*ing. The pace, or tempo, slows and slows. The group drags it down. If the leader chooses to change what she sings aloud, the *kahal* often overrides. The group's voice often does not match the tempo of the *chazzan*. We as a group do not pay attention.

My cousin, Steve Katz, who *daven*ed here occasionally several years ago, brought a favorite cassette to play during a long car trip home to Columbus. He started listening and went nuts. Unbeknownst to me, my car's tape player was working at 90% of normal speed. I had grown so used to it, I didn't even notice anymore. But I had wondered why some of my favorite tapes were not so favorite anymore.

The waves don't come in evenly generated forces. The energy here often feels like it is a clock winding down instead of the winds stirring the ocean forward. We chose to alternate *daven*ers so that we could be stirred by variety. But as a group we are teaching a flat curve.

The beat or tempo of the *daven*ing affects many things. First of all, it creates a mood. Shabbat is a joyous time. An energy leaping forward to reach to God, to the *Shechina*. Second, it can energize us – or deflate us. The more upbeat, the more invigorating. A slow, thoughtful tune is only inspirational in contrast to a quicker pace elsewhere. Third, a few minutes here and a few minutes there, and suddenly *daven*ing has stretched out very late. This reinforces people coming late. They come early if they feel like they will miss out.

There is an internal score to the symphony of the service. *Psukei, Shacharit*, taking out the Torah, the reading, putting it back, *Musaf, Adon Olam*. It builds up, opens our hearts, serves up the epiphany, and reminisces. When we arrive late, we lose the internal rhythm. We have missed the ascent. When we wander heedlessly in and out during sacred moments, when we gossip at quiet spots, we cause others to stumble in their concentration.

My challenge to the Minyan is for each of us to pay attention to the tempo and rhythm of our *daven*ing. Let's put energy and vigor into the *kevah* of the weekly words to make them holy, so that the *kavanah* comes together to reinvigorate us.

Let us hear more voices singing and leading as well. Then let us listen to these messengers and follow their lead.

We have chosen not to have a single *chazzan*, to be able to listen to many voices.

It is good to be disquieted by music and *daven*ing. This is when we remember it stirs man's soul and speaks to God. If we wish to find *kavanah*/meaningful reflection in our *daven*ing, we need to also find a way to listen to ourselves, to fill our mouths with God's praise with the variety of the waves of the sea.

Just as inspiration often arrives from unexpected connections and careful listening, so *kavanah*/special concentration surprises us as the reward for attention to details of ritual.

Eelo pinu malei shir cayam/If only our mouths were as full with song as is the sea.

Shabbat shalom.

Naso (II)

Richard Tupper[1]

In *Naso*, the priestly blessing is recounted (Num. 6:22-27). Thereafter follows what has to be one of the least riveting parts of the Torah, the description of the gifts brought to the Tabernacle by the tribal chieftains. A friend of mine imagines that thousands of years ago members of each tribe would lean forward eagerly as the account was read, waiting to hear their own tribe mentioned. Somehow I doubt that.

If the account is not put in for its entertainment value, what is its purpose? Perhaps it seeks to teach the equality among the tribes. If, instead of one leader from each tribe bringing gifts, every member of each tribe had brought gifts, the gifts of the more numerous tribes would have far outnumbered those of the smaller tribes. Of course, inherent in this procedure is the biblical view of society as made up of groups as opposed to atomized into individuals, a "corporate" view of society that we today often fail to appreciate. However, by making the gifts of each tribe of equal value, a fact made abundantly clear by the twelve time repetition of the gifts, the ineluctable conclusion is that every tribe – and hence each member of every tribe – stands on equal footing before HaShem.

One might, however, detect subtle distinctions of rank in the process. For example, the tribe of Judah goes first and Ephraim seventh. However, the tribes are repeatedly listed in the Bible, and the seventh position in the lists doesn't seem to be of particular importance. As for Judah going first, the rabbis note that only Nahshon son of Amminadab is not designated as a

---

[1] Actually, this *d'var Torah* was not delivered at the Minyan. Tupper wrote it up but because members had debated for so long whether to continue duchening (they decided to continue it), Reb Oren persuaded Tupper not to give it. Better to let sleeping dogs lie. But now, Reb Oren won't know that Tupper has snuck this into this anthology until it is too late!

"chieftain" (7:12), unlike all the others. Moreover, it appears that the order that the gifts were presented reflects the ordering of the camp in chap. 2 (see also chap. 10). Since Judah was the largest tribe (1:26), it made sense for Judah to march first and to occupy the camp's most critical defensive position, the eastward position in front of the entrance to the Tabernacle.

However, one tribe is accentuated by its glaring absence, Levi. The Levites are different simply because HaShem chose them. HaShem plainly states (8:14 [NJPS]), "the Levites shall be Mine." With that choice went certain obligations. The Levites inherited the awesome responsibility of guarding the Tabernacle against encroachment and transporting it when the camp was on the move. From among the tribe of Levites, the house of Aaron was given even greater responsibilities, officiating over the sacrifices and teaching Torah to Israel.

Today there is no Temple. Consequently, the *kohanim* (priests) and the Levites have fewer responsibilities. Today *kohanim* and Levites receive few perquisites; being called first to the Torah comes to mind. The *kohanim* still must observe restrictions with respect to funerals and marriages that the rest of us do not. Those restrictions are maintained, however, for our benefit so that the *kohanim* can fulfill their responsibilities. The one major obligation that still rests upon *kohanim* and Levites is the delivery of the priestly blessing. Levites are obligated to help the *kohanim* prepare to recite the blessing, and the *kohanim* are obligated to recite the blessing when called to *duchen*.

Just as Israel must observe mitzvot, such as *kashrut*, that *goyim* need not simply because HaShem has chosen Israel and has given us specific mitzvot, so too the *kohanim* and the Levites are obligated to deliver to us the blessing set out in *Naso*. Performing a mitzvah sanctifies, failing to do so profanes. If we as Israel fail to observe the mitzvot, we become "*chol*"/common, indistinguishable from gentiles. If *kohanim* and Levites fail to deliver the priestly blessing, they become indistinguishable from the rest of Israel. But just as is the case with sacrifices, so, too, the priestly blessing was not instituted for the benefit of the *kohanim* and the Levites, but rather for the benefit of all Israel. Our *kohanim* and Levites have been given this mitzvah, not because they are better than us, but because HaShem has chosen to sanctify them by this mitzvah and through the performance of this mitzvah to bring blessing to all Israel. Israel, by keeping the mitzvot, is meant to be a blessing to all the peoples of the world. So, too, the *kohanim* and the Levites are meant to be a blessing to us, Israel, by delivering the priestly blessing.

Naso (II)

May our *kohanim* and *Leviim* fulfill their ancient and sacred obligation, and may we all enjoy HaShem's blessing.

Shavuot

Steve Oren

The Status of Non-Jews

It is well known that the world's population is divided into Jews and non-Jews. The Jewish tradition does not always have a positive outlook regarding non-Jews. For instance, we read in *M. Avodah Zarah* 1.1:

> Three days before the festivals of non-Jews[1] it is forbidden to do business with them, to give things to them and to ask from them, to lend to them and to take loans from them, to repay their loans and to accept repayment from them. Rabbi Yehuda [middle 2nd century CE] says "We may accept repayment from them because it is a trouble to him [the individual non-Jew]." They [the Rabbis] said to him "Although it is a trouble to him now, he will rejoice after a while."

Nor is it only on festivals that there are restrictions. For instance, we read in *M. Avodah Zarah* 2.1:

> One may not put an animal in a stable of [owned by] non-Jews because they are suspected of bestiality. A woman may not be alone with them because they are suspected of sexual immorality [*'arayot*]. And a man may not be alone with them because they are suspected of bloodshed. A Jewish woman may not be a midwife for a non-Jewish woman

---

[1] Some texts read "Non-Jews" (*Goyim*), others "star-worshippers (*Ovdei Kochavim*) but in context they both mean the same thing.

> because she is giving birth to a child of idol worship. A Jewish woman may not nurse the child of a non-Jewish woman, but a non-Jewish woman may nurse the child of a Jewish woman in her [the Jewish woman's] residence.

Note that even this last point is a concession. There are Midrashim about how Pharaoh's daughter had to get a Jewish nursemaid for the young Moses as he refused the milk of a non-Jewish woman.[1]

These views are not just found in ancient times. For instance the Rambam (Moses Maimonides [Spain/Egypt 1135-1204]) writes (*Mishneh Torah. Nezikin, Rotzeach* 7.11):

> But idol worshippers [see note 1 on the previous page] with whom there is not between them and us war and Jewish shepherds of small animals [who were suspected of stealing] and similar individuals, it is forbidden to plan their deaths and it is forbidden to save them if they are in danger of dying. For instance, if one sees one of them that fell into the sea, one may not lift him up as it is said "You shall not stand by the blood of your neighbor" [Lev. 19:16]. And this one is not "your neighbor."[2]

While these views seem somewhat narrow, please notice that they are also inconvenient – especially once Jews are dispersed in a non-Jewish world. Imagine, for instance, being the Jewish owner of a department store who must close three days before Christmas! And this is the start of the quite different approach of Menahem HaMeiri (S. France 1249-1306).

The Meiri begins by observing[3] (page 3) that as to the restrictions listed in the first source "but in these times no person is careful of these matters at all even as to the day of their festivals." In other words, he holds that the fact that Jews do or do not observe a supposed prohibition tells us something

---

[1] See Rashi to Exodus 2:7 citing *b. Sotah* 12b.

[2] It was pointed out that since the Rambam himself worked as a physician for non-Jews; he presumably held it was permissible to save the lives of non-Jews if you were paid for it.

[3] References to the Meiri, cited by page, are to Menahem HaMeiri *Beit HaBehira al Mesechet Avodat Zarah* (ed. Avraham Schreiber) (Jerusalem, Qedem 1964).

about the status of that supposed prohibition. Nowadays, this seems to be a matter in dispute between spokespeople for Orthodox and Conservative Judaism, and it is interesting that a leading medieval authority, and he is by no means the only one, takes what is in effect the Conservative side.

Still, he asks, what is the justification for the fact that people do not observe these rules? He discusses at some length the theory that it is because of 'hate' (that if we kept these rules, it would endanger our status in a non-Jewish majority society) and concludes that that theory is not sufficient. Hence, he writes (p. 4), "And it appears to me that these things were not said except in regard to worshippers of idols, and their pictures and these statues, but nowadays they are completely permissible." In other words, the non-Jews of the Meiri's time are *not* idol-worshippers. Indeed, he is then faced with an explicit reference in the *Gemara* to *Notsrim* (Christians), and he argues (with greater ingenuity than history) that the "*Notsrim*" of the *Gemara* are not Christians but an ancient sect of sun-worshippers.

Now the Meiri may feel that at this point things are "apparent and clear" (p. 4), but the rest of us may be a little confused. Let us look, then, to the Meiri's discussion of the second source. Again, he observes that these rules are not generally observed.[1] "We see many wonders at these times when no person is careful as to these matters" (p. 59). He explains that these prohibitions applied to the ancient nations that "were not limited by the ways of the religions."

At this point, we notice something odd. The non-Jews of the Meiri's time are, in his view, clearly different from those of the times of the Talmud. But, he states this difference only negatively. The non-Jews of his day do not worship idols. He does not say that the non-Jews of his time are monotheists. The "We all worship the same God" argument of our modern defense agencies is not made by the Meiri.

Why not? The Meiri has already told us that all of the non-Jews he would encounter have this status of "non-idol worshippers." Whom, in the city of

---

[1] By contrast he affirms the ongoing force of other ritual restrictions, such as that on the wine of non-Jews, which were apparently observed in his day. It is quite possible that the Meiri would today arrive at different conclusions as to these ritual restrictions.

Perpignan, would the Meiri have encountered at the start of the 14th century?[1] There would have been Catholics, there might have been a visiting Muslim from southern Spain, there would have been Waldensians, forerunners of the Protestant churches. And, there would have been Cathars; the Perpignan region was one of their strongholds. Now, they believed in two gods. One, an evil god who was identified with YHWH of the Tanach, had created all material objects, including the human body. But the human body was a prison for the human soul which had been created by the good God.

The Meiri quite clearly does not differentiate between the Cathars and other non-Jews of his day. One cannot argue he would not have known about them. The Meiri was a businessman, lending money to the non-Jews of the region, rather than a scholar cloistered in a yeshiva. If believing in two gods is not "idol-worship," what is? Notice that it cannot be argued that having statues in one's place of worship and showing respect to those statues makes one an idol-worshipper. For while the Cathars had no such statues (and no such formal places of worship), the Catholics did. If having a multiplicity of gods does not make one an idol-worshipper and if showing respect to statues does not make one an idol-worshipper, what does – for the Meiri clearly believes that idol worship existed?

Let us look at the Meiri's comments on our third source. He writes, "The non-Jews and the Jewish shepherds of small animals that may be assumed to be constantly engaged in stealing and are sunk in it until they become through this as those who throw off the yoke of the Torah . . . we are not commanded to engage in saving them" (p. 59). First, notice the difference with the Rambam. For the Rambam, saving non-Jews is prohibited. For the Meiri, if you wish to, you may do so.[2] Then the Meiri says,

> And even as to this concerning non-Jews, you must inspect what we said before as to what kind of non-Jew is

---

[1] The following discussion is based on Emmanuel LeRoy Ladurie *Montaillou: The Promised land of Error* (trans: Barbara Bray) (New York, Vintage Books 1979) and Steven Runciman *The Medieval Manichee: A study of the Christian Dualist Heresy* (Cambridge, Cambridge University Press 1949).

[2] This distinction is actually quite frequent. For instance, the Rambam holds that it is optional (*reshut*) to lend money to non-Jews but that if you do, you *must* charge interest. In contrast, Meiri holds that lending to non-Jews, other things being equal, is a command (mitzvah) and that if you do so you *may* charge interest.

being spoken of here. That is to say, it speaks of idol worshippers who were not restricted by the ways of the religions and, on the contrary, all sins and all hateful things were fine in their eyes. And already, the chief of the philosophers [Aristotle] said that one who has no religion should be killed. Hence, all who are worshippers of divinity, even though they are not in the category of [our] religion [*i.e.*, Judaism], are not subject to this law [of not being saved], Heaven forefend!

(pp. 59-60)

The Meiri here bases himself on the *Gemara* which asks how people can be so silly as to worship idols.[1] And it answers that people are not that silly but they make themselves silly in order to be able to engage in sexual immorality. The idol worshipper is a danger to society because he does not think he is commanded to be moral. In this respect, he is like the Atheist. Hence, says the Meiri, whenever you see people, such as the Christians, Muslims, and Cathars of his day, who are not immoral, who do not steal and will not rape a Jewish woman who walks into their store, you know they are not idol-worshippers. Hence, the restrictions as to idol-worshippers outlined in our starting sources do not apply to them.

I want to end by asking a different question: why does it matter? What we have here is a theory of tolerance which is certainly remarkable for early 14th century Europe. This is not the tolerance of the 19th century Mill, who included atheists among those who should be tolerated.[2] It is, however, at least as extensive as anything found in John Locke at the start of the 18th century, 400 years after the Meiri.

Where does "modernity" come from? One theory, widely held in the 19th and early 20th century, was that modernity was the offspring of western

---

[1] *B. Sanhedrin* 63b "Says Rav Yehuda says Rav [Iraq – late 3rd century CE] 'Israel knew as to idol worship that there was no substance in it and they did not worship idols except to make sexual immorality publicly permissible to them.'"

[2] A number of listeners were disturbed by the Meiri's failure to tolerate those without any religion. But, the Meiri was in scientific matters a follower of Aristotle. If one believes in Aristotle's physics, as Europe and the Middle East did during the Middle Ages, then God's existence is easily demonstrable (as the Rambam does in *The Guide to the Perplexed*) and atheism the view of an imbecile.

Christianity. On this view, before a Muslim, Hindu, or Jew can become "modern," they must become "Christian." This theory is also quite prevalent among Orthodox Jews who regard any "modern" Judaism as inauthentic. "Modernity" and "Judaism" are opposites.

But, there is another way of looking at the matter. And that is seeing modernity as something implicit in each of the world's religious traditions.[1] That is, looking back from our modern perspective at each of the religious traditions of the world, we can find modern values within it. This is certainly as true of Judaism as any other tradition. By looking at the Meiri's views, we see how modernity can be thought of not as the opposite of Judaism but as the continuation of it.

---

[1] This is the argument of Joshua Cohen "Minimalism about Human Rights: The most we can hope for?" *Journal of Political Philosophy* XII:2 (April 2004) 190-213, of Amartya Sen *Development as Freedom* (New York, Anchor 1999) and, with special reference to the history of Judaism, Gershom Scholem "Redemption Through Sin" (trans: Hillel Halkin) in Gershom Scholem *The Messianic Idea in Judaism* (New York, Schocken 1971).

Shavuot (II)

Bev Fox

The Three Wives of Rabbi Akiva

Many of you have asked me to share a little of my experiences in Israel. The best way for me to do that is to share some of the learning I did. One of my favorite classes was with Avigdor Shinan. He was teaching a class on *Aggadah*, taught in Hebrew at the University, and both Rhonda and I took it. He was a great lecturer, quite engaging, very funny and most importantly he gave a good overview of the various places where we find *Aggadic* literature.

You might ask me to begin by defining "*Aggadah.*" My guess is that he would translate it as something akin to "lore" or "stories." Basically, *Aggadah* are the stories not in the Torah that help elucidate the characters and values of our people. Some *Aggadah* can be found in *Mishnah* or Talmud, others are found in their own collections, and some are viewed as midrash or what I call "filling in the blank spaces" left in the stories of the Torah. One of the most important things I learned from Shinan was that different traditions of midrash developed at different periods to help the people "solve the problems" of their time. The stories had a particular "*hashkafa* for the time" and they were created to teach current values. Therefore, a student of midrash can learn a lot about changing cultural values by studying stories that come from different time periods or different locales.

Rhonda and I enjoyed Shinan so much that we invited him to dinner, just before Pesach, and invited our children to come and "learn at his feet." Deena had just arrived in Israel – we had Deena, Becca, Tamar, Rachel, and one of Renana's teachers who had been over for dinner the Friday before, and, when he heard about our planned dinner party, asked to be included. Quite an interesting discussion ensued, which later inspired Tamar to feature him as a keynote speaker in an "imaginary" Shabbaton she was planning for college students. At that dinner he gave me a copy of an article he had written on the three wives of Rabbi Akiva, and this article will be the basis of my discussion today.

The story I grew up knowing about Rabbi Akiva comes from the *Bavli*, Tractate *Ketubot*. R. Akiva worked as a shepherd for Kalba Savua. When Kalba Savua's daughter saw that there was something extraordinary about R. Akiva, she said, "If I am willing to be betrothed to you, will you attend a house of study?" R. Akiva said yes and she betrothed herself to him in secret. When Kalba Savua learned what she had done, he drove her out of his house and vowed that she was not to benefit from any of his property. She went and married Akiva. When winter came they had to sleep in a barn. R. Akiva picked the straw from her hair and said, "If I had the means, I would give you a Jerusalem of gold." This story was also given by Naomi Shemer as the inspiration for her song by the same name.

The story goes on to say that Kalba Savua's daughter insisted that R. Akiva go and learn Torah. He went away, and for twelve years he studied with R. Eliezer and R. Joshua. At the end of twelve years, he came home bringing with him 12,000 disciples. When his wife heard of his arrival she went out to meet him. Her neighbors told her to go borrow some clothes and be presentable. She replied that a righteous man will recognize his loyal wife. When she approached him, she fell upon her face and was about to kiss his feet. His disciples tried to push her aside but R. Akiva shouted, "Let her be – all that is mine (my learning) and yours are rightly hers." Another story suggests that he overheard her say that he should study for another twelve years, and so he returned to his studies without having any married life with her until after twenty-four years of study.

Her father, on hearing that a great man had come to town, said, "I shall go to him and perhaps he shall release me from the vow I made not to support my daughter." R. Akiva asked him, "Would you have made your vow if you had known that her husband was to become a great man?" The father said, "Had her husband known even one chapter, even one *halakhah*, I would not have made such a vow." R. Akiva said, "I am your daughter's husband." The father fell on his face and kissed R. Akiva's feet and then gave him his wealth.

When I first learned this story, it was supposed to be a prototype for positive women role models in the Torah. Here was a woman who believed in study so much that she would both give up her inheritance and forego actually living with her husband so that he could go and really learn. Other values here – R. Akiva praised his wife and recognized her sacrifice. His father-in-law realized his mistake and R. Akiva forgave him. I guess this

Shavuot (II)

could be a good story for a Yom Kippur *d'var* on *teshuvah*, but we'll focus on the study component to make it appropriate for Shavuot.

The modern poetess, Dalia Rabikovich, wrote a poem about R. Akiva. In it she describes R. Akiva as a modest shepherd who cared for Kalba Savua's sheep until he was forty. Then he meets Rachel, Savua's daughter, who sees him as a modest scholar and who offers to marry him if only he agrees to go and study Torah. They were poor and lived in a hut filled with straw. In the mornings, Akiva would have to pick the straw out of her hair. She urged him to go away and study. He was gone for twenty years and in that time her hair turned white. When he returned, his students wanted to push her away, but he told them that she was his Holy Torah.

In Rabikovich's poem, the woman referred to in the earlier story from the Babylonian Talmud is identified as Rachel, not just as Kalba Savua's daughter. A few other differences: R. Akiva studied for twenty years; her hair turned white; he was forty years old when they met; he longed for her while he was away; and the final words changed from "what are mine and yours are rightly hers" to "she is my holy Torah." This is a more romantic version. R. Akiva is gone for longer. His wife really ages while he is away and yet he longs for her. When he returns, he compares her to the Torah, attributing to her even higher value than the Jerusalem of gold.

Another story comes from the Jerusalem Talmud, Tractate *Nedarim*.

> R. Akiva was betrothed to the daughter of Kalba Savua. When Kalba Savua heard, he swore an oath forbidding his daughter from benefiting from any of his wealth. She went and married him. In the winter they slept in a barn and he used to pick the straw from her hair. He said to her, "If I would, I would give you a Jerusalem of gold." Eliyahu came to them dressed as a human. He asked them to give him some straw because his wife was about to give birth and she didn't have anything to lie on. Rabbi Akiva said to his wife, "Look this man doesn't even have straw." She said to him, "Go and study." He went and studied for twelve years . . . .

This story is different in that they marry after they have already heard Kalba Savua's vow following their betrothal. In this case, Akiva's study wasn't a condition for their marriage. He went to study after they had lived together for a while. Only when he realized that others could live in a situation even worse than his, was he willing to go and leave his wife in poverty for the sake of studying Torah. At first perhaps he felt guilty because of the vow, but later he realized that study was the most important.

From Tractate *Ketubot* we learn that betrothal was conditional on study of Torah. From Tractate *Nedarim* we learn that the goal of studying Torah grows out of a full marriage that has existed for a while.

In the second story we see the love Akiva has for his wife, their poverty and his wish that he wanted to be able to provide for her, to take care of her and to honor her . . . to give her a Jerusalem of gold. In a sense Akiva is showing that he feels that his wife gave up a lot for him, and he makes it appear that wanting gold and a better lifestyle is good. But she didn't choose from all the rich men in the city, she chose him – the author brings in Eliyahu to make his point. Eliyahu helps R. Akiva realize that there are others in the world worse off than he. When he understands that he doesn't have anything to complain about, his wife can take advantage of the opportunity and let him know that what she wanted from this marriage was not riches, but a *Talmud Chacham* (Talmudic sage) and he should go and study.

Dalia Rabinovich has managed to put these two different stories and the values they teach together into one story.

However, there are two details that come from Rabinovich's songs that don't come from either of these stories, the name Rachel and the idea of Akiva's age being forty. These come from another piece called *Avot Divrei Natan* (which comes from *Eretz Yisrael* as opposed to Babylonia).

A story is told about the beginnings of R. Akiva. Up to the age of forty, he had not yet studied a thing. Once when standing by a well he asked, "Who hollowed out this stone?" And was told, "Haven't you heard that water wears away stone?"

R. Akiva asked himself, "Is my mind harder than this stone? I will go and study at least one section of Torah." He went to a school house and he and his son began reading from a child's tablet. He and his son each took hold of one of the tablets; his teacher wrote out the aleph bet for him and that is how he learned until he learned the whole Torah.

Each day R. Akiva would gather a bundle of twigs – half he would sell to provide food for himself and the other half he would use for his personal needs. His neighbors said, "You are choking us with smoke. Sell us the twigs, buy oil, and study by the light of a lamp." He replied, "I find many uses for the twigs. To begin with I study by the light they give, then I keep warm by their heat, and finally I sleep on some of them." He went and studied for thirteen years. Then he gave his wife golden sandals and a golden tiara. His disciples said he put them to shame by what he did for her, but he replied, "Much suffering did she endure with me for the sake of the Torah."

In this story, he is an older man of forty, a father – he studies Torah like a child, and the whole time he lives with his family. He combines his Torah study with the work of cutting wood so that he can provide for his family. She doesn't send him away to study, but she encourages him, and for this he wants to honor her with golden sandals and a golden tiara.

The name Rachel comes from the ending of this version where it says:

> In the future R. Akiva required even the poor to study. And if they ask why, you should say, "Rabbi Akiva was even poorer than you." And if they ask about the children, say, "Rabbi Akiva had sons and daughters." And then say, "For the merit of Rachel, his wife, was he able to study."

Shinan wants us to look at these differing views of R. Akiva's wife, not as different people, but as different expressions of the historical times through literature. The key question here is what is to be put first, maintaining the house or study of Torah. The *Yerushalmi* story comes to teach us that only with the wife's permission can a man go out and study Torah for a month, but the *Bavli* says that you don't need the wife's permission and you can go out for even twelve years. It seems clear that the conditions of life, the distances, the geography, the character of the people and the community, and the distances between the *Bati Midrash* all affected the amount of time one could study Torah. What the rabbis have done with the different *Aggadic* stories is point out that one must make a decision about how much Torah one is allowed to study based upon the realistic needs of one's own community. The Jews living in Jerusalem were poorer, and the father needed to stay at home and work to support them. Those living in Babylonia were more accustomed to sending the real scholars out to a yeshiva to study and to leaving the wife at home working to support the family.

Then there is a third story about R. Akiva's wife – the Roman woman. This story takes place during the time of the Bar Kochba rebellion. Tineius Rufus was then ruling the city. This story comes from the Babylonian Talmud, Tractate *Avodah Zarah*. Supposedly, when R. Akiva saw the wife of Tineius Rufus, he spit, he ground his teeth, and he cried. He spit because when he saw her, he released a drop of sperm. He ground his teeth because he knew her future was to convert and to marry him. He cried because she was so beautiful and some day she would deteriorate into the ground. There is a question as to why this story was brought at all, but some feel that it was brought to deal with the question of someone being a convert. There is some feeling that the objective of this story was to bring into the fold of Judaism those women who had converted to marry Jews. If R. Akiva, the *gadol* of this generation, could have married a convert, then so could others. This is another way that the rabbis used midrash to help deal with changes in the society. Understanding this third story in this way also makes us want to go back and look at the other story and see whether we can read into them what the message for their generation was to be.

Each of these stories can be used by a different type of person to explain his situation. The wise man who wants to leave his house to go and study will use the *Bavli* version. The wise man who wants to promote the idea of staying at home and working while studying will use the *Eretz Yisrael* version (*Yerushalmi*). The one who wants to set as the example a wise man who marries a convert will use the story of the Roman woman.

What I have said up until now is a summary review of Shinan's article. What I want to add is a fourth perspective. Shinan wants us to understand *Chazal – Chachameinu Zichronam Livrocho*/Our Sages of blessed memory – in terms of what each story teaches us about a wise man, one who wants to study Torah. I want to suggest that the three women also can serve as different models for what we see is important in a wife. In the first story, the *Bavli*, the wife stands up for her convictions. She wants a wise husband and will do whatever it takes to make him go and study. She values having a strongly educated and Jewishly committed husband more than she honors "respect of her elders." She is willing to give up her ties to her family in order for her husband to be a *Talmud Chacham*.

The second story I see as portraying the romantic woman who loves her man and is willing to live in poverty with him. But she is somewhat like Rebecca, she has a goal for her husband (in Rebecca's case, for her son Jacob) and she bides her time until she can convince him of the importance of her goal. Finally, Elijah is sent by God to come to her aid. With his request for straw for his wife, he helps to show R. Akiva the importance of study, and Akiva is willing to leave her on her own.

The third story is most interesting to me because it shows R. Akiva as what I might call a modern husband – studying together with his son and working to make a living by selling wood. This is a more egalitarian story. The family works together to survive, and the wife supports the husband's need to study. I would have liked to see them in an egalitarian *Beit Midrash* (like the one at the Conservative Yeshiva) studying together and ultimately she would be the woman in the back room who figured out the hardest

Shavuot (II)

questions and whispered the answers to her "wise" husband, but then . . . I didn't write this story.

Rabikovich's song brings up another view. First, you have a younger woman falling in love with an older man. She proposes with a condition that he study Torah, but they live together in poverty for a short while before he goes off to study. She is convinced he will be a great Torah scholar and happily sends him away. He studied for twenty years, she grew old and yet he still longed for her. When he returned his students thought she was an old beggar, but he recognized her and praised her as being his holy Torah. So what do we learn about a good wife – she likes older, smarter men, is willing to wait for them and to sacrifice for them, and, in the end, she will be rewarded for her patience. Now I'm not quite sure that if I were giving Deena, Tamar or Renana some pre-dating advice this would go over well. A bit too small "c" conservative for our family.

The connection to Shavuot is easy – the value of studying Torah is paramount for Jews. I would go so far as to say that second only to observing Shabbat, studying Torah and being people of the book is what being Jewish is all about. I encourage everyone to find some way to be involved in some sort of ongoing Torah study, whether it be Ben's class, a personal *hevruta*, the Melton program, a local course, *Daf Yomi*, or just individual study. If you can squeeze in a visit to Jerusalem and the Conservative Yeshiva, even better.

Tikkun Leil Shavuot shouldn't stop with the sunrise. Rather we should all commit ourselves to deepening our Jewish knowledge and ultimately our Jewish souls.

Behaalotecha

Richard Tupper

In *Behaalotecha*, we have the interesting portrayal of the offering of the tribe of Levi. (Objective or subjective use of "of"? Keep listening!) In a way, it parallels the offerings of the princes described in *Naso*.

The repetitive format of the princes' offerings in *Naso* seems to stress the equality among the tribes and the people before HaShem. However, noticeably missing from the offerings brought in *Naso* was any offering brought by the tribe of Levi. In *Behaalotecha*, we find out why. In fact, we see that Levi brings no offering but instead becomes an offering. The tribe of Levi becomes an offering of all the tribes, and the procedure by which the people of the other tribes place their hands on each of the Levites is meant to drive home that the individual Levites are the offering of the individual members of the other tribes, paralleling the customary way you offered animals – pressing your hand on the animal you were to offer.

In short, we offer Levi as our offering and what does Levi offer? It offers its service. So, their service becomes part of our offering. Again, one aspect of this passage parallels the point of *Naso*, and that is, while there may be differences in status or function between and among us, before HaShem we are equal. When the Levite performs his service to HaShem, his actions are viewed not only as his offering but as ours as well. The Tabernacle/Temple service was part of a symbiotic relationship among all of Israel: without the other tribes, the priests and the Levites could not function; and without the priests and the Levites, the tribes would have no Temple/Tabernacle service. For the sacrificial system then and our more modern method of worship today to work, all of us are needed.

Shelach Lecha

Carol Grannick

I have thought a lot about journeys this year. There were many; there always are. My mother's life shifted in palpable ways that moved her from "older" to "old"; a big group of our Minyan children moved from elementary school to high school; I became a bionic woman; our country sent young men and women to war. Millions of journeys for millions of lives.

I read the commentary in *Etz Hayim* (bottom right, p. 840): "God seems to be saying, 'I have told you already that the land is good and that I will give it to you. If you need human confirmation of that, go ahead and send scouts.'" Something stirred in my mind. Something seemed awfully familiar.

I understand the need of the Israelites to scout out the land. To live in uncertainty is to teeter in a delicate balance between the familiar and the unknown. It is easier to try to work out some sort of blueprint for what will happen on whatever journey we embark — the first year of high school, a hip replacement, marriage, raising children, heading out for errands for that matter.

Many of us want to know what we can expect, what obstacles we may meet along the way. We have a natural fear of the unknown. The Israelites in *Shelach Lecha* are a wonderful example of this. They wanted to know what they were getting into. "Check it out," says Moses. "Are the people strong or weak, few or many? Is the country good or bad? Are the towns open or fortified? Is the soil rich or poor? Is it wooded or not? Oh, and get some grapes while you're there."

The only problem is that fear fuels their exploration, and so, colors the outcome. Ten of the scouts disagree with Caleb, and have determined that the Israelites cannot overcome the obstacles. "Okay, then let's go back to Egypt!" is the overwhelming response.

Caleb's and Joshua's scouting, however, is fueled by faith. Caleb does not even mention what he's seen. He simply says, "Absolutely – let's go!" And soon Joshua says, "It is a good land – have no fear!" Faith-based scouting sees no obstacles.

On the other hand, those who have used the scouting to gather negative, "anti-faith" information present obstacle after obstacle. After a somewhat amusing dialogue with God involving an exchange that sounds a lot like "You can't do that – what will the neighbors think?," God decides to let the unbelieving and disobedient Israelites die off naturally in the course of forty years of desert wandering, rather than killing them off immediately.

The message that came across loud and clear to me in this *parsha* is that journeys embarked upon with faith are God's preference. God puts up with the human need to scout out the territory – "go ahead if you must" – but then shows us how it backfires.

As I thought about the journeys in my own life – physical, intellectual, spiritual, psychological – they have never been as I imagined they would be. When I was younger, I never knew how to deal with these obstacles and changes. Like the Israelites, I "sent scouts" out, predicting and imagining dangers and obstacles, and limiting my journeys because of this. Scouting out the future was a sure way to die in the desert.

Gradually I learned to let up on the blueprints and maps, and embark on life's journeys – and the journey of life – as a faith-based adventure. Disappointments, obstacles, traps, detours are reminders to me that I am not in charge of planning out how my journeys will go. I see each obstacle as "God's little reminders" that I am not in charge of all the details of the journey, and that I will be capable of handling the challenges that come.

I recently took an online course in picture book writing, and, on one of the twenty intense days, we read and wrote about "Journey" books. It is notable that in many of the books – *all* the ones that I happened to choose to read and analyze that day – journeys are embarked upon with faith. There is no plan in any of these books. The protagonist wants to go somewhere new and better (geographically, intellectually, spiritually, psychologically), to move *from* some type of slavery *to* some type of freedom.

As Bob and I talked about well-known literary journey-stories, and well-known human journeys, this capacity to "go up into the land" without knowing exactly what lies ahead is at the basis of all the journeys we could think of.

I recently began reading a book because Adam asked me to – I was one-third of the way through the book, planning ahead for it to continue to be a carnival of special effects, beloved by my son, but not always by me. But because I promised, I continued, and before I knew it, I was lost in the dark

Shelach Lecha

journey of Jim and Will and Dad in the incredible and profound story, beneath the special effects, of Ray Bradbury's *Something Wicked This Way Comes*. The dark carnival was the setting for an intense and moving story of friendship, the longing for closeness between a boy and his dad, the presence of evil in all of us, and the dad's brilliant discovery for combating it. Adam was right – the book took my heart somewhere I never planned to go.

Faith-fueled journeys are adventures – as Ellen reminded me, creative adventures . . . . They may frighten us, surprise us, shock us, thrill us, and even take our breath away.

For the millions of journeys – tiny and huge, physical, spiritual, intellectual, psychological – that we all have during our lifetimes, God reminds us in *Shelach Lecha* that sending out scouts does not help, but rather inhibits.

Attempting to anticipate all the obstacles – scout them out – may be an attempt to avoid pain, fear, difficulty, and even discomfort, but it also avoids the possibility of surprise, thrill, and the rapture of life. Each journey gives us another opportunity to have faith, and leap ahead to the promised land.

Shelach Lecha (II)

Richard Tupper

In today's *parsha*, specifically in Numbers 15:22-31, HaShem gives Moses instructions about the *chattat*/purification offering. Of course, we all recall that HaShem already gave Moses instructions regarding the *chattat* in Lev. 4. But when we compare the instructions here in *Shelach Lecha* with those in Lev. 4, we notice some striking differences. For example, the instructions in *Shelach* describe only the *chattat* to be brought by the individual or the community, but Lev. 4 describes the *chattat* that must be brought not only by the individual and the community but by the high priest and the *nasi*/chieftain as well. Moreover, the sacrifices differ. In *Shelach Lecha*, if the community sins, they must bring a bull for an *olah*/whole burnt offering, accompanied by a meal and a drink offering, as well as a he-goat for a *chattat*. In Lev. 4, if the community sins, they must bring a bull as a *chattat*, not a he-goat, and there is no mention of an *olah* or any accompanying meal and drink offering.

How can these apparent inconsistencies be reconciled? Typically, modern scholars reconcile the inconsistencies by positing different sources, either two completely independent sources or a later source reworking an earlier source. This approach yields interesting results but of course it is not typical of the traditional rabbinic approach which assumes that the Torah is a divinely given unity. The great biblical commentator Ibn Ezra offers, as is frequently the case with him, a unique approach. He suggests that Lev. 4 deals with violations of prohibitive commandments (thou shalt nots), since in Lev. 4:2 (NJPS) it states that the *chattat* is brought when a person unintentionally violates "any of the LORD's commandments about things not to be done." In contrast, Ibn Ezra suggests that Num. 15, at least with respect to individuals, deals only with violations of positive commandments ("thou shalts). After all, Num. 15:22 (NJPS) begins, "And should you err and *not do* all these commandments that the LORD spoke to Moses . . . ." However, the Ramban rejects Ibn Ezra's interpretation, noting that Num. 15:24 begins, "and should it happen that it was *done* as in errancy . . . ." This verse says the person has sinned by having done something, not by having failed to do something; in other words, the sin involved violating a prohibitive mitzvah, not a positive mitzvah.

Of course this apparent discrepancy did not escape the notice of the rabbis of the Talmud, who are close readers of the Torah *par excellance*. The rabbis resolve the apparent discrepancies by positing that the two passages are dealing with different types of sins. Based upon Lev. 4:2, the rabbis conclude that Lev. 4 is aimed at violations of prohibitive mitzvot.[1] However, focusing on Numbers 15:22, the rabbis note that it says,

וכי תשגו ולא תעשו את כל-המצות האלה אשר דבר ה' אל-משה

"And should you err and not do all these commandments that the LORD spoke to Moses . . . ." The rabbis focus on the phrase "all these commandments." They ask, "which is the commandment that is as weighty as all the other commandments? Surely it is that of idolatry" (*b. Hor.* 8b). The *Sipre* takes a somewhat similar approach:

> You say the text refers to idolatry, but maybe it refers to [any]one of the commandments of the Torah. Scripture says: "If you unwittingly fail to observe all the commandments . . . ." Scripture states "*all* of the commandments" so as to give instruction about a single commandment. Just as the one who transgresses all the commandments also breaks the yoke and violates the covenant, and brings dishonor to the Torah, so also the one who breaks one commandment breaks the yoke, violates the covenant, and brings dishonor to the Torah. And which commandment is this? That of idolatry.[2]

The rabbis bring various verses in support of their interpretation, but for our purposes the important point is that the rabbis view Lev. 4 as the general rule and Num. 15 as the exception to the rule which is addressed solely to the sin of idolatry.

---

[1] And in particular, only those mitzvot for which the penalty for intentionally violating is *karet*/excision.

[2] Translation by Gary Anderson in "Purification Offering in 11Q Temple," *Journal of Biblical Literature* 111 (1992), 17-35.

Shelach Lecha (II)

While viewing Lev. 4 as the general rule and Num. 15 as the exception is one way of resolving the apparent inconsistencies, it was not the only option available to the rabbis. A modern biblical scholar, Gary Anderson, has studied the Temple Scroll that was discovered at Qumran and has argued that the community which produced the Temple Scroll viewed the matter exactly opposite to the rabbis. For the authors of the Temple Scroll, Anderson argues, Num. 15 was the general rule and Lev. 4 was the exception. For reasons I won't go into here, Anderson believes that the authors of the Temple Scroll viewed the *chattat* described in Lev. 4 as applicable only in the instance of the ordination of the priests. For all other sins, the authors of the Temple Scroll believed Num. 15 described the general rule.

What difference does it make whether we view Lev. 4 as the general rule and Num. 15 as limited only to idolatry or Num. 15 as the general rule and Lev. 4 as limited to the ordination of the priests? The "rubber hits the road," so to speak, in Num. 15:30-31. Num. 15:22-29 is dealing with a person who inadvertently sins. However, Num. 15:30-31 deals with a person who sins "with a high hand," in other words, brazenly. The person who sins brazenly, Num. 15:30-31 says, will suffer the punishment of "*karet* – being cut off." For the rabbis, then, the only persons who will be cut off for sinning intentionally are those who commit the sin of idolatry, a sin which in rabbinic times was thought to be virtually non-existent among Jews after returning from the exile. In contrast, the authors of the Temple Scroll apparently believed that the person who intentionally violated any mitzvah ought to be cut off. In short, the rabbis' approach to interpreting Lev. 4 and Num. 15 was inclusive, one that would exclude very few Jews from the community, whereas the approach of the authors of the Temple scroll was exclusive, one that would exclude almost all Jews from the community.

We Jews today are heirs of the rabbis' inclusive approach. The community which produced the Temple scroll is no more. We today ought to take to heart the lesson of the rabbis from long ago.

Shabbat shalom!

Korach

Tamar Fox

The story of the Korachite rebellions is famous for, among other things, its vivid imagery. The punishment doled out to Datan, Abiram, and *b'nei Korach* for their rebelliousness is spectacular and terrifying. According to Num. 16:32, "and the earth opened its mouth and swallowed them and their households and every human being that was Korach's and all their possessions." The mental image of people being swallowed alive by the ground is often equated with an earthquake, but the rabbis in the midrash go to great lengths to explain that this was not a natural phenomenon. Among other things, they report that a hole opened under each individual person, and it widened where the person was wider, and narrowed where he was narrower. It at first swallowed them all only up to their chests so the rest of Israel could hear their cries of agony. As soon as they went under ground, the land returned exactly to the way it had been before.

I'm fascinated by this idea of people falling or being pulled down, literally, to their demise. Why does it happen? What does it mean?

In this case, a closer look at the Korachite rebellions reveals the base of the problem. There are four conflicts, according to Jacob Milgrom's commentary in the JPS Torah Commentary: the Levites against Aaron, Datan and Abiram against Moshe, the tribal chieftains against Aaron, and the entire community against Moshe and Aaron. Korach, though, is the instigator of all of these conflicts, and according to tradition, he attempted to use all these venues to secure more power for himself. Korach's problem, then, was a personal one. He didn't like Moshe and Aaron being in charge. But he dealt with this personal problem in four very public ways. In every instance where Moshe or Aaron was being confronted it was done in front of a large group, thus humiliating the leaders, and forcing them to deal with an angry mob, rather than one power-hungry man. This required that Moshe and Aaron respond in a communal setting. Note Korach himself was not the object of any of God's wrath, rather his community of rebels. When Korach refused to keep private things private, when he, in fact, put the spotlight on them (gathering 250 chieftains of the community, according to 16:3), he was punished by having his community fall down into Sheol alive. This public/private mix-up is clearly important.

There is another instance in Judaic literature of someone falling down to their demise because of their inversion of the public/private balance. The story is found in the Babylonian Talmud, *Ketubot 63a*. The discussion surrounding the story concerns how often a man is allowed to leave his wife to study without "performing his marital duties." According to the *Gemara*,

> Rav Rehumi was a regular in the entourage of Rava in Mehoza. He used to go home on the eve of the Day of Atonement. One time, he was absorbed in his studies. At home, his wife was waiting for him, [thinking] "now he is coming, now he is coming," but he did not come. Her mind was weakened; a tear fell from her eye. He was sitting on a roof when the roof caved in below him, and he died.

Rav Rehumi, intentionally or unintentionally, replaced something private – sleeping with his wife – with something public – Torah study at Rava's yeshiva. The fact that this mistake was due to his concentration on Torah is not considered a valid excuse. Elevating the public experience over the private one was a costly mistake. Rav Rehumi found himself with the world caving in under him, much like the camp of Korach in our *parsha*.

As I looked at these two stories, I was reminded of my favorite novel, *The Bridge of San Luis Rey* by Thorton Wilder. The following sentence opens the book, "On Friday noon, July the twentieth, 1714, the finest bridge in all Peru broke and precipitated five travelers into the gulf below." This, too, is a story of people falling down alive. After a few paragraphs, Wilder introduces us to a Franciscan monk named Brother Juniper, who happened to witness the bridge snapping as he went about his work:

> At all events he felt at peace. Then his glance fell upon the bridge, and at that moment a twanging noise filled the air, as when the string of some musical instrument snaps in a disused room, and he saw the bridge divide and fling five gesticulating ants into the valley below. . . . And on that instant Brother Juniper made the resolve to inquire into the secret lives of those five persons, that moment falling through the air, and to surmise the reason of their taking off.

Korach

The next hundred pages or so are dedicated to the stories Brother Juniper gathers about these five people in an attempt to discover exactly why they died, when, and how they did. He gathers the inconclusive information in a book, but when the town judges hear of it, he and his book are deemed heretical, and they are both condemned to be burned in the town square. Brother Juniper takes the news well. Wilder tells us, "He was not rebellious. He was willing to lay down his life for the purity of the church, but he longed for one voice somewhere to testify for him that his intention, at least, had been for faith." After he is gone many of the people he spoke to when gathering information for his book begin to think about him and their lost loved ones. In the final paragraph of the novel a nun comments on the state of life,

> We ourselves shall be loved for a while and forgotten. But the love will have been enough; all those impulses of love return to the love that made them. Even memory is not necessary for love. There is a land of the living and a land of the dead and the bridge is love, the only survival, the only meaning.

Love seems to be the vital connection of many tenuous relationships. Love will clarify what is meant to be private, and what is meant to be public. If we are without it, we fall, literally, to our own demise.

Hukkat

Gail Golden

Moses' Big Mistake

And the community had no water, and they assembled against Moses and against Aaron. And the people disputed with Moses, and they said, saying, "Would that we had perished when our brothers perished before the LORD. And why did you bring the LORD's assembly to this wilderness to die here, we and our beasts? And why did you take us out of Egypt to bring us to this evil place, not a place of seed or fig tree or vine or pomegranate, and no water to drink?" And Moses, and Aaron with him, came away from the assembly to the entrance of the Tent of Meeting and fell on their faces, and the LORD's glory appeared to them. And the LORD spoke to Moses, saying, "Take the staff and assemble the community, you and Aaron your brother, and you shall speak to the rock before their eyes, and it will yield its water, and I shall bring forth water for them from the rock and give drink to the community and to its beasts." And Moses took the staff from before the LORD as He had charged. And Moses and Aaron gathered the assembly in front of the rock, and he said to them "Listen, pray, rebels! Shall we bring forth water for you from this rock?" And Moses raised his hand and he struck the rock with his staff twice and abundant water came out, and the community, with its beasts, drank. And the LORD said to Moses and to Aaron, "Inasmuch as you did not trust Me to sanctify Me before the eyes of the Israelites, even so you shall not bring this assembly to the land that I have given to them." These are the waters of Meribah, where the Israelites disputed with the LORD and He was sanctified through them.

(Numbers 20: 2-13)

What on earth is going on here? The story starts out with a very typical sequence – the Israelites are whining, Moses and Aaron take the people's complaints to God, and God tells the two leaders what to do. But then the plot goes off the rails. Instead of following God's instructions, as he had done so many, many times before, Moses decides to improvise. In fact, he resorts to a tactic which had previously worked (Ex. 17:3-7) – he strikes the rock. And God gets *very* angry. It is difficult to imagine a harsher punishment than the one he imposes on Moses and Aaron, namely that they will not live to see the fulfillment of their dream.

For me, the story raises two basic questions: 1) What was so terrible about what Moses did? and 2) Why did he do it? The commentators, not too surprisingly, go to town with this story. One of them lists thirteen different sins that Moses committed in this episode. It seems to me that the essence of Moses' misdeed is that he lost his temper in an ugly and public way, showing disrespect to the people and, ultimately, to God. This leads me to explore previous episodes of anger in Moses' life, and the role anger played in his intimate and complicated relationship with God. Here is a brief review of a few of the highlights.

As a young man, Moses sees an Egyptian beating a Hebrew, looks around, and, seeing no one watching, strikes down the Egyptian (Ex. 2:11-15). I find this incident very troubling. Moses makes no attempt to restrain or reason with the Egyptian, even though the next day he uses reasoning with two Hebrews who are fighting. And his looking around for witnesses first suggests that it is a calculated rather than an impulsive act. He gets in trouble with the Egyptians for this killing, but does God reprimand or punish him? Not a word. Does the episode prevent God from choosing Moses as the leader? Nope. Hmmm.

The next episode is the Golden Calf. God sees what the people are up to and proposes to destroy the lot of them and create a new nation from Moses. This time, Moses restrains God. Interestingly, his argument is that it will be bad PR for God – the Egyptians will say that He delivered His people from Egypt with evil intent, only to kill them off in the mountains (Ex. 32:9-13). So God spares the people, but Moses himself makes quite the display of anger – smashing the tablets, burning up the calf, grinding it to powder, mixing it with water, and making the people drink it (Ex. 19-20). Once again, God expresses no disapproval of Moses' rage.

Shortly thereafter, Moses carves the second set of tablets and goes back up on the mountain. God passes before him, proclaiming His own qualities. The one that caught my eye was "slow to anger" (Ex. 34:6). In this context,

Hukkat

the description seems a little surprising! And interestingly, later on when God is once again ready to destroy the people, Moses calms Him down by reminding him of the very description (Num 14:11-18).

There is the episode with Nadab and Abihu. There is Korach, which we studied last week. There are numerous other episodes in which either Moses or God or both of them become furious. And yet it seems as if there is a curious tension between them, a teaching and learning about the delicate balance between legitimate expression of anger and self-restraint of excessive rage. Without meaning any disrespect to either Moses or God, it seems to me that together they learn and move toward greater maturity around how to handle anger.

Until Meribah – when Moses blows it. He is not responding to injustice, as he was with the slave master. He is not reacting to outrageous idolatry, as he was with the Golden Calf. He is just ticked off, fed up, worn out, and he acts with no regard for the consequences of his anger. A lifetime of leadership, of service, of holiness – and he blows it.

Why? What went wrong that day? To my mind, the answer lies in the sentence which immediately precedes the story. "And the Israelites, the whole community, came to the Wilderness of Zin, in the first month, and the people stayed at Kadesh. And Miriam died there and she was buried there" (Num 20:1). Miriam, Aaron's beloved older sister, is the first of the siblings to die. Now I want you to listen carefully to the accounts of Aaron's and Moses' deaths, and hear what is missing from the account of Miriam's death.

> . . . and Moses came done, and Eleazar with him, from the mountain. And all the community saw that Aaron had expired, and all the house of Israel keened for Aaron thirty days. (Num 20:28-29)
> And Moses was a hundred and twenty years old when he died. His eye had not grown bleary and his sap had not fled. And the Israelites keened for Moses in the steppes of Moab thirty days . . . . (Deut 34:7-8)

Aha! For both Aaron and Moses, the community stopped to grieve for thirty days. But for Miriam – no mention of observing *shloshim*. For whatever reason, Moses and the community went right on after she died, and tragedy was the result.

As a psychologist I know that it is a grave mistake to not take time to mourn. We live in a culture which does not honor mourning. Most people take one or two days of bereavement leave, and then they are back at work as if nothing had happened. We take tranquilizers to mask our grief, and get irritated at people who seem to be carrying on too obviously or too long about their loss. And we pay a terrible price in unresolved grief, which leads to emotional and physical symptoms which plague us long afterwards.

We are so lucky as Jews to have a tradition which obligates us to take the time to mourn. And we must be grateful to our great teacher and rabbi, Moses, who on what was probably the worst day of his life taught us that even the holiest and wisest of leaders is a human being who must pay attention to his emotional needs and take time to grieve for his loved one.

Shabbat shalom.

Hukkat (II)

Andrew Kirschner

We certainly have a lot going on in *parshat Hukkat*: the Israelites do battle with the Amorites and the Canaanites, God sends serpents, we have the death of Aaron and Miriam, and the story of Moses and Aaron hitting the rock! And to start off this action-packed *parsha* we have the story of the Red Heifer (*parah adumah*). So I have chosen the story of this mysterious decree as the highlight of my *d'var Torah*.

First of all the ritual of the Red Heifer is a *hok*, which makes it a decree from God that we don't necessarily understand or that may not make much sense at all. The decree itself is the ritual performed in order to prepare the ashes used to purify a person who has touched a corpse. It is one of the most mysterious *hukkim* of the Torah. The ashes are used to remove an impurity, but anyone involved with the ritual becomes impure himself. The cow must be completely red (as few as two hairs of a different color would disqualify it). Indeed these were very rare animals. The Torah commands that it be slaughtered outside the city of Jerusalem (in contrast with other *korbanot*, which must be slaughtered in the courtyard of the Temple). However, it must still be slaughtered within the sight of the Temple and its blood sprinkled "toward the Holy of Holies" (Chabad.org).

In my research, I was unable to find an explanation for the reasoning or meaning of this ritual. I did find a story of Jochanan ben Zakkai who was questioned by a Roman about the meaning of this ritual. Ben Zakkai replied by referring him to a pagan analogy:

> "Just as a person afflicted by melancholy or possessed by an 'evil spirit' is freed of his disease by taking certain medications or by the burning of certain roots, in the same manner the ashes of the Red Heifer, prepared in the prescribed way and dissolved in water, drive away the 'unclean' spirit of defilement resulting from contact with the dead." The Roman was satisfied with the answer, and went

Leaves from the Garden

his way. Thereupon the pupils of Jochanan said to him: "That man's attack thou hast warded off with a broken reed, what answer hast thou for us?" "By your lives," said the Master, "the dead man doth not make impure, neither do the ashes dissolved in water make pure: but the law concerning the Red Heifer is a decree of the All-holy, Whose reasons for issuing that decree it behooves not mortals to question."

(Quotation taken from *Hertz*, p. 652)

Even though I was not able to find a reason for the *hok* of the *parah adumah* I did develop an explanation of why it is here in this portion. With all the action-packed story line of the reading it seems out of place to have a ritual involving creating ashes for the purification of one who has touched a corpse. But if you will allow me to humbly bestow my opinion on some interesting parallels to the story of Moses and Aaron hitting the rock.

First of all, God told Moses and Aaron to take the rod, gather up the congregation, and talk to this rock in order to bring out water for the congregation. It is something that makes no logical sense, just like the ritual of the Red Heifer. However, just as we are obligated to observe the ritual as one of God's decrees, so should Aaron and Moses have listened to what they were told to do.

There is a great mystery surrounding the ritual, just as there is a great mystery surrounding the nature of the sin that Aaron and Moses committed that ultimately led to their severe punishment. Rashi says that it was because they hit the rock versus talking to the rock that they were punished. Some rabbis say that it was because he hit the rock twice. Maybe the water didn't come out right away when he hit it the first time, and he hit it again displaying a lack of faith. The Rambam insists that it was because Moses says "hear ye rebels." Calling the Chosen People of Israel rebels for demanding a basic need such as water was not his right.

The third parallel comes with the punishment itself. In Numbers 19:13 it says, "Whosoever touches a dead body, a human being who has died, and does not cleanse himself, he defiles the LORD's Tabernacle, and that person shall be cut off from Israel, for riddance water was not thrown upon him. He is unclean; and his uncleaness is still in him." So, anyone who enters the Tabernacle of the LORD without having gone through the ritual after having touched a corpse, that person shall be cut off from Israel. In Numbers 20:12 it says, "Inasmuch as you did not trust Me to sanctify Me before the eyes of the Israelites, even so you shall not bring this assembly to the land that I have

Hukkat (II)

given to them." Moses and Aaron too were cut off for not following a direct order from God.

Well, getting back to a more reputable source of interpretation, other than me, there is a midrash that again does not explain the mystery of the Red Heifer, but made me more comfortable with the whole thing.

In the time of the Temple, the *Kohen Gadol* (High Priest) used to wear a breastplate with a jewel for each of the twelve tribes of Israel. Each jewel was a specific color and cut to a specific measurement. One day it was discovered that one of the jewels was missing and needed to be replaced. So, they searched all over Israel and could not find a match for the missing jewel. They even searched beyond the borders of Israel and they heard that a non-Jew named Gamma Ben Nessina, a master craftsmen, might have the jewel they were looking for. They traveled hundreds of miles to his house, knocked on his door, and explained the situation. Ben Nessina said that he was pretty sure he had the jewel, and it was locked in his safe. He retreated to another room and came back a few minutes later empty-handed. He explained that he was almost certain that he had the jewel in his safe, but the safe was locked. The key to the safe was under a pillow that his father was sleeping on. He did not want to wake his father, so they would just have to wait.

The sages thought this was simply a ploy to get more money, so they immediately offered him 50 percent more money. Ben Nessina insisted that he didn't want any more money; he just did not want to disrespect his father by waking him. So they offered him even more money: double, and even, 200 percent, but he would not wake his father. Just then, an old man peered into the room and looked like he had just woken up from a nap. Ben Nessina ran into the other room, got the key and retrieved the jewel from the safe. It was the right jewel and he only charged the sages the original amount, because he did not want to profit from observing a custom to respect his parents.

Several years later, it is said that Gamma Ben Nessina was rewarded by having a red cow in his field. These were so rare they only came once every three or four generations. So word spread quickly that he had the red cow, and the sages returned to buy it. They paid him a huge sum of money for the red cow.

Now, the angels in heaven cried up to God and asked, "Why do we need the Jews? Even a non-Jew can follow your commandment to honor your mother and father. What is so special about the Jews?" God replied, "Anyone can honor their parents because this is a mitzvah that makes sense. You are raised by your parents. They feed you, they clothe you, they protect you. It is natural to want to respect them. Anyone will honor their parents, but only the Jews will travel hundreds of miles and pay an extraordinary amount of money for a mitzvah that they don't even understand!"

In the Torah we have many mitzvot. Many are *mishpatim*, or laws. They generally make sense to us, like don't steal, or don't kill. Some are *hukkim* or decrees that don't have an inherent meaning, like don't eat pork, or don't wear wool and linen. I came across a story on the Internet about a rabbi who was giving a lecture about the practice of putting on *tefillin*. A student stood up in the back of the room and shouted, "How can you expect me to put on *tefillin* when I don't even believe in God!" The rabbi retorted, "Put on *tefillin* and I assure you will start to believe in God."

I will leave you with a question. If we observe the *hukkim* of the Torah, despite our lack of understanding, doesn't that make the laws we do understand that much more special to observe?

Balak

Joel Teibloom

The story of Bilaam is told at length, being played out over almost the entire *parsha*. But who is Bilaam? We are conflicted in our assessment of Bilaam as he is presented in two strikingly different and contradictory depictions both within the biblical text itself and in the midrash.

I. Bilaam as a servant of Hashem

Initially, I admit to a certain pre-disposition toward Bilaam as a "good guy" since on the surface much of what he does is admirable. It is also easy to believe that much of the strong and even extreme condemnation of Bilaam in our tradition comes from a certain xenophobic bias. Let us first portray Bilaam in the most positive light:

He states clearly that he cannot be hired without the consent of Hashem. It is noteworthy that Bilaam is familiar with Hashem, not merely a generic name for God such as Elohim, which is often used when referring to non-Israelites addressing God.

Bilaam clearly states that he cannot be bought. All the gold and silver will not dissuade him from saying the word of God, which is put into his mouth. On the surface, this seems to be a man of principle. Similarly, he restates that he won't say a word without God's approval.

Of course when the moment of truth comes, Bilaam lives up to this promise. He not only refuses to curse Israel for Balak but, in what is described by some commentators as true prophecy, he exceeds the actual words of God and has his own vision of Israel. It is noteworthy that his language "*mah tovu ohalecha Yaakov* – How goodly your tents, O Jacob" – is not only such beautiful poetry that it is included in the liturgy, but that it is one of the very first things we say in the morning *daven*ing.

This positive vision of Bilaam is also seen in the Midrash. Some commentators see him as the equal of Moshe, and some say, perhaps shockingly, he was even better. For example, it is pointed out that Moshe did not recognize the voice of God when he was called from the burning bush, but Bilaam has no problem divining God's presence and comprehending him. Similarly, it is pointed out that Moshe did not know when God would speak to him, but Bilaam knew to draw aside when God wanted his attention. Lastly, it has been pointed out that Bilaam had the ability to communicate with God whenever he chose, but Moshe had to wait to be called. Plainly, there is a strong strand in our tradition of Bilaam as (at least at this point in our story) true to the word of God and even incorruptible.

II. Bilaam as the schemer and curser of Israel

Those whose view of Bilaam is negative in our tradition see him as a schemer and a potential curser of Israel. He would have sold out the people but for God's vigilance in protecting us from his plain intention to say something evil about the people and collect the promised reward. They view his protestations that he is unable to do anything beyond the word of God as either a negotiating tactic to increase the promised reward, or said with a wink and an outstretched hand.

There is certainly textual support for this view as well. God is straightforwardly described as being angry when Bilaam goes on the mission after receiving the second group of dignitaries. Certainly, if God is angry with you, there is reason to believe that you did *something* wrong. This is not an implicit or interpretive verse. It explicitly says God was angry!

Additionally, one interpretation of the fact that Bilaam left "early" to go on his mission with the dignitaries is that he was eager to get going and to see if he could find a way to manipulate the situation to get the big reward. This is a common interpretation of the "early to rise" phenomenon in biblical travel planning. Another midrash suggests that Bilaam intended to circumvent God's will in this manner and always intended to say whatever was necessary to get the reward. (This school of thought views the initial protests of Bilaam to the dignitaries as a negotiation tactic.)

Another view of Bilaam's departure as revealing his negative intent is based on reading God's instruction to him as an illusory choice. When God tells him he may go, but only if he does what God wants, he should know that there is no way to satisfy his prospective employers and still be true to God's command. Therefore he should refuse to participate in any way. His agreement to go with them – and doing so in apparent eagerness by leaving early in the morning – suggest (this view would maintain) that he failed to understand the immutable nature of God's will. Perhaps, he believes that he can manipulate even God's will to his own ends, a distinctly un-Jewish view.

The main reason to believe that Bilaam is off to a questionable start is God's apparent need to teach him a lesson. The famous episode of the talking ass is a literary mechanism for humiliating Bilaam by mocking his special skills. His claim of prophetic sight is specifically mocked by his inability to perceive the angel and the sword that even his ass can see. Similarly, his prophetic speech is questioned by putting words into the mouth of a "dumb beast." Bilaam is forced to make an admission ("I did not know") that contradicts his claim of wisdom.

There are several other delicious ironies in the episode. First, the mighty wordsmith cannot defeat his own donkey in verbal duel and must draw a sword. Similarly, what does it say about a man whose power is so great that his words have been hired to defeat an entire army, when he must resort to brute strength to defeat an ass? This is highlighted with the comic touch of Bilaam seeking a sword when one is directly in front of him.

This view is best summed up by this quotation from the commentary in Excursus 57 of the JPS Torah Commentary to *Bemidbar* (Yes, Tup, it was written by Jacob Milgrom): "In truth, Balaam is depicted on a lower level than his ass: more unseeing in his inability to detect the angel, more stupid in being defeated verbally by his ass, and more beastly in subduing it with his stick whereas it responds with tempered speech."

The view of those who see Bilaam as evil is strengthened, of course, by the subsequent misdeeds attributed to him in later biblical stories.

III. Sorcerer v. diviner

The views of Bilaam are parallel to two differing perceptions of him: whether he is a sorcerer or a diviner. Divination is the science of reading omens. One who merely divines the will of God is not an offense to the biblical view of the world; he is attempting to discern the immutable will of God, and may even be a prophet. A sorcerer, however, is one who attempts to manipulate future events (read: the will of God) through various arcane and secret procedures. This, of course, is contrary to the biblical view and is indeed anathema. God's will is not subject to manipulation by trickery or parlor games.

The tension in the biblical story is the conflict between these two competing ideas. Bilaam (with the possible exception of the donkey story) clearly portrays himself in this *parsha* as one who is a diviner. He can only recount the words that God puts in his mouth and cannot do anything of his own accord. He cannot even accept a commission unless God consents.

Balak, on the other hand, clearly perceives Bilaam as one who has the power to change future events (*i.e.*, a sorcerer). Balak wants to hire a sorcerer, one who can manipulate the coming events to defeat Israel. Despite even Bilaam's own protestations, Balak believes this is what he does so well and will do for hire. Even in the face of repeated blessings in lieu of curses, Balak clings to this belief. (Excursus 59 (in the same JPS volume; yes, Tup, also by Milgrom) wonderfully flushes out this topic.)

IV. Later biblical and post-biblical views

These views of Bilaam are more commonly negative. Deuteronomy is less accepting of the idea that prophecy can exist outside Israel and therefore is more inclined to demonize Bilaam. In Talmudic stories, Bilaam is seen as helping Pharaoh, the archetypal villain (never mind the geographic and temporal displacement).

V. Conclusion

We are still left with differing views of Bilaam. When in doubt, however, turn to *gematria*. Consistent with some of the parallels drawn between Bilaam and Moshe we compare them numerologically. Bilaam = 142; Moshe = 345. The difference is 203 or "Ger" (convert or stranger). This may be the only difference.

Alternatively, the site for both Moshe and (some of) Bilaam's encounters with God is on the mountain, God's remote and preferred location for talking to mere humans. The Hebrew word for mountain or "*har*" is 205. if you remove the prophetic portion of the encounter ("*navi*" or prophet = 63), we are left with 142, or the *gematria* for Bilaam. All that is left after removing the prophecy is a mere human.

Or perhaps, Bilaam is both good and evil at various times, like so many others of the human species. As with so much else, the image of what we are viewing is ultimately defined in the eyes of the beholder.

Pinchas

Shira Eliaser

The first time we meet Shimon and Levi, they are "rescuing" their sister from a smooth-talking rapist, and by "rescuing" we mean "savagely murdering the perpetrator, massacring his entire clan, and enslaving the survivors." When their father accuses them of provoking reprisals and putting the entire family in danger, they reply, *"Ha'chzonah na'aseh et achoteinu?"* Should our sister be treated like a whore? We're living in a country where some guy thinks he can take her and rape her and then say, "It's OK, I'll pay you for her!" We didn't make this danger, Dad, it's been here all along. What were we supposed to do, sit and discuss the situation by committee? Write to the newspaper about the nationwide decline in moral fiber and family values? They done us wrong! Let's get 'em!

The brothers make a very compelling argument, but neither time nor reflection bears them out. "They done us wrong! Let's get 'em!" has never been a motto endorsed by Judaism. Yes, it's important to defend your family, but, however real the danger may have been, there was no excuse for that kind of bloodbath. Shimon and Levi's readiness to destroy anyone who stood in their way, their readiness to write their own international law, to do what they thought was right in spite of their father's remonstrations is totally condemned by the Tanach. Shimon and Levi become the villains of rabbinic literature. They are condemned throughout the Torah *sh'bichtav* (Written Torah) and vilified throughout the Talmud and Midrash. Later in *Bereshit*, when Joseph chooses to imprison Shimon while his ten brothers return to Canaan, Rashi comments that Joseph was really just trying to separate Shimon and Levi; he figured if they were allowed to work together, they'd probably try to assassinate him too! Rashi doesn't trust Shimon and Levi to do so much as bring home the groceries without stopping to whack someone along the way. Shimon and Levi's insistence that they alone can dispense justice, whenever and however they feel like it, breaks the family apart and creates a world where no one can trust anyone else. At the end of the patriarchal period, Shimon and Levi are cursed instead of blessed: *"arur apam kee az v'evratam kee kashatah* – Cursed be their fury so fierce, and their wrath so remorseless! *Achaklem b'Yaakov v'afitzem b'Yisrael* – I will divide them in Jacob, disperse them in Israel."

Flash forward several centuries. Shimon and Levi themselves are dead and gone, but the things that they stood for remain very much alive. In their lifetimes, they passed their ideals on to their families, and those families have grown and flourished. Shimon and Levi have left an enduring legacy in the tribes that bear their names, two great clans of passionately judgmental extremists who think with their hearts, follow their instincts, and believe that aggression is a solution. But Jacob's curse has come true: Shimon and Levi are separated, dispersed. They are no longer acting as a team. Each of them has taken these instincts in a different direction.

Route 152 down Memory Lane. Next stop: The Golden Calf.

I hate to say it, but Cecil B. DeMille got this one right. When the moo cow gets brought out, Aaron tries to proclaim a Festival for the LORD, but the ringleaders take the matter in a different direction and say, "These are your gods, O Israel, who brought you up from the land of Egypt!" "*Vayeshev ha-am l'echol v'shatu v'yakumu l'tzachek* – the people sat down to eat, and they drank, and they got up to . . . party" [Eds.' note: Shira's translation]. *L'tzachek* – loosely translated "to party" – is not a nice verb in Hebrew. There's no real equivalent in English, but when Sarah sees Yishmael doing it, she has him thrown out of the house within 24 hours. When King Avimelech sees Isaac and Rebekah doing it, he calls them in and says, "Ergh!!! Why did you say she was your sister? That lady is your wife!" It's what the Philistines do to Samson when they capture him as a P.O.W. Abu Gharib, anyone? These guys with the Golden Calf are not just dancing the hora here.

"*Vayar Moshe et ha am ki forah hu, ki faro Aharon l'shmitzah b'kameyhem.* And Moses saw that people, that it was let loose, for Aaron had let them loose as a shameful thing to their adversaries. *Vayaamod Moshe b'shaar hamachaneh yayomer, mi l'Adoshem elai, v'yeasfu eilav kol b'nei Levi.* And Moses stood at the gate of the camp and said, 'Whoever is for the LORD, to me!' And the Levites gathered round him."

Moshe is about to give a terrible order. He's going to tell the people who have joined him to put down the rebellion, to end this mayhem by any means necessary. Anyone who can party like this after having stood at Sinai and heard God's voice in their head telling them not to murder and not to commit adultery is a lost cause, and their presence is endangering not just certain

Pinchas

people in the community, but the very existence of the community itself. Their appalling disregard for the basic rules of human society is preventing the formation of any kind of Godly community around them. *"Koh amar Adoshem elohei Yisrael*: Thus said the LORD God of Israel, 'Put every man his sword on his thigh, and cross over and back from gate to gate in the camp, and each man kill his brother and each man his fellow and each man his kin.' "

Levi's children willingly follow these orders – and not just because they're Moshe's relatives and they want their boy to look good on camera. Levi's spirit is still the spirit of action, and he still is using violence to achieve his ends. He's the one who's going to slam the door on the committee for the investigation of Goldencalfgate, and go do something about it. But something in Levi has changed. It's no longer about us and our people, about who done us wrong and what we're gonna do to them now. It's no longer an issue of protecting one's family at the expense of an entire city. Levi is looking at the whole of society, not just his particular friends and relatives. Levi is putting this passion, this aggression, in the service of a higher ideal. He is fighting not for himself, his ego, and his family honor, but for his community, his principles, and his God. He's still ready to defy the majority, to fly in the face of the older generation and do what he thinks is right, but he's not doing it because someone done him wrong, he's doing it because God asked him to and because the consequences of what's he's doing will benefit everyone in the long run. In stark contrast to the episode at Shechem, where Levi did what he did because he wanted his family to come out on top, Levi now has more important things on his mind than factionalism and blind loyalty. Now he's willing to go against his heart, to take a stand against his own family if he has to, for the sake of a better tomorrow.

What about Shimon? Where has Shimon been during all of this? When Moshe is looking for a few good men to do a dirty job, Shimon is nowhere to be found. The tribe of Shimon is strangely silent whenever Moshe and Aaron identify a threat to the community and call for retaliation. The next time we hear from Shimon, it isn't even the tribe who's springing into action, it's one lone member. Something Shimon has done has fractured his tribe from one unified entity into a collection of disparate individuals.

Route 152 down Memory Lane. Last stop: the end of last week's *parsha*.

In the face of a national crisis, when Jewish men are being seduced by Midianite women and assimilating into the fertility cult of *Baal-Peor*, when Moshe has executed several leading officials for idolatry, when even Moshe is calling for violence as a solution, Zimri ben Salu, chief of the clan of Shimon . . . brings a Midianite gold-digger to shul.

The only member of the tribe of Shimon to have anything to do with this unpleasant cause isn't trying to solve the problem, he's deliberately exacerbating it! What's almost worse, he's not even trying to rally his tribe in communal support of the Free Love movement ("All we are saying is give Baal a chance . . ."). Communal support and national unity mean nothing to Zimri ben Salu! He has lost all sense of clan connection, all sense of community responsibility, all sense that the actions he takes can affect the lives of people around him. Anyone who doesn't like what he's doing can talk to the hand, because they hain't got no call to bring down his groove.

Not only has Zimri abandoned his moral fiber and his God, he's also abandoned his fellow human beings. Zimri has to be stopped and he has to be stopped fast, before even one other Jew considers the advantages of his carefree lifestyle. And to everyone's surprise, the one who takes up the spear to stop him isn't his sworn enemy from the tribe of Menashe or Ephraim, isn't his father defending the honor of the family, it isn't even Moses, who's got a pretty big stake in all this. Shimon's chief is ultimately stopped by Pinchas ben El'azar ben Aharon haCohen, great-great-grandson of Levi. "*Vayar Pinchas ben El'azar ben Aharon haCohen, vayakam mitoch ha-eidah, vayikach romach b'yado. Vayavo achar ish Yisrael el ha-kubah vayikod et shneihem, et ish Yisrael v'et ha-ishah el kavatah.* Pinchas took in this scene and rose up from the midst of the crowd, taking his spear in his hand. He followed the Israelite man into the chamber and skewered them both, the Israelite man and the woman, through the stomach" [Eds.' note: Shira's translation]. The patriarchal curse has been fulfilled in the most gruesome of terms. Shimon and Levi are separated, all right: instead of brothers and partners, they are blood enemies.

What happened? Where was the rift? When did Shimon and Levi stop seeing the world through the same eyes? When did one of them get on the wrong end of the spear?

Levi turned outward; Shimon turned inward. Like Levi, he's stopped looking at the world in terms of us *vs.* them. Shimon no longer thinks about us and who done us wrong, but instead, he's thinking about me and who's in my face. Levi has reined in his instincts and holds himself back until God gives the word; Shimon follows each and every instinct wherever it takes him. Shimon is a man who follows his heart, no matter what society says; he'll defy the older generation and take an aggressive stand for what he believes in, but he's not doing it for the community or even for his family.

Pinchas

He's not doing it for the good of anybody except himself! The fact that casual sex with strange women is creating a serious assimilation problem – as well as a mysterious plague that's circulating around the camp – is not an issue for Shimon. He's following his heart! He's taking a stand! And that's what's important!

Shimon has held onto everything that his ancestor did wrong in the massacre at Shechem. He's headstrong, he's aggressive, he's totally sociopathic, and he springs into action because his comfort level is on the line. And these days, when he's defying the big guys and doing what he thinks is right, he's not looking out for his sister, kidnapped and raped and taken from her family, he's doing it for his current squeeze. The devastation he's wreaking is no less then what he's caused in the past, but now he's not even dignifying this behavior with any kind of honorable motive.

Levi, on the other hand, is headstrong and aggressive and totally sociopathic, but he springs into action because the community is falling apart and he wants to be the one who pulls it together. He's defying the crowd and doing what he thinks is right, not for his sister, but for his principles, his nation, and his God. His sister will never get treated like a whore, not because he's going to massacre the relatives of anyone who breathes on her, but because he's going to build a society where she can walk the streets without fear.

God places the tribe of Levi in charge of the sanctuary. The old curse is still in full force – they are still going to be dispersed and landless among the tribes – but these living arrangements are no longer a punishment, they're a privilege! Levi has a job in the sanctuary – he doesn't have to worry about little things like agriculture. Levi's children have shown that they can rise above his tendency to think about every issue in terms of his team, that they can protect ideals as well as individual people; they are rewarded by becoming the perennial protectors of the nation's spirituality. By using his own worst and most dangerous tendencies – aggression, ruthlessness, rage – in defense of society rather than in spite it, Pinchas transforms Levi's curse into a blessing. "*Lachen emor hinneni noten lo et briti shalom* – Therefore say: 'I hereby grant him My covenant of peace.' "

Mattot

Steve Oren

Some of you will have noticed that Sam Fox read two *aliyot* today. When I sent an e-mail to the Fox family, asking for their help, I said that this was an appropriate time for them. For *Mattot* is the start of the three weeks of mourning that leads up to Tisha b'Av, when we remember the destruction of the Temples and read *Eichah*. And what does it say in *Eichah*? "On Mt. Zion that is destroyed, the Foxes walk upon it" (Lamentations 5.18).[1] When else might such an appeal be timely? On Pesach – for on that holiday we read *Shir HaShirim* and what does it say there? "Let us take for ourselves the Foxes" (Song of Songs 2:15).

What do we see from this? There is a curious and dialectical link between Pesach, the season of our redemption, and Tisha b'Av, the anniversary of the destruction. There are many such links. In the calendar, the first day of Pesach is *Alef*, the first letter of the Hebrew alphabet. Tisha b'Av starts with a *Tav*, the last letter. Yet, they always fall on the same day of the week. In today's *haftarah*, God appoints Yirmiyahu as a prophet – as the prophet of the destruction (see esp. Jer. 1: 14-15). But, when Yirmiyahu first speaks to *Klal Yisrael*, what does he say in God's name? "I remember the loving-kindness of your youth" (Jer. 2:2) – he is talking about Pesach. Indeed, Moshe, the prophet of redemption, and Yirmiyahu, the prophet of destruction, are the only two prophets who at first refuse to be prophets (compare Jer.1:5-10 with Ex. 3). In *Melakhim* and *Yirmiyahu*, Tisha b'Av is when the Jews leave the Land of Israel; in *Yehoshua*, Pesach is when they enter it. Nor is it an accident that Ruth, the grandmother of the Messiah, enters the land of Israel at Pesach time.

When we move from *pesuqim* to logic, we see why this connection must be so. Pesach and Tisha b'Av both represent times of danger for the Jewish

---

[1] Eds.' note: in this *d'var Torah*, all translations from the Hebrew are Reb Oren's.

people. But how are they different? At Pesach, God comes to our aid and saves us. At Tisha b'Av, he does not do so. The issue is then to distinguish, among times of danger, Pesachs from Tisha b'Avs.

Indeed, that was the problem in Yirmiyahu's time as well. Yirmiyahu did not just have a message of destruction. He did not just have a religious message of repentance. He had a political message. Do not rebel against Babylon. Do not put yourself into danger. But everyone knew that this was a time of danger. The central episode is the confrontation in Chapter 28 between Hananiyah[1] and Yirmiyahu. Hananiyah accepts that this is a time of danger. But, he argues, God is a mighty god. We are the people of God. This city is the City of God. This temple is the Temple of God. Therefore, He will come to our aid and break the yoke of the Babylonians as I break this rod of wood. And Yirmiyahu's answer was: you may indeed break the rod of wood but a rod of iron will be substituted for it. God is not coming to our aid.

The confrontation between Hananiyah and Yirmiyahu is not one for that generation only. It is being played out today: most obviously as Hananiyah's Hasidim march out in orange. For the entire logic of staying in Gaza depends upon the assumption that we live in a time of Pesach, where eight thousand settlers can sustain themselves among 1.3 million Palestinians, where less than 1 percent of Gaza's population can seize 25 percent of Gaza's land.

Yet, the problem is not the settlers, they are but a symptom. They did not spring up out of nothing. Rather, the problem is the assumption that modern Zionism is but the adaptation of Jewish messianism, as if Bar Kokhba, Shabbetei Tzvi, and Ben Gurion form a chain – but this time it worked. This spirit is seen in circles far removed from the settlers. Arthur Hertzberg comments on the ideology of American Jewish organizations that they believe, "There is no God and He gave us the Land."[2] It is also the spirit behind the phrase that has come into our liturgy, that Israel is the *"reshit smikhat geultatano* / the beginning of the process of our redemption." Now,

---

[1] Consistency would require that if I speak of Yirmiyahu, I speak of Hananiyahu. Or, if I speak of Hananiyah (as the text in 28 does), I speak of Yirmiyah (as the text in 28 does). But most of the rest of the book uses the long form Yirmiyahu and he is more familiar to us by that name. Hence, I have chosen to be inconsistent.

[2] Arthur Hertzberg A *Jew in America* (San Francisco, Harper 2002), p. 360. Looking this up, I found the actual quotation is "There is probably no God but He chose the Jewish people for a very special destiny and He gave them the Holy Land."

that is a fine poetic phrase – it should be as it was written by Shai Agnon. But if taken, not as poetry, but as fact, it is a very dangerous phrase. It suggests that Israel is something more than a mere state. States are after all boring contrivances with no purpose except to stop Reuven from killing Shimon and Levi from raping Dinah. They are not vehicles of redemption. To say that they are is to adopt the language of Pesach – and to put us in danger of a Tisha b'Av.

Gershom Scholem, who knew a thing or two about Jewish mysticism, has an essay[1] in which he argues that Zionism is not a continuance of Jewish messianism. Rather, it is a break with that messianism. It says not that God will save us but that we live in an age in which God is silent, an age in which Jews must act to advance their interests, realizing that they are subject to the same laws and rules as all the nations of the earth. It is by following that advice, by realizing that the Israeli state is not the King Messiah and that we do not live in Messianic times, that we can follow the advice of Yirmiyahu. It is by avoiding the idea that this is Pesach that we avert turning our day into a Tisha b'Av.

---

[1] "The Politics of Mysticism: Isaac Breuer's New Kuzari" in his *The Messianic Idea in Judaism* (New York, Shocken 1971), pp. 325-334.

Mattot (II)

Jesse Bacon

I initially intended to only speak about our trip to Mexico, but I don't get to do these very often, and I couldn't pass up the actual content of the *parsha*. I am not someone who believes we should sugarcoat or explain away the passages which are troubling to a modern ear. Rather, by considering them, even with unavoidably biased modern minds, we can make meaning for the present.

I am going to read excerpts from the relevant passage (Numbers 31) because I don't want anyone to miss out on the language. Here it is:

> And Moses spoke to the people, saying, "Send forth a vanguard of men from you for the army, for them to be against Midian to exact the LORD's vengeance from Midian . . . ." And they arrayed against Midian, as the LORD had charged Moses, and they killed every male . . . . And Moses was furious with the commanders of the force . . . who came from the battling army. And Moses said to them, "You have let every female live! Look, these are the ones who led the Israelites by Balaam's word to betray the LORD's trust in the affair of Peor, and there was a scourge against the LORD's community. And now, kill every male among the little ones, and every woman who has known a man in lying with a male, kill. And all the little ones of the women who have not known lying with a male, let live.

The slaughter of the Midianite women seems an extreme act of vengeance even by the standards of Torah. I feel that if I were not to use the great opportunity of a *dvar* to comment on it, I would be remiss. One *dvar* I read that dealt with another portion of this *parsha*, the ability of a husband to annul his wife's vow, focused in on the fact that if he doesn't speak up, his silence is taken as an assent. In a skillful repositioning of the theme for a modern audience, the commentator focused less on the issues of sexism here in favor of the much more progressive idea that we need to speak up or have things continue on without us.

However, I don't want to focus on the issue of marital vows, thrilled as I am to be reunited with Karey and thus able to immediately take issue with something she says. Nor do I want to tell you how against the slaying of Midianite women I am. What I would like to do, instead, is pose three questions that I think are incumbent on us as the contemporary inheritors of the legacy of these acts. These questions apply to any military action. For me they draw on principles that are both universal and Jewish, and I would like to pose them to this *parsha*. I hope you will at least agree that the questions are interesting, and come up with your own answers.

The first question is in some ways the most difficult to have an interesting conversation about. That is, "Is this moral?" Clearly our modern mores do not permit the wholesale slaughter of women. However, I would be interested to study the rules of warfare in the Torah and figure out how exceptional it is. Indeed, next week we will read that women and children were killed in Heshbon. Part of what seems to set this passage off is that Moshe gives the direct order after the battle is over. Of course, at this point, Moshe is speaking directly with God, and certainly has no one to challenge his authority, so the question of morality doesn't really come up.

The second question for me is, "Is it proportionate?" This is a term straight out of international law, but for me it has Jewish roots as well. We all learn the clichéd version of "An Eye for an Eye" as an undesirable or savage concept, but at its heart is the idea that the response to a crime must be proportionate to the severity of the crime itself. Of course, though the concept is introduced in Exodus, there is not yet a functioning legal system. Nonetheless, if we accept proportionality as a fundamental value, we can still try to apply it in this case. The problem I see is that in the original crime, the Israelites paid for the sins by suffering a plague, and a man and a (Midianite) woman are executed by the same thrust. So the actions seem less about the actual crime of the Midianites and more a tactic by Moshe to increase the soldiers killing ardor. Incidentally, the heresy was actually with the Moabites, not the Midianites. But in the fog of war, who can tell them all apart?

My final question that I think we should always ask in such matters is, "Will this extreme action have the desired effect?" In this case, it seems to have, as the Israelites do conquer the Midianites utterly and go on to take possession of the Promised Land. However, Midianites pop up again in the

Mattot (II)

Book of Judges, calling into question whether they have really been completely vanquished. And, of course, the problem of idolatry persists in the biblical narrative. So while it was successful in the short term, I would question whether the ultimate goal of security and religious purity was attained by the action, and, thus, whether it was worth it.

So we are left with an episode that does not fare well morally or pragmatically, one that takes place in the heat of battle. We have the luxury of not physically being present in the battlefield (though, of course, there are many around the world who are present in the battlefield). We can use the framework I have outlined or an alternative one, but I would argue that we need to engage in this type of thought. Whatever we think of various leaders, they are not Moshes, and they do not have a hotline to God. We need to make sense of their actions even in the most troubled times.

Shabbat shalom.

Mattot (III)

By Joshua Burton

"*Bli neder.*" We all know that vows are trouble. Later this summer in *Ki Teitze*, we learn there is no sin in forbearing to vow, and the Quakers, for example, take this so seriously that "I solemnly swear *or affirm*" has become an American courtroom cliche. The single best-attended service of the Jewish year is a legal formula designed to release us from the bonds of our rash vows.

Yet the sanctity of the *nazir*, and of many of our prophets, inheres in the vows that they take, and the yoke of Torah itself came upon us through the vow at Sinai: "we shall do and we shall hear," a vow taken under duress but later, in the time of Ezra, freely affirmed as binding upon us all.

In today's *parsha*, we encounter a qualification that is not congenial to our egalitarian sentiments: a woman who vows does so at the pleasure of her father or husband, who can absolve her of her most solemn vow at a word. The Mishnah adds to this a law (which, by *Hagiga* 1:8, "hovers in the air with nothing to support it" in written Torah) to permit a sage to release a vow by annulment, under a fiction that the vow was taken without full awareness of its implications. The idea that any mortal can have this *full* awareness is, of course, absurd: this is where the old parable of the evil vow always begins.

Many cultures tell this cautionary tale: the Greek Eurydice, the Norse Freya, and our own Jephthah's daughter were all victims of their loved ones' imprudent vows. But the most vivid telling I know is in the *Silmarillion*, the detailed Elvish mythology Tolkien built as a backstory to the *Lord of the Rings*. The first of Elvish artisans, Fëanor, has been robbed of his masterwork, and he *really* wants it back.

> Then Fëanor swore a terrible oath. His seven sons leapt straightway to his side and took the selfsame vow together, and red as blood shone their drawn swords in the glare of the torches. They swore an oath which none shall break, and

none should take, by the name even of Ilúvatar, calling the Everlasting Dark upon them if they kept it not; and Manwë they named in witness, and Varda, and the hallowed mountain of Taniquetil, vowing to pursue with vengeance and hatred to the ends of the World Vala, Demon, Elf or Man as yet unborn, or any creature, great or small, good or evil, that time should bring forth unto the end of days, whoso should hold or take or keep a Silmaril from their possession.[1]

You just know this is going to end badly, don't you? And of course it does: the oath pursues Fëanor and his sons to the end of the world, and to the final wreck of all that is good. The last two survivors, twisting in their folly, try to break the oath at last, but fate conspires against them and even in this they fail; the Silmarils are destroyed.

Why would the Torah even expose us to this danger? What is the good in a vow, that we should even be put in the way of temptation to its proverbial evil?

I think the crucial clue is in the first verses of today's *parsha*, in that paternal (and paternalistic) absolution clause. What to us may seem mere sexism must be viewed in the context of a society where most women were under the authority of a father or husband; the *parsha* is quite clear that a widow's vow must stand, so it is not the daughter's or wife's feminine frailty but rather her position in society that makes her vow erasable. And similarly, every man who vows is provided in the oral law with an escape clause, through the authority of a sage. Extending this notion, we can characterize Moriah not only as the physical binding of Yitzhak, but also as the binding of Avraham by a vow of one word, "*hineni*," from whose black consequences he is also released by heavenly authority. And in fear that our vow at Sinai might also be annulled by its Author, the Rabbenu Gershom ben Yehuda tried to convert it into a marital vow, binding on husband (*haShem*) as well as on wife (Israel) by a ban on giving a forced *get*. In a coequal partnership, it seems, there is no longer authority to annul a vow.

Here's what I think is going on. A vow is a self-imposed present constraint against future action: it allows the vower, for the sake of the vow, to guard against his own future weakness – to do, not what he will want to do, but what he feels he *should* want to do. If we had infinite foresight and wisdom, this would be all there is to vowing. But in the real world, a vow binds the vower not only against himself but against unforeseen future

---

[1] J. R. R. Tolkein, *The Silmarillion* (Houghton Mifflin Co. 1977), p. 83.

Mattot (III)

reality: it permits him to make promises that he would have disavowed *at the time they were made* if he had only known then what he knows later. This is how vows in the bad stories always bite the hand that swore them.

How then can we keep the machinery of the vow as a fence against weakness, without turning it into a goad to folly? It's no good to say that the *vower himself* should be allowed to annul, for a vow from which I can withdraw at will is no fence at all against a future defect in my will. Nor can a servant who submits *to me* help me out of my trap. (Odysseus cried out to his comrades to untie him when he heard the Sirens; had the men been slaves at his command, all would have been lost.) But what if someone to whose authority *I* have submitted – a spouse, a sage, a voice from heaven – sees that my oath has gone astray? Yielding self-sufficiency and embracing trust, I find my only hope of rescue from myself. And it is in One who stands in authority over all Creation that our trust must ultimately reside. Have no fear; He will provide the burnt-offering.

Shabbat shalom!

Massei – Rosh Chodesh

Richard Tupper

When the Moon Hits Your Eye . . . .

This Shabbat is *Rosh Chodesh*. Back in *parshat Bo*, God tells Moses, "This month is for you head of months, it is the first for you of the months of the year" (Ex. 12:2). This is by all accounts the first mitzvah that God gives to the nation of Israel.

Why the need for inaugurating a calendar? Shadal suggests that prior to this time, the people were slaves and thus time was not their own, but belonged to their masters. Their masters worried about time, the people only had to do what they were told when they were told. Now as a free people, time is theirs and they must determine how to use it.

Why a lunar calendar? Why not a solar calendar? I have heard it suggested that unlike the sun, the moon changes; it waxes and it wanes. So too, the people of Israel, like the moon, can change. We can increase or decrease. We celebrate the arrival of the new moon because it is then that the moon begins to wax and we, too, hope that we will increase and not decrease.

In the days of the Tabernacle and the Temple, the arrival of *Rosh Chodesh* required certain *korbanot*, offerings, to be brought as set out in Numbers 28:11-15. Nowadays, unable to offer these *korbanot* on account of the destruction of the Temple, we read these verses instead in the synagogue, as we read them today.

Like every other *yom tov*, holiday, the Torah requires that the *korbanot* brought on *Rosh Chodesh* include a *chattat*, traditionally translated as "sin offering."

Why the need for a *chattat*? The *chattat* purges the altar of the *tuma'ot*, impurities, that pollute it, caused by the people's moral failings or severe physical impurities. On a *yom tov*, many more people than usual would come to the Temple and so it was more likely that the altar of burnt offerings would be polluted by some unintentional infraction of the people.

However, in Numbers 28:15, the rabbis notice a unique phrase in the description of the offerings to be brought on *Rosh Chodesh*. The verse says that there must be offered "one he-goat for a *chattat l'Adonai*." Generally, this is translated as "one he-goat for a sin offering to the LORD." Elsewhere when a *chattat* is required, it simply says "*chattat*" but not "*chattat l'Adonai*." Why "*l'Adonai*?" the rabbis ask.

One answer is that the *chattat* is "*l'Adonai*" because it is brought for sins which only HaShem knows of. You may have unwittingly eaten something you should not have and polluted the altar unawares, yet God knows of it. Rambam, on the other hand, suggests that it is "*l'Adonai*" because the Torah wants to stress that you are offering the *chattat* to HaShem and not to the moon.

Nevertheless, in the *Gemara, Chullin* 60b, the rabbis offer an even more intriguing explanation of why the *chattat* is brought "*l'Adonai*." The verse should be read as "a *chattat* for the LORD" rather than "to the LORD." Why must the *chattat* be brought for the LORD? What is it that HaShem did wrong that requires a *chattat* to be brought on HaShem's behalf? The *chattat* must be brought for HaShem because, says Resh Lakish, HaShem reduced the size of the moon!

In *Chullin* 60b, Rabbi Shimon ben Pazi finds a contradiction in Gen.1:16, which begins by saying, "And God made the two great lights" but then immediately follows with, "the great light to rule the day, and the small light to rule the night; and the stars." Rabbi Shimon ben Pazi asks, if God created two great lights, how is it that we then have a "great light" and a "small light"?

The rabbis say that originally the moon was the same size as the sun. However, when the Moon saw that it was not bigger than the sun, it complained to HaShem, saying, "two kings cannot wear the one crown." In response to the Moon's complaint, HaShem said to the Moon, "then make yourself smaller." The Moon, rankled by Hashem's response, said to HaShem, "Master of the Universe, because I said something that is true, I must reduce myself?" (Said with a strong Yiddish accent no doubt!)

Remarkably, HaShem did not discount the Moon's criticism but tried to appease the Moon. HaShem told the Moon that although he would be reduced in size, he would still appear during the daytime. This did not satisfy the Moon because, as the Moon said, who needs the moon when the sun is out? All right then, said HaShem, the people of Israel will use you to

Massei – Rosh Chodesh

determine their months. Again the Moon was not appeased because the Moon pointed out that while the arrival of the new moon might signal the beginning of the new month, the Sun would be used to set the seasons. Well then, said HaShem, people will be named after you, like David who is referred to as "haKaton" and like Rabbi Joseph HaKatan. When the Moon still was not appeased, HaShem said, "Then they will bring a *chattat* for Me every new moon." And that is why we offer the *chattat l'Adonai* every new moon.

What is all this about? The Moon talking to HaShem, the Moon complaining and HaShem trying to appease it. What is all this about?

Rabbi Shlomo Riskin brings down that this reported exchange between HaShem and the Moon must be understood as a metaphor. A metaphor for what? A metaphor for the fact that HaShem created an imperfect world!

Why is the Moon complaining? Because HaShem made the Moon the same size as the Sun, and the Moon doesn't want to share the honor. He is greedy or jealous. Look at Cain and Abel. Cain envies his brother Abel and what happens? Cain kills Abel. So many of our world's problems are caused by one person or one group of persons envying another – they want what the others have or don't want to share what they have. In part God is responsible for this because He created a world in which there is the potential for one to envy another. He created a world in which there is shortage and disaster. As a result, there is terrible injustice and suffering. God imposes the requirement of the *chattat* for Himself in recognition of the fact that He created the world, knowing full well that it could have terrible results simply because of the way it was made.

But why would God knowingly make such a world? Why not make a world in which everything was perfect? Where there was no occasion for jealousy or envy? Where everyone did what was right and there was no injustice or suffering?

Why? Because if there were no possibility of doing wrong, then there would be no opportunity to do right. If everyone automatically did what was right, then we would just be automatons, and there would be no occasion to do good. There would be no good to do.

Because God made a world in which there can be injustice and greed and envy, there can also be a world in which humans right wrongs, love instead of hate, and care for the oppressed rather than oppress the weak. In other words, God purposely made an imperfect world, a world in which there could be wrong, for our benefit. Because we are made in God's image, we can be just and merciful, faithful and kind, and forgiving wrong. We can visit the sick, feed the hungry, clothe the poor and bury the dead. As my friend Irv HaCohen would say, "This imperfect world is the perfect world for us."

Having chosen to create this imperfect world for our benefit, God has placed a great responsibility upon us. It is up to us to perfect the world, to complete the creation, by emulating God's justice, mercy, kindness and faithfulness.

We pray with each new month, "May it be Thy will, LORD my God and God of my fathers, to readjust the deficiency of the moon so that it may no longer be reduced in size, may the light of the moon again be like the light of the sun as it was in the first seven days of creation." Building on Rabbi Riskin's interpretation, Rabbi Stanley Kroll of the Chicago Loop Synagogue says that when we pray these words, we are praying for the world to be perfected, for a time when men "shall beat their swords into plowshares, and their spears into pruninghooks; nation shall not lift up sword against nation, neither shall they learn war any more" (Isaiah 2:4). But that can only be done by us, with God's help, through keeping the mitzvot, because it is through the observance of the mitzvot that we repair the world. In short, this story is not only about Creation but Re-Creation.

Devarim

Al Hobscheid

A Land Flowing with Milk and Honey – What's That All About?

One of my earliest memories connected with my introduction to Judaism (1991 or so – I am a convert by the way) was listening to Rabbi Maralee Gordon, currently Chief Rabbi of McHenry County, Illinois, who at the time was the Education Director of the religious school of McHenry County Jewish Congregation, during her welcoming assembly at Sunday school – playing guitar and singing songs, such as *Ufaratza, David Melech Yisrael*, and *Mayim*. What these songs were about was pretty much a mystery to me as my Hebrew was non-existent, but they certainly got you rocking on a Sunday morning. Another popular selection that got a lotta *ruach* going was this one:

ERETZ ZAVAT CHALAV

Eretz zavat chalav,	(rest for two counts)	*chalav u-d'vash*
Eretz zavat chalav,	(rest for two counts)	*chalav u-d'vash*
Eretz zavat chalav,	(rest for two counts)	*chalav u-d'vash*
Eretz zavat chalav,	(rest for two counts)	*chalav u-d'vash.*

(I have been conducting an informal national survey on how that rest is handled by the singer of the song: do you say or do nothing? clap twice? or say "ooh-aah"? The results of this survey will be released at some later point. Stay tuned . . . .)

The Tanakh, especially *Devarim*, is quite littered with references to this "land flowing with milk and honey" that *b'nei Yisrael* was about to conquer. But really, what is the meaning of this reference? I think a lot of us have the same answer, as if part of some collective Jewish memory. I was taught early on that this adage is merely God's way of saying that this land that is being given over is bountiful and very good. This is how it was taught to me, but

Leaves from the Garden

with one additional bit of information – and don't get this part wrong – the honey doesn't mean bee's honey; oh, no it means date honey. Hmmm! Okay, it seemed to me that some of this makes sense and some of it is kinda odd. First, why "milk" and why "honey"? Why not a land flowing with "olive oil and hummus"? And what is date honey? And why can't it be bee's honey? Whenever I get to one of these junctures, I find a little literature review is in order.

To support the standard explanation that is stated above, I found a good example on the 'net. It was provided in the form of a response to an ask-the-rabbi segment on some Ortho website I had found:

> **. . . and this from Miriam of Montreal, Canada. And she writes:**
>
> *Dear Rabbi,*
> *I have known for some time that in the phrase "eretz zavat chalav u'dvash - a land flowing with milk and honey" the "dvash" refers to date honey (not bee honey). What is the chalav? Certainly it was not cow's milk. Was it goat's milk or could it be some other type of milk? Does this have some inference that honey and milk should be our main food sources?*
>
> The Rabbi responds:
>
> *Dear Miriam,*
> *The milk referred to is cow's or goat's milk. The honey is fruit honey, such as from figs or dates.*
>
> *This doesn't mean that milk and honey should be our main food sources, but rather that the Land of Israel is overflowing with everything good.*
>
> *The Talmud relates that our Sages saw goats eating from fig trees. The figs were so luscious that they were dripping with juice; the goats' udders were so full that milk flowed out. These two liquids mingled into a sweet stream, and the land was literally "flowing with milk and honey."*
>
> *Ramban notes that regions with good air, good pasture and good water, such as mountainous regions, produce the healthiest animals which give the best milk (witness Swiss cheese and Swiss chocolate). But these types of climates don't usually produce top quality fruits (ever heard of Swiss plums?). The Torah stresses that the Land of Israel has both.*

Devarim

So here we have affirmation from a well-founded source (among a ton of others) that all say pretty much the same thing: the symbolic idea that the land is strongly connected to bounty and wealth, and that the honey refers to dates, or some fruit, and not bee honey.

This is all well and good, but when it comes to matters of the flora and fauna of Israel I must necessarily go to a higher source, to Nogah Hareuveni, the founder of Neot Kedumim, the nature preserve of biblical heritage, located in Kiryat Ono. His famous, well-respected research of Tanakh is always rooted in the reality of the land itself; the physicality of the land informs the text. In his seminal text, *Nature in Our Biblical Heritage*, he discusses the meaning of *chalav ud'vash* from a purely physical geographical perspective. He kicks off his thesis with this apparent duality. He quotes from Torah: "... bless Your people Israel and the soil that You have given us as You swore to our fathers, a land flowing with milk and honey" (*Devarim* 26:15). The widespread assumption that the phrase "a land flowing with milk and honey" is a description of the bounty of the land of Israel and of its agricultural fruitfulness stems from these passages and others like them in the Bible. In the eyes of the prophet Isaiah, on the other hand, abundance of milk and honey is seen as the direct result of the destruction of the land (by the Assyrians).

> And it shall come to pass in that day, that a man shall rear a young cow, and two sheep; and it shall come to pass, for the abundance of milk that they shall give, he shall eat curd; for curd and honey shall every one eat that is left in the midst of the [desolated] land. And it shall come to pass in that day, that every place, where there were a thousand vines at a thousand pieces silver, shall even be for briers and thorns. With arrows and with bow shall one come thither; because all the land shall become briers and thorns.
> (Isaiah 7:21-24)

So how can desolation *and* bounty relate to an abundance of milk and honey? According to Hareuveni, the answer is found in the land itself. To recall the spies' report in *parshat Shelach Lecha*, the passage portrays clearly the situation during the time of Israelite settlement in the middle of the thirteenth century BCE: the fertile valleys were inhabited by the Canaanites, while much of the hilly region was uninhabited and retained the natural cover of forest and thicket. To corroborate, according to most biblical archaeologists, the Israelites were the first inhabitants of what is referred to as the "hill country."

Over time, cows and goats were domesticated and raised for milk, and the connection between abundant forage found in the wide-ranging pastures of the hill country and increased milk production became clearly evident.

And what of honey? Here are two oft-heard references from Tanakh:

First from Proverbs 25:16: "Have you found honey? Eat so much as is sufficient for you, lest you be filled with it, and vomit." (If there is any chance to say *"vomit"* in a *d'var Torah*, I go for it.)

And from Judges 14:8-9, ". . . and he [Samson] turned aside to see the carcass of the lion; and, behold, there was a swarm of bees in the body of the lion, and honey. And he scraped it out into his hands, and went on, eating as he went, and he came to his father and mother, and gave unto them, and they did eat . . . ."

As in nearly all references to honey in the Tanakh, it is clearly of that produced by bees and not fruit. These bees, however, are clearly wild bees as there is no reference to apiculture whatsoever in Tanakh. Apiculture apparently didn't exist in Israel until the Talmudic period. But the connection between milk and honey is reinforced. The same pastures, rich in greens for the cow, the goat and the sheep, also sustained abundant wildflowers, their nectar supporting copious bee honey production.

After their conquest of the hill country, the Israelites cleared the forests and built terraces, thus turning the mountains into productive agricultural land. This action essentially removed or marginalized native plants and wildlife, including the bee population found there. The numerous references to lions and bears stalking several verses of the Tanakh are testament to what was once the fauna of Israel prior to settlement and agriculture.

From Hareuveni, "The phrase 'a land flowing with milk and honey' describes uncultivated areas covered with wild vegetation and a profusion of flowers. **It was a positive and alluring description to the Israelites while they were still shepherds.** However, after they settled the land of Israel by clearing the 'milk and honey' areas for cultivation, **the same phrase became a frightening description associated with the destruction of productive farmland,**" *especially as a result of warfare and the destruction of Israel* (his bold, my italicized insertion).

To me, there is an intriguing duality built into *eretz zavat chalav ud'vash* beyond what Hareuveni has offered. It speaks to a conflict that has on the one hand the need for a society to sustain an agricultural base, which is, of course, the lifesource of its people, and from which all other activities,

Devarim

including the maintenance of a religion, are made possible. And on the other hand, I would argue, there is an equally human need to maintain and preserve our native habitats and as the Torah ably demonstrates (as usual) that Creation demands that we seek some sort of balance in order to remain connected to our heritage. Israel, just as every country of the world, must bring sensibility and sensitivity in dealing with this bedeviling duality. This is especially significant at this season. With Tisha b'Av fresh in our consciousness, it is important to be reminded that just as baseless, causeless hatred destroyed the Temples and sent Israel into destruction and diaspora, so will the needless and causeless destruction of our environment place Israel in a predicament that will threaten its existence.

So that's how I'm gonna connect to this image of a "land of milk and honey." But what of "milk" and "honey" in and of themselves? I have presented evidence to you that these are products of great significance to the shepherd and are emblematic of the children of Israel, but what meaning do they have to the rest of us – us non-shepherding, urban types?

We are all aware that milk is equated with goodness. It is our initial sustenance and it is true sweetness to newborns. Honey, of course, is the ultimate in sweetness, but it is also mythic in its healing properties and it appears magical in that it is the only food that does not spoil. But as valid Jewish symbolism, I found a little midrash that I found enlightening (although I am not sure of the veracity of the statement). It is said that milk (mother's milk, that is) and honey are the only two kosher substances that are derived from non-kosher sources (*i.e.*, people and bees are not kosher). It is surely more than coincidence. The implication is that the Land of Israel has the spiritual energy to purify even the impure. *Shabbat shalom.*

Vaetchanan

Miriam Berele[1]

I would like to thank everybody that Yaakov thanked and also Nava Cohen for volunteering to do whatever was necessary in the service. I also thank Neil Brill and Carole Groover for helping to prepare Yaakov. Also Yaakov for working so very hard and being my first child to allow me to make a speech at his *bar Mitzvah*. Also Nathaniel for taking part in the service.

I picked this *Shabbes* for Yaakov's *bar Mitzvah* because I wanted to wait until after the three weeks when he was born and, frankly, because I was a little greedy for a *parsha* and *haftarah* with so much of interest. After Yaakov and I studied them for a while, they began to remind me of Yaakov. Yaakov is like Moshe Rabbenu – in the beginning we were very worried that he could not speak clearly enough but now it's easy to get exasperated when he says the same thing for the umpteenth time and say, "*Al tosef dabber eilai od badavar hazeh*" – don't mention that to me again. And the *haftarah* reminds me of Yaakov and of this Minyan because of the end which says, "*ish lo needar*" – not one is left out (Isaiah 40:26).

On the one hand, the *parshat Vaetchanan* has a lot in it – a model prayer, the *Tochechah*, the *sh'ma*, the Ten Commandments, *etc*. On the other hand, it is in *sefer Devarim*, with its stifling, cloying insistence that good is always rewarded and evil always conclusively punished. The concept of total immediate divine justice does not ring true to human experience, and Jewish tradition has various limits and counterbalances for it. We see some protest against it in the *haftarah*. The *mefarashim* have already noticed that the double punishment mentioned in the second verse is inconsistent with divine justice. But more than that, what in the prophet's vision will it take to get a glimpse of the divine glory? What will it require to bring the divine justice in

---

[1] Miriam delivered this *d'var Torah* on the occasion of her son, Yaakov, becoming a *bar Mitzvah*.

which the good is truly rewarded? Nothing less than a reversal of creation. Psalm 104 speaks of hills rising and the valleys descending at the creation of the world, whereas our *haftarah* yearns for the humbling of all the hills and the exultation of all the valleys, for equality and justice even in the natural order.

Vaetchanan (II)

Steve Oren

Two weeks ago, we spoke about the *Irei Miqlot* – the cities of refuge. In this week's *parsha*, they appear again. At the start of *shlishi*, we read (Deut. 4:41-43), "Then, Moses separated three cities in Transjordan . . . : Betzer in the plain of the Reuvenite, and Ramot in Gilead of the Gadite, and Golan in Bashan of the Menashite" [Eds.' note: Steve's translation]. Now this is very strange. First of all, in the text Moshe has been generally mentioned in the first person. Here, it switches to third person. Second, this is the one command associated with settling the land of Israel that Moshe is said to have done. Why this one command? It cannot be that he was especially concerned with the accidental murderer, for our Rabbis explain that until all six cities were set out, none was protected. He could have waited for the entire land to be conquered, and then set up all six cities (which the text of Joshua says happens in the time of Joshua). In this connection, it is a bit ironic to remember that of the six cities only one, Qadesh in the Galil, is in modern Israel.

But, it turns out that this mitzvah is not merely connected with settling the land of Israel. It also has eschatological significance. In Isaiah 63:1 we read, "Who is this that comes from Edom, with crimsoned garments from Batzrah." In context, this is clearly a savior[1] who comes, and there is a dispute as to whether it is the Messiah, the Angel Michael (the heavenly officer of Israel) or God himself (see Ibn Ezra). But, why should this figure be coming from Batzrah, a city in Edom?

---

[1] Robert Graves cites this verse in one of his two Claudius novels.

Leaves from the Garden

B. Makkot 12a tells a strange story.

> Says Resh Laqish, "Three errors the heavenly officer of Rome [other texts: Edom[1]] will in the future make as it is written (Isaiah 63:1), 'Who is this that comes from Edom, with crimsoned garments from Batzrah.' He will err for it does not protect but Betzer [one of the cities which Moshe set aside] protects and goes in exile to Batzrah. He errs because it does not protect except for accidental murderers and he is a deliberate murderer. He errs because it does not protect except for people and he is an Angel."

R. Yitzhaq Abravanel explains that the Jewish People are like someone who has been murdered, and God is their *Goel HaDam*, their avenger of blood. That is why the heavenly officer of Rome thinks to flee to a city of refuge. This also explains why Moshe does this particular mitzvah, because despite all the gloomy things he says in Deuteronomy, it shows his belief in the ultimate salvation of the Jewish people.

Well and good. But, what suggested this story to the Rabbis? Notice that the three errors are not cumulative – any of them would have been enough. There is clearly a suggestion here that the "heavenly officer of Rome" has something of a *goyishe kop*. But, again, why? Someone at my house asked why the "heavenly officer of Rome" could not simply read the same *Gemara* we do? Shmuel answered that he could not for it is well known that the angels do not understand Aramaic (although this particular passage is in clear Hebrew). But there is something else. After all, the first error is simply a failure in reading the text of Tanach. But, suppose a Roman of the time of Resh Laqish (late 3rd century CE)[2] wanted to read Tanach. It had not yet been independently translated into Latin (St. Jerome would do that in the fifth century). He would have to read either a translation from the Greek or the

---

[1] Of course, for the Rabbis, Edom equals Rome and this "heavenly officer" probably partakes of both, being the angel who wrestled with Yaaqov just before his confrontation with Esau and the officer in charge of the Roman Empire. It appears, however, that those texts which read "Edom" here do so because of censorship.

[2] And, who, it will be noted, is a Palestinian rather than a Babylonian figure. He comes from an environment which is part of the Roman Empire and in which there are many Greek speakers – some of whom, by his time, are Christians reading the Bible in Greek.

Vaetchanan (II)

Greek itself. And if we turn to the Greek, what do we find? For both Betzer, in our *parsha*, and Batzrah, the Greek text has Beta-omicron-sigma-omicron-rho: Βοσορ ("Bosor"). Hence, someone who was dependent on the Greek text would in fact make the first error of confusing the two cities. Thus, this story not only serves to explain why Moshe is said to have picked this command rather than any other command associated with settling the land of Israel, but also serves as a polemic in favor of the Masoretic Text and against the Greek text.

Eikev

Richard Tupper

The Golden Calf story is recounted briefly in Deut. 9:8-21 and described in more detail in Ex. 32. The Golden Calf incident is perhaps Israel's greatest sin while in the wilderness. It is easy and therefore popular to criticize Israel in the wilderness. We often picture them as backsliders, weak and lacking faith, but my guess is that most of us, had we been there, would not have behaved any better. We must remember that Israel spent forty years in the wilderness and so from that perspective their national sins are relatively few, or at least relatively few are reported. Indeed, the prophet Hosea has high praise for Israel in the wilderness.

We must remember, too, that the stories of Israel's sins in the wilderness are recorded in the Torah for a purpose. In *Eikev*, the purpose is explicit: Moses, like a parent sending out children to be on their own, is warning Israel not to repeat the mistakes of the past. Consequently, Moses focuses on Israel's sins so that they serve as warnings and guidance. However, no story has only one lesson. The story of Little Red Riding Hood can be told as a story about the danger of talking to strangers; it can also be told as a story about the triumph of good over evil. Either or both of these lessons can be emphasized when telling the story, and whether either or both are emphasized depends upon the storyteller's purpose. And so, I would like to focus on what I think is another lesson embedded in the Golden Calf story.

In *Eikev*, we have a very condensed version of the Golden Calf story. Moses relates that God told him to hurry back down because the people had gone astray by making a molten image. God tells Moses to leave Him alone so that He can wipe out Israel. Moses then relates how he came down the mountain and saw how the people had made the Golden Calf and had gone astray. He tells how he smashed the tablets and spent forty days and nights fasting, trying to persuade HaShem not to destroy the people. He concludes by saying that he destroyed the Golden Calf, burning it and grinding it to dust, and tossing it into the stream that ran down from the mountain.

Moses also mentions a fact not included in Exodus, namely that God was angry with Aaron, and Moses had interceded on Aaron's behalf. I like to think of this *d'var Torah* as my intercession on behalf of the Israelites in this instance against their many modern day critics who find it so easy to self-righteously condemn them.

Exodus 32 relates many more particulars, but I will only focus on a few. In v. 8, we are told more details of God's accusation against Israel. He tells Moses that not only have the people gone astray, but also that they had made a golden calf and had prostrated themselves before it, sacrificing to it and saying, "These are your gods,[1] O Israel, who brought you up from the land of Egypt." We are also told in v. 20 that Moses made the people drink the water into which he had strewn the dust of the destroyed Golden Calf. Moses then calls out for whoever is on God's side to come to him, and the zealous Levites jump to Moses' side. At Moses' direction, the Levites kill three thousand Israelites. Moses then returns to HaShem to intercede, ultimately successfully, on Israel's behalf, but we are also told in v. 35 that HaShem sent a plague among the people.

Many commentators have noted that in this story as told in Exodus 32, Israel is portrayed as an unfaithful wife and HaShem as a jealous husband. The most obvious evidence for this is Moses' requirement that the people drink the water that contains the dust of the destroyed Golden Calf. This part of the story unmistakably resembles the *sotah* ritual described in Num. 5:12-31, where, if a jealous man accuses his wife of adultery but lacks witnesses, the wife must drink bitter waters. If she is guilty, the waters will sicken her; if not, the waters will have no effect on her.

There is, however, other evidence for understanding this story as modeled on an accusation of adultery. In vv. 21, 30 and 31, Moses describes Israel's conduct as "*chataah gedolah*/a great sin." In the ancient Middle East, this phrase "a great sin" is a term of art for adultery. Indeed in the story of Avimelech and Avraham (Gen. 20), Avimelech accuses Avraham of bringing "a great sin" upon him (Gen. 20:9) by passing off his wife Sarah as his sister so that Avimelech takes Sarah into his household. Furthermore, in Ex. 32:8, HaShem is clearly accusing the people of worshipping another god; in other words, He is accusing them of being unfaithful to Him. Some suggest that Moses' breaking of the tablets is akin to annulling a betrothal agreement or granting a divorce. I also find striking God's remark to Moses in v. 9 to leave Him alone so that His fiery anger can blaze forth and consume the people. It

---

[1] NJPS: "This is your god . . . ."

Eikev

is perhaps a pointed parallel to Judah's order that Tamar be burnt to death when she is accused of harlotry (Gen. 38:24).

So, the story presents God as a jealous husband who accuses His wife, Israel, of unfaithfulness by worshipping another god. Moses' language – his talk about Israel committing a great sin – and his actions – employing the quasi-*sotah* ritual – surely indicate that Moses understands God's accusations in these terms. But the real question is: was all Israel guilty of worshipping another god? Of gross unfaithfulness?

There are many theories as to what Israel was guilty of. Some argue that Israel did not want another god, but that they only wanted a replacement for Moses as v. 1 seems to indicate, and that they saw the Golden Calf as the visible equivalent to an angel. Some say that the calf was only meant as a pedestal upon which HaShem's presence would invisibly rest, just as HaShem's presence would rest between the cherubim in the *Mishkan*. Others say Israel was guilty of making an image, which they had been commanded not to do, but that the image was supposed to represent HaShem. Of course, others do argue that Israel was, in fact, guilty of worshipping a false god in the form of the Golden Calf.

I say, "the proof is in the pudding." The Levites kill only three thousand men. How did the Levites know whom to kill? Ibn Ezra argues that the quasi-*sotah* ritual employed by Moses was designed to identify the true sinners, those who had actually intended to worship another god when they bowed down before the Golden Calf and offered sacrifices. Indeed, Nahum Sarna suggests that the plague sent by God (v. 35) is the sickness that results from the people drinking the water mixed with the dust of the Golden Calf. Even if we assume that there were deaths from the plague in addition to the three thousand slain by the Levites, it is highly unlikely that the number in relative terms was very high. We are told that when Israel left Egypt there were approximately 600,000 adult males (Ex. 12:37). When the census is taken after the Golden Calf incident, we are told that there were 603,550 adult males (Ex. 38:26). When the census is taken again in Numbers, there were 603,550 adult males (Num. 2:32) and an additional 22,000 Levites (Num. 3:39). Thus, even assuming that there were deaths resulting from the plague in addition to the three thousand slain by the Levites, the total number of Israelites killed because of the sin of the Golden Calf would have been a tiny fraction of the total population.

The implication? In the Golden Calf story, what at first blush seems to be apostasy on a national scale was not. Only a relative handful actually was worshipping another god. The others who were not killed were not worshipping another god. They had sinned, to be sure, by making the image of the calf, but their sin was a *chet*, a mistake, and not an *avon* or a *pesha*, an intentional or flagrant sin.

I would like to draw a parallel to the incident involving Nadav and Avihu related in Leviticus 10. Nadav and Avihu were slain by divine fire emanating from the *Mishkan* when they attempted to make an offering of incense with "strange fire," something, the Torah tells us, HaShem had not commanded them to do (v. 1). Later in the same chapter (vv. 16-20), Moses demands of Aaron why Aaron and his sons had not eaten the meat of the purification offering as God had commanded them to do. Aaron's answer is rather cryptic; he says (v. 19): "See, this day they brought their purification offering and burnt offering before the LORD, and such things have befallen me! Had I eaten the purification offering today, would YHWH have approved?" This answer satisfies Moses (v. 20).

Why were Nadav and Avihu punished but Aaron was not? In a previous *d'var Torah*, I argued that Nadav and Avihu's use of the strange fire is crucial to understanding their punishment. Every offering that is offered up on the inner or outer altar of the *Mishkan* must be burnt with the divine fire that must be kept burning on the outer altar at all times. When the sacrificial cult was inaugurated in chapter 9, divine fire blazed out from within the *Mishkan* and consumed the burnt offering on the outer altar (v. 24). It is this divine fire that must be kept burning perpetually on the outer altar and must be used to incinerate every offering. Thus, when divine fire is used to consume Israel's sacrifices, it manifests God's acceptance of Israel's offerings. However, when Nadav and Avihu use alien fire to make their incense offering, they are making an offering to something or someone other than HaShem. They are engaged in *avodah zarah*, alien religion.

In contrast to Nadav and Avihu who did something that God had not commanded them to do, Aaron, by not eating the purification offering, has refused to do what God had commanded him to do. Admittedly, Aaron's explanation is somewhat opaque, but the best explanation that I have heard for his refusal is that Aaron believed that the carcass of the purification offering had become so polluted due to its proximity to Aaron's dead sons that he should not eat it. (See Milgrom, *Leviticus, ad loc.*)

The key, however, to understanding why Aaron is not punished is that, even though he refuses to do what God commanded him to do, his refusal is rooted in his desire to do what he understands to be God's will. Indeed, we are expressly told that Moses approved of Aaron's refusal to eat the meat of the purification offering (10:20).

Eikev

What is striking about Nadav and Avihu on the one hand and Aaron on the other is that to the human eye the strange fire used by Nadav and Avihu is indistinguishable from divine fire. No one can simply look at fire and tell whether it originated from the outer altar. In contrast, Aaron's refusal to eat the meat of the purification offering appears to the human eye to be nothing short of flagrant disobedience. The significance is: we see only the external action but HaShem sees the heart (see, I Sam. 16:7). What may outwardly appear to be the sincerest form of piety may actually be apostasy, and what may outwardly appear to be flagrant disobedience may actually be the sincerest piety.

These lessons from the Golden Calf incident and that of Nadav, Avihu and Aaron are very apt for us today. Among Jews it is fair to say that with respect to what can be called the ethical mitzvot there is a great deal of agreement, and, if not agreement, then common ground. However, when it comes to ritual mitzvot there are almost as many differences as there are Jews. When we see our fellow Jews observing the ritual mitzvot differently than we do, their *kashrut* or Shabbat or *taharat hamishpachah* observance differs from ours, we should not be quick to condemn them as bad Jews. We must remember that we see only the outward differences in how the ritual is observed; we do not see the heart that motivates the difference. When our fellow Jews differ from us over these ritual mitzvot, it may be that their difference springs from true apostasy as in the case of Nadav and Avihu and the three thousand or so that died in the Golden Calf incident. It may be that their difference springs not from apostasy but simply a mistaken belief as to what HaShem wants, as was the case in the vast majority of the Israelites at Sinai; their sin was a *chet* and not an *avon* or a *pesha*. It may also be that their difference in observance, though it appears to us to be a flagrant disregard for God's mitzvot, is actually, like Aaron's, the truest form of piety. Because we see only the outside and not the heart, let us be charitable, one with another.

Reeh

Benjamin Sommer[1]

Today's *haftarah* contains a familiar line (Isa 54.13; *EH* 1085, bottom; *Hertz*, 818, middle):

וְכָל-בָּנַיִךְ לִמּוּדֵי ה' וְרַב שְׁלוֹם בָּנָיִךְ:

Where do we know this line from? (The quotation from the Talmud in the *Siddur* towards the end of *Musaf – Slim Shalom*, p. 182.)

That quote is a midrash that connects several biblical verses that seem unrelated.

Because midrash is one of the most misunderstood but also most important aspects of Judaism, I thought it might be a good idea to take a closer look at the way this midrash interprets the verse from today's *haftarah*.

Read the whole passage from the *siddur*; note how random it initially seems. Forced, arbitrary.

It's trying to make a connection between wisdom and peace, but it's not so clear how the verses quoted really do that.

Reread the beginning of the passage including אל תקרי. It seems to get the quoted text to support what it is saying by changing the quote!

Note the two translations.

Which is right? In the context here, and in the biblical text.

In the context here: "those who have understanding" seems better, since we are talking about learning and Torah.

In the biblical text itself, summarize the idea of the passage, which really begins in verse 1 and goes through verse 17[2]: Jerusalem or Zion is portrayed

---

[1] Eds.' note: this outline of Ben Sommer's *d'var Torah* ought to be read with the following books open in front of you: *Slim Shalom, Etz Hayim* ("*EH*"), and *Hertz*.

[2] The whole passage is in the *haftarah* of Noah, so take a look there. *EH* 64; *Hertz* 41.

Leaves from the Garden

as a woman. She is childless (*i.e.*, without inhabitants) and apparently forsaken by her husband (*i.e.*, the LORD). However, this passage assures her that God remains her husband and protector and that she will soon have abundant children. Jerusalem, which is now empty, will soon be crowded once again.

Let's read the passage. As we go through it, think about whether it is plausible that בניך really could mean either "those who build" or "those who understand."

Before we do, let me note a tendency of this particular prophet: he does love to pun, to use the same word twice with two different meanings. For example, see

⇨ 40.12-13 (*EH* 1034; *Hertz* 778): מִי־מָדַד בְּשָׁעֳלוֹ מַיִם וְשָׁמַיִם בַּזֶּרֶת *תִּכֵּן*, וְכָל בַּשָּׁלִשׁ עֲפַר הָאָרֶץ; וְשָׁקַל בַּפֶּלֶס הָרִים וּגְבָעוֹת בְּמֹאזְנָיִם. מִי־*תִכֵּן* אֶת־רוּחַ ה' וְאִישׁ עֲצָתוֹ יוֹדִיעֶנּוּ. – NRSV: 12 "Who has **measured** the waters in the hollow of his hand and marked off the heavens with a span, enclosed the dust of the earth in a measure, and weighed the mountains in scales and the hills in a balance? 13 Who has **directed** the spirit of the LORD, or as his counselor has instructed him?" [The verb can mean "measure" or "correct, arrange, set in order," as the parallel with "give counsel" shows.]

⇨ 56.1 (*EH* 1336, top; *Hertz* 1037, middle): כֹּה אָמַר ה' שִׁמְרוּ מִשְׁפָּט וַעֲשׂוּ *צְדָקָה*: כִּי־קְרוֹבָה יְשׁוּעָתִי לָבוֹא וְ*צִדְקָתִי* לְהִגָּלוֹת. Note the parallelism!

⇨ 63.3,6 (*EH* 1193; Hertz 886): פּוּרָה דָרַכְתִּי לְבַדִּי וּמֵעַמִּים אֵין־אִישׁ אִתִּי, וְאֶדְרְכֵם בְּאַפִּי וְאֶרְמְסֵם בַּחֲמָתִי וְיֵז *נִצְחָם* עַל־בְּגָדַי וְכָל־מַלְבּוּשַׁי אֶגְאָלְתִּי... וְאָבוּס עַמִּים בְּאַפִּי וַאֲשַׁכְּרֵם בַּחֲמָתִי וְאוֹרִיד לָאָרֶץ *נִצְחָם*. NJPS: 3 "I trod out a vintage [lit. "winepress"] alone; Of the peoples no man was with Me. I trod them down in My anger, Trampled them in My rage; Their life-blood bespattered My garments, And all My clothing was stained. 6 I trampled peoples in My anger, I made them drunk with My rage, And I hurled their glory to the ground." In both cases it could be "juice" (blood) but the second could be "eminence, everlastingness."

With this in mind, let's go to the *haftarah* and see what it is talking about (read Isa 54.11, 12, 14; *EH* 1085, bottom; *Hertz* 818). What are they talking about here? Rebuilding Zion – in which case, the midrash's sugestion to read this as if it were בוניך (builders) actually makes sense – it is a typical Deutero-Isaianic pun.

The point is that as long as the builders are wise, are committed to being a student or disciple of God, then their work will succeed.

Reeh

But now focus on verse 13 itself: what is it talking about? About למודי ה' – in which case, the other pun as understood in *Slim Shalom* makes sense.

The point is that Zion's children (*i.e.*, the Judeans living there) will be wise. Therefore, this time around, they will not be exiled: as long as they are committed to being a student or disciple of God, they will endure.

The verse from our *haftarah* is a three way pun: בניך means "children"[1] but also hints at once at "builders" and "wise ones."

In other words, we've come to two conclusions about the midrash that we read right before עלינו:

• The usual understanding of the midrash, that בוניך means "builders", and the less usual one found in *Slim Shalom* that it means "wise ones" are both right.

• The midrash's understanding of our verse is not forced at all. It is actually the פשט: Deutero-Isaiah really wants us to understand בניך to mean several things at once.

While we're there, let's quickly look at the rest of the passage (in *Slim Shalom* p. 182). How does it fit?

⇨ The first verse in Ps 119.165: שָׁלוֹם רָב לְאֹהֲבֵי תוֹרָתֶךָ וְאֵין-לָמוֹ מִכְשׁוֹל. Does this fit into a theme? Yes, peace and Torah (*i.e.*, peace and wisdom) go together. These are themes that show up in our *haftarah*, and they are the main themes of the midrash.

⇨ The next verse is Psalm 122.7-9:

יְהִי-שָׁלוֹם בְּחֵילֵךְ   שַׁלְוָה בְּאַרְמְנוֹתָיִךְ.
לְמַעַן אַחַי וְרֵעָי   אֲדַבְּרָה-נָּא שָׁלוֹם בָּךְ.
לְמַעַן בֵּית-ה' אֱ-לֹהֵינוּ   אֲבַקְשָׁה טוֹב לָךְ.

How does that fit? It becomes clear when you look at the beginning of the psalm (in *Slim Shalom*, p. 251):

שִׁיר הַמַּעֲלוֹת לְדָוִד
שָׂמַחְתִּי בְּאֹמְרִים לִי   בֵּית ה' נֵלֵךְ.
עֹמְדוֹת הָיוּ רַגְלֵינוּ   בִּשְׁעָרַיִךְ יְרוּשָׁלָ ִם.
יְרוּשָׁלַ ִם הַבְּנוּיָה   כְּעִיר שֶׁחֻבְּרָה-לָּהּ יַחְדָּו.

This psalm is quoted because it deals with what theme? The connection of peace and building!

---

[1] That makes sense especially in light of the opening verses of this chapter, which are in the *haftarah* for כי תצא (*EH* 1138; *Hertz* 847): Isa 54.1, 4-5. What's the issue here? Her loss of children and their sudden reappearance!

Leaves from the Garden

But it also deals with wisdom and Torah as well, since it goes on to say:

שֶׁשָּׁם עָלוּ שְׁבָטִים שִׁבְטֵי־יָ-הּ--*עֵדוּת* לְיִשְׂרָאֵל: לְהֹדוֹת לְשֵׁם ה'.
כִּי שָׁמָּה יָשְׁבוּ כִסְאוֹת לְמִשְׁפָּט: כִּסְאוֹת לְבֵית דָּוִד.
שַׁאֲלוּ שְׁלוֹם יְרוּשָׁלָ͏ִם; יִשְׁלָיוּ, אֹהֲבָיִךְ.

The word עֵדוּת = Torah.[1]

The themes that were present in today's *haftarah*, the connection between wisdom, rebuilding, and the peace for Jerusalem, also show up in Psalm 122! The fact that the midrash quotes this verse is not random – in fact, it seems to me that this midrash *has to quote* this verse – it's too perfect to let it go.

⇨ The last verse is from Psalm 29: ה' עֹז לְעַמּוֹ יִתֵּן; ה' יְבָרֵךְ אֶת־עַמּוֹ בַשָּׁלוֹם.
How is this related? What relevant themes show up?
Clearly, peace does.
But what about עֹז? How does that relate?
For the rabbis, עֹז is a synonym for Torah.

And remember that Psalm 29 talks about God's קוֹל, (which manifests itself as thunder and causes mountains to shake) (*Slim Shalom*, p. 20):

קוֹל ה', עַל־הַמָּיִם. אֵ-ל־הַכָּבוֹד הִרְעִים..
קוֹל־ה' בַּכֹּחַ; קוֹל ה', בֶּהָדָר....
וַיַּרְקִידֵם כְּמוֹ־עֵגֶל; לְבָנוֹן וְשִׂרְיֹן כְּמוֹ בֶן־רְאֵמִים....
קוֹל ה', יָחִיל מִדְבָּר; יָחִיל ה', מִדְבַּר קָדֵשׁ.

It's not a stretch to see why the rabbis would see this psalm as alluding to the giving of the Torah, and hence why the rabbis of the midrash can understand the final words of this psalm ה' עֹז לְעַמּוֹ יִתֵּן; ה' יְבָרֵךְ אֶת־עַמּוֹ בַשָּׁלוֹם as referring to the Torah.

Thus this verse is about the connection of Torah and peace: by giving us Torah, God gave us peace, or the ability to create peace.

Okay, to sum up: what have we seen? I hope I shown something about midrash.

The midrash that we say every Shabbat before עלינו is making a point about Torah and peace, wisdom and well-being, and the rabbis support that point with several biblical verses.

---

[1] See Psalm 19.8 (p. 87 of *Slim Shalom*):

תּוֹרַת ה' תְּמִימָה, מְשִׁיבַת נָפֶשׁ; עֵדוּת ה' נֶאֱמָנָה, מַחְכִּימַת פֶּתִי.

Reeh

- Now, many people think that when the rabbis want to make a point they just choose any old verse out of a hat and claim it says what they want it to say – changing its wording if necessary!
- In fact, what we've seen is quite the opposite. They fit together perfectly.

But to see how they fit together perfectly, we have to do some work. We have to look not just at the verses themselves, but at the verses that come before them or after them – a rabbinic method of citation. The midrash isn't just about the verse quoted; it is often about the whole context.

- People think of midrash as creative, the rabbis as building what they want to build.
  - This is not entirely inaccurate.
  - The rabbis do not create midrash from whole cloth. They create by paying incredibly close attention to the texts they are reading – by making themselves disciples to the Tanakh, by making it clear that they come second and the Tanakh comes first, by making it clear that they are the children and God is the parent, and that their first job is to acknowledge the difference.

In other words, the essence of midrash is that we can build something wise out of what we've been given only if we make ourselves disciples and children first. בינה and בניין result from humbling ourselves, making ourselves בנים before anything else.

- The rabbis see themselves not just as בונים but first of all as בנים.
- This is a central aspect of midrash we modern Jews tend to forget.

Shofetim

Bernard Weisberger

I was delighted when Robert asked me to do this particular *d'var*, and wondered whether he had developed the gift of divination (in addition to his many others) because the *parsha* is one of my special favorites in the *Chumash*. "You shall appoint magistrates and officials," it begins in the *Etz Hayim*[1] translation, an opening that sounds as exciting as clause six, subparagraph nine, section eight of a municipal code, but a few words later it suddenly takes off and soars: "and they shall govern the people with due justice/ *mishpat tzedek*." Bear that phrase in mind. "You shall not judge unfairly: you shall show no partiality; you shall not take bribes, for bribes blind the eyes of the discerning and upset the plea of the just." And then, hammered home with deliberate repetition and an active verb, "JUSTICE, JUSTICE SHALL YOU PURSUE, that you may thrive and occupy the country that the LORD your God is giving you." Not "administer," or "pronounce," or "render," or something bureaucratic. Pursue. A verb that runs instead of walks – that says as loudly and clearly as a bullhorn, "NOW HEAR THIS!"

If we are ever really going to put quotations from the Hebrew Bible in our American courtrooms, a bad idea in a pluralistic society if ever there was one, I'd certainly choose that one as far more appropriate in the halls of justice than the more generalized and diffused Decalogue. *Tzedek t'rdof*, in a sense, sums up a whole catalogue of demands for procedural equity on Israel's judges-to-be in the Promised Land. Do not make distinctions between rich and poor, between foreigner and native, between the influential and the obscure, the popular and the disdained. Don't fear the opinions of the

---

[1] Eds.' note: Bernie uses the *Etz Hayim* translation in the first paragraph; thereafter Robert Alter's translations have been substituted for the *Etz Hayim*.

multitude – "the face of man," as the literal Hebrew of Deut. 1:17 puts it, – "for judgment is God's." The whole idea of fair and impartial trial is to make a leap to a higher level of substantive justice – to found your decisions on eternal principles of right and wrong implicit in God's universe, not on the shifting sands of opinion-making authority in human communities.

We presume that God has made those principles visible, clear and unmistakable through revelation in the Torah itself – and that, therefore, the tasks of jurisprudence should be easy – find what The Law says, weigh the facts of the controversy presented against those holy dictates, press the button marked "Calculate," and shazzam! – a just verdict will appear in the read-out column! It is the way some American conservative jurists who preach the doctrine of "originalism" now argue that we ought to read the Constitution. They seem to have forgotten the fact that the Founding Fathers did not think they were taking down God's dictation on stone tablets. They were putting together an improvised, compromise government to meet immediate needs; they changed their own draft versions many times; and they expected that succeeding generations would sooner or later revise the final product of their sweaty summer of 1787 deliberations.

But of course, the Torah IS written by a Divine author, and supposedly is beyond erasures and insertions. All the same, it is not beyond interpretation. It can only be understood through human apprehension, unaided – or at least mostly unaided since the death of Moses – by further direct word from Sinai. In its detailed application to the shifting circumstances of human life, specific decisions are necessary, even when specific instructions are lacking. The key then becomes to look at what specific mandates there are, and to judge them within a context. What's their overall thrust? What, so to speak, is God's "original intent" in revelation? We can only find out by close attention to details of whatever clear mandates are in the Torah itself. That's the key that opens the door to constant study as a form of prayer and a holy activity – that search for the intent and purpose of the mandated mitzvot.

In the early chapters of Exodus, and in the great recapitulation in Deuteronomy, we find plenty of rules that bear on the theme of justice, and that for me, at least, are far closer to the heart of Judaism than the elaborate regulations for ritual and sacrifice – though I know that they are supposed to be of equal weight, and yes, I recognize the importance of repeating them to preserve our connections with our unique past and special chosen status. But my heart isn't exactly kindled by hearing about the priest's vestments in a way that it is by the order not to hold back the wages of a laborer overnight. Not to glean the corners of your field so as to leave something for the poor.

Shofetim

Not to take usurious advantage of others' needs. Not to shame and dehumanize even the sinner. Not to have separate and unequal laws for the stranger and for yourself. Not to take an egg from under the mother bird. And, to shift to the positive side, to rest the land itself in jubilee years and restore it to the community, to free the bondservant, to give a fresh start to debtors, to remind oneself that one is the steward, not the owner of wealth. All of these, to my mind, point to a potential definition of "*mishpat tzedek*" that implies a sense of what is due to all of God's creation – to the earth itself and its products, to the beasts that God's will has brought into being and over whom God has given humankind dominion in return for their contributions to humanity's work and to its sustenance. What is due to them? Respect, care, benevolence, non-destructiveness. That is the justice that is implicit in the cosmos – balance among the rights of every part of it, preservation of consideration for every part of it, recognition of the interconnectedness of every part of it and for God's desire that all of it be united in harmony.

I am, of course, putting this in the best light. When it comes to what is necessary to occupy the Promised Land, there are some significant exceptions about how its occupants are to be treated – and exceptions within the exceptions – but we will not go there today. And God's benevolence toward God's own handiwork, when considered in the light of tsunamis and hurricanes – but no, we will not go there today, either. There will be other times and other occasions to wrestle, as sincere believers should and must, with the mysteries of suffering in what is conceived of by our religion and many others as a fundamentally benevolent universe. For now, let me get back to the *parsha* and its major elements.

It begins by creating a hierarchy of officialdom in whose hands the administration of justice may lie. First, magistrates and judges, the "*shofetim*" themselves. Some specific rules are laid down for them to follow and apply – the prohibitions against erecting altars, offering blemished animals for sacrifice, and, as always above all, worshipping strange gods, for which the penalty is death – but only on the testimony of two witnesses who must themselves take the responsibility of casting the first stone. When there are really hard cases, especially involving assault and homicide, they can be appealed to the priests, OR a magistrate. And the appeal to the priests does not seem to rest on the assumption that they are privy to direct communication with Heaven, but to their learned and pious qualities (although there are plenty of High Priests in the Tanakh who fall considerably short in that department). Their verdicts, however, cannot be appealed.

Leaves from the Garden

After that comes a digression on how a king should behave if the Israelites should choose to have one. It is intriguing that the choice is left to them to be like other nations in this respect if they so choose. But that emphasizes that the royal figure is essentially of human, not divine, substance. The king himself is subject to the Law, and, unlike Pharaoh and Roman Emperors and the monarchs of ancient Eastern principalities, he is in no way in himself a god or manifestation of God or powerful forces of Nature like the sun. And he, like the *shofetim*, must govern justly.

After this, we are advised of what is properly due as compensation to the levitical priests.

And then we get to the intriguing part. We are on the edge of a huge transition. Until now, God has spoken with patriarchs and prophets, and most especially Moses, face to face, in direct communication of God's intent. And humanity, through these special figures, has even been free to argue with God in God's own person – and in one case, to remind God that he is bound by the very principles he himself proclaimed. There is Abraham in that wonderful passage where he is trying to preserve Sodom and, continually protesting that he knows he is a mere dust-bunny on the floor of creation, gets God to agree that even if a handful of non-sinners can be found in that city, for the sake of those innocents it will not be destroyed. "*Chalilah lecha*, Abraham says, *l'hamit tzadik im rashah*" – "Far be it from you . . . to bring death upon the innocent as well as the guilty." And that truly superb line: "*hashofayt kol haaretz lo yaaseh mishpat?*" – "Shall not the Judge of all the earth deal justly?" God wins the argument in the end; he can't even find ten righteous in the city (though I wonder, were little children included in the count?) – but God wins most of the argument, and at least concedes the principle. Moses, too, talks God out of destroying the Israelites in the wilderness for their stiff-necked qualities, their backsliding and whimpering and lack of confidence – their insufferable kvetching – by reminding him not only that it will look to the heathen as if God could not complete God's promise to take them to the Promised Land but that, after all, it takes two to make and to keep a Covenant.

Ah, but now, God is withdrawing from direct communication with the children of Israel. Moses is going to die, and there will be no prophet like him that will arise in Israel – that is, none who speaks face to face with God. But there will be other prophets to whom God will reveal the Divine intentions. These prophets are carefully distinguished from soothsayers, augurs, diviners, astrologers, readers of chicken-guts and presiding officers over bizarre rituals. Genuine prophets will not promise to manipulate the

Shofetim

future or controvert the order of nature by miracles – although some of them can and do work miracles, like Elijah filling the widow's cruse, or Elisha reviving the dead young man. They will be known because their prophecies – or really, their announcements of God's wishes and plans – come true. They, in short, will be the guardians and messengers of that "original intent" for which the *shofetim* are searching.

All right, then, let's look at the prophets – and extract what seems to be an essential essence of the prophetic message. Now, what do we find in many of the most outspoken? Predictable auguries of backsliding and wickedness, of woe to come, and of ultimate redemption from a merciful God when shown true repentance. Also, some bold examples of speaking truth to power. Elisha tells Jezebel where to get off; Nathan lets David know of how he has wronged Uriah. Comforting the afflicted and afflicting the comfortable is in the job specs of a Hebrew prophet, and they perform up to high expectations.

But in some of the best-known later prophets, the wickedness of which the Israelites are accused is not merely building altars to strange gods or neglecting what is due to *Adonai*. It is vanity, greed, a comfortable feeling that good fortune is their own doing instead of the LORD's – and it is, especially, injustice to the poor! I call on today's *haftarah* as my witness, and also remind you of the fine, scholarly *d'var* we had last week from Ben Sommer. He pointed out that the use of parallel expressions, often using the same language, in different parts of the Bible is meant to link those books together in the consciousness of the Israelites – to stitch together a running theme from disparate passages that sound like each other.

Well, turn to that *haftarah* of consolation in Isaiah 52, and take note of the concluding two verses. When Israel returns to Zion from her exile she won't be fleeing, but departing in pride, with head held high, carrying the furniture of the Temple back to its rightful place. And the LORD will be marching before them, the God of Israel will be their "rear guard" – "*Ki holach lifnayhem Adonai, umaaschem Elohay Yisrael.*" Six chapters later, in Isaiah 58, comes a section that we will read on Yom Kippur, which is close ahead. In this one, God is reproaching the Israelites for observing the forms but not the substance of worship. They have done the right rituals, they have fasted on fast days, but they have not changed their behavior. And so, says God to them through Isaiah, do you think that's what I wanted? That you should starve yourselves, bow down like a bulrush, wear sackcloth? Is that repentance? No. Unlock the fetters of wickedness, free the oppressed, share your bread with the hungry and your roof with the naked, don't turn away from your own kin. Then, says Isaiah 58: 8 (NJPS), "Then shall your light burst through like the dawn/ And your healing spring up quickly;" and – listen! – *"V'holaych lfanecha tzidkechah, k'vod Adonai yaasfechah*/ Your Vindicator shall march before you,/ The Presence of the LORD shall be your rear guard." The NJPS translates *tzidkechah* in this case as "[y]our Vindicator," I'm not sure why, but KJV says "righteousness." Light is cast ahead on your path by the LORD – the metaphor is almost the same – and this time the rear guard is not defending against pursuit, but it is behind Israel as a support. Good deeds and righteousness will create a history on which you can advance and build. And while the same close parallelism does not show up, it's fairly recently that we read the *haftarah* for *Balak*, drawn from Micah, who asks, in another of my favorite passages, what does the LORD ask of you? *"Ki im asot mishpat, v'ahavat chesed, v'hatsnaya lechet im Elohechah"* – to do *"mishpat,"* love mercy – whose difference from *mishpat* is subject for a different *d'var* – and to walk in humility in God's path.

So the prophetic message resounds and reverberates almost constantly with the theme of justice. And if God no longer sends prophets to warn, threaten, and exhort us – if God has withdrawn from direct intervention in the moral world just as God withdrew from manipulation of the physical world through miracles – then it's up to us to keep looking on our own. Perhaps there are prophets among us whom we don't recognize. Perhaps the rabbis and sages and Torah scholars who compiled the Talmud are the latest incarnations of those who bring us signals of God's fundamental intent to have us imitate Him in benevolence – or at least to imitate God's more benevolent aspects. The signals are there for the reading. Time forbids my summary of the rest of the *parsha*, and I am sorry because it is so rich in further definitions of "due justice."

But the commandments for goodness are not self-interpreting or self-executing, because they are uttered to men who live and behave in a real world of murder, rape, incest, theft, greed and deceit – a world of morally imperfect people. And so courts and judges must exist, civil suits and criminal prosecutions must take place, witnesses must be summoned, evidence presented, something as near to truth as possible must be unveiled in the course of deciding, instance by instance, whether the law applies specifically to the precisely defined behavior under scrutiny. And the decisions must be codified, studied, parsed and re-parsed in each succeeding generation in light of its experience and understanding. This is not to say that rabbis can "make" law as they please. But between "anything goes" and "set in concrete," there is a vast terrain to explore and to map. And it is the work not only of rabbis and scholars, but of thinking Jews at any time. Only my

Shofetim

reluctance to trench on the territory of whomever will do the *d'var* on *Nitzavim* a couple of weeks from now prevents me from elaborating on two more favorite verses, those which say that the law which Moses is now relaying from God to the Israelites at the entry gate of Zion is neither in Heaven, and accessible only to mystics and seers, nor in some foreign province of scholars far from the understanding of plain men and women, but is near every listener's heart and in every listener's mouth to hear and to do. But that, too, requires a minimum at least of interpretation in the light of reason. The only certainty is that you cannot ask an angel or a soothsayer for the answer; you must ask the text, and reason with fellow human beings who may derive a different meaning from it. That is the process of interpretation over time, which preserves a living Torah – and it's another story entirely.

I began this discussion by quoting the verse demanding the pursuit of justice. As we close our Torah study and put the scrolls away for this morning, we'll say a prayer for peace which implores whoever it is to whom we address prayer to let justice flow like a mighty stream. That re-invocation of the word seems to be as good a place to stop as any.

Shabbat shalom.

Ki Tetze

Nava Cohen

I would like to thank Richard Tupper and Ellen and Alan for nagging me for a very long time to give a *d'var Torah*. I would especially like to thank Tupper for helping my vanity overcome my reluctance, when he told me about six weeks ago that I needed to give a *d'var Torah* so that it could be published in the book.

"*Ki tetze l'milchama al oyvecha.*" "Should you go out to battle against your enemies" (Deut. 21:10). These are the words that begin our *parsha*. I'd like to take you back a chapter and a half, towards the end of last week's *parsha*, *Shofetim*. If you look at the beginning of chapter 20, you see that we encounter the exact same five words there. "*Ki tetze l'milchama al oyvecha.*" It seems to me that the repetition of this phrase provides bookends for us to understand not only how you go to war, but also how you return from war.

"*Ki tetze l'milchama al oyvecha*" opens a discussion of what happens prior to commencing battle: who should not take part in the battle, the process for attempting to conquer a city peacefully, and, finally, setting siege to a city. What is allowed in a siege and how the soldiers are supposed to treat the inhabitants and trees of the city complete chapter 20. "*Ki tetze l'milchama*" speaks about how soldiers must behave as they engage in war.

Parshat Shofetim ends with the beginning of chapter 21, the case when one finds a dead body in a field. Why does the found corpse follow the discussion of war? What is the connection between these two situations?

About three quarters of the way into *War and Peace* (pp. 915-916 in my copy, which is the Ann Dunnigan translation), we get the following passage:

> Pierre got out of his carriage and, walking past the toiling militiamen, climbed up onto the knoll from which the doctor had told him he could see the battlefield.... All that Pierre saw to the right and left of him was so indefinite that no part of the scene before his eyes satisfied his expectations. Nowhere was there a battlefield such as he had imagined, but

only meadows, woods, glades, troops, the smoke of campfires, villages, knolls, and streams; try as he would, he could descry no military position in this landscape teeming with life, and could not even distinguish our troops from the enemy's.

What is the intrinsic difference between a field and a battlefield? There is no difference. By an accident of history, we come to know certain areas, be they fields, cities, or regions, because of what happens in them. How many of us would know the names Fallujah, Sadr City, Nazariah, Kandahar, or Mazar-i-Sharif were it not for the newsworthy events taking place in those cities? We know those names, not because they are intrinsically important or because they were destined to be famous, but because it turned out that things happened there. However, all famous cities are surrounded by other, more anonymous cities, and to return home from those famous cities, soldiers must pass through the anonymous areas. This is where our corpse in the field begins to make sense to me.

Who is it who finds this corpse? The Torah just says *"Ki Yimatzeh"* and doesn't tell us who it is who finds it. I believe that it is our returning soldiers. As our soldiers begin to return home from war, they must pass through fields. Our soldier or soldiers have passed out of the fields surrounding the warring city and are now in a no man's land that could have been one of the battlefields, but, by happenstance, was not. They find a corpse, a sight too familiar to warriors. This corpse is not in the context of war, but neither is it in a domestic setting. This is the midpoint of the soldiers' return. They are half-way between war and peace. From here they will continue into a more domestic setting.

Now we come to our *parsha*. In the middle of chapter 21 (Deut. 21:10), our *parsha* opens with our bookend phrase *"Ki tetze l'milchama al oyvecha."* This time, however, we do not find a discussion of the ethics of war. Instead, it seems to me that we find a discussion of the life of a soldier who has just returned from war.

"Ki tetze l'milchama al oyvecha, un'tano Hashem Elokecha byadcha vshavita shivyo." Our soldier takes captives and finds a woman he desires. Despite the guidelines for his behavior given in chapter 20, our soldier has, nevertheless, been in an environment where he does not need to control his impulses as strictly as he must when at home. Rashi says that the Torah allows the soldier to marry the captive woman because he would marry her whether he was allowed to or not! The Torah is allowing the expression of the man's *yetzer harah* because the reality is that he will follow his impulses

Ki Tetze

anyhow. The Torah is concerned for the soul of our returning soldier. This acknowledgement that a man returning from war is likely to have difficulties following the strictures of polite society demonstrates an understanding of the psyche of a returning combatant and a desire to reintegrate him into society, even if that means changing society to a certain extent.

The text also understands that the attraction to the captive woman may be fleeting and that, once the soldier has adjusted to being home, he may lose interest in her. He is not allowed to sell her or use her as a slave, however. In this way, the Torah does rein in some of what may be the soldier's improper impulses. He is not free to do whatever he pleases.

Rashi continues that if the soldier marries the captive, he will end up hating her, bringing us to the next topic in the *parsha*, the case of the two wives, one loved, and one hated. This issue evokes Rachel and Leah, as well as Penina and Chana, although in those cases the beloved wife was barren and the "hated" wife had children, and in this case both wives have children. Rashi assumes that it is the captive wife that the man will hate, probably because this discussion is immediately after the discussion of what you may not do if you grow uninterested in your captive wife. But I wonder whether it is the pre-war wife who becomes hated because she is less exotic than the new wife or perhaps jealous of her. Or perhaps it is the captive wife who becomes hated, when the man takes an even newer wife in an attempt to find some solace. Whatever the case is, the dynamic of this family is not peaceful, and it makes sense that a returning soldier might face strife in his family life.

In the intensely gritty, disturbing, and vile HBO series *Rome*, a fictional soldier returns to his wife after not seeing her for seven years. He does not know how to speak to her and she fears him. His daughters can barely raise their heads around him, and they fear that he may kill them, which was allowed to Roman fathers. In short, the household is filled with discord upon his return. This type of situation was probably a very common one in the ancient world, and must still be common in military families. What the Israelite soldier has, however, that the other ancient and modern soldiers do not, are instructions from the Torah, guiding him in how he must behave towards his children (albeit, only in terms of their inheritance), no matter what his inner turmoil or outer dysfunction is.

The next issue in chapter 21 features a son who does not listen to his parents or obey them. Now, this is not a "clean-up-your-room" or "finish-your-homework" type of disobedience. This is the rebellion that comes from a profoundly unhappy child whose parents cannot control him. To my reading, this is the type of disobedience that may come from living in a household with a father who has been to war, who hates at least one of his wives, and who might, if allowed, disinherit you. This *ben sorer u'moreh*, "wayward and rebellious son," is the result of a fractured society, or at least a fractured family, and, if he is not dealt with, the entire society is likely to suffer. Our modern ears cringe at the punishment this boy receives: death. However, what I take from this situation is the idea that the Torah gives guidelines for what we should do when the dysfunction of a society has become so great that it ruins our children. Rather than wade around in uncertainty and further misbehavior, the family is instructed on exactly what they must do. And, of course, as we might expect, Hertz states, "The Rabbis tell us that this law was never once carried out . . . . Its presence in the Torah was merely to serve as a warning . . ." (*Hertz*, p. 842).

The final issue of chapter 21 involves a man who has been executed and how his body is to be treated with respect. At this point, if we are to continue with the narrative of our soldier, the worst has happened. He, or perhaps his erstwhile repentant son, has committed a sin worthy of death. Rashi indicates that this is what will happen to the *ben sorer u'moreh*, if his parents do not take care of him. Yet, even though all has been lost, and there no longer exists any hope of a peaceful, domestic existence for this family, there are still guidelines for what must be done. "[Y]ou shall not let his corpse stay the night on the tree but you shall surely bury it on that day . . . ."

From here the *parsha* moves on to thoroughly domestic issues: a wandering ox, proper apparel, birds, roofs, and mixtures of seeds, animals, or fabrics. The Torah has done what it could to provide for our soldier's return to civilian society. Now it turns to the details of that civilian society.

From wedding to marriage to children to death, the beginning of *Ki Tetze* sketches a return to domesticity for our soldier. It is not a contented domesticity; in fact, it is one of increasing horror, but it is also one that is governed by boundaries and rules. Those boundaries and rules form an environment that at least has a chance of reintegrating a soldier into civilian society.

It seems to me that were we living in a society and under an administration that was truly concerned with what Scripture says, we would be able to discern it by this proof: the integration of our soldiers and their families back into civilian society would be a high priority.

Shabbat Shalom Lanu u'lchol HaOlam
Sabbath peace to us and to all the world.

Ki Tavo

Richard Tupper

Ki Tavo is a difficult *parsha* to read. In chapter 27, we read the list of twelve curses that will befall those who violate certain mitzvot. Then in chapter 28, we read the relatively short passage of benedictions that Israel will enjoy if it keeps the covenant, followed by the much longer passage of maledictions should Israel violate the covenant. From a literary and historical perspective, the maledictions reach their climax at v. 68:

> And the LORD will bring you back to Egypt in ships, on the way that I said to you: "You shall see it again," and you will put yourselves up for sale there to you enemies as male slaves and slavegirls, and there will be no buyer.

Thus HaShem, who miraculously redeemed Israel from bondage in Egypt by a mighty hand and an outstretched arm, will send Israel back to Egypt, where they will be so miserable that they will not be thought fit even to be slaves. The people of Israel will have come full circle, brought out of Egypt and then brought back to Egypt in an even worse condition.

I would like to discuss three thought-provoking questions that arise from this verse and offer answers to two of them. First, what is the significance of returning to Egypt in ships? Second, when did HaShem tell Israel not to go back to Egypt? And finally, when if ever is this malediction fulfilled?

The reference to boats is curious. In the Tanakh, at least, there is no reference to Israel returning in boats to Egypt. Neither Rashi nor ibn Ezra discusses this aspect of v. 68 in their commentaries. The Ramban, however, says this verse applies to the Romans deporting Jews after the destruction of the Second Temple, though he does not specifically address whether those deportations were by boat.

Some modern scholars take a very different approach. Some have suggested that the word *"bo-oniyyot"* can be revocalized as *"ba-aniyyot,"* the plural or, as Tigay describes it in the JPS Commentary on *Devarim*, "an abstract plural of *aniyah* – 'mourning, lamenting.' " Thus Israel would be returning to Egypt with lamentations or in a state of mourning. On the other hand, if we do not revocalize the word, perhaps the use of boats here is meant to stress that Israel's return to Egypt will be much swifter than its departure long ago. Frankly, I haven't made up my mind about this one.

So on to the next two questions: When does HaShem tell Israel not to return to Egypt and when does this curse come true? With respect to the first question, modern biblical scholars tend to focus on two verses, one in *Shemot* and the other in *Devarim*. Thus for example, Jeffrey Tigay in the JPS commentary on *Devarim* translates v. 68 as "a direction, or destination [*derekh*], I promised you would never see again" and states:

> This verse seems to combine elements of [*Devarim*] 17:16, "the LORD has said to you, 'You must [or will] never go back that route [*derekh*] again" and Exodus 14:13, "The Egyptians whom you see today you will never see again."

There are problems with both of these references. The verse from *Devarim* seems to say that HaShem has already told Israel not to go back to Egypt, but there is no earlier injunction in *Devarim* against returning to Egypt. As for the verse in *Shemot*, it seems to be referring to the fact that HaShem will destroy the Egyptians and that is why Israel will not see them again. It doesn't appear to be an injunction against going back to Egypt.

A modern biblical scholar, Richard Friedman of *Who Wrote the Bible* fame, suggests that we look elsewhere. II Kings 25 reports how the Babylonians had installed the non-Davidide Gedaliah as their governor over the Jews that remained in Judah after the exile to Babylon. However, some in Judah were violently opposed to Gedaliah and vv. 25-26 report:

> But it came to pass in the seventh month, that Ishmael the son of Nethaniah, the son of Elishama, of the seed royal, came, and ten men with him, and smote Gedaliah, that he died, and the Jews and the Chaldeans that were with him at Mizpah. And all the people, both small and great, and the captains of the forces, arose, and came to Egypt; for they were afraid of the Chaldeans.

Here is the reversal: Israel who had come out of Egypt now flees back to Egypt, going back whence they came.

Ki Tavo

But, you say, there is no warning here against going back to Egypt nor does it appear that HaShem has brought the people back. For this, we have to turn to the longer report in the book of Jeremiah. Chapters 42 and 43 report what happens after Gedaliah is assassinated. The people are clearly afraid of retribution by the Babylonians so they go to Jeremiah. Chapter 42 begins:

> **1** Then all the captains of the forces, and Johanan the son of Kareah, and Jezaniah the son of Hoshaiah, and all the people from the least even unto the greatest, came near, **2** and said to Jeremiah the prophet: "Please accept our request, and pray for us to the LORD your God, even for all this remnant; for we are left but a few of many, as your eyes do behold us; **3** that the LORD your God may tell us the way wherein we should walk, and the thing that we should do." **4** Then Jeremiah the prophet said to them: "I have heard you; behold, I will pray to the LORD your God according to your words; and it shall come to pass, that whatsoever thing the LORD . . . shall answer you, I will declare it to you; I will keep nothing back from you." **5** Then they said to Jeremiah: "The LORD be a true and faithful witness against us, if we do not even according to all the word wherewith the LORD your God shall send you to us. **6** Whether it be good, or whether it be evil, we will hearken to the voice of the LORD our God, to whom we send you; that it may be well with us, when we hearken to the voice of the LORD our God." **7** And it came to pass after ten days that the word of the LORD came to Jeremiah.

What does HaShem tell them? HaShem tells them in no uncertain terms not to go back to Egypt, but to stay in the land and not to fear retribution from the Babylonians.

What do we have here? It's a mini-Sinai experience. The people send not Moses but Jeremiah as their representative to HaShem to receive HaShem's command. Jeremiah reports to them HaShem's command, but do the people obey? No, they accuse Jeremiah of lying and refuse to obey. So, they pack up and go to Egypt, taking the prophet Jeremiah with them, who continues to prophesy in Egypt, which has implications of its own.

So where does HaShem tell Israel not to return to Egypt? Right here, as clearly as can be. But is it HaShem who brings the curse of return to Egypt upon the people? It must be said that sometimes the curses we experience inhere in the very choices we make.

Nitzavim-Vayelech

Steve Oren

On Rosh HaShanah, Rabbi Kanarek spoke about the *Yud-Gimel Midot*, the thirteen attributes of God. Among other things, she drew our attention to the seeming duplication at the start "HaShem, HaShem." She mentioned a midrash that was also a favorite midrash of my teacher, Rabbi Yosef Ber Soloveichik, of blessed memory. The midrash explains the duplication of "HaShem, HaShem" in this way. "HaShem, HaShem: I am HaShem before a person sins and I am the same HaShem after a person repents." The question was asked "If so, where is God in the intermediate time, between the time that a persons sins and the time that the person repents?" In answer, Rabbi Kanarak quoted from this week's *parsha* (Deut. 31:18), "*VaAnochi Hastar Astir Panai* – I will surely hide My face."

This is a remarkable verse. Notice that a few weeks ago in *Ki Tavo*, we also read about the really horrifying consequences of sin: war, hunger, and disease. But, this threat "I shall surely hide My face" is not there. The passage in *Ki Tavo* is a parent who says, "I don't want you doing something, and, if you do it, I will scold you/slap your hands/spank you." In our passage the threat is much more serious. The passage here is a parent who says, "If you do that, that behavior is so terrible that it ends our relationship. I will no longer be your parent. I am abandoning you." The human example would be the Jewish parent who sits shiva when his/her child marries a non-Jew. "My child," the parent says, "is dead. And this one that has the name and face of my child is a stranger."

Most of the Jewish holidays are mentioned in the Torah. One of the few that is not is Purim. Yet, the Rabbis asked, "Where can Purim be found in the Torah?" And they answered with this same verse, "*VaAnochi hastar <u>Astir</u> (Esther) Panai*." Part of this is a pun on Astir/Esther – a pun that directs our attention to the non-Jewish sources of the Purim story (for Anglo-Saxons: Esther/Easter). But, part of it is very serious. If you look in the *Megillah*, you will not find the name of God in it. The world of Purim is a world which God has abandoned, in which everything arises from human desires and causes. And, of course, it is a world in which there is no redemption. That is actually one explanation of why we do not say *Hallel* on Purim. The Jews are subject to the Persian monarchy as much at the end of the story as at its start.

But, what is being described is a process. God withdraws from the world. From whose prospective is the story told? In *Devarim*, the story is told from God's perspective. Let us suppose one were to describe the same process from the point of view of humanity. This would be the process of the "Death of God" described by Hegel and Nietzsche. God no longer acts in the world, and humanity does not believe that God could act in the world or, perhaps, God no longer acts in the world BECAUSE humanity does not believe that God could act in the world. We are accustomed to thinking of "theism" (belief in a God) and atheism (belief in no God) as alternatives. In a recent (but unoriginal) book, Daniel Dennett suggests that the real distinction is between God-as-essence and God-as-conscious-supernatural being (a God who can hear and answer prayer). Once God is simply "essence," once it is universally agreed that all events in the world are the consequences of other events in the world (Spinoza's *Deus sive Natura*), the question of whether or not there is a God becomes unimportant. Dennett suggests that religions that believe in God-only-as-essence (Unitarianism as well as Conservative and Reform Judaism are mentioned) have only limited prospects since "only divine beings DO anything."

There is another pun which the Rabbis made. What is Yom Kippur? *Yom-ki-purim*: a day like Purim. How is Yom Kippur like Purim? Purim is the holiday of God's absence from the world. Surely, that is not the nature of Yom Kippur? But what has God said? Although it appears I have totally abandoned you, in fact I have not done so. I am still listening to you and waiting for you to decide that you want to resume our relationship. Since I gave you free will and since you are the one who ended the relationship, I, the Creator of the Universe, am powerless. It is you who must act. And if you will return, if you will do *Teshuvah*, then I will return to you. Yom Kippur is our chance to be reminded of our sins, to do *Teshuvah*, and to cause God's return to His world.

Haazinu

Richard Tupper

No, I'm not telling you to listen up, that's just the name of the *parsha* – *Haazinu* – give ear (Deut. 32). We read it this week on *Shabbat Shuvah*, the Sabbath of Repentance or "Re/Turning." We come to shul on *Shabbat Shuvah* and the question is – Where is God?

In the 60's, the fashionable answer to that question was that God was dead. Man was too sophisticated, too knowledgeable, too cynical to believe in God. But Moses in this week's portion has a much more intriguing response to that question – God is hiding! In the Song of Moses, Moses recounts God saying, "Let Me hide My face from them" (32:20). This notion of God hiding His face from *b'nei Yisrael* already appeared in the preceding chapter where God says to Moses, Deut. 31:17-18:

> 17 And My wrath will flare against them on that day, and I shall forsake them and hide My face from them, and they will become fodder, and many evils and troubles will find them, and they will say on that day, "Is it not because our God is not in our midst that these evils have found us?" 18 And as for Me, I will surely hide My face in that day for all the evil that they have done, for they turned to other gods.

As is clear from verse 18 of chapter 31 as well as from the earlier verses of the Song of Moses (32:15-18), what causes God to hide from Israel is Israel's idolatry. And what causes Israel to turn away from HaShem and to turn to "no-gods"? Prosperity.

One theme in Deuteronomy is that while many material blessings result from obedience to the Covenant, the material blessings of the Covenant are, to be cute, "mixed." Not because there is anything wrong with material blessings *per se* but because Israel tends to become so caught up in the material prosperity that Israel forgets its source, HaShem, and turns away from HaShem and the Covenant either to false gods or to inflated notions of their own importance (*e.g.*, 32:15).

Interestingly, the structure of the poem itself intimates how prosperity leads to disruption. In a Torah scroll, the poem is laid out in two columns and each poetic verse is one or two lines. The result is that each poetic verse begins on a new line on the right and is completed at the end of the same or next line on the left. However, midway in the poem, this format breaks down and each poetic verse begins and ends in the middle of the lines. Which is the verse with the extra half line that causes the disruption? Verse 14, the verse that heaps the material blessings on Israel. Thereafter, Jeshrun waxes fat and kicks.

Moses' description of God hiding His face and why is no less true today. We generally are relatively (as compared to other people in the world) prosperous. In part because of our achievements, we know about evolution, astronomy, geology, anthropology, Higher Criticism (!) *etc* . . . . As our human explanations for the reality around us expand, God's role seems to shrink until *poof* God disappears or, as they said in the 60's, dies.

In place of the living God who created heaven and earth, covenanted with Abraham and liberated us from Egypt, we set up new gods. In place of HaShem, the source of all reality, we worship abstractions – truth, justice, liberalism, you name it. If not that, then we even substitute worshipping Jews for worshipping God so that Judaism is not about God and us but about Jews and their perception of what is best and true. Or sadly, sometimes we substitute worshipping wealth for HaShem.

Just like the poem, we're out of whack, estranged from God. How do we get back on track?

In the Song of Moses, the poetic lines get back "on track" in verse 39 where God declares in no uncertain terms to Israel that He and He alone is their God. It is this announced fact that then puts the poem back into the form it began.

How do modern Jews come to that certain fact that HaShem is indeed real and is indeed our God? The poem tells of one way – God wreaks terrible punishments upon Israel until beaten down and miserable they acknowledge that HaShem is God. As they say, "there are no atheists in foxholes."

But in addition to suffering, God promises Israel that if you seek Him "with all your heart and with all your being," "you shall find Him" (Deut. 4:29). That's good advice but how do you seek God? How do you find Him when He is hiding? Where do you go?

Haazinu

The best way to go is in the way that God has prepared for us to walk to return to Him. Repeatedly, God tells Israel to "walk in all His ways" (Deut. 5:30; 10:12; 11:22). And of course we walk in His ways by following the mitzvot, the commandments or directions that God has given us. This too must be done with all our heart and with all our soul. *Na'aseh v'nishma*/We will do and we will hear, says Israel (Ex. 24:7). From the doing of the mitzvot comes the hearing of God's voice.

Will it work? If lighting candles on Friday night becomes not a routine but the onset of the Sabbath, the day of rest rooted in creation and in liberation, if our mezzuzot are not merely decorative but calls to obedience, if we work to repair the world through justice and mercy so that peace is as a river and righteousness like the waves of the sea (Is. 48:18), will God's presence return? Will He "make His face to shine upon [us]" (Num. 6:25 [OJPS])?

We will never know unless we try. But if we try, and wait to see, we will be in good company because God too is waiting to see how we will end up. "And He said: 'Let Me hide My face from them, I shall see what their end will be'" (Deut. 32:20).

"*Shuvu alai*/Return to me," HaShem says, "*v'ashuv aleichem*/and I will return to you" (Zech. 1:3).

Let's hope we meet.